Essential Economics
for Cambridge IGCSE® & O Level
Third Edition

Robert Dransfield
Terry Cook
Jane King

Oxford excellence for Cambridge IGCSE® & O Level

OXFORD
UNIVERSITY PRESS

Great Clarendon Street, Oxford, OX2 6DP, United Kingdom

Oxford University Press is a department of the University of Oxford. It furthers the University's objective of excellence in research, scholarship, and education by publishing worldwide. Oxford is a registered trade mark of Oxford University Press in the UK and in certain other countries

© Oxford University Press 2018

The moral rights of the authors have been asserted.

First published in 2018

All rights reserved. No part of this publication may be reproduced, stored in a retrieval system, or transmitted, in any form or by any means, without the prior permission in writing of Oxford University Press, or as expressly permitted by law, by licence or under terms agreed with the appropriate reprographics rights organization. Enquiries concerning reproduction outside the scope of the above should be sent to the Rights Department, Oxford University Press, at the address above.

You must not circulate this work in any other form and you must impose this same condition on any acquirer.

British Library Cataloguing in Publication Data
Data available

978-019-842489-5

10

Paper used in the production of this book is a natural, recyclable
product made from wood grown in sustainable forests. The manufacturing process conforms to the environmental regulations of the country of origin.

Printed and bound by CPI Group (UK) Ltd, Croydon, CR0 4YY

Acknowledgements
COVER: 3DDock/Shutterstock; p6: STR/AFP/Getty Images; p7: Paolo Fridman/Bloomberg/Getty Images; p12 (T): STR/AFP/Getty Images; p12 (B): Danita Delimont/ Gallo Images/Getty Images; p2: tropicalpixsingapore/iStock; p4: Yuri Turkov/Shuttesrtock; p8: Nik Niklz/Shutterstock; p14: OUP ; p16: Alberto Loyo/Shutterstock; p22: Dpa Picture Alliance Archive/Alamy Stock Photo; p50: China Daily CDIC/Reuters; p52: Glowimages/Getty Images; p58: Sturti/iStockphoto; p60: JON HRUSA/EPA; p24: RZ_Images/Alamy Stock Photo; p27: G Richardson/Robertharding/REX/Shutterstock; p38: Dmitry Melnikov/Shutterstock; p28: ROB ELLIOTT/AFP/Getty Images; p30: RafalStachura/iStockphoto; p46: Bill Brooks/Alamy Stock Photo; p32: Tomohiro Ohsumi/Bloomberg/Getty Images; p34: Vladimir Weiss/Bloomberg/Getty Images; p54: Oatpixels/iStockphoto; p36: Tuul/Robertharding/Getty Images; p40: ParthSanyal/Reuters; p42: Sandy Marsall/Nelson Thornes; p44: Oliver Thornton/Nelson Thornes; p48: Shawn Banton/NelsonThornes; p80: Keystone Pictures USA/Alamy Stock Photo; p68: Suzanne Long/Alamy Stock Photo; p70: David R. Frazier Photolibrary, Inc./Alamy Stock Photo; p72: Hamad I Mohammed/Reuters; p90: India View/Alamy Stock Photo; p74: MyLoupe/Universal Images Group/Getty Images; p76: Zhenghua Zhuhai China/Moment/Getty Images; p92: Andrey Rudakov/Bloomberg/Getty Images; p78: Angelo Giampiccolo/Shutterstock; p82: Buena Vista Images/ The Image Bank/Getty Images; p84: Paul Prescott/Fotolia; p86: Alex Treadway/Getty Images; p94: Notey; p88: Farjana K. Godhuly/AFP/Getty Images; p96: Xia Yuan/Moment/Getty Images; p98: Sinopix/REX/Shutterstock; p100: PIERRE VERDY/AFP/Getty Images; p102: Ryan Pyle/Corbis/Getty Images; p103: Supergenijalac/iStockphoto; p108: Laurence Griffiths/Getty Images; p110: BobElsdale/Stone/Getty Images; p112: RosaIreneBetancourt 10/Alamy Stock Photo; p114: Thomas Imo/Alamy Stock Photo; p116: Andyleeadams/iStockphoto; p118: PhotoEdit/Alamy Stock Photo; p122: Jon Arnold Images Ltd/Alamy Stock Photo; p130: Graham Crouch/Bloomberg/Getty Images; p128: Paul Andrew Lawrence/Alamy Stock Photo; p136: Sheng Li/Reuters; p132: Jeremy Sutton Hibbert/Alamy Stock Photo; p138: ROSLAN RAHMAN/AFP/Getty Images; p140: YASUYOSHI CHIBA/AFP/Getty Images; p142: AMINU ABUBAKAR/AFP/Getty Images; p148: Agence France Presse/Getty Images; p150: Stockbyte/Getty Images; p154: Joerg Boethling/Alamy Stock Photo; p156: Dominic Harris/Alamy Stock Photo; p158: Robyn Beck/AFP/Getty Images; p160: Boniface Mwangi/Bloomberg/Getty Images; p164: Hirkophoto/iStockphoto; p166: Dansin/iStockphoto; p176: Dave G. Houser/Corbis Documentary/Getty Images; p178: Nordicphotos/Alamy Stock Photo; p180: Namas Bhojani/Bloomberg via Getty Images; p181: Dean Purcell/Getty Images; p182: Universal Images Group North America LLC/Alamy Stock Photo; p184: Marie Hippenmeyer/Afp/Getty Images; p186: ImageMore/Age Fotostock; p188: Stuart Price/AFP/Getty Images; p190: Images & Stories/Alamy Stock Photo; p192: BrentWinebrenner/Getty Images; p194: Alain Evrard/Robert Harding; p196: Campus Life/Getty Images; p206: HeliRy/iStockphoto; p204: Ermess/Shutterstock; p226: Lou Linwei/Alamy Stock Photo; p208: China Newsphoto HAN/DY/Reuters; p212: DarioEgidi/iStockphoto; p214: PatrickPoendl/iStockphoto; p216: David Pearson/REX/Shutterstock; p218: Arko Datta/Reuters; p220: Peter Harrison/Photolibrary/GettyImages; p222: FrancaCallegari/iStockphoto; p224: Dpa Picture Alliance/Alamy Stock Photo;

Although we have made every effort to trace and contact all copyright holders before publication this has not been possible in all cases. If notified, the publisher will rectify any errors or omissions at the earliest opportunity.

Links to third party websites are provided by Oxford in good faith and for information only. Oxford disclaims any responsibility for the materials contained in any third party website referenced in this work.

Introduction

This book is designed specifically for Cambridge International Examinations (Cambridge) IGCSE® & O Level Economics. Experienced examiners have been involved in all aspects of the book, including detailed planning to ensure that the content adheres to the syllabus as closely as possible.

Using this book will ensure that you are well prepared for the exam at this level, and also studies beyond the IGCSE level in Economics. The features below are designed to make learning as interesting and effective as possible:

STUDY TIP

These give you hints on how to avoid common errors or provide useful advice on how to tackle questions.

TOPIC GUIDANCE

These are at the start of each spread and will tell you what you should be able to do at the end of the spread.

SUMMARY QUESTIONS

These questions are at the end of each spread and allow you to test your understanding of the work covered in the spread.

CASE STUDY | Subject

These are real-life examples to illustrate the subject matter within the unit, and are accompanied by questions to test your understanding.

KEY POINTS

These summarise the most important things to learn from the spread.

DID YOU KNOW?

These are interesting facts chosen to stimulate your interest in business studies. Make sure you read them all, as some "Did you know?" facts are needed for the examination.

At the end of each chapter, you will find examination-style practice questions, as well as general revision questions. These include both short-answer summary questions to test your understanding and learning of the unit just covered, and longer-answer questions preceded by a short scenario.

All the questions feature the command words that you will find in the exam. Explanatory notes on these, along with some guidance on answering the questions, are provided here.

The questions, example answers, marks awarded and/or comments that appear in this book and on our website were written by the authors. In examination, the way marks would be awarded to answers like these may be different

At the end of the book, you will find a glossary of the key terms highlighted in bold in the text.

Contents

Unit 1: The basic economic problem: economic goods, choice and the allocation of resources   1
1.1 The nature of the economic problem   2
     1.1.1   The economic problem   2
     1.1.2   Economic and free goods   4
1.2 The factors of production   6
     1.2.1   Factors of production and their rewards   6
     1.2.2   Mobility, quantity and quality of factors of production   8
1.3 Opportunity cost   10
     1.3.1   Definition and examples of opportunity cost   10
     1.3.2   Opportunity cost and economic decision making   12
1.4 Production possibility curves   14
     1.4.1   The production possibility frontier   14
     1.4.2   Movements along and shifts in a production possibility curve   16
     Test yourself   18

Unit 2: The allocation of resources: how the market works and market failure   21
2.1 Microeconomics and macroeconomics   22
     2.1.1   The difference between microeconomics and macroeconomics   22
2.2 The roles of markets in allocating resources   24
     2.2.1   The market system   24
     2.2.2   Resource allocation decisions   26
2.3 Demand   28
     2.3.1   Price and demand   28
     2.3.2   Causes of shifts in the demand curve   30
2.4 Supply   32
     2.4.1   Price and supply   32
     2.4.2   Conditions of supply   34
2.5 Price determination   36
     2.5.1   Market equilibrium   36
2.6 Price changes   38
     2.6.1   Causes and consequences of price changes   38
2.7 Elasticity of demand   40
     2.7.1   Price elasticity of demand   40
     2.7.2   Elasticity of demand and total spending/product revenue   42
2.8 Elasticity of supply   44
     2.8.1   Price elasticity of supply   44
2.9 Market economic systems   46
     2.9.1   The market economic system   46
     2.9.2   Merits and weaknesses of a market system   48
2.10 Market failure   50
     2.10.1   The nature of market failure   50
     2.10.2   Private and social costs and benefits   52
     2.10.3   Causes of market failure   54
2.11 Mixed economic systems   56
     2.11.1   The nature of a mixed economy   56
     2.11.2   Government influence on micro-economy: regulation   58
     2.11.3   Government influence on micro-economy: subsidies   60
     2.11.4   Government influence on micro-economy: indirect taxes   62
     Test yourself   64

Unit 3: Microeconomic decision makers: banks, households, workers, trade unions, firms   67
3.1 Money and banking   68
     3.1.1   Money   68
     3.1.2   Commercial banks   70
     3.1.3   Central banks   72
3.2 Households   74
     3.2.1   Influences on spending, saving and borrowing   74
     3.2.2   Income and expenditure patterns   76
3.3 Workers   78
     3.3.1   Factors affecting occupation choice   78
     3.3.2   Wage determination   80
     3.3.3   Differences in earnings   82
     3.3.4   Division of labour/specialisation   86
3.4 Trade unions   88
     3.4.1   Nature and purpose of trade unions   88
3.5 Firms   90
     3.5.1   Classification of firms   90
     3.5.2   Small firms   92
     3.5.3   Growth of firms   94
     3.5.4   Mergers and integration   96
     3.5.5   Economies and diseconomies of scale   98
3.6 Firms and production   100
     3.6.1   Demand for factors of production   100
     3.6.2   Labour-intensive and capital-intensive production   102
     3.6.3   Production and productivity   104

3.7 Firms' cost, revenue and objectives — 106
- 3.7.1 Fixed and variable costs — 106
- 3.7.2 Total and average costs — 108
- 3.7.3 Output and costs — 110
- 3.7.4 Revenue — 112
- 3.7.5 Objectives of firms — 114

3.8 Market structure — 116
- 3.8.1 Competitive markets — 116
- 3.8.2 Monopoly markets — 118
- **Test yourself** — 120

Unit 4: Government and the macroeconomy — 123

4.1 The role of government — 124
- 4.1.1 Government roles — 124

4.2 Macroeconomic aims of government — 126
- 4.2.1 Macroeconomic aims — 126
- 4.2.2 Conflicts between government aims — 128

4.3 Fiscal policy — 130
- 4.3.1 Elements of fiscal policy — 130
- 4.3.2 Classification of taxes — 132
- 4.3.3 Principles and impacts of taxation — 134
- 4.3.4 Fiscal policy and government aims — 136

4.4 Monetary policy — 138
- 4.4.1 Monetary policy measures — 138

4.5 Supply-side policy — 140
- 4.5.1 The effects of supply-side policy — 140

4.6 Economic growth — 142
- 4.6.1 Measuring Gross Domestic Product — 142
- 4.6.2 Economic growth and recession — 144
- 4.6.3 Illustrating growth and recession — 146
- 4.6.4 Government policies for economic growth — 148

4.7 Employment and unemployment — 150
- 4.7.1 Patterns and levels of employment — 150
- 4.7.2 Full employment — 154
- 4.7.3 Causes of unemployment — 156
- 4.7.4 Consequences of unemployment — 158

4.8 Inflation and deflation — 160
- 4.8.1 The Retail Prices Index and inflation — 160
- 4.8.2 Causes of inflation — 164
- 4.8.3 Consequences of inflation — 166
- 4.8.4 Causes and consequences of deflation — 168
- 4.8.5 Policies to control inflation and deflation — 170
- **Test yourself** — 172

Unit 5: Economic development — 175

5.1 Living standards — 176
- 5.1.1 Indicators of living standards — 176
- 5.1.2 Comparing living standards and income distribution — 180

5.2 Poverty — 182
- 5.2.1 Causes of poverty — 182
- 5.2.2 Policies to alleviate poverty — 184

5.3 Population — 186
- 5.3.1 Factors that affect population growth — 186
- 5.3.2 Reasons for different rates of population growth — 188
- 5.3.3 Problems of population change — 190
- 5.3.4 The effect of changing population sizes on an economy — 192
- 5.3.5 Changes in population structure and their effect on an economy — 194

5.4 Differences in economic development between countries — 196
- 5.4.1 Different rates of development — 196
- 5.4.2 Factors affecting development — 198
- **Test yourself** — 200

Unit 6: International trade and globalisation — 203

6.1 International specialisation — 204
- 6.1.1 Advantages and disadvantages of specialisation — 204

6.2 Globalisation, free trade and protection — 206
- 6.2.1 Globalisation — 206
- 6.2.2 Multinationals — 208
- 6.2.3 The benefits of free trade — 210
- 6.2.4 Methods of protection — 212
- 6.2.5 Reasons for protection — 214

6.3 Foreign exchange rates — 216
- 6.3.1 Exchange rates — 216
- 6.3.2 Causes of foreign exchange rate fluctuations — 218
- 6.3.3 Consequences of fluctuations — 220

6.4 The balance of payments — 222
- 6.4.1 The current account of the balance of payments — 222
- 6.4.2 Current account deficit and surplus — 224
- 6.4.3 Policies to achieve balance of payments stability — 226
- **Test yourself** — 228

Glossary — 232
Index — 237

Additional resources are available online at:
www.oxfordsecondary.com/9780198424895

Syllabus match

This student book is fully aligned to the Cambridge International Examinations (Cambridge) IGCSE® (0455) & O Level (2281) Economics syllabuses.

UNIT NUMBER		SYLLABUS REFERENCE
1	**The basic economic problem**	1
1.1	**The nature of the economic problem**	1.1
1.1.1	The economic problem	1.1.1
1.1.2	Economic and free goods	1.1.2
1.2	**The factors of production**	1.2
1.2.1	Factors of production and their rewards	1.2.1
1.2.2	Mobility, quantity and quality of factors	1.2.2/1.2.3
1.3	**Opportunity cost**	1.3
1.3.1	Definition and examples of opportunity cost	1.3.1
1.3.2	Opportunity cost and economic decision making	1.3.2
1.4	**Production possibility curves**	1.4
1.4.1	The production possibility frontier	1.4.1
1.4.2	Movements along and shifts in the PPC	1.4.1/1.4.3/1.4.4
2	**The allocation of resources**	2
2.1	**Microeconomics and macroeconomics**	2.1
2.1.1	The difference between macro and microeconomics	2.1/2.2
2.2	**The role of markets in allocating resources**	2.2
2.2.1	The market system	2.2.1
2.2.2	Resource allocation decisions	2.2.2/2.2.3
2.3	**Demand**	2.3
2.3.1	Price and demand	2.3.1/2.3.2/2.3.3
2.3.4	Causes of shifts in the demand curve	2.3.4
2.4	**Supply**	2.4
2.4.1	Price and supply	2.4.1/2.4.2/2.4.3
2.4.2	Conditions of supply	2.4.4
2.5	**Price determination**	2.5
2.5.1	Market equilibrium	2.5.1/2.5.2
2.6	**Price changes**	2.6
2.6.1	Causes and consequences of price changes	2.6.1/2.6.2
2.7	**Elasticity of demand**	2.7
2.7.1	Price elasticity of demand	2.7.1/2.7.2/2.7.3
2.7.2	Elasticity of demand and total spending	2.7.4/2.7.5
2.8	**Elasticity of supply**	2.8
2.8.1	Price elasticity of supply	2.8.1/2.8.2/2.8.3/2.8.4
2.9	**Market economic systems**	2.9
2.9.1	The market economic system	2.9.1
2.9.2	Merits and weaknesses of a market economic system	2.9.2
2.10	**Market failure**	2.10
2.10.1	The nature of market failure	2.10.1
2.10.2	Private and social costs and benefits	2.10.1
2.10.3	Causes of market failure	2.10.2/2.10.3
2.11	**Mixed economic systems**	2.11
2.11.1	The nature of a mixed economy	2.11.1
2.11.2	Government influence on micro-economy regulation	2.11.2
2.11.3	Government influence on micro-economy subsidies	2.11.2
2.11.4	Government influence on micro-economy indirect taxes	2.11.2
3	**Microeconomic decision makers**	3
3.1	**Money and banking**	3.1
3.1.1	Money	3.1.1
3.1.2	Commercial banks	3.1.2
3.1.3	Central banks	3.1.2
3.2	**Households**	3.2
3.2.1	Influences on spending, saving and borrowing	3.2.1
3.2.2	Income and expenditure patterns	3.2.1
3.3	**Workers**	3.3
3.3.1	Factors affecting occupation choice	3.3.1
3.3.2	Wage determination	3.3.2
3.3.3	Differences in earnings	3.3.3
3.3.4	Division of labour specialisation	3.3.4
3.4	**Trade unions**	3.4
3.4.1	Nature and purpose of trade unions	3.4.1
3.5	**Firms**	3.5
3.5.1	Classification of firms	3.5.1
3.5.2	Small firms	3.5.2
3.5.3	Growth of firms	3.5.3
3.5.4	Mergers and integration	3.5.4

3.5.5	Economies and diseconomies of scale	3.5.5	4.8	Inflation and deflation	4.8
3.6	**Firms and production**	3.6	4.8.1	The retail price index and inflation	44.8.1/4.8.2
3.6.1	Demand for factors of production	3.6.1	4.8.2	Causes of inflation	4.8.3
3.6.2	Labour intensive and capital intensive industries	3.6.2	4.8.3	Consequences of inflation	4.8.4
3.6.3	Production and productivity	3.6.3	4.8.4	Causes and consequences of deflation	4.8.3/4.8.4
3.7	**Firms' costs, revenue and objectives**	3.7	4.8.5	Policies to control inflation and deflation	4.8.5
3.7.1	Fixed and variable costs	3.7.1/3.7.2	**5**	**Economic development**	**5**
3.7.2	Total and average costs	3.7.1/3.7.2	5.1	**Living standards**	5.1
3.7.3	Output and costs	3.7.1 and 3.7.2	5.1.1	Indicators of living standards	5.1.1
3.7.4	Revenue	3.7.3/3.7.4	5.1.2	Comparing living standards and income distribution	5.1.2
3.7.5	Objectives of firms	3.7.5	5.2	**Poverty**	5.2
3.8	**Market structures**	3.8	5.2.1	Causes of poverty	5.2.1/5.2.2
3.8.1	Competitive markets	3.8.1	5.2.2	Policies to alleviate poverty	5.2.3
3.8.2	Monopoly markets	3.8.2	5.3	**Population**	5.3
4	**Government and the macroeconomy**	**4**	5.3.1	Factors that affect population growth	5.3.1
4.1	**The role of government**	4.1	5.3.2	Reasons for different rates of population growth	5.3.2
4.1.1	Government roles	4.1.1	5.3.3	Problems of population change	5.3.3
4.2	**Macroeconomic aims of government**	4.2	5.3.4	Changes in population structure and their effect on an economy	5.3.3
4.2.1	Macroeconomic aims	4.2.1	5.4	**Differences in economic development between countries**	5.4
4.2.2	Conflict between government aims	4.2.2	5.4.1	Different rates of economic development	5.4.1
4.3	**Fiscal policy**	4.3	**6**	**International trade and globalization**	**6**
4.3.1	Elements of fiscal policy	4.3.1/4.3.2/4.3.3	6.1	**International specialisation**	6.1
4.3.2	Classification of taxes	4.3.4	6.1.1	International specialisation	6.1.1/6.1.2
4.3.3	Principles and impact of taxation	4.3.5/4.3.6	6.2	**Globalisation, free trade and protection**	6.2
4.3.4	Fiscal policy and government aims	4.3.7/4.3.8/4.3.9	6.2.1	Globalisation	6.2.1
4.4	**Monetary policy**	4.4	6.2.2	Multinationals	6.2.2
4.4.1	Monetary policy measures	4.4.1/4.4.2/4.4.3	6.2.3	Methods of protection	6.2.4
4.5	**Supply side policy**	4.5	6.2.4	Reasons for protection	6.2.5/6.2.6
4.5.1	The effects of supply side policy	4.5.1/4.5.2/4.5.3	6.3	**Foreign exchange rates**	6.3
4.6	**Economic growth**	4.6	6.3.1	Exchange rates	6.3.1/6.3.2
4.6.1	Economic growth, measuring GDP	4.6.1/4.6.2	6.3.2	Causes of foreign exchange rate fluctuations	6.3.3
4.6.2	Economic growth and recession	4.6.3/4.6.4/4.6.5	6.3.3	Consequences of fluctuations	6.3.4/6.3.5
4.6.3	Illustrating growth and recession	4.6.3	6.4	**The balance of payments**	6.4
4.6.4	Government policies for economic growth	4.6.6	6.4.1	The current account of the balance of payments	6.4.1
4.7	**Employment and unemployment**	4.7	6.4.2	Current account deficit and surplus	6.4.2/6.4.3
4.7.1	Patterns and levels of employment	4.7.1/4.7.2/4.7.3	6.4.3	Policies to achieve balance of payments stability	64.4
4.7.2	Full employment	4.7.2/4.7.3/4.7.6			
4.7.3	Causes of unemployment	4.7.4			
4.7.4	Consequences of unemployment	4.7.5/4.7.6			

How to use the practice questions and Command words explained

The questions at the end of each unit in the book are to help you practise your examination technique after completing all the work in the unit. You should answer them without referring to the information in the book or your notes.

The short-answer questions test your knowledge and understanding of what you have learnt. Generally, these will ask you to state, identify, define and/or explain one or a number of factors, differences or meanings. Your answers will be fairly brief, perhaps bullet points, but avoid single-word 'lists', especially where an explanation is required. Do not spend too long or write too much – 2–4 lines is sufficient for these answers. Where an example is required, give one from your own experience, either as a consumer or as an observer of your local business environment.

The longer-answer questions introduce you to the 'case study' approach, in which questions are based on a specific business scenario. Read the material carefully, because this will help you to give an answer that is appropriate to the business concerned. So, for example, do not recommend TV advertising for a small business; do not suggest 'access to raw materials' as a location factor for a retail business, as this is only really applicable to a production business. Read the case study carefully and try to put yourself in the role of the business person in the text.

Make sure you can answer the following:

- Is this business large or small?
- Who owns this business?
- What are they selling – a product or a service?
- Is the business objective profit or another, such as public service?
- Who are the customers?
- What challenges does the business face (e.g. competition)?

Make sure you refer to the circumstances of the business, rather than just mentioning the company or owner by name. If you are asked to make a decision about the future way forward for the business, consider a range of options and come to a supported conclusion.

The instruction in the question is given by the command word: as the term suggests, this tells you what is required. The following is a list of the command words you are likely to see in your examination.

Calculate, e.g. 'Calculate the gross profit margin of a business.' You need to do some mathematics to produce an answer. Always show your workings.

Consider, e.g. 'Consider the two options given in the case study.' You need to weigh up the merits of a situation or decision and give the opposing view as well.

Define, e.g. 'Define market research.' State the exact meaning of the term; this will be a short answer, sometimes including an example to illustrate it.

Explain, e.g. 'Explain what is meant by a price elastic demand.' This term enables you to show your understanding of a term or topic. You can do this by including an example or a descriptive development.

Identify, e.g. 'Identify two factors a company should consider before deciding to issue more shares.' 'Identify' (or 'State') requires you to select from a number of possibilities. Only a brief answer is necessary, so a list may be fine, but if you are unsure, include a sentence of clarification or an example.

Justify, e.g. 'Should company X buy more machinery? Justify your answer.' This is a longer answer in which you should support your answer with reasons. Outline, e.g. 'Outline the main features of a business partnership.' You should give a short description (in this example, of the main features of the partnership).

Recommend, e.g. 'Recommend which option the company should take.' You should make a positive suggestion, with reasons that support, or justify your decision.

1 The basic economic problem: economic goods, choice and the allocation of resources

Unit 1 introduces the basic economic problem: insufficient resources to meet all our needs and the choices that have to be made as a result. It is explained that while the earth is a very rich source of raw materials that support human life, most of these resources are limited – in particular, oil, gas and fertile agricultural land. Goods that are scarce relative to the demand for them are termed economic goods.

The unit looks at how the resources of land, labour, capital and enterprise are used to become factors of production. The example of a successful entrepreneur illustrates how factors can be combined to generate wealth and opportunity for growth in an economy.

The unit develops the idea of choice with the introduction of the concept of opportunity cost. Explanations are given of how every economic decision involves a choice, and that when choices are made, the sacrificed alternative become the opportunity cost.

The unit shows how the production boundaries of an economy can be illustrated by means of a production possibility curve.

TOPIC COVERAGE

Students will cover the following topics:
- The nature of the economic problem (finite resources and unlimited wants)
- Economic and free goods
- Factors of production and their rewards, mobility of factors
- Opportunity cost and how it influences decision making
- Production possibility curves
- Movements along and shifts in production possibility curves

1.1 The nature of the economic problem
1.1.1 The economic problem

TOPIC GUIDANCE

Students should be able to:
- define the term 'economic problem'
- give examples of the economic problem
- understand the meaning of scarcity and choice.

The economic problem

The economic problem arises because the people that make up society have **unlimited wants**, while society only has access to a **finite resource base**. As a result, we cannot have everything we want, and so we have to make choices.

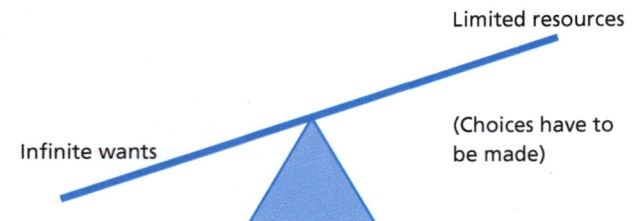

Wants are infinite because once some of our wants have been met, we often want something better. Our resources are finite because:

- many resources are limited in quantity, e.g. land
- when resources are in use, they often cannot be used for something else at the same time.

There are a number of types of resource (Figure 1.1.1).

Forest resources in Haiti are extremely scarce because forests have been cut down to meet human needs and wants

Natural resources	Human-made resources	Human resources
Soil, climate, water, minerals, forests and fisheries	Machinery, buildings and equipment	People and their skills

Figure 1.1.1 Types of resource

STUDY TIP

Every country faces the economic problem. You will come across this in various places throughout this book and you should be able to discuss it in different contexts.

If society had all the land, labour, raw materials and other resources it needed, we could produce all the goods we wanted without making sacrifices. In reality resources are **scarce**. When we use resources to produce an item, we are taking away these resources from producing something else. All societies face this problem. An important distinction is made between needs (those things we have to have for survival, such as basic food items and shelter) and wants (those things we desire that may include needs, but may also include things such as luxury foods).

Decision-making over the use of resources involves:
- making a **choice** (we can do one thing *or* the other)
- making a **sacrifice** (if we choose to do this with a resource, we cannot also do the other).

> **DID YOU KNOW?**
> Sustainable use of resources means using them in such a way that future supplies of these resources are not reduced.

CASE STUDY | Deforestation in Haiti

Haiti is a large Caribbean island economy that was once covered in forest but has been almost stripped bare to make way for agriculture, house-building materials and charcoal burning. Wood fetches very high prices, so trees have been cut down with terrible consequences – including mudslides during heavy rains, as there are no tree roots to hold the soil together. The Haitian government is now seeking to address this problem by setting large tracts of land aside for tree planting.

A challenge for Haiti is to replant its forests in a sustainable way, so that future generations have more resources to meet their wants and needs.

Questions
1 Why is forest land so scarce in Haiti today?
2 How does scarcity of forest and wood resources illustrate the economic problem of unlimited wants and limited resources?
3 What difficulties do you think the Haitian government may face in tackling this issue?

> **STUDY TIP**
> Another way of thinking about choice and sacrifice is in terms of time. For example, what are you going to do this evening: stay in and do your homework or go out with friends? You cannot do both at the same time. You need to fully understand the implications of making a choice in terms of what has to be given up.

Making choices

Gathering scarce fuelwood is a very important activity in Haiti, particularly for poor people. Collecting driftwood that has been washed ashore on beaches takes a lot of time. People have to choose whether to allocate time to this activity or to something else. Alternatively, they can buy wood for building, and charcoal made from wood for cooking. However, this is expensive because of the scarce nature of the resource.

The economic problem is a constant issue for Haitians and for citizens of all countries. Our daily lives involve thousands of choices that involve how we spend our time and money.

- Time is a scarce resource – there are only 24 hours in a day.
- Money is a scarce resource – we only have a limited amount.

Daily life involves solving **economic problems** in which choices have to be made. Imagine you have to decide whether to buy a book or borrow it from a library. If you buy the book, you 'sacrifice' the opportunity to buy something else. If you borrow it, you sacrifice the opportunity to own the book. Unit 1.3 explores this further in terms of the cost of the sacrifice – the **opportunity cost**.

> **KEY POINTS**
> 1 The economic problem is one of finite resources and unlimited wants.
> 2 Resources are scarce; this requires individuals and societies to make choices.
> 3 Making a choice involves a sacrifice.

> **SUMMARY QUESTIONS**
> 1 What resources do you think are particularly scarce in your country?
> 2 Give an example of a situation in which your own finite resources have forced you to make a choice.
> 3 In what situations does your school make choices because the wants it has are greater than the finite resources available to it?

1.1.2 Economic and free goods

Most of the resources we use are scarce. As a result we have access to very few free goods. A **free good** is one which is so abundantly available that no sacrifice has to be made to supply or use it. Examples of free goods include air and seawater. In an island economy people have as much access to clean air and fresh seawater as they want. The fact that one person can enjoy these resources doesn't stop someone else from enjoying them too. Similarly, everyone who lives near to a park can enjoy it.

However, in the modern world there are limits to these free goods. For example, some factories cause pollution when they use air and seawater resources. By creating pollution then they spoil some of the air and water for other people. In some cities people wear masks over their faces so that they are protected from polluted air. Seawater may be polluted and parks can be spoiled by overuse.

Economic goods

An **economic good** is a good or resource that is scarce in comparison to the demand for that good or resource. Therefore, to acquire an economic good, a sacrifice must be made – often in the form of an outlay of effort or money. Nearly all goods, services and resources are scarce relative to demand, and therefore should be classified as economic goods. The existence of economic goods gives rise to the economic problem (see section 1.1.1).

As resources and goods are scarce relative to the demand for them, they will be able to command a price – people will be willing to pay to use them.

> **TOPIC GUIDANCE**
>
> Students should be able to:
> - define economic and free goods
> - illustrate the differences between an economic and a free good.

The Estadio Santiago Bernabéu is the stadium of the Spanish football club Real Madrid. On a match day it has seats for 85 454 spectators. Tickets are economic goods because seats are relatively scarce in relation to the demand for them

> **DID YOU KNOW?**
>
> Just because a good is given away for free does not make it a 'free good'. For example, a supermarket may offer goods that it wants people to try out for free. However, these are not free goods in the economic sense, because resources have been used to produce these goods and these resources could have been used for something else.

> **ACTIVITY**
>
> Choose an example of a good that is sold for a very low price at your local supermarket. Explain why this should be regarded as an economic good rather than a free good.

> **CASE STUDY** | Ticket prices to watch Real Madrid versus Barcelona
>
> Spectators travel to stadiums such as the Estadio Santiago Bernabéu in Madrid from all over the world. You might think there would be plenty of room for everyone who wanted to watch a match to be able to do so. However, this is far from the case. When Real Madrid play their rivals Barcelona there are as many people who cannot get tickets as those who are successful – even though the price of tickets can be very expensive.
>
> Watching top teams play football is another example of an economic good. Clubs such as Real Madrid know that they can charge high prices because people's wants and needs to watch top-class football are greater than the availability of the good.
>
> **Questions**
>
> 1 Why is watching Real Madrid play football at the Bernabéu an example of an economic good?

2 Why do you think that Real Madrid are able to charge relatively high prices for tickets?

3 For a good to be an economic one, what does the availability of a resource or a product need to be scarce in relation to?

	Economic goods	Free goods
Definition	Goods that are scarce relative to the demand for their use	Goods that are superabundant
Sacrifice	A sacrifice is made when using an economic good	No sacrifice is made in using a free good
Examples	Food items, machine tools, football tickets, clothes	Seawater and air

> **STUDY TIP**
>
> Most resources, goods and services are 'economic goods'. You should be able to explain why specific examples can be classed as economic goods. Remember that free goods are ones that are abundant; there is no sacrifice incurred when a free good is used.

CASE STUDY | 'The tragedy of the commons'

'The tragedy of the commons' written by the American biologist Garrett Hardin in 1968 provides a powerful example of man's increasing use of economic goods. In this story, shepherds graze their sheep on a common piece of land. When there are a small number of them, this is not a problem. However, there comes a point at which one too many flocks of sheep is grazed on the land, and the pasture is destroyed, meaning everyone loses out. What appeared to be a free good (the pasture) is in fact an economic good – a finite resource with multiple demands.

Questions

1 Why is farmland that is shared by multiple owners an economic good rather than a free one?

2 Can you think of other examples where overuse leads to losses for all users of that resource?

> **DID YOU KNOW?**
>
> One of the best-known quotes of Mahatma Gandhi was: 'God forbid that India should ever take to industrialism after the manner of the west… keeping the world in chains. If [our nation] took to similar economic exploitation, it would strip the world bare like locusts." This quote highlights the nature of scarcity on a global scale and problems associated with so-called economic development.

KEY POINTS

1 Goods can be classified a 'economic' or 'free' goods.

2 Nearly all goods are economic goods because using them involves a sacrifice of time or other resources.

3 A free good would be one that is superabundant so that there is no sacrifice incurred in using it.

SUMMARY QUESTIONS

1 Why are the clothes that we wear considered an economic good?

2 Why might a private beach be seen as an economic good, while a public beach might be seen as a free good? Can you think of any exceptions to this?

3 If you have to pay to use a resource, is it more likely to be an economic good or a free good? Explain why.

1.2 The factors of production

1.2.1 Factors of production and their rewards

TOPIC GUIDANCE

Students should be able to:
- define the factors of production
- explain and give examples of land, labour, capital and enterprise.

Imagine that you are visiting a modern food-processing plant. It is processing vegetables to put into cans. What do you see?

The most obvious sight will be large areas of land and factory buildings. Inside, you will see machinery, equipment and employees. Some workers will be looking after the equipment. In the production area you will see people preparing the vegetables. Other workers will be loading and unloading supplies and finished goods.

The **factors of production** are what make the business work: **land**, **labour**, **capital** and **enterprise**.

- In the plant, the land includes the site on which the factory is built.
- The labour is the factory employees.
- The capital is the buildings and machinery that are used to make the canned vegetables.
- Finally, enterprise is the factor that takes the risk in bringing the factors together to produce goods in order to make profits.

A canning factory brings together land, labour, capital (machinery and buildings) and enterprise to create the finished product

ACTIVITY

Talk to the owner of a small local business. Find out how the business uses its land and capital, the type of labour employed and the enterprise skills needed to ensure that the enterprise is successful.

STUDY TIP

The concept of capital in economics can sometimes appear confusing. In some senses, it can mean money, but in relation to the factors of production, it means any human-made aid to production.

Definitions

Over the years the four factors of production have come to mean more than the examples used above.

- **Land** is now used to refer to all natural resources, e.g. farmland, water, coal.
- **Labour** is used to refer to all the physical and mental contributions of an employee – so it is more than just the physical effort of digging coal or making car parts. It also includes the mental effort of an accountant or the services provided by a bank clerk.
- **Capital** includes all those items that go into producing other things, e.g. a machine manufactures products, tools contribute to this process, and so on.
  Machines, tools and buildings are all examples of physical capital.
- **Enterprise** is the factor that brings the other factors together to produce goods in order to make profits.

CASE STUDY | Combining the factors of production

Lakshmi Mittal is a well-known entrepreneur. He founded the Mittal Steel company in India (now part of ArcelorMittal). The company has expanded to take over a network of steel producers from across the world. Today the company headquarters are in Luxembourg. Mittal brings together factors of production in effective combinations to create the only truly global steel company. To run his enterprise Lakshmi Mittal rewards certain features.

Lakshmi Mittal

- **Labour with wages**: attractive salaries and wages have to be paid to workers in each of the countries while production takes place.
- **Land with rent**: ArcelorMittal has to pay rent on some of the sites on which its factories are located.
- **Capital with interest**: like most other businesses, ArcelorMittal borrows money from banks to fund its activities. Interest must be paid at regular intervals on the loans.
- **Enterprise with profits**: profits are a reward for enterprise. The profits of ArcelorMittal are shared out among shareholders (or reinvested in the business).

Questions

1 Which factor is responsible for bringing together the other factors of production?
2 Why is labour so important to a giant steel company?

STUDY TIP

Textbooks used to leave out 'enterprise' and refer to only three factors of production. Don't make that mistake; when discussing the factors of production, make sure that you can refer to all four.

DID YOU KNOW?

ArcelorMittal was created in 2006 by the merger (joining together) of Luxembourg-based Arcelor with Lakshmi Mittal's global steel business. The company employs about 200 000 people.

ACTIVITY

Think of an entrepreneur in your own country who brings together the factors of production in a particular company. Research and write a short report about your chosen person.

KEY POINTS

1 Factors of production are combined to produce goods.
2 Enterprise is responsible for bringing together land, labour and capital.
3 Factors are rewarded in the form of incomes, e.g. wages for employees.

SUMMARY QUESTIONS

1 Choose a familiar product and describe how factors of production are brought together to produce it.
2 What are entrepreneurs? What do they do?
3 What type of capital do the following work with?
   a farm workers
   b factory workers
   c teachers.

1.2.2 Mobility, quantity and quality of factors of production

TOPIC GUIDANCE

Students should be able to:
- understand and explain the influences on the mobility of factors
- outline the causes of changes in the quantity and quality of factors.

Physical units of capital can be moved from one country to another to improve the capital stock of the receiving country

DID YOU KNOW?

The occupational mobility of labour depends on people's willingness to learn new skills. An example of occupational immobility can be found in the US car industry. Here, high paid jobs were lost, and workers struggled to find similarly paid jobs that used the same skills. This was compounded by many workers' unwillingness to move geographically.

Some factors of production can be moved from one area to another quite easily. This is referred to as the **geographical mobility** of a factor.

Some factors of production can be moved from one use to another. This is referred to as **occupational mobility**. Other factors are less mobile.

Land

Some types of land are geographically immobile. For example, it is difficult – but not impossible – to move an area of farmland from one location to another.

You might need to move an area of land to a new location if it is in greater demand there. For example, as new cities develop, farmland is required to provide the population with fresh food. In the Netherlands, sea walls (dikes) were created in low-lying areas (polders) to create new areas of farmland. As a result, 2,700 square miles of land was reclaimed from the sea. China has created double this amount.

Many types of land can have their use changed (occupational mobility). Land use can change from farming to urban construction, or from forest resources to agriculture (as in the Amazon rainforest in Brazil).

Labour

Workers sometimes need to move from one area to another, but may be reluctant to do so for a variety of personal reasons. To persuade workers to move from one area to another, businesses and governments need to offer incentives, both to encourage workers to move and to cover higher costs of living (as is the case in cities such as London, New York and Mumbai).

Capital

Some units of captial, e.g. small machines, are easily moved from one place to another. Even larger items can be shipped to other countries. However, much bigger items of capital, e.g. steel rolling mills, are immobile.

Many items of capital are occupationally mobile – a generator can be used to provide electricity to many types of industry. However, capital becomes obsolete (replaced by more modern versions) over time.

Enterprise

Enterprise can be one of the most mobile factors. Entrepreneurs can be flexible, moving from one location (geographical mobility) and industry (occupational mobility) to another. However, this may be restricted internationally by citizenship and passport restrictions, or by specific knowledge required by specialist industries.

| CASE STUDY | Shipping diesel trains from New Zealand to Mozambique |

In 2017 the Auckland (New Zealand) Transport Authority shipped 17 diesel trains to Mozambique. Auckland bought these passenger trains in 1993 from Australia, where they were then going out of service. In 2017 Auckland is converting from diesel to electrical and battery-powered trains which are faster, cleaner and less costly to maintain. However, for Mozambique the diesel trains are a step up from the present stock of steam locomotives.

Questions

1 What factor of production are diesel trains?
2 What type of mobility of factors is illustrated in this case study?
3 How might diesel trains improve the capital stock of Mozambique?

Quantity and quality of factors of production

The quantity of a factor of production is the amount of that factor available in a specific economy. For example, in Caribbean island economies such as Saint Lucia or Saint Kitts and Nevis, the quantity of physical land is severely restricted, although there is greater access to sea resources in the form of fish stocks in the Caribbean Sea.

China has huge areas of land available for various land uses, e.g. forestry, agriculture and mining. The amount of capital depends on the accumulation of capital over time, so economies that industrialised relatively early (such as the UK and France) have been able to accumulate extensive capital stocks.

However, perhaps more important to an economy is the quality of factors of production available to it. High quality factors of production the following.

- **Skilled labour force** – education and training improve the quality of labour. In addition, the quantity and quality of labour is improved by immigration of more skilled labour.
- **Highly productive land** – the quality of land is improved by investment, e.g. by application of fertiliser in agriculture.
- **Highly productive capital** – capital is improved by increased investment and application of new technologies.
- **Highly productive entrepreneurs** – economic systems that educate and encourage entrepreneurs will improve enterprise – whereas petty regulations will stifle enterprise.

KEY POINTS

1 Occupational mobility relates to change in the use of factors. Geographical mobility refers to change in geographical location of factors of production.
2 Some factors are relatively mobile, whereas others take time to change their use or location.
3 The quantity of factors of production can be enhanced by increased mobility of factors and the quality can be improved by investment, e.g. in training and education.

SUMMARY QUESTIONS

1 How can the mobility of factors of production be increased?
2 Identify key obstacles holding back the mobility of each of the factors of production.
3 How can the quantity of factors and the quality of factors of production be increased?

1.3 Opportunity cost
1.3.1 Definitions and examples of opportunity cost

> **TOPIC GUIDANCE**
>
> Students should be able to:
> - define opportunity cost
> - give examples of opportunity cost.

The opportunity cost to a poor family's children spending time in school may be thought of as a loss of wages from that child not working

Opportunity cost

The **opportunity cost** of choosing to buy a particular product or to carry out a particular economic action is the next best alternative that is given up. The opportunity cost is the sacrifice that is made. In simple terms, opportunity cost can be defined as the cost of a missed opportunity.

Opportunity cost is relevant to each of the participants that we focus on in this book – that is, consumers, workers, firms and governments (see section 1.3.2).

> **CASE STUDY** | Sava and the supermarket
>
> Sava has recently made some important purchasing decisions. She wanted to buy a new dress for an important event. After looking at all the options, the choice came down to a full-length blue evening gown or a mid-length green one. She chose the green one.
>
> She also needed to purchase some new sports trainers and found it difficult to choose between an excellent lightweight pair costing $49.99 and a more conventional pair costing the same price. She chose the lightweight pair. Sava works part-time in the local supermarket. Her supervisor has recently offered to increase her hours from 15 per week to 20, but this will clash with the time she spends practising basketball. Sava decides against working the extra hours because she loves playing basketball.
>
> The supermarket that Sava works for is called LowCost. The company has recently decided to replace the fresh products it sells on one of its aisles with 'ready meals'. It believes this will increase profitability. For the same reason, it has stopped selling toothpaste manufactured by a company called Brighter Smiles and replaced this with toothpaste produced by the Shinier Teeth company.
>
> The government imposes a tax on business profits. It uses the money from this tax to pay for a range of government spending, e.g. on health services and education. It has decided to reduce this tax on small businesses in order to create more jobs, but this will mean it has less money to spend on education and health.
>
> | Who is making the choice | What they chose | Opportunity cost (what they could have had, i.e. the next best alternative) |
> |---|---|---|
> | *Sava (consumer)* | green evening gown | blue evening gown |
> | | lightweight trainers | conventional trainers |

Who is making the choice	What they chose	Opportunity cost (what they could have had, i.e. the next best alternative)
LowCost supermarket (firm)	to increase profits by selling 'ready meals' and Shinier Teeth toothpaste	the profits that could have been made from fresh produce profits from Brighter Smiles products
The government	to reduce taxes on small businesses	additional spending on education and health

Questions

1 How do the decisions we make involve an opportunity cost?
2 Identify two choices you have made recently that involved an opportunity cost. What was the opportunity you gave up? Why should this be considered a cost?
3 How do business and government decisions involve an opportunity cost?

Opportunity cost in education

Opportunity cost is particularly important in education. For example, in Bangladesh successive governments have had the target of **universal education** (that is, for all children to go to school). To achieve this aim, the government initially provided food subsidies to poorer families to encourage school participation. More recently these subsidies have been replaced by payments to families to encourage schooling. For poor families, the opportunity cost of schooling is the loss of income from children going to work, e.g. in seasonal agriculture, textiles or construction. Government payments to families are designed to compensate for the opportunity cost of lost wages.

In the UK a number of studies have shown that going to university increases the lifetime average earnings of graduates. However, many young people make the economic decision not to go to university, choosing to earn a full-time wage from the age of 18.

SUMMARY QUESTIONS

1 Dalvinder has saved $10 to spend on clothes. She has written a list of what she would like and ranked the items from 1 to 3, with 1 being the most desirable.

	What I want to buy	Price ($)
1	two T-shirts	US$9.50
2	bracelet	US$10.00
3	skirt	US$10.00

What is the opportunity cost if she buys the T-shirts?
2 Why should opportunity cost be considered when making economic choices?
3 In what way is time significant in making economic decisions?

STUDY TIP

Decisions in economies involve opportunity costs – choosing a particular course of action always involves a sacrifice. This is the opportunity cost.

DID YOU KNOW?

One of the most important choices an individual can make is how much time to spend studying. Research shows that spending more time in education leads to better-paid jobs in the long term. The opportunity cost of choosing not to study might be the loss of earnings resulting from a lower-paid job.

ACTIVITY

Identify:
- two recent situations when you had to decide how to use your time
- a situation where you had to decide how to spend your money.

Explain how opportunity cost was involved in each choice.

KEY POINTS

1 Opportunity cost is the next best alternative that is sacrificed when making an economic choice.
2 The opportunity cost is the real cost of any economic decision.
3 Purchasing decisions and decisions about how to make use of time involve an opportunity cost.

1.3.2 Opportunity cost and economic decision-making

TOPIC GUIDANCE

Students should be able to:
- show how decisions made by consumers, workers, producers and the government are influenced by opportunity cost.

Opportunity cost – the next best alternative to the Chinese government spending on hospitals could be spending more on primary schools

ACTIVITY

Think of some of your most recent purchases. Did all of them involve thinking about the sacrifices involved in making your choice? Were there some purchases in which you gave greater consideration to opportunity cost than others?

Volkswagen switches production plant from Europe to Brazil

Government increases spending on education – defence cuts likely

Workers in South Korea choose to work fewer hours as incomes rise

More shoppers buying luxury brands

Newspaper headlines illustrating choices involving an opportunity cost

Economic actions

Economic choices are made every day: an employer may choose to hire a young apprentice or a more experienced worker; consumers may choose to spend part of their income on rice rather than on potatoes.

The main groups that make up the economy are:
- consumers (people who buy goods and services)
- workers (people who supply labour in exchange for a wage)
- producers (people who make and sell goods and services)
- the government (which acts both as a producer and consumer, and as lawmaker).

You need to understand how the actions of each of these groups involve an opportunity cost. You also need to evaluate the implications of the choice – in other words, understand any effects of the choice of one alternative over another.

Consumers

Everyone is a consumer, whether they are individuals or part of a household that uses goods or services produced in the economy.

The opportunity cost of making any decision about consumption is the next best alternative that is sacrificed. When you buy a cup of coffee, the opportunity that you are giving up is the next best alternative that you could have spent your money on. This might be a cup of coffee from an alternative supplier, or it might be another item that you could have bought.

Workers

Workers provide labour to enable production to take place.

A key decision is how much labour time to provide in exchange for a wage. There are two contrasting effects that a worker will consider. As wages increase, the opportunity cost of leisure will increase, and so we would expect workers to work longer hours. However, in most countries in the world labourers are choosing to work shorter hours, and this is because as wages increase, people will consume more of the things they enjoy, including leisure.

Producers

Decisions made by a producer include:

- what to produce
- where to produce, e.g. whether to set up a bottling plant in Germany or Brazil.

For example, when a farmer decides to grow maize in a particular field, the opportunity cost is the next best crop that could be grown, e.g. onions.

Business activity is often criticised for failing to consider some elements of the opportunity cost of its activities that affect others. For example, the opportunity cost of creating pollution and waste is the cleaner environment that would otherwise exist.

Government

Governments receive income in the form of taxes and other revenues. Led by the finance minister, a government must then decide how to spend the money. The finance minister works with the various government ministries, e.g. health, education, defence and transport, to allocate government funds. There will be a minister in charge of each key area, and each will make a case for more spending for his or her department.

In each case it is necessary to identify the opportunity cost: if US$100 million extra is spent on education, that money cannot also be spent on health or road building. You can see how detailed discussion is necessary to make choices about how best to spend government money.

> **STUDY TIP**
>
> The concept of opportunity cost is important. In terms of pollution and its effect on the environment, you should understand that cleaning up the effects of pollution costs money, and could possibly lead to an increase in prices charged by a firm.

> **STUDY TIP**
>
> Government spending decisions involve opportunity cost, e.g. the implication of spending less on defence and more on education. You should be able to apply the concept of opportunity cost to such decisions.

KEY POINTS

1. The main groups in the economy consist of consumers, workers, producers, government and financial institutions.
2. Decisions made by these groups involve an opportunity cost.
3. Taking into account the opportunity cost of decisions means that the real cost of economic activity can be assessed.

SUMMARY QUESTIONS

1. Describe a choice made by a:
   a. consumer
   b. worker
   c. producer
   d. government.

   Explain the opportunity cost.

2. Why is it important to consider opportunity costs in economic decision-making?

3. Outline the implications to a government in terms of the opportunity cost of deciding to build more schools.

1.4 Production possibility curves

1.4.1 The production possibility frontier

Production possibility curves

A **production possibility curve** (or **frontier**) shows combinations of goods that can be produced in an economy at a particular time, utilising all resources.

In an economy, it is only possible to produce a given number of goods at a particular moment in time. The number that can be produced is shown on the production possibility curve.

For example, a territory could use its land to grow two main types of crop – bananas or sugar. If it used all the land to grow bananas it could grow 100 000 kg per year. Alternatively it could use all of its land to produce sugar and produce 50 000 kg per year. A third choice would be to use some of the land for growing bananas and some for growing sugar. For every extra kilogram of bananas grown the economy would have to give up half a kilogram of sugar. If each area of land was identical, the production possibility curve would be a straight line (Figure 1.4.1).

However, land is not identical. Some land is more suitable for growing bananas and some for sugar. If farmers want to produce more bananas they will first use the land that is best for growing bananas and least good for growing sugar. In this case the production possibility frontier is a curve rather than a straight line (Figure 1.4.2). The nearer we are to the end of the curve the steeper it is, because to grow more of one crop will involve a greater sacrifice of the other. The more bananas we grow, the larger the reduction in sugar output required to produce a few more bananas.

> **TOPIC GUIDANCE**
>
> Students should be able to:
> - define the term 'production possibility curve' and identify points on a production possibility curve.

To convert agricultural land to hotels involves giving up agricultural output

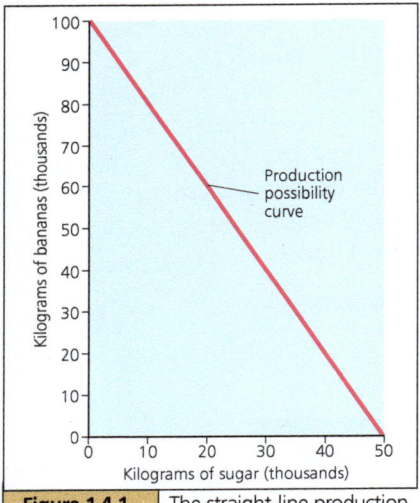

Figure 1.4.1 The straight-line production possibility curve: substituting sugar for bananas where land is identical

> **STUDY TIP**
>
> You should be able to demonstrate that you understand why a production possibility curve is usually drawn as a curve rather than as a straight line.

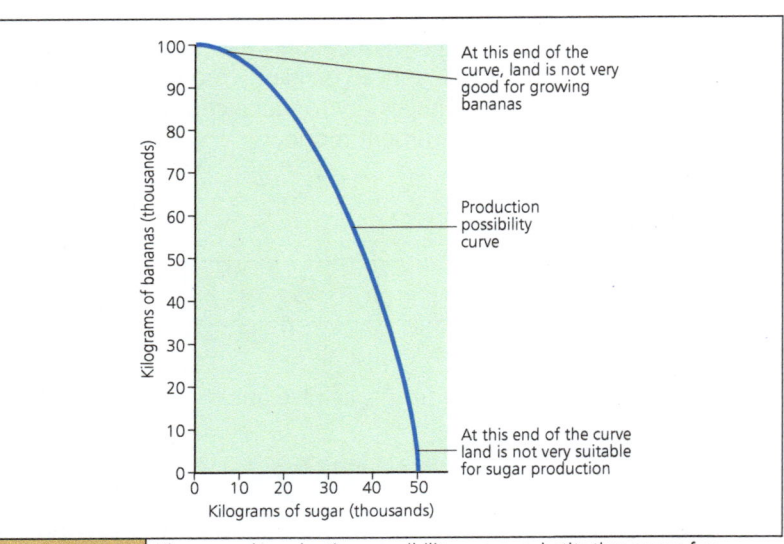

Figure 1.4.2 The curved production possibility curve: substituting sugar for bananas where some land is more suitable for banana and some for sugar production

Illustrating choice and resource allocation

A production possibility curve can be used to illustrate choices made in an economy and the resultant impact on resource allocation. For example, many island economies such as Mauritius, Sri Lanka, Jamaica, Barbados and Trinidad have had to weigh up how much land should be committed to agricultural purposes and how much to tourism. Figure 1.4.3 shows three alternatives. A is a situation where most of the land is allocated to tourism, B is a situation with a fairly even distribution of land between agriculture and tourism, and C is where most of the land is allocated to agriculture. If we start from position B and choose to allocate more land to tourism, we will have to sacrifice some agricultural land. Conversely, if we were to choose to allocate more land to agriculture we would have to reduce the area of land available for tourism.

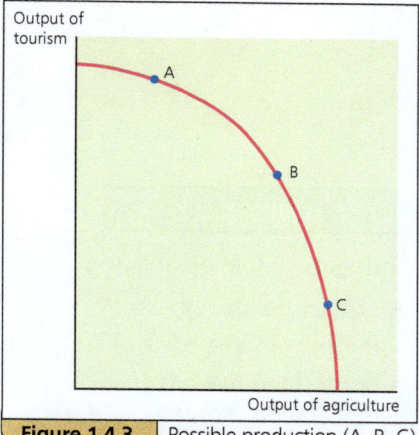

Figure 1.4.3 Possible production (A, B, C)

Illustrating opportunity cost

The concept of opportunity cost can be illustrated in the form of production possibility curves. In the production possibility curve shown in Figure 1.4.4 we can consider what happens when agricultural land is converted to hotels and leisure activities. The distance shown by the arrow (A1–A2) on the horizontal axis shows the value of agricultural production sacrificed to increase the value of tourism income by the value illustrated with an arrow on the vertical axis (T1–T2). The greater the proportion of resources already allocated to tourism, the greater the quantity of agricultural output that will have to be sacrificed to use more land for tourism. In other words, the greater the proportion of resources used for tourism, the higher the opportunity cost (measured in agricultural output) required to increase resource use for tourism.

> **STUDY TIP**
>
> You should by now realise the importance of opportunity cost in economics. A production possibility curve is an excellent way of showing that you understand how the concept can be applied to two products.

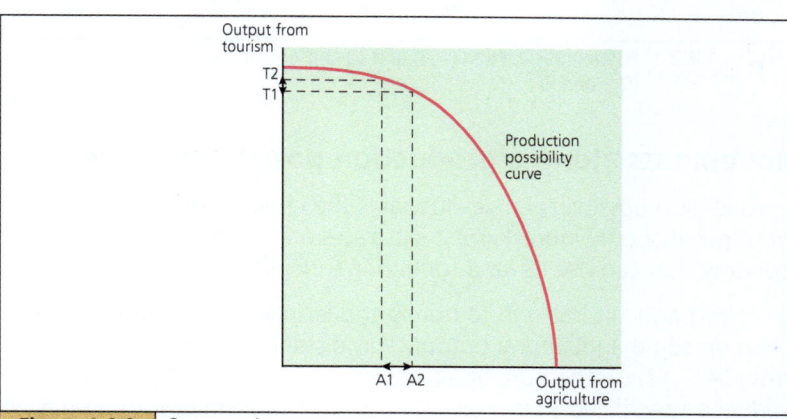

Figure 1.4.4 Opportunity cost

SUMMARY QUESTIONS

1. What do points on a production possibility curve represent?
2. What is the impact on resource allocation if a country chooses to use more land for producing tea and less for producing coffee?

KEY POINTS

1. A production possibility curve illustrates quantities of two goods that can be produced with existing resources at a point in time.
2. The curve shows different choices that can be made about how to allocate existing resources.
3. Opportunity cost can be measured along the curve in terms of the sacrifice in the quantity of one good when you choose to allocate more resources to an alternative good.

1.4.2 Movement along and shifts in a production possibility curve

TOPIC GUIDANCE

Students should be able to:

- explain points under a production possibility curve
- understand reasons for movements along a production possibility curve
- understand reasons for shifts in a production possibility curve.

Converting land for hotel construction involves sacrificing the previous land use

DID YOU KNOW?

Climate can have a major impact on the production possibility frontier. For example, hurricane Irma in 2017 had a massive effect in the Caribbean, to the extent that 95 per cent of the buildings in Barbuda were badly damaged, leaving over half of the island's population homeless. It can take years for an island economy to recover from such devastation.

Points under a production possibility curve

The production possibility curve illustrates how much of two goods can be produced, assuming all resources are being fully employed. We can illustrate this by taking the example of an economy that can use its land for tourism or agricultural production.

On the production possibility curve shown (Figure 1.4.2.1) points A, B and C show combinations of agricultural and tourism output that could be produced. However, points D, E and F illustrate points where some resources are not being used. They represent inefficient situations, which is why the points lie under the curve.

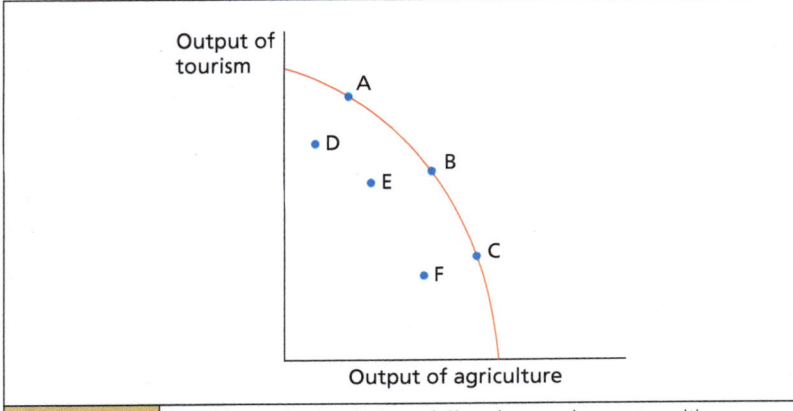

Figure 1.4.2.1 Possible production (A, B, and C) and unemployment positions (D, E and F)

Movements along a production possibility curve

A production possibility curve illustrates the choices that can be made about production. Figure 1.4.2.2 illustrates an example of an island economy that can use its land for either agricultural or tourist use.

To convert agricultural land to hotels and leisure activities will involve giving up some agricultural output. This distance shown by the arrow (A1–A2) on the horizontal axis shows the value of agricultural production sacrificed to increase the value of tourism output by the value illustrated by the arrow on the vertical axis (T1–T2). The greater the proportion of resources already allocated to tourism, the greater quantity of agricultural output that will have to be sacrificed.

Economists use the term 'movement' along a production possibility curve to describe the impact (in terms of output) of the substitution of one form of land use for another. For example, when tourism production is increased (from T1 to T2) at the expense of a reduction in agricultural output (from A2 to A1), we would move along the curve (from point X to point Y).

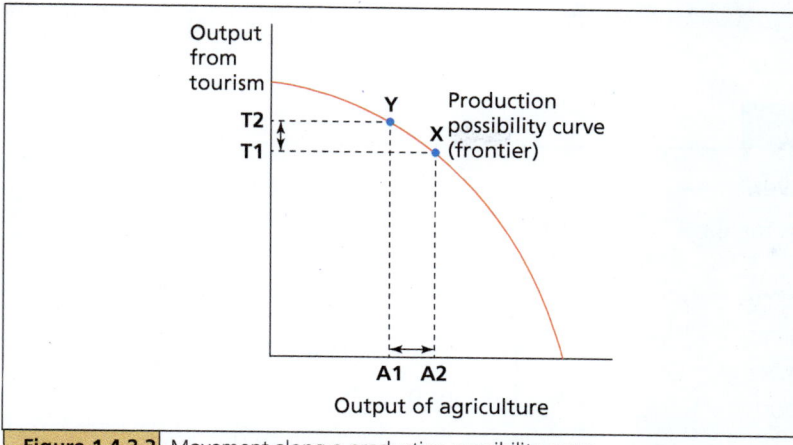

Figure 1.4.2.2 Movement along a production possibility curve

Shifts in the production possibility curve

The production possibility curve will shift to the right as a result of economies becoming more efficient, leading to economic growth. An example of this would be an island economy producing increased quantities of agricultural and tourism output with its resources.

Over time, economies become more efficient. This generally results from investing resources, e.g. by building new hotels or investing in new agricultural equipment. Increased efficiency is represented by a shift to the right in the production possibility curve. Assuming the original frontier is the curve PP, increased efficiency is represented by P1P1. To illustrate that P1P1 is more efficient, look at a point where 'X' of agricultural goods is produced (Figure 1.4.2.3). On PP, only 'Y' of tourism output can be produced. However, on P1P1, 'Y1' of tourism output can be produced.

The production possibility curve could also move from P1P1 to PP (a downward movement). For example, the economy could become more inefficient as a result of a hurricane. Two main factors affect the production possibility curve: a change in the amount of resources and a change in the productivity of existing resources.

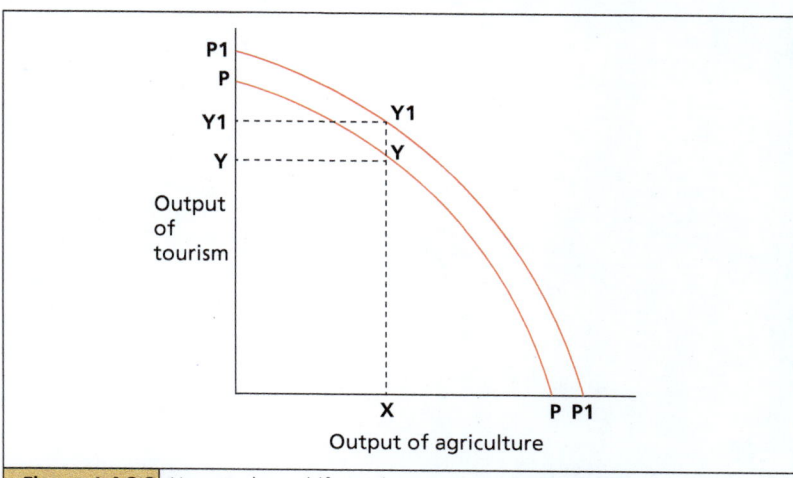

Figure 1.4.2.3 How to show shifts and movement on a production possibility curve

STUDY TIP

A production possibility curve shows combinations of two outputs that can be produced with existing resources. It can shift to the right when resources are more efficient or more plentiful. It will shift to the left if the resources become less efficient or scarcer.

KEY POINTS

1. Points that lie below a production possibility curve show an inefficient use of existing resources compared with what is possible.
2. Movements along a production possibility curve illustrate the substitution of one type of output for another with a given resource base.
3. Shifts in the production possibility curve represent either increased efficiency (shifts outwards) or decreasing efficiency (shifts inwards).

SUMMARY QUESTIONS

1. Why is it better for economic output to be on the production possibility curve rather than to lie below it?
2. What is the impact on the production possibility curve of shifting from one type of production to another?
3. Under what circumstances would a production possibility curve shift upwards and to the right?

Unit 1 — Test yourself

SECTION 1: Multiple-choice questions

Each question has ONE correct answer.

1. Which of the following BEST describes the basic economic problem?
   a. Limited needs and unlimited resources
   b. Unlimited wants and scarce resources
   c. Limited incomes and spending power
   d. Unlimited choices of consumer goods

2. Which of the following is a *human-made* resource?
   a. A production worker
   b. A forest
   c. A field of wheat
   d. A factory

3. Which of the following is an opportunity cost of using farmland to allow animals to graze?
   a. The cost of animal feed
   b. The price that the animals can be sold for
   c. The use of the land to grow crops
   d. The cost of preparing the land for grazing

4. Which of the following is NOT a *factor of production*?
   a. Labour
   b. Money
   c. Enterprise
   d. Capital

5. Which of the following is the reward to an entrepreneur?
   a. Profit
   b. Wages
   c. Revenue
   d. Employment

6. Which of the following illustrates the sustainable use of resources?
   a. Discovering new sources of oil for fuel
   b. Recycling soft drink bottles
   c. Burying rubbish in landfill
   d. Replanting trees following use for fuelwood

7. Which of the following is an example of opportunity cost as applied to consumers?
   a. The cost of an item bought regularly
   b. The ability to buy more when prices are lower
   c. The decision to buy a book instead of a toy
   d. The cost of a present bought for a friend

8. Which of the following is NOT a decision made by producers?
   a. Which goods or services to produce
   b. Where to locate a factory
   c. How to produce the goods or services
   d. How much of the good or service will be bought

9. Why must a government consider the opportunity cost of spending decisions?
   a. To get the best value for money
   b. Because the money comes from taxation
   c. Because a choice must be made between alternative uses
   d. To meet all the people's needs

10. Which of the following is NOT a scarce resource?
    a. Air
    b. Land
    c. Money
    d. Oil

SECTION 2

Country B is a developing nation whose economy has been growing at an average of 7 per cent a year for the last four years. The older industries are in the manufacturing sector, mainly based on cotton textiles and related products. Newer industries include computer games software development and customer call centre facilities for multinational banks. These organisations are owned and run by a growing group of 'new entrepreneurs'. There is a big demand for wood and other building materials throughout Country B, and this is leading to the loss of many square kilometres of forest. Generally the forest is not replanted, but used for farmland.

- The population is growing at approximately 4 per cent a year, although this is hard to measure as there is no formal census.
- The unemployment rate is very low, with jobs available for anyone who wants one. Wages are increasing as employers try to attract workers to their businesses.
- The average price level is increasing at a rate of 2 per cent per annum as firms raise prices in order to pay higher wages which have been increasing at a rate of 3 per cent per annum. People on a fixed income are having to think very carefully about how they spend their limited money as prices rise.
- The government of Country B has recently raised the age of compulsory schooling to 14 and is investing in new school buildings in rural areas.

1 a Explain what is meant by *human resources* and give an example from the text. (2)
   b Explain what is meant by *human-made resources* and give an example from the text. (2)
   c Explain ONE likely reason for the increased demand for resources in Country B. (2)
   d Discuss whether the use of labour in the new call centre industry in Country B may benefit the economy more than the established textiles factory jobs. (6)
   e Calculate the increase in real wages. (2)
   f Discuss the possible opportunity cost of the use of wood from forests in Country B for building materials. (6)
   g Using the example of a new call centre business, explain how the four factors of production may be used. (4)
   h Using the concept of opportunity cost and information in the text, discuss whether the government of Country B is wise to spend money on increasing education provision for the population. (6)

Total: 30 marks

SECTION 3

1. Country A is a small island nation in Asia, whose native population is growing at 5 per cent a year. The main town is situated in the south of the island and is growing fast, as many jobs are based there. The country is a popular tourist destination and beach resorts are located in the coastal areas. Several big hotel chains have built hotels and there are others that would like to buy land to build all-inclusive leisure resorts, with numerous facilities for guests. Apart from tourism, the main industry is fish canning, and a large factory is situated in the west of the island. The fishing boats bring their catch into the small port and much of
the canned produce is exported to Europe and the US.

   a. Explain why the resources of the island need to support more people than just the native population. *(4)*
   b. Identify and explain TWO examples of scarce resources mentioned above. *(4)*
   c. Using the information given, identify and explain TWO examples of natural resources that are being used by the people of Country A. *(4)*
   d. Discuss what sacrifices, in terms of resource use, may need to be made if the government of Country A wants to increase tourism. *(8)*

2. Fishing and tourism are the main industries in Country A. The government would like to welcome more tourists to the island.

   a. Identify the four *factors of production* as used in the fishing industry in Country A. *(4)*
   b. Choose THREE of the factors you have identified in A and explain the likely rewards to the owners of these. *(6)*
   c. Identify the four *factors of production* as used in the hotel industry in Country A. *(4)*
   d. Discuss how the proposed increase in tourism may affect the fishing industry and those employed within it. *(6)*

3. The main town on the island is becoming very busy and congested with traffic, which is also causing air pollution. For business, it is virtually impossible to find a shop or office to rent and many local residents are moving to quieter areas outside town, where new apartments are being built. They then need to spend time and money to travel into town by bus or car to work.

   a. According to the extract, what has been the opportunity cost of using more buildings in the town for offices and shops? *(4)*
   b. Describe TWO opportunity costs to local residents who choose to move out of town. *(4)*
   c. Describe TWO possible opportunity costs to the owners of the land where the new apartments are being built of the choice to provide homes for local residents. *(4)*
   d. Discuss how the government of Country A might use its resources to reduce congestion and pollution in the town. *(8)*

4. Two large international holiday companies have been planning to build hotel and leisure facilities for tourists on one of the island's beaches, which is also a popular day-trip destination for local families. The government tourism minister is keen to encourage these new developments in order to 'make the best use of our resources'. He also believes that if the hotel companies take their money elsewhere, this could lead to a loss of tourists coming to Country A.

   a. Explain what is meant by 'our resources' in this instance. *(4)*
   b. Explain the minister's view that more hotels will 'make the best use of our resources'. *(4)*
   c. State TWO possible opportunity costs to the island of a decision in favour of the hotel developments. *(2)*
   d. Using the concepts of scarce resources and opportunity cost, discuss whether increased tourism may be the best use of the island's resources in the long term. *(10)*

Total: 80 marks

2 The allocation of resources: how the market works and market failure

Unit 2 looks at how markets work. The market brings together buyers (who demand goods and services) and producers and sellers (who supply goods and services). It explains how the market helps to decide how scarce resources, such as 'land' and 'labour', will be used. Demand is the quantity that buyers are willing to buy at different prices and supply is the quantity that suppliers are prepared to sell at these prices.

Unit 2 also shows how price elasticity affects market prices. Elasticity is a measure of how quantities demanded and supplied in the market respond to changes in price.

The notion of market failure is also introduced. This shows how markets may not necessarily allocate resources in the most efficient way and may fail to meet the needs of members of a society. The alternative of a mixed economy is introduced, blending together market forces with some government intervention. Throughout unit 2, graphs and diagrams illustrate the points under discussion.

TOPIC COVERAGE

Students will cover the following topics:
- Micro- and macro-economics
- The market system and resource allocation decisions
- Introduction to the price mechanism
- The nature of demand, individual and market demand
- The nature of supply, individual and market supply
- How prices are determined, market equilibrium and disequilibrium
- Causes and consequences of price changes
- Price elasticity of demand (PED) and determinants of PED
- Price elasticity of supply (PES) and determinants of PES
- The market system, its advantages and disadvantages
- The nature of market failure
- Causes and consequences of market failure
- The mixed economic system
- Government intervention to address market failure

2.1 Microeconomics and macroeconomics

2.1.1 The difference between microeconomics and macroeconomics

> **TOPIC GUIDANCE**
>
> Students should be able to:
> - define microeconomics and macroeconomics
> - understand the difference between the two
> - outline the key decision-makers involved in each.

Micro and macro perspectives

To understand how economies work, it is helpful to make a distinction between:

- **microeconomics**: the study of smaller-scale units, markets and individual decision-making within the economy
- **macroeconomics**: the study of the major units and **aggregate** decisions that make up the economy.

Microeconomics

Microeconomic decisions are made on a small scale and involve the making of economic choices – that is, those involving scarcity – by businesses, individuals and consumers.

Examples of microeconomic decisions include those made:

- by a firm, e.g. how much to produce and what price to charge
- by an individual, e.g. how much time to spend on leisure activities
- by a consumer, e.g. what to buy, where to buy from, when to buy.

As individuals we make thousands of decisions every day that have a microeconomic dimension to them – whether or not to go into a particular shop, how long to spend there, what items to look at, which items to buy, etc. Many of these personal microeconomic decisions involve how we spend our money. Firms come into contact with large numbers of consumers who are in the process of making individual purchasing decisions. Firms have to decide how to respond to consumers' wishes – what products to make available, when and where to supply, how much to charge, etc. The decisions made by very large numbers of customers impact the decisions made by large numbers of suppliers in a market economy (see Unit 2.2).

Macroeconomics

Macroeconomics is concerned with aggregate decisions such as the total level of consumer and investment spending in an economy, and the impact these have on indicators that affect us all, such as:

- the level of inflation (rate at which prices are changing)
- the growth of the economy (as measured by the total level of output or incomes)
- changes in employment and unemployment
- the total level of exports and imports
- the level of development within an economy.

Central banks such as the Indian government's Reserve Bank of India are major macroeconomic decision-makers, setting the price of borrowing money (the interest rate) in the economy

Key decision-makers in the macro-economy

The main decision-makers in the macro-economy are as follows.

- Groups of consumers: their combined spending can be aggregated so that we can study the impact of the general level of spending on the economy. Sometimes economists refer to consumers as 'households'.
- Groups of producers or firms: as a group, businesses make decisions that impact on the economy, e.g. how much to produce within the national economy and how much to invest.
- Exporters (and importers): these are a subset of firms whose collective decisions impact on the international economy.
- The government: government decisions impact all firms and households in an economy.

  Governments:
  - make spending decisions, e.g. how much to spend on infrastructure and public services
  - tax households and firms to raise revenue for specific purposes, e.g. to discourage pollution
  - create laws that impact on other decision-makers, e.g. relating to competitive practices.
- The financial sector: banks and other financial institutions look after business and personal savings and lend money to economic decision-makers. This sector is regulated by the central bank (the government's bank), which sets the interest rate.
- International government bodies and non-government organisations (NGOs): a number of international bodies create the frameworks for international economic relations. For example, the World Trade Organization (WTO) establishes frameworks for trading between countries, and the International Monetary Fund (IMF) creates borrowing and lending frameworks to help countries to manage international payments.

DID YOU KNOW?

The term 'aggregate' is used in macroeconomics to signify a grouping of components to arrive at, for example, totals for aggregate demand (the total level of demand in the economy) and aggregate supply (total level of supply). Macroeconomics is concerned with the interplay between these aggregates and the measurement of aggregate figures, e.g. gross domestic product (GDP) aggregates the total level of output (or income in the economy).

STUDY TIP

The three main sectors in any economy are firms, households and the government. Individual decision-makers in these sectors make microeconomic decisions e.g. which firms to buy from. The sectors as a whole also make macroeconomic decisions.

SUMMARY QUESTIONS

1. Which of the following is studied by microeconomics and which by macroeconomics?
   a. the price of fish charged by a retailer in a fish market
   b. the total supply of goods in the Malaysian economy
   c. how many hours an individual works.
2. Which of the following is not a macroeconomic indicator?
   a. the level of inflation in Brazil
   b. the supply of goods by a local retailer
   c. global economic output.

KEY POINTS

1. Macroeconomic decisions are large whereas microeconomic decisions are small.
2. The main microeconomic decision-makers are firms, individuals and consumers.
3. Macroeconomics is concerned with aggregates such as national spending and national output.

2.2 The roles of markets in allocating resources

2.2.1 The market system

TOPIC GUIDANCE

Students should be able to:
- explain how a market system works
- show how the market allocates resources
- contrast market equilibrium and market disequilibrium.

A market system

A **market** is any situation in which buyers and sellers interact with one another. The market brings together buyers and sellers. This might be in a traditional market, where buyers and sellers come together to trade for vegetables, meat, clothing and other items. The term also describes any other situation in which buyers and sellers contact each other. They might do this over the telephone or on the internet.

The market brings together two sets of people: those who are willing and able to buy products (**consumers**), and those who are willing and able to supply products (**suppliers**).

Prices of fresh vegetables at Soroti fruit and vegetable market in Uganda are influenced by supply factors such as transport delays and drought

CASE STUDY | Soroti vegetable market

The local fruit and vegetable market in Soroti, Uganda supplies a range of fresh fruit and vegetables. The sellers are small stall holders who source their supplies from their own gardens (*shambas*) and from suppliers in the surrounding countryside. The produce deteriorates quickly, so it is important to sell it on market day.

Buyers range from householders buying a few items to eat on the day to commercial buyers looking to stock hotel and restaurant kitchens. Suppliers will look around to see what competitors are charging: they cannot pitch their price much above the daily market price or they will have unsold stocks at the end of the day. Consumers will want high-quality fresh produce at the best prices. They will also look around to make sure they are not paying more than the market price. The result of all this competition is that a market price is reached – that is, suppliers offer very similar prices. The two forces of demand and supply thus interact to create a market price.

The market price for different types of vegetables will vary from month to month, depending on which are in season and the ease of supply. When potatoes are plentiful, for example, there will be lots of sellers, leading to more competition and lower prices. When potatoes are less plentiful there will be fewer sellers and consumers will pay higher prices. Recently, prices for fresh vegetables such as cabbages and tomatoes have increased significantly because of drought, and also because the reliability of some lorries bringing vegetables to market has suffered due to poor road conditions.

Questions

1. Who are the suppliers and consumers at Soroti vegetable market?
2. What is likely to happen to the price if the quantity of cabbages coming to the market falls over time? Why?
3. What is likely to happen to the price if the number of consumers coming to the market increases over time?

STUDY TIP

Make sure that when you explain market disequilibrium you can do so both in terms of changes in supply and of demand.

Market allocation of resources

The economy has a range of resources available for use. These resources include the factors of production: land, labour, capital and enterprise. If the prices of cabbages and potatoes at Soroti vegetable market increase, then there is an incentive for farmers (entrepreneurs) in the Soroti area to plant more cabbages and potatoes (providing they have access to adequate water supplies). The market signals through higher prices that consumers want more of specific products. Transport companies may invest in more robust lorries (capital) in order to be able to supply the market.

At the same time there may be other produce, e.g. beans, that is becoming less popular. There will be fewer consumers of beans and the prices will fall. Farmers will therefore notice this signal and perhaps take some of the land they previously used for bean cultivation and use it to grow cabbages and potatoes.

Market equilibrium and disequilibrium

The term 'equilibrium' refers to a state where there is no tendency to change. However, markets are rarely like this. Most markets are characterised by disequilibrium states. This is because either demand or supply forces are in a state of change. Typical examples of forces for change will include changes in demand and supply.

- **Demand changes:** tastes and fashions change so that more or less of a good is demanded. Incomes rise, enabling people to afford more of particular product.
- **Supply changes:** weather impacts on supply – drought conditions lead to decreases and good conditions lead to increases in crop supply. Development of new technologies enables increased supply from the same or fewer resource inputs.

Changes in these market forces lead to rises or falls in price, which encourage further changes in demand and supply. When the market is in disequilibrium prices will change, as will the forces of demand and supply. We will examine market equilibrium in detail in section 2.5.1.

As we will see throughout this unit, the market is constantly seeking to move towards an equilibrium state where demand is matched by supply. When the market signals through rising prices that suppliers are supplying too little, they will seek to supply more. When the market signals through falling prices that suppliers are supplying too much, they will reduce supply.

KEY POINTS

1. The market consists of buyers (consumers) and sellers (suppliers).
2. Prices act as signals communicating the wishes of consumers to suppliers.
3. The market is more likely to be in a state of disequilibrium than equilibrium because demand and supply conditions continually change.

ACTIVITY

Use the example of a street market in your local town or other marketplace. Show how prices of fresh fruit in this market are determined by demand and supply. Who are the sellers? How many of them are there? What determines the prices they charge? Who are the buyers? What determines who they will buy from? How do the buyers influence prices?

SUMMARY QUESTIONS

1. What will be the impact on the price of soya beans of the following?
   a. more fertiliser is used on soya growing land
   b. the demand for soya based products increases
   c. a drought reduces soya harvests.
2. How might soya bean farmers react in the following situations?
   a. the price of soya beans increases on world and local markets
   b. the cost of water used for land irrigation increases
   c. soya becomes an even more fashionable food product.
3. Why is disequilibrium likely to be more common in food markets than equilibrium states? Give reasons for your answer.

2.2.2 Resource allocation decisions

> **TOPIC GUIDANCE**
>
> Students should be able to:
> - describe how the allocation of resources involves answering questions of what to produce, how to produce and for whom.

Allocation of resources

Resources can be used to make goods. Some, such as timber or water, are provided by nature. Others, such as tools and equipment, are human-made.

The table indicates some of the decisions that have to be made in an economy about allocating resources – that is, deciding how they will be used to produce goods and services.

Decisions involving allocation of resources	Examples
What resources will be used to produce goods and services	Type of energy (nuclear, coal, wind, solar) to use in power industry and homes
How the resources will be used	For example, whether energy supplies will be available for industrial production, e.g. in factories, or for private use (in homes)
Who decides how the resources will be used	Whether government-owned or private businesses will generate energy
Who benefits from the use of the resources	Whether the energy resources are available for just a few people or for all

> **DID YOU KNOW?**
>
> An economic system refers to the ways in which resources are allocated in an economy.

Government influence on economic decision-making

In some countries the government plays a major role in decision-making. In North Korea, for example, industries are government-owned and officials working for the government decide what will be produced, the methods of producing goods and the prices charged. In contrast, the government in most other countries plays a smaller part in this type of decision-making. Figure 2.2.2.1 gives some examples of countries and the different levels of **government intervention** in their markets.

> **STUDY TIP**
>
> These are the three key allocation questions:
> - What to produce?
> - How to produce?
> - Who to produce for?

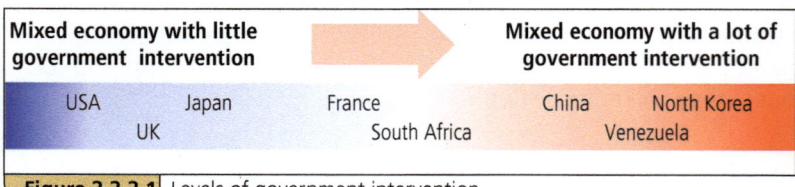

Figure 2.2.2.1 Levels of government intervention

The market and economic decision-making

In a **market economy** goods and services are freely exchanged and **prices** are decided by individual suppliers. Buying and selling decisions are made by buyers and sellers. Prices act as a guide.

- If prices are high enough, suppliers will be willing to supply to the market. High prices create profit and increased supply.
- If buyers think that prices give good value for money, they will buy goods. The lower the price, the more customers will buy.

Supporters of the market system argue that it is decentralised and automatic. The allocation of resources is determined by the wishes of individual consumers and suppliers.

A mixed economy

In most countries, decisions are made by a combination of government decision-making and the market. This is a **mixed economy**.

CASE STUDY | Mauritius

Mauritius is an island economy in the south-west Indian Ocean. The market is an important part of economic life in Mauritius. Mauritius is a trading economy that imports and exports large quantities of textiles. Companies on the island produce t-shirts and designer clothes for famous brand names such as Lacoste and Nike. Other industries include sugar cane and tea plantations owned by private companies. There are also thousands of small businesses producing household goods.

Most economic decisions are made by businesses and consumers. However, the government does play a part. One example is the payment of subsidies (sums of money) to encourage 'derocking': rocks are taken from the land to increase the quantity of fertile soil for growing sugar cane. Another example is management of the island's water shortage in the form of a government limit on water use at certain times of the year.

Questions

1 What economic decisions will be made by private businesses?
2 Why do you think that the government gets involved in the economy of Mauritius?
3 Does Mauritius have a mixed economy? Give a reason for your answer.

DID YOU KNOW?

Adam Smith was one of the earliest economists, and he described the price system as an 'invisible hand'. His theory was that if consumers and producers are allowed to choose what to buy and sell, prices will settle at a level that benefits individuals and their community.

In a mixed economy like that of Mauritius, most decisions are made by the market. However, the government does intervene by subsidising 'derocking' to help farmers increase sugar cane production

KEY POINTS

1 In a market economy buyers and sellers interact and this decides how resources are allocated.
2 Prices act as signals to buyers and sellers.
3 In a mixed economy the government makes some of the decisions about how resources will be used.

ACTIVITY

What types of goods and services are provided by government businesses in your country? Which ones are provided by private businesses?

SUMMARY QUESTIONS

1 Who are the main participants in a mixed economy?
2 What are economic resources?
3 Who decides on the use and allocation of resources in a market economy?

2.3 Demand

2.3.1 Price and demand

TOPIC GUIDANCE

Students should be able to:
- define and explain the term 'demand'.

The lower the price of roasted nuts sold from a stall, the higher demand for them will be

DID YOU KNOW?

When price falls and demand increases, this is referred to as an extension in demand. When price rises and demand falls, this is referred to as a contraction in demand.

STUDY TIP

It is important to understand that a movement along a demand curve (either an extension or contraction in demand) is caused by changes in the price of a product with everything else held constant.

Demand for goods and services

The **effective demand** for a good or service is a **want**, supported by the money to purchase it. If a good is in great demand, there will be a lot of people wanting to buy it at the current price.

Business organisations try to predict how much the demand for their products will be at different prices. They can then decide how much to make in order to meet demand.

Recording demand

The demand for a product can be recorded in a table which shows how many items would be demanded at given prices. It is also useful to record the demand for a product on a graph. A **demand graph** shows that larger quantities of any good will be bought at lower prices, and lower quantities at higher prices. Common sense and personal experience help to explain this: when goods are sold at a lower price, more people can afford to buy them. Existing purchasers will be tempted to buy more because they have to give up less of their income to make the purchase.

The table below shows the demand for bananas at different prices per kilogram. Figure 2.3.1 shows the same figures transferred onto a **demand curve**.

Price per kg	Quantity demanded
45 cents	1,000 kg
35 cents	3,000 kg
25 cents	4,500 kg
15 cents	6,500 kg

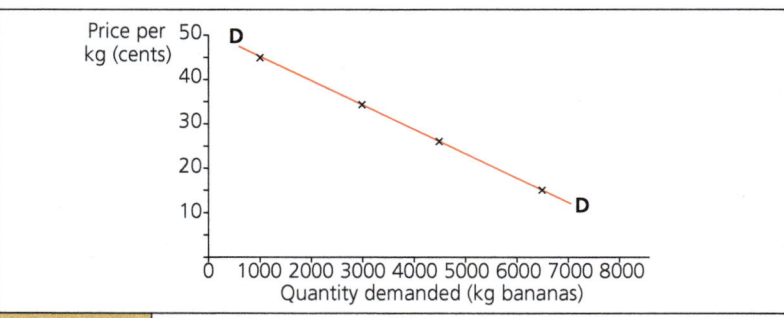

Figure 2.3.1 Demand for bananas at different prices per kg

The demand curve is constructed by showing prices on the vertical axis and quantities demanded along the horizontal axis. You can see that:

- higher prices lead to lower quantities being bought
- lower prices lead to higher quantities being bought.

CASE STUDY — Market demand

Demand for a product can be found by adding together the demand of all the consumers in the marketplace.

Rajesh sells small packets of roasted nuts from a stall in his village. It costs him 10 cents to grow the nuts that go into each packet. He sells the nuts to the other villagers, who come from five families. He has calculated the demand by asking the families how many packets they would buy from him per week at different prices.

Price per packet	Demand from the families					
	Family Panwar	Family Singh	Family Patel	Family Rai	Family Jain	TOTAL
10 cents	15	15	20	20	15	85
15 cents	12	12	20	15	11	70
20 cents	8	8	15	10	9	50
25 cents	7	7	12	9	5	40
30 cents	6	6	9	7	2	30
35 cents	5	4	6	5	–	20
40 cents	–	2	3	–	–	5
45 cents	–	–	–	–	–	–

Questions

1. Illustrate the information provided in the table in the form of a graph.
2. What is the relationship between price and quantity illustrated in the table and the graph?
3. How would you explain this relationship?
4. Why might it be more sensible for Rajesh to charge 25 cents per packet of nuts rather than 10 cents or 40 cents? Work out how much revenue (price × quantity sold) Rajesh will make at each price level.

Straight-line demand curves

Although in reality demand curves have a curved or irregular shape, economists find it convenient to draw them as a straight line (Figure 2.3.2) – it is quick and easy to draw. They are still referred to, however, as demand 'curves'. Price is shown on the vertical (*y*-axis) and quantity demanded on the horizontal (*x*-axis).

KEY POINTS

1. Effective demand is a want or need backed up by the ability to make a purchase.
2. At lower prices, greater quantities will be demanded than at higher prices.
3. A demand curve usually slopes down from left to right.

STUDY TIP

Make sure that any diagrams you produce are clearly drawn and labelled, including having correctly labelled horizontal and vertical axes.

ACTIVITY

Identify one good that you or your family have recently bought more of because its price has fallen. Identify another good that you have bought less of because its price has risen. Compare your findings with others in your group.

DID YOU KNOW?

Demand for products in a mixed economy is made up of demand from individuals, businesses and the government.

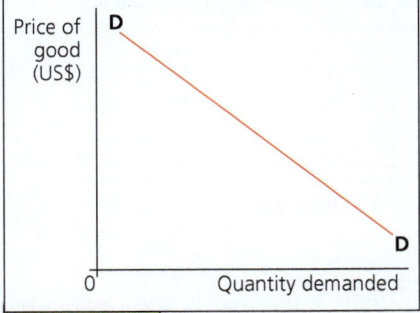

Figure 2.3.2 Straight-line demand curve

SUMMARY QUESTIONS

1. What is the difference between want and demand?
2. How would you illustrate a demand curve for pencils?
3. How does knowledge of demand help businesses?

2.3.2 Causes of shifts in the demand curve

TOPIC GUIDANCE

Students should be able to:
- describe the causes of changes in demand conditions
- contrast shifts in demand with movements along the demand curve.

If the use of highlighter pens becomes more popular among students, the demand curve for them will shift upwards to the right – this will lead to a rise in price

Movement along the demand curve

A demand curve shows the relationship between demand and price, all other factors remaining the same. When the price of a good rises or falls there is a movement along the curve. The movement is down the curve (**contraction**) for a rise in price, and up the curve (**expansion**) for a fall in price.

Changes in the conditions of demand

In addition to price, there are a number of factors that influence the demand for a product. If one of these factors alters, the conditions of demand are said to have changed. These factors include:

- popularity or fashion
- income
- the age distribution of the population
- the price of substitute and complementary goods (**complements**).

Changes in one (or a combination) of these factors will cause a **shift in the demand curve**. The demand curve will shift to the left if smaller quantities are wanted than before at given prices. A shift to the right indicates that larger quantities are wanted than before at given prices.

Popularity

Figure 2.3.2.1 shows that originally a quantity of 600 highlighter pens would be bought per month at 80 cents. However, if the pens become more popular with students, more will be demanded at all prices, so that, for example, at 80 cents perhaps 800 will be bought each month.

STUDY TIP

Make sure that you clearly show in a diagram which direction a demand or supply curve is shifting. This can be done through arrows and through clear labelling, such as: a shift from DD to D1D1.

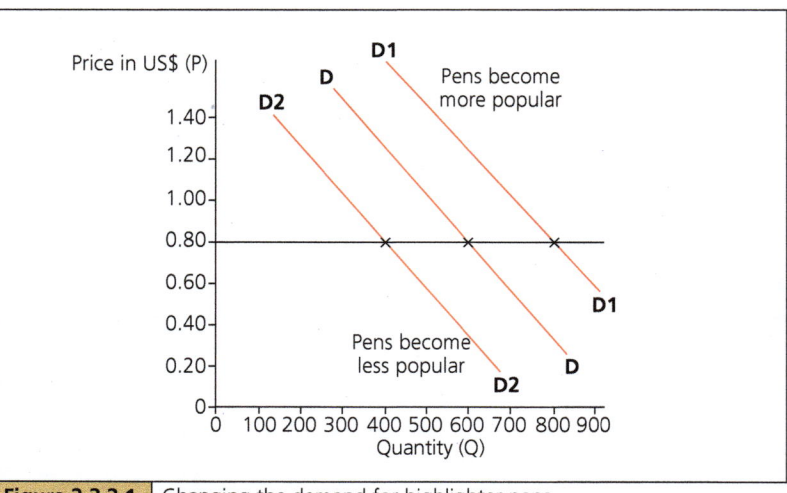

Figure 2.3.2.1 Changing the demand for highlighter pens

Alternatively, if the highlighters become less popular, fewer will be bought at all prices so that at 80 cents, 400 highlighters will now be demanded.

Income

It is obviously easier to buy goods if you have money to spend. The amount of income people have to spend on goods is known as their **disposable income**. Average incomes tend to rise over time, which leads to a general increase in demand for most goods, noticeably expensive branded goods. An increase in incomes leads to a shift in the demand curve to the right.

However, some products may become less popular as income rises: they may be regarded as inferior as spending power increases. So a bicycle may be replaced by a motor scooter or car. In the case of inferior goods, demand shifts to the left when incomes rise.

Age distribution

The **age distribution** of the population can affect demand. Many products appeal to certain age groups. For example, trainers or sneakers are particularly popular among young people across the world. The rising number of young people in many countries such as Brazil, China and Saudi Arabia has led to an increase in demand for trainers.

Price of other products

The demand for products that have close **substitutes** will often be strongly influenced by the price of the substitutes. This would be the case, for example, with different brands of tinned fruit or different brands of petrol, because there are many different brand names from which consumers can choose.

The demand curve for a product is likely to shift to the right if a substitute product rises in price. The demand curve for a product is likely to shift to the left if a substitute product falls in price.

Some products are used together (**complementary goods**) so that the demand for one is linked to the price of another. An example of this might be cars and car radios: if the price of cars falls, this is likely to lead to an increase in demand for car radios.

KEY POINTS

1. Movements along a demand curve result from changes in price.
2. Shifts in demand result from changes in factors other than price.
3. Shifts in demand result from changes in the popularity of goods, in disposable incomes, changes in the age distribution of the population and changes in the prices of complements and substitutes.

ACTIVITY

Identify two goods that you use that are complements. How does this affect your demand for both goods when the price of one of them falls?

STUDY TIP

Make sure you understand that a shift of a demand curve takes place when something happens in a market other than a change in the price of a product. A common error is confusion between movements along a demand curve and a shift of a demand curve to the right or left.

SUMMARY QUESTIONS

1. Give three examples of situations in which the demand curve for mobile phones would shift to the right.
2. What is an inferior good? Give an example. What would happen to demand for this good if incomes rise?
3. Give three examples of competing substitute products. What would happen to the demand for one of these as a result of a fall in the price of a substitute?

2.4 Supply

2.4.1 Price and supply

TOPIC GUIDANCE

Students should be able to:
- define and explain the term 'supply'
- contrast individual and market supply curves.

The higher the price an airline can charge people wishing to fly, the greater the number of flights it will be willing to supply

STUDY TIP

Make sure that when you are drawing a demand and supply diagram, you clearly label these. The demand curve will usually slope downwards from left to right and the supply curve will usually slope upwards from left to right.

The **supply** of a product is the quantity that a supplier is willing to provide at different prices. Typically suppliers will supply more at higher prices than at lower prices. Higher prices enable producers to cover costs and make increasing profits.

For example, every year large numbers of pilgrims fly from Delhi to Mecca for the annual pilgrimage, the Haj, an important festival in the Islamic calendar. Groups from the various mosques in India charter flights – that is, they hire airlines to provide special flights.

A charter airline might run six flights between Delhi and Mecca a day when pilgrims are prepared to pay US$200 for the return journey. However, if pilgrims are willing to pay US$300 each, the airline might buy more planes and run nine planes a day. At US$400 it might run 12 planes.

Supply of flights by the airline can then be illustrated on a **supply curve**, as shown in Figure 2.4.1.

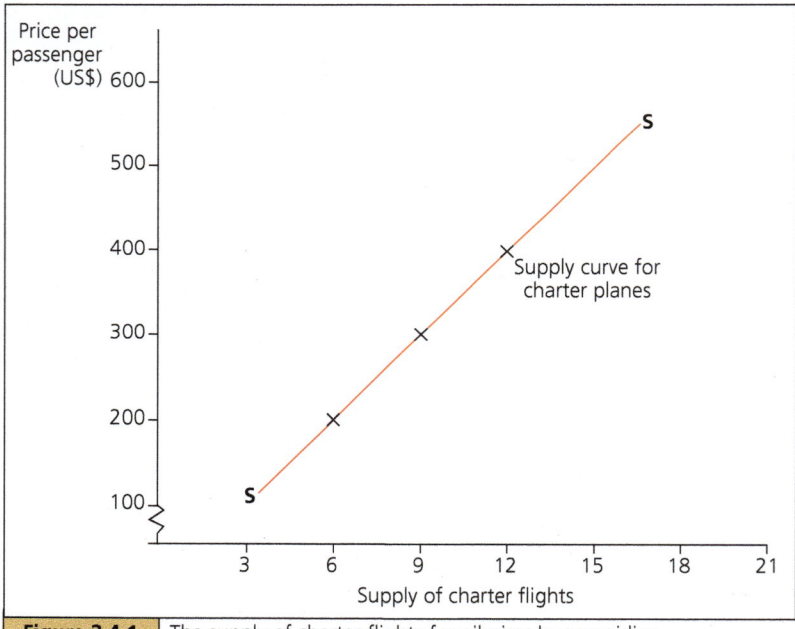

Figure 2.4.1 The supply of charter flights for pilgrims by one airline

Individual and market supply

Figure 2.4.1 illustrates the supply curve in an individual airline. To find out the **market** supply curve we need to add the individual supply curves of all the airlines supplying flights to Mecca. The same principle applies to the supply of any product to its market.

If there are three airlines supplying charter flights, the individual and market supply curves might look like those in Figure 2.4.2.

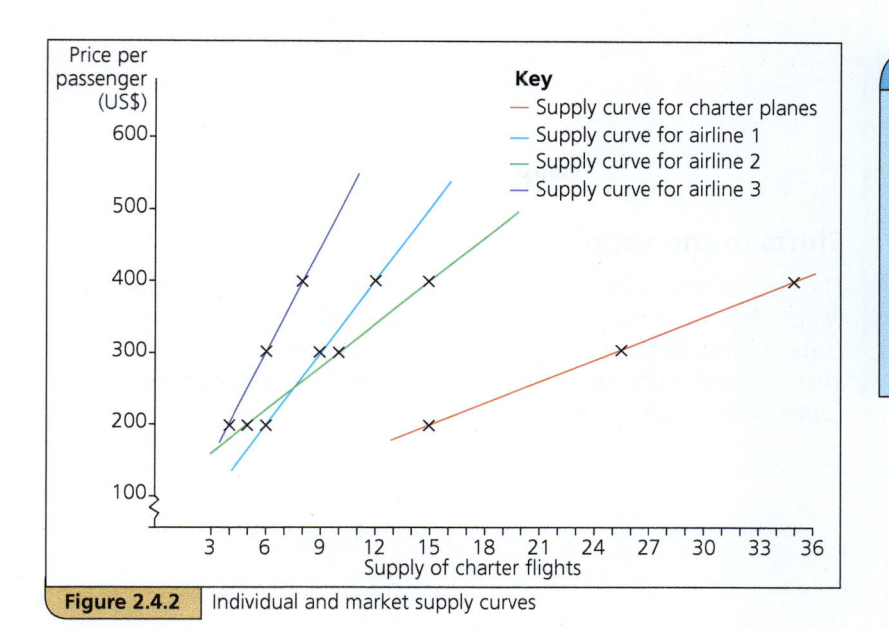

Figure 2.4.2 Individual and market supply curves

Price per seat (US$)	Supply by airline 1 (flights/day)	Supply by airline 2 (flights/day)	Supply by airline 3 (flights/day)	Market supply (flights/day)
200	6	5	4	15
300	9	10	6	25
400	12	15	8	35

Extensions and contractions in supply

In the example above we looked at how the supply of a product changes as a result of an increase in its price. This is referred to as an **extension in supply**. Should the price that pilgrims are prepared to pay rise from US$200 to US$400, this would lead to an increase in flights from 15 to 35 per day. In Figure 2.4.3 this is illustrated by the movement from Q to Q1. Supply extends from Q to Q1. In contrast, a fall in the price of charter flights would lead to a **contraction in supply**.

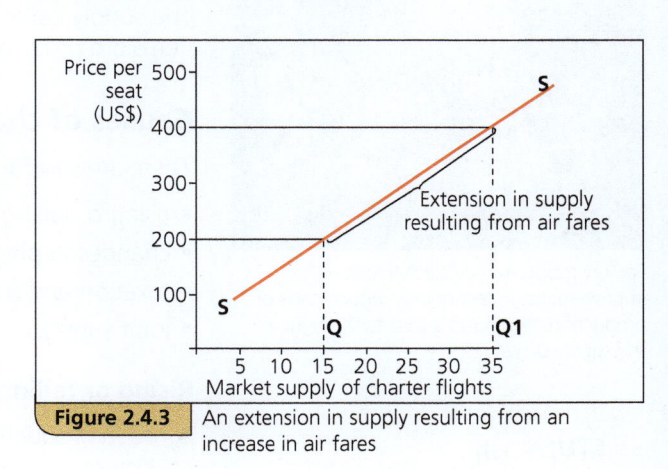

Figure 2.4.3 An extension in supply resulting from an increase in air fares

DID YOU KNOW?

Extension and contraction can be used to refer to both extensions in supply and demand and contractions in supply and demand. This relates to changes in the quantity supplied, or the quantity demanded, resulting from changes in the price of a good.

KEY POINTS

1. Supply is the quantity that producers provide to the market at different prices.
2. Producers supply more at higher prices than at lower ones.
3. The supply curve slopes up from left to right on a supply diagram.
4. Extensions and contractions in supply result from changes in the price of a product.

SUMMARY QUESTIONS

1. Describe the relationship between quantity supplied and price.
2. How does a rise in price lead to an extension in supply?
3. How does a fall in price lead to a contraction in supply?

2.4.2 Conditions of supply

TOPIC GUIDANCE

Students should be able to:
- describe the causes of changes in supply conditions
- analyse changes in supply to identify effects in the market.

Factory robots in the Czech Republic: improvements in technology reduce costs of production, leading to a shift to the right in the supply curve

STUDY TIP

Oil is a vitally important resource in most countries. It is useful to know whether the general price of oil is going up or down, and to demonstrate that you are up to date with current events.

Shifts in the supply curve

The cost of producing an item is determined by the price of the various inputs, including the raw materials and machinery used to make it. Rises in the prices of some of these resource inputs will increase production costs, which in turn results in a reduction in supply at each price rise (see Figure 2.4.2.1).

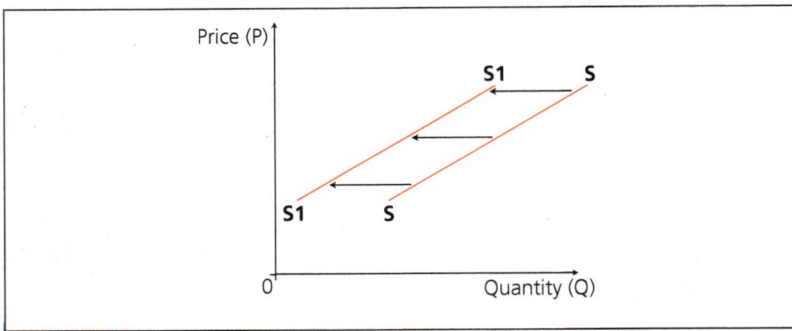

Figure 2.4.2.1 Effect of a shift in the supply curve

The supply curve shifts to the left when, at any given price, fewer items are produced and offered for sale.

Causes of changes in supply conditions

There are several factors that can cause **changes in supply**:
- rising or falling production costs
- changes in physical conditions
- taxation and subsidies
- joint supply.

Rising or falling production costs

A rise in production costs pushes the supply curve to the left (it will cost more to produce each level of output), and a fall in production costs pushes the supply curve to the right.

Production costs fall when the price of resources falls. So when the price of oil falls, for example, energy costs for all industries are reduced. Rising resource prices lead to rising production costs. Wars and conflicts can restrict the supply of important resources such as oil, and can lead to rapid increases in production costs. In recent years economic growth in China has led to price rises for many important industrial metals across global markets.

The development of new technology, in the form of computer-based processing systems and computer-controlled machinery, has reduced production costs in many industries.

Physical conditions

Changes in the weather, the quality of soil and natural disasters such as flooding and drought can have a major impact, particularly on agricultural products. Climate change means that it is increasingly difficult to grow crops in drier areas of the planet.

Taxation and subsidies

Rises in taxation and **subsidies** pull in opposite directions on the supply curve. A production tax of 10 cents per unit on a good would increase the cost of its production by 10 cents per unit. In contrast, a subsidy would reduce the costs of production. Supply will therefore shift to the left as a result of rising taxes on a product, and to the right as a result of a subsidy (see Figure 2.4.2.2).

Joint supply

Some production processes create more than one product (**joint supply**): when oil is refined the process creates by-products that can be used to manufacture goods such as synthetic carpets and soap. Increases in oil supply will therefore drive down the price of these by-products as more of them are supplied to the market.

ACTIVITY

The following headlines have appeared in newspapers. State in each case the likely impact on supply in the relevant industries or areas.

- Wages fall in printing industry
- South Africa – good wine-growing conditions reported
- High-tech start-up businesses – new subsidies announced
- Brazil – poor coffee harvest
- South East Asia earthquake – latest news

Effect of changes in supply on the market

An increase in supply results in a fall in the price of a product. This leads to a movement along the demand curve (more is bought in response to the lower price).

A decrease in supply results in a rise in the price of a product. This leads to a movement along the demand curve (less is bought in response to the higher price).

KEY POINTS

1. The supply curve shifts to the right as a result of increases in supply at each price.
2. The supply curve shifts to the left as a result of a fall in supply at each price.
3. Shifts in supply result from changes in costs of production, physical conditions and changes in joint supply.

DID YOU KNOW?

In the Middle East and North Africa (MENA) area, an increasingly scarce resource is water. Yemen is the country most affected. There are 400 million people in the MENA area with a desperate need for water. In many areas water is delivered in tankers or sold in bottles. Increasing scarcity for businesses drives up this important cost of production.

DID YOU KNOW?

A subsidy is a sum of money given by the government to support a particular purpose or activity. For example, a subsidy might be 10 cents per unit produced.

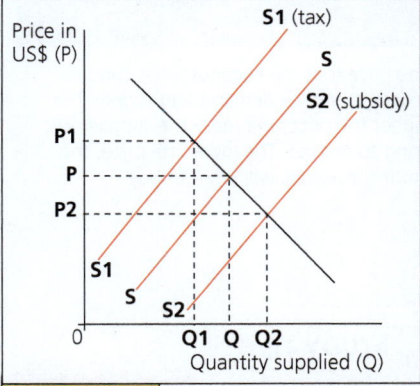

Figure 2.4.2.2 The impact of taxes and subsidies on the supply of a product

SUMMARY QUESTIONS

1. Explain and illustrate the effect of the use of improved manufacturing technology in the car industry.
2. How might a fall in the supply of oil have a multiple effect in many markets?
3. Explain joint supply by giving an example of a locally produced product.

2.5 Price determination

2.5.1 Market equilibrium

TOPIC GUIDANCE

Students should be able to:
- demonstrate the principle of equilibrium price and analyse simple market situations with changes in demand and supply.

The price that the coconut seller charges is determined by demand and supply. The higher the price, the more the supplier will bring to market. The lower the price, the more consumers will want to buy

STUDY TIP

The equilibrium position in a market will be where demand and supply intersect. When you draw this in a diagram, you should make sure that you clearly show the equilibrium price on the vertical axis and the equilibrium quantity on the horizontal axis.

Equilibrium price

Equilibrium means a state of balance. **Equilibrium price** occurs when there is a balance between demand and supply: the quantity demanded by consumers is equal to the amount that suppliers are willing to provide. For example, Ramesh and his family collect fresh coconuts in a plantation that they own. They sell them at a local holiday beach. The higher the price they can get, the more they will supply. The lower the price that Ramesh charges, the more customers will buy his coconuts (they can always buy from rival sellers).

The table of demand and supply schedules shows the weekly demand and supply for Ramesh's coconuts:

Price of Ramesh's coconuts (US$)	Supply per week	Demand per week
2.50	500	200
2.00	400	400
1.50	300	600
1.00	200	800

These demand and supply curves can be illustrated on a single drawing, as in Figure 2.5.1.1.

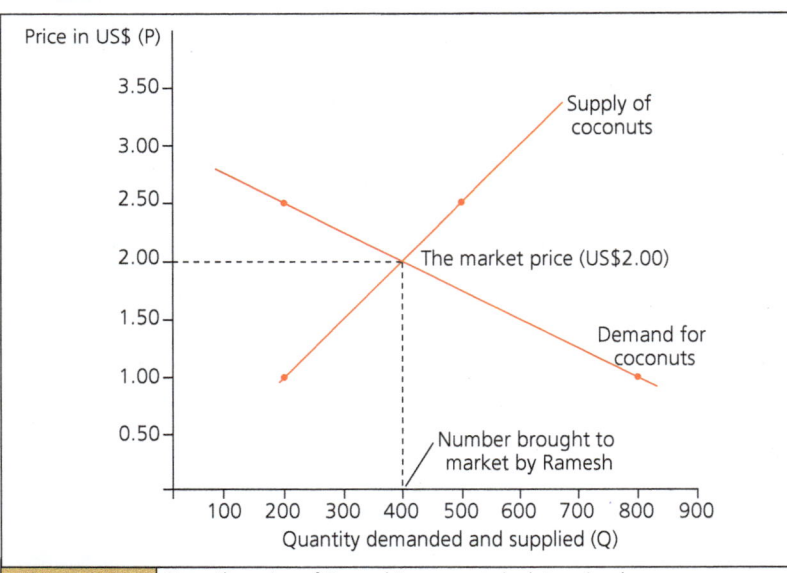

Figure 2.5.1.1 How the price of Ramesh's coconuts is determined

You can now see that, at a price of US$2.00 per coconut, 400 would be bought each week. At this price Ramesh's customers would be happy to buy all 400 and Ramesh would be happy to supply this quantity. This is the equilibrium price, as both seller and buyer are happy with the price.

You can see why this point is an equilibrium one by considering non-equilibrium points. For example, at US$2.50 Ramesh would be prepared to supply 500 coconuts, but buyers would only be prepared to purchase 200 (leaving 300 unsold). Alternatively, if we examine a price below the market one (US$1.00), customers would be willing to buy 800 coconuts, but Ramesh would only be prepared to bring 200 to sell. Customers would soon bid the price back up to the equilibrium price.

The market price is often referred to as the **market clearing price**, because demand matches the quantity supplied. Therefore the market would be 'cleared', with no coconuts remaining and no dissatisfied customers.

> **ACTIVITY**
>
> Identify some food items in a local shop or market that are being sold off at the end of the day. It is possible that the prices charged earlier in the day above the equilibrium price. Try to identify food items that have run out as well – it may be that the price charged was too low.

> **DID YOU KNOW?**
>
> Market disequilibrium exists when the forces of demand and supply do not balance each other, leading to a tendency to change. For example, oversupply to the market leads to a fall in price, which in turn will lead to reductions in supply.

CASE STUDY Demand and supply for Sweet Pastilles

Sweet Pastilles are a popular type of sweet sold from a variety of shops and small kiosks. The following table sets out the demand and supply schedules for different prices of Sweet Pastilles.

Price per packet (cents)	Demand (million packets per year)	Supply (million packets per year)
10	320	0
20	240	80
30	160	160
40	80	240

Questions

1 Set out the figures in the form of a graph.
2 a What is the equilibrium price?
   b Why is this the equilibrium price?
3 What volume of sweets will be supplied at the equilibrium price?
4 Explain why neither 10 cents nor 40 cents is the equilibrium price.

> **STUDY TIP**
>
> The idea of a market clearing price is very important. Make sure you understand that this will bring demand and supply together at a particular price without any need for government intervention.

KEY POINTS

1 At the equilibrium price demand and supply are in balance.
2 The equilibrium price is also known as the market clearing price.
3 The market clearing price can be illustrated by demand and supply curves.

SUMMARY QUESTIONS

1 Why is the equilibrium price the best price for suppliers to charge?
2 What would happen if the price were higher than the equilibrium price?
3 What would happen if the price were lower than the equilibrium price?

2.6 Price changes

2.6.1 Causes and consequences of price changes

TOPIC GUIDANCE

Students should be able to:
- identify changing market conditions as causes of price change
- draw demand and supply diagrams to illustrate changes in market conditions.

Changes in market conditions

Changes in demand and supply will impact on the price of goods and services.

This can be summarised in the following table:

	Effect on equilibrium market price	Effect on equilibrium market quantity
Demand shifts to right	increases	increases
Demand shifts to left	falls	falls
Supply shifts to right	falls	increases
Supply shifts to left	increases	falls

Table 2.6.1 Effect of demand and supply changes

Figure 2.6.1 illustrates the effect of an increase in demand for an expensive brand of trainers. This might be triggered by the rising popularity of the brand, an increase in consumers' incomes, an increase in the population of consumers (mainly young people) or a fall in the price of a good that complements the sneakers, e.g. designer clothes or tracksuits. The diagram illustrates the impact of the change. Demand shifts from DD to D1D1, leading to an increase in price from P to P1 and an increase in the quantity traded on the market from Q to Q1.

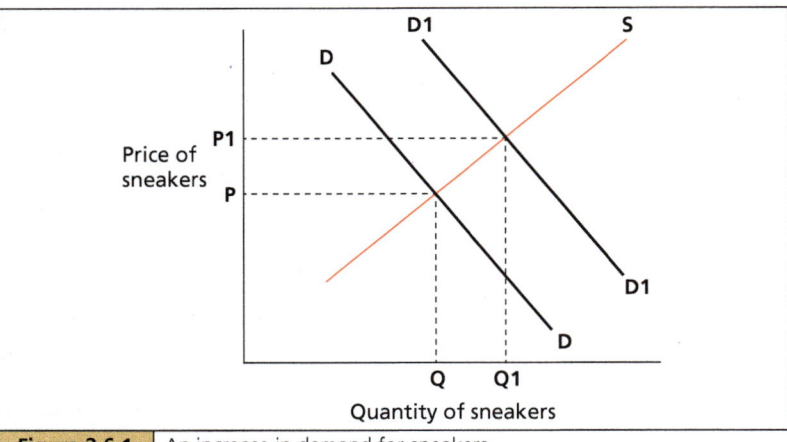

Changes in demand for items like trainers can bring about changes in market equilibrium

Figure 2.6.1 An increase in demand for sneakers

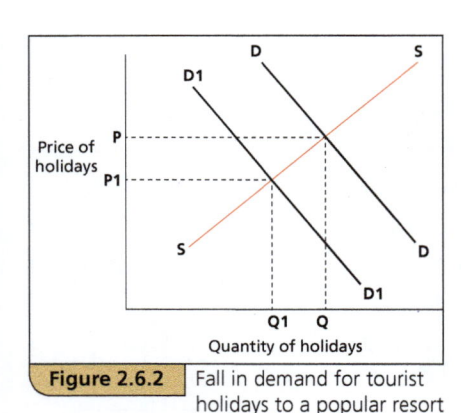

Figure 2.6.2 illustrates the effect of a fall in demand for holidays to a popular destination. This might be a result of adverse weather conditions in the region or steep price rises in the visitors' home market. You can see that the market price charged by tour operators would fall from P to P1 and the quantity of holidays traded in the market would fall from Q to Q1.

Figure 2.6.2 Fall in demand for tourist holidays to a popular resort

Figure 2.6.3 shows the impact of a shift in the supply of tomatoes to a vegetable market in Tripoli, Libya. There are a number of reasons why the supply might increase, including an improvement in growing conditions, an increase in the use of fertiliser, the use of better techniques for growing (including better equipment such as greenhouses), a fall in distribution costs, e.g. cheaper fuel, or a subsidy paid by the government to encourage small farmers.

Figure 2.6.3 Increase in the supply of tomatoes to vegetable market

Figure 2.6.4 Fall in supply of sugarcane to the regional market

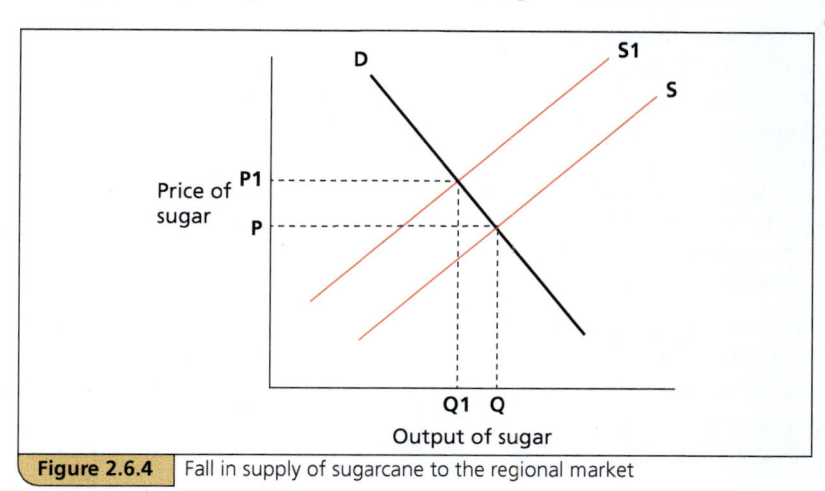

Figure 2.6.4 shows the impact of a reduction in sugar cane production in the Caribbean on the regional sugar market. What factors can you think of that would cause the supply curve to shift to the left?

KEY POINTS

1. A change in the quantity demanded or supplied results from a change in its price.
2. A change in demand or supply results from a change in the conditions of demand or supply.
3. A change in demand or supply leads to a new market quantity and a new market price.

STUDY TIP

It is important to understand the difference between a change in demand and a change in the quantity demanded. A change in demand involves a shift in the demand curve. A change in the quantity demanded results from a change in the price of that good. The same distinction can be applied to a change in supply and a change in the quantity supplied.

SUMMARY QUESTIONS

1. What is the difference between:
   a a change in demand, and
   b a change in quantity demanded?

   Explain your answer with reference to the demand for meals in a popular restaurant.

2. What is meant by the market environment? Who are the main decision-makers in this environment?

3. How does a change in price affect demand for a product in the market?

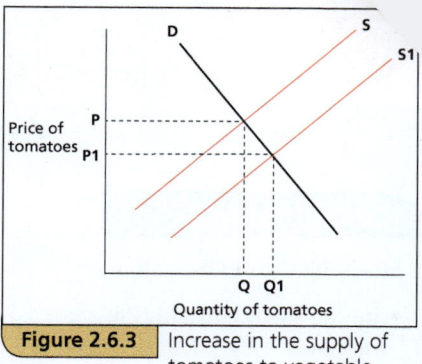

Elasticity of demand

2.7.1 Price elasticity of demand

TOPIC GUIDANCE

Students should be able to:
- define price elasticity of demand
- perform simple calculations.

By cutting the price of rail fares, Indian Railways has substantially increased revenues, because demand is elastic

DID YOU KNOW?

Price elasticity measures how much the demand for a product alters in response to a change in its price. Demand for a product is elastic when it alters by a larger proportion than the change in price. Demand is *in*elastic when it alters by a smaller proportion than the change in price.

What is price elasticity of demand?

A restaurant owner who is considering increasing prices will first want to know what effect this will have on the customers. Will there be no effect, a small fall in customers or a large fall? If the number of customers remains the same or falls by a smaller percentage than the price change, the business will make more revenue and profit. The calculation used to estimate this is **price elasticity of demand**, which measures how demand for a product responds to a change in its price. Anyone wishing to raise or lower prices should first estimate the price elasticity.

It is useful for a government to know the effect of raising taxes on particular goods. If it raises taxes a little and customers continue to buy as many goods as before, tax revenue will rise without harming the demand. However, if the tax leads to a substantial fall in demand this could lead to:

- a fall in tax revenues
- a substantial fall in sales for makers of the taxed goods.

CASE STUDY | **Indian Railways lowers prices**

Railways in India are government-owned. Indian Railways is India's largest employer.

At the beginning of the 21st century, India's railway network was running at a loss and was on the edge of bankruptcy.

Instead of raising fares, the Railway Board decided to cut them. This led to much higher passenger numbers. At the same time, the trains were lengthened. Now that each train pulls more carriages, the cost per passenger has fallen. By 2017 Indian Railways was making a profit in 10 of its 17 operating zones. Profits on freight tend to compensate for losses on passenger traffic. Costs are high because of the large number of employees.

Questions

1. Why do you think the decision was taken to cut rail fares?
2. What would have been the effect on revenues and profit of cutting rail fares? (Note that revenue refers to the money received by Indian Railways principally from the sale of rail tickets.)

Measuring price elasticity

Where falls in price have a more than proportional effect on demand, as in the Indian Railways case, demand is said to be **elastic**. If instead demand changes by a smaller proportion than the change in price, it is said to be **inelastic**. Price elasticity of demand is calculated as follows:

$$\text{Price elasticity of demand} = \frac{\text{\% change in quantity demanded}}{\text{\% change in price}}$$

Making simple calculations

1. First calculate the percentage change in quantity demanded (the demand would be an estimate). This is the change in demand as a percentage of the quantity originally demanded (i.e. before the price change).
2. Next calculate the percentage change in price. This is the change in price as a percentage of the original price (i.e. before the price change).
3. Divide the percentage change in demand by the percentage change in price.
4. Remember to include the minus sign. However, when deciding whether demand is elastic or inelastic you should ignore the minus sign and focus on the absolute number (as shown in point 5 and the examples below).
5. If the absolute value of the figure is greater than 1, demand is relatively elastic. If the absolute value of the figure is less than 1, demand is relatively inelastic.

Example 1: A railway company reduces rail fares from US$1 to 90 cents. Daily demand for tickets rises from 100 000 to 120 000.

$$\frac{20 \text{ per cent}}{-10 \text{ per cent}} = -2$$

Price elasticity is therefore −2. As the absolute value is greater than 1, demand is elastic.

Example 2: A bus company reduces bus fares from US$1 to 90 cents. Daily demand for tickets rises from 10 000 to 10 500.

$$\frac{5 \text{ per cent}}{-10 \text{ per cent}} = -0.5$$

Price elasticity is therefore −0.5. As the absolute value is less than 1, demand is inelastic.

SUMMARY QUESTIONS

1. Why should a business estimate elasticity of demand before changing its prices?
2. Calculate the price elasticity of demand for melons sold from a fruit store: the owner reduces prices from 20 cents to 15 cents per melon, and daily demand increases from 100 to 150.
3. Why is price elasticity of demand represented by a minus figure?

DID YOU KNOW?

Price elasticity of demand is always a minus figure. This is because an increase in price (+) leads to a fall in demand (−). A fall in price (−) leads to a rise in demand (+). Another way of putting this is that there is an *inverse relationship*.

STUDY TIP

A common mistake is to state that a particular good is elastic, e.g. a CD. Make sure you can understand that it is not the CD that is elastic, but the demand for it.

KEY POINTS

1. Price elasticity of demand measures the responsiveness of demand to price changes.
2. Price elasticity of demand is calculated by dividing the percentage change in quantity demanded by the percentage change in price.

2.7.2 Elasticity of demand and total spending/product revenue

TOPIC GUIDANCE

Students should be able to:

- demonstrate the usefulness of price elasticity in particular situations such as revenue changes and consumer expenditure.

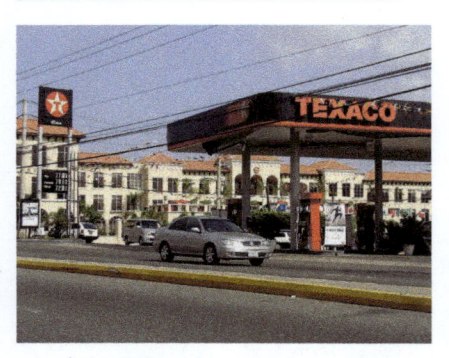

Knowledge of elasticity enables governments to decide how much tax can be levied on products such as petrol to maximise tax revenues

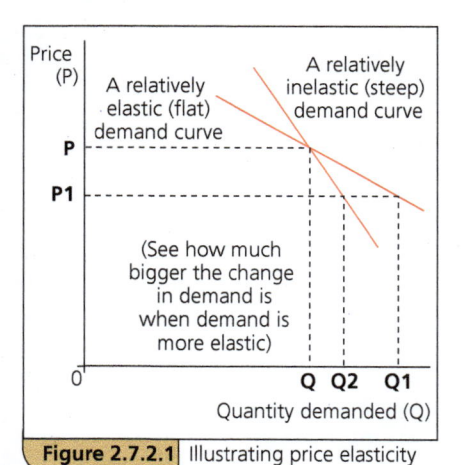

Figure 2.7.2.1 Illustrating price elasticity of demand

ACTIVITY

Interview someone who has a small business to find out how knowledge of consumer demand influences the prices charged for products.

Illustrating price elasticity of demand

In section 2.7.1 we saw that price elasticity of demand measures the responsiveness of changes in the quantity demanded to changes in price. Where demand for a product is relatively elastic, this is represented by a shallow sloping demand curve. Where demand is relatively inelastic the demand curve will be steeper (see Figure 2.7.2.1).

Comparing the same price change – a fall from P to P1 on the graph – the change in quantity from Q to Q1 is much larger for the good with the elastic demand than for the one with the inelastic demand (Q to Q2).

Revenue implications

The **revenue** of a business is the sum of money that it receives from sales of goods.

Revenue = Quantity sold × Price per item

For example, if a business sells 5,000 items at US$30 per item, its sales revenue will be US$150 000.

Knowledge of price elasticity enables sellers to calculate revenues at different prices. For example, Yin Qiang is going to import radios and is deciding on a price to charge. He has carried out research that reveals the following:

Price US$	Demand per month	Sales revenue
50	1,000	50 000
40	2,000	80 000
30	5,000	150 000
20	6,000	120 000

Using this information he will be encouraged to charge a price of US$30, because this will yield the most revenue.

The price elasticity of demand is particularly elastic between US$40 and US$30. The price elasticity is −10. When price is reduced from US$40 to US$30 (a price change of 25 per cent), quantity demanded increases by 250 per cent (from 2000 to 5000).

$$\frac{250 \text{ per cent}}{-25 \text{ per cent}} = -10$$

(a reduction in price from $40 to $30 is 25 per cent)

Yin Qiang would also need to take into consideration the cost of importing the radios before deciding on the price to charge.

Factors that influence the price elasticity of demand for products include:

- whether consumers see the product as essential or as a luxury: demand for necessities, e.g. basic foodstuffs such as rice, noodles and potatoes, is relatively inelastic

- how much consumers spend on the item: if they spend only a tiny fraction of their income on an item, demand may be more inelastic than for goods they spend a lot on, such as matches (relatively inelastic) or luxury foods (relatively elastic).

Total revenue

When producers and sellers reduce or lower prices they want to know what the impact is on total revenue. In both situations the ideal is to increase total revenue. The table to the right shows the impact on total revenue of a change in price. The table relates to elasticity for the specific price change.

	Elastic demand	Inelastic demand
Price increase	Revenue will fall	Revenue will rise
Price fall	Revenue will rise	Revenue will fall

Knowing whether demand is elastic or inelastic in relation to a change in market price will help a firm to make a pricing decision

Tax decisions

Knowledge of price elasticity is also important for a government when it levies taxes on goods. As we shall see in Unit 4, a government has a number of objectives when raising taxes. One of these is to bring in revenue to finance government spending. Taxes need to be levied at rates that maximise these revenues. A number of goods taxed by governments have inelastic demand: the demand for petrol in the UK, for example, is unaffected by a price that includes tax of more than 70 per cent. The government therefore needs to be careful not to overtax items to the point at which they become so expensive that demand for them becomes relatively elastic.

Exchange rate changes

In Unit 6.3 we explain the importance of the exchange rate. The **exchange rate** is the rate at which the currency of one country will exchange for the currency of another country. When the exchange rate of a currency rises or falls this affects prices for firms that buy and sell internationally. In section 6.3.3 we explain how price elasticity of demand affects revenues as a result of changes in exchange rates.

STUDY TIP

Make sure that you understand why knowledge of price elasticity of demand is useful to a business. If demand is price elastic, a business should lower the price to increase revenue. If, however, demand is price inelastic, a business should raise the price to increase revenue.

KEY POINTS

1. Knowledge of price elasticity of demand helps decision-making.
2. Businesses should identify price elasticity of demand in order to maximise revenues.
3. Governments can use knowledge of price elasticity to set tax rates on goods.

DID YOU KNOW?

An important factor affecting price elasticity of demand is whether there is a substitute for a product. If there are no substitutes, the product is likely to have an inelastic demand (and a high price). This is the case with a number of important medicines developed by pharmaceutical companies. The companies take out legal protection in the form of a patent. A **patent** is a licence granted to an inventor preventing others from copying the idea.

SUMMARY QUESTIONS

1. Describe two situations in which knowledge of price elasticity would help a decision-maker to set prices.
2. If a business raised the price of a product with an inelastic demand, what would be the effect on sales revenue?
3. How would knowledge of price elasticity of demand for petrol help a government in deciding how much tax to levy on it?

Elasticity of supply
2.8.1 Price elasticity of supply

TOPIC GUIDANCE

Students should be able to:
- define price elasticity of supply
- perform simple calculations.

For goods that cannot be stored for long, such as these fresh fruits and vegetables in a market in Dominica, price elasticity of supply is reduced

DID YOU KNOW?

The term 'perfectly inelastic supply' refers to a situation in which, however much price increases, it is impossible to increase supply by a single unit.

DID YOU KNOW?

We use the term 'price elasticity of supply' because quantities supplied are responding to changes in the price of a good. The raised price gives an incentive to, or encourages, producers to supply more.

Changes in supply

When the price of a good rises or falls, this leads to an **extension in supply** – that is, a movement up or down the supply curve. The extent to which supply responds to a change in price is determined by how elastic supply is.

Price elasticity of supply

Price elasticity of supply is the extent to which supply alters in response to a change in price. It is measured by the formula:

$$\text{Price elasticity of supply} = \frac{\%\text{ change in quantity supplied}}{\%\text{ change in price}}$$

In the case of supply there is a positive relationship between the two variables. As a result price elasticity of supply will typically be represented by a + sign.

Elastic supply occurs when the percentage change in quantity supplied is greater than the percentage change in price, e.g. if supply increased by 10 per cent as a result of a 5 per cent drop in price.

Factors influencing price elasticity of supply

The main factor influencing price elasticity of supply is time. At a particular moment in time it may be impossible to increase supply, e.g. reprinting a popular book, however much price increases. Supply in this instance is perfectly inelastic. In the short term it may be possible to increase supply using existing equipment and machinery. In the longer term it may be possible to increase supply further by acquiring more machinery and equipment. The longer the period of time, the more elastic supply is in response to a price change (see Figure 2.8.1.1).

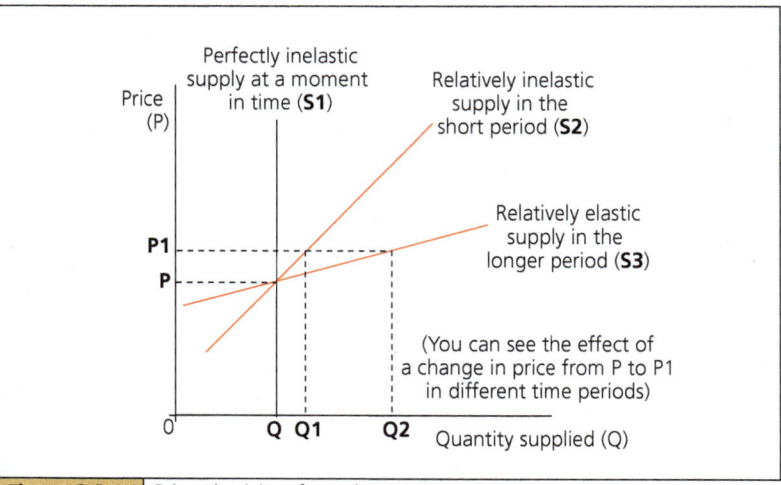

Figure 2.8.1.1 Price elasticity of supply and time

In Figure 2.8.1.1, S1 shows **perfectly inelastic supply** at a moment in time, S2 shows relatively inelastic supply in the short period, and S3 represents relatively elastic supply in the longer period.

Other factors affecting price elasticity of supply are:

- the ease with which a product can be stored: if stores of a product can be kept easily, supply will be more elastic, e.g. coffee can be stored in jars (making supply elastic), but fresh strawberries go off very quickly (making supply more inelastic)
- the cost of increasing supply: the less costly it is to increase supply, the more elastic supply will be.

Making simple calculations

Example 1: A rise in the price of rice in a country from US$1 per bag to US$1.20 per bag leads to an increase in supply by farmers from 1,000 bags per month to 1,300 bags per month.

$$\text{Price elasticity of supply} = \frac{30 \text{ per cent}}{20 \text{ per cent}}$$

$$= 1.5 \text{ (relatively elastic supply)}$$

Example 2: There is a shortage of flour in a country. A rise in the price of bread from 50 cents to 60 cents a loaf leads to an increase in supply by bakers from 1,000 loaves per month to 1,100 loaves per month.

$$\text{Price elasticity of supply} = \frac{10 \text{ per cent}}{20 \text{ per cent}}$$

$$= 0.5 \text{ (relatively inelastic supply)}$$

STUDY TIP

Remember that when producers are not manufacturing at full capacity, they could always produce a little more if the price increased. So when businesses have unused capacity, supply tends to be more elastic than if they are producing at full capacity. In a period of recession, supply can be quite elastic, in that producers have the ability to supply more.

KEY POINTS

1. Price elasticity of supply measures the responsiveness of supply to changes in price.
2. Price elasticity of supply is a positive number.
3. Price elasticity of supply is calculated by dividing the percentage change in quantity supplied by the percentage change in price.

SUMMARY QUESTIONS

1. If rail services are suddenly cancelled on a particular day, why might the supply of bus journeys be inelastic in supply?
2. If the rail service remains closed, why might the supply of bus journeys become increasingly elastic over time?
3. Increasing demand for melons in a city pushes up the price from 20 cents to 25 cents per melon. This leads to an increase in supply of melons per day from 2,000 to 2,500. Calculate the price elasticity of supply.

DID YOU KNOW?

Where elasticity of supply is relatively high, producers will be able to increase supply quickly when prices rise. Where supply is relatively inelastic, consumers will not be able to access extra supplies in times of high demand, and so will experience rising prices. The government monitors markets where supply is inelastic, e.g. energy markets and healthcare for the elderly, because an increase in demand can lead to shortages.

2.9 Market economic systems

2.9.1 The market economic system

TOPIC GUIDANCE

Students should be able to:
- define the term 'market economic system'
- explain the roles of the private and public sectors
- show how the system works in a variety of countries.

Even in a market system like Barbados there is a public sector. Government blue buses provide a key service on important routes competing with private sector buses.

ACTIVITY

Identify services in your country where there is direct competition between government providers and private providers (like the bus service in Barbados).

The nature of a market economic system

In a **free market** or **capitalist** system individuals set up their own enterprises to produce goods and services. The US is most frequently cited as an example of a free market economy that encourages private initiative (although the government does intervene, e.g. supporting some sectors of US agriculture and car manufacturing). Barbados is another example of an economy operating largely on free enterprise lines.

The advantage of this system is that individuals are free to choose what they want to purchase, and can spend their own money to gain maximum advantage for themselves. Land and businesses are privately owned rather than being owned by the government. The key decisions in this system are as follows.

- **What to produce:** this is determined by independent businesses that seek to make a profit from producing the goods that consumers are prepared to purchase.
- **How much to produce:** businesses seek to produce levels of output that will maximise their profit; customers signal to businesses which product they want by showing that they are willing to pay the current market price.
- **Who gets the products:** consumers can acquire products through purchasing (some people think this is unfair, as it favours those with the highest incomes, who can buy the most desirable products).

CASE STUDY | The market system in Barbados

Barbados is a good example of an efficient market system. Barbados is an island in the Caribbean whose economy was previously reliant on sugar production. Today Barbados has a dynamic economy with a number of flourishing sectors, including tourism and offshore industries. Major exports include liquor and dried fish. There are many small businesses in activities such as retail, transportation, entertainment, cosmetics, farming and fishing. Key aspects of why the market economy is so efficient in Barbados include:

- the domination of business in the economy by small and medium-sized privately owned businesses – some companies are large in scale such as Barbados Light and Energy Company, which provides electricity supply within the country
- an effective legal system so that business disputes are quickly resolved
- very low levels of corruption
- property rights (citizens own their own land and property)
- transparent dealings in business
- a free-running price system to determine what is produced.

As with all market systems, the government does have a part to play, e.g. in levying business and income taxes and regulating the banking system through the Central Bank of Barbados (the government's bank). The government also runs some key business sectors, such as the Post Office and a government-run bus service.

The bus service provides a good example of the coexistence of the public and private sectors. Government blue buses compete with rival companies on key routes on the island. The fares on blue buses are set by the government.

The government also intervenes to encourage new industries to develop, by providing grants and subsidies to encourage new enterprises, e.g. in the field of e-commerce, informatics and financial services.

Questions

1 What makes Barbados a market economy?

2 Who makes the decisions about what and how to produce in Barbados?

3 How does the market economy in Barbados combine both the private and public sectors?

Sectors in a market economy

There are two main sectors in the market economy.

- **The private sector:** this consists of small, medium and large-scale businesses. The owners of these businesses are individuals who have set up on their own (sole traders), those who have formed partnerships, and shareholders who are the owners of companies. Individuals set up companies principally to earn a profit and for the pleasure of running a business and being their own boss. They might also have wider social concerns, such as to provide essential services, e.g. hearing aids for the hard of hearing or incomes for those in need of a job. Private sector businesses seek to anticipate customer requirements and respond to signals provided by the market in the form of demand and prices.

- **The public sector**: this consists of enterprises owned and run by the government. In many countries the government will own and run key utilities such as rail and bus companies, as well as oil, gas and electricity industries, and the central bank. Government departments directly run by government officials, such as the tax department, are also part of the public sector.

KEY POINTS

1 In a free market economy, most decisions are made by consumers and producers.

2 The market (demand and supply) determines what will be produced in a market economy.

3 Most goods are produced by companies seeking profits in a free market economy. Examples of free market economies are the US, Barbados and Hong Kong.

SUMMARY QUESTIONS

1 To what extent could your territory or country be described as a free market economy? What elements of the free market economy exist there?

2 In a market economy, what is the role of:
   a prices
   b private businesses?

3 What is the role of the private sector in a market economy?

2.9.2 Merits and weaknesses of the market system

TOPIC GUIDANCE

Students should be able to:
- evaluate the merits of the market system.

The market

In this unit we have been looking at how the market works. We have explained how the forces of demand and supply determine market price. Changes in demand and supply lead to changes in the market price. The main groups involved in the market system are consumers, the government and other businesses.

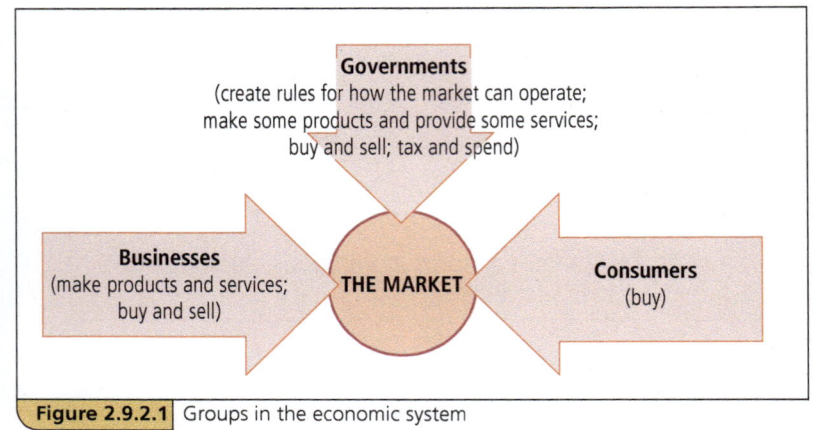

Markets such as this one in Kingston, Jamaica bring together buyers and sellers. Through demand, buyers are able to show their preferences for goods they want to be supplied

Figure 2.9.2.1 Groups in the economic system

- **Governments** (create rules for how the market can operate; make some products and provide some services; buy and sell; tax and spend)
- **Businesses** (make products and services; buy and sell)
- **THE MARKET**
- **Consumers** (buy)

Bringing together buyers and sellers

The **market** brings together buyers and sellers. This might be in a traditional market, where buyers and sellers come together to trade for vegetables, meat, clothing and other items. The term 'market' also describes any other situation where buyers and sellers contact each other. They might do this over the telephone or on the internet.

The price the seller sets helps buyers to decide what and how much they want to purchase. Buyers show what they prefer by their choice of purchase. This is **effective demand**.

Allocating resources to goods in demand

Every day millions of buying and selling decisions are made. For example, when you go shopping you may make a decision (a choice) to buy a particular type of canned drink.

If many consumers decide to buy a new type of drink, then a manufacturer may react by switching resources (such as labour, machinery and materials) into making that type of drink. Figure 2.9.2.2 shows how, as the demand for the new drink continues to rise, suppliers are willing to increase supply – a movement up the supply curve from Q to Q1 and then to Q2, and then Q3.

Figure 2.9.2.2 Supply and demand for canned drink

Coordinating decision-making

One of the greatest efficiencies of the market system is that it coordinates billions of decisions. Across the world, every second, billions of consumers are making purchasing decisions. They may be persuaded by fashion or advertisements, but the decision is ultimately theirs. They then make their decisions known through the purchases that they make. Sellers then make their own decisions about what to produce and sell based on what is selling well.

Providing plenty of choice

In a market that is working well, customers have **choices**: there will be plenty of competing rivals providing goods. For example, in most countries there are rival companies providing different mobile phone services, and there are rival firms producing household goods such as soap, washing powder and cooking oil.

Keeping prices down

Competition in the market helps to keep prices down. Rival businesses will seek to beat the competition by providing lower prices than those offered by rivals.

Weaknesses of the market economy

- The market economy emphasises individual initiative so there is no automatic mechanism for protecting the interests of weaker members of society, e.g. the elderly, or society as a whole.
- The pursuit of profit may be at the expense of employee safety, environmental standards and ethical behaviour.
- The market economy is subject to periodic falls in macroeconomic activity, referred to as the trade cycle.
- Market failure is a potential weakness (see section 2.10.1).

STUDY TIP

Make sure you understand that in a pure market system, there would be no need for a government to intervene to allocate resources.

DID YOU KNOW?

One country with a fast-growing competitive telecoms market is Pakistan, with 100 million mobile phone subscribers and 10 million landlines. There is plenty of choice for consumers, with six major competitors in the mobile market: Mobilink; Ufone; Telenor Pak; Warid Telecom; Zong; Instaphone. The market is regulated by the government's Pakistan Telecom Authority, which makes sure that consumers get a fair deal. Prices are low because there is so much competition.

ACTIVITY

Identify a product market where you have lots of choice of goods and prices are competitive. Compare this with a market in which there is less choice and prices seem high. How could the uncompetitive market become more like the competitive one?

KEY POINTS

1. The marketplace is any situation in which buyers and sellers come into contact.
2. Producers and sellers supply the market provided they can make a profit.
3. The market allocates resources, coordinates buyer and seller decisions, provides choice and helps to keep prices down.

SUMMARY QUESTIONS

1. How does the market help both consumers and producers or sellers?
2. How does the market help to channel resources into goods where demand is increasing?
3. What would be the features of a smooth working market?

2.10 Market failure

2.10.1 The nature of market failure

> **TOPIC GUIDANCE**
>
> Students should be able to:
> - describe the concept of market failure
> - explain the reasons for its occurrence.

> **DID YOU KNOW?**
>
> There is no automatic mechanism in the market system for protecting the environment. Environmental resources such as rivers and lakes are often used for dumping industrial and household waste. Government regulation, taxes and fines are therefore required to prevent pollution, because the market often fails to protect the natural world.

> **STUDY TIP**
>
> 'Public good' and 'merit good' are useful terms for conveying the idea of market failure.

Market failure

Markets are said to fail when they are inefficient. This would arise if:

- they fail to produce goods that consumers want
- they fail to produce the quantities of goods required
- they fail to produce goods at acceptably low prices.

A good example of **market failure** is in the provision of treatment for children for HIV and AIDS. Large numbers of children in poorer countries are born with HIV/AIDS. These children are in desperate need of the drugs required to protect them. However, the prices of these medicines is very high, so most families cannot afford them. The market therefore fails these children.

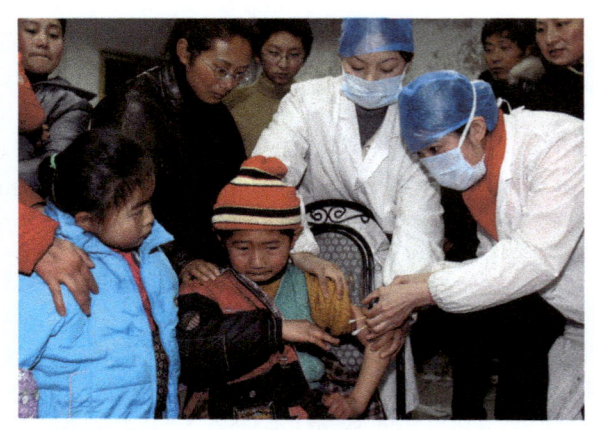

Inoculating children against harmful diseases not only benefits the children, but the whole community too

It is important to identify some of the failures of the market system. Criticisms can be levelled in two main ways:

- the market system does not always produce 'desirable' outputs. For example, it could be argued that cigarettes and fast or junk food, such as fatty burgers, are bad for health.
- the market system does not always work. Some of the worst failures of the market system are outlined below.

Not producing public or merit goods

A **public good** is one that must be provided to the whole of a community or not at all, e.g. a police force. Individuals would be reluctant to pay for such a service because people who chose not to pay (free-riders) would still benefit from the service. Public goods are therefore provided by the government, which usually funds them by means of taxes.

A **merit good** is one with substantial benefits (sometimes referred to as positive external effects or externalities) for society as a whole rather than being restricted to individuals, e.g. inoculation against a particular disease. A merit good exists as a result of information failure; a government is better informed than consumers about what is good for them. Everyone benefits if these are provided at low cost.

CASE STUDY | Providing vaccinations and family planning services

Many illnesses can have severe effects across wide populations. Some diseases can spread rapidly across the globe. Many of the inoculations required to protect against these diseases are very expensive and many people cannot afford them. On its own the market would fail to provide for the poorest sectors of the community.

Governments and international bodies can help to combat market failure. The international body responsible for looking after the health of people worldwide is the World Health Organization (WHO). The WHO provides funds and supports governments across the globe by providing free inoculation against serious diseases. International efforts have helped to eradicate smallpox and polio from most countries.

The WHO also supports programmes of family planning across the world. Families are given advice and support to limit the number of children they have. Both of these initiatives provide benefits to the wider community.

Questions

1 Why does the market fail to meet the health needs of the poor in many situations?

2 In what ways are inoculation against smallpox and free family planning merit goods?

3 Why does the government sometimes need to step in when the market is failing?

The market system will often fail to provide essential goods and services that benefit the wider public, such as street lighting, good roads, a police force and a fire service. The market often does not provide these goods because it is very difficult to get the people who benefit to pay for them.

KEY POINTS

1 Market failure involves inefficiency in producing goods that consumers want at prices they can afford.

2 The market may produce 'undesirable' goods.

3 Public goods and merit goods require government provision.

DID YOU KNOW?

Some people think that persuading consumers to buy goods that they do not really need does not always benefit the market. Large businesses can also restrict competition by undercutting the prices of smaller rivals and forcing them out of business.

ACTIVITY

Create a poster with the heading 'Market Failure'. On the poster illustrate market failure by providing examples from your local area.

SUMMARY QUESTIONS

1 Define market failure. Illustrate your answer with two recent examples.

2 State which of the following are public goods: street lighting, soap, motor cars, flood defence systems, police services, chocolate.

3 In what circumstances might the market system be unstable?

4 Why is the market not a good protector of:
   a the environment
   b poorer people?

2.10.2 Private and social costs and benefits

TOPIC GUIDANCE

Students should be able to:
- define private and social costs and benefits.

Building a new factory in Thailand has both private and social costs and benefits – it is not just the factory owners who will benefit or make a loss from the new venture

Private costs and benefits

When a business, small or large, makes a decision, it will first consider the **private costs** and **private benefits** – in other words, the financial advantages and disadvantages. In the table below the example of a business owner in Thailand considering whether to set up a new factory is used to show the costs and benefits that help the owner to make a decision.

Private costs of building and operating a factory in Thailand	Private benefits of building and operating a factory in Thailand
Cost of borrowing the necessary finance to build the factory	The revenues earned by the factory
Cost of building the factory and equipping it with machinery	The savings to the business resulting from operating in Thailand rather than at a higher-cost location
Cost of labour	
Cost of raw materials	

To work out the profit from running the factory, an accountant will calculate the net financial return in the following way:

   Private benefits – Private costs = Net private benefit or profit

This method does not take into account social costs and benefits and is a very narrow way of looking at the impact of the decision. It does not consider **externalities**.

DID YOU KNOW?

Some practices, such as industrial activities that create a lot of pollution, would be stopped if the social costs were taken into consideration.

STUDY TIP

Make sure that you are able to refer to the distinction between private and social costs and benefits.

Externalities

An externality is the result of economic activity, such as building a new factory, that is not taken into account by the individuals who make a decision. In other words, it is the external, or 'outside', effect of a decision. For example, the new factory may provide local jobs, but it may force an existing local factory to close down, with the loss of some jobs. The favourable effect is a **positive externality**. The effect on the rival factory is a **negative externality**.

Social costs and benefits

Social benefits include the private and other benefits that result from a particular business activity or decision. **Social costs** are the private costs to the company, say of building a factory, plus all the other costs resulting from this, such as traffic noise affecting local residents. The overall net benefit of an economic activity can be calculated by:

(Private benefits + External benefits) – (Private costs + External costs)

The table below illustrates some of the external costs and benefits of setting up a factory in Thailand.

External costs of building and operating the factory	External benefits of building and operating the factory
Jobs lost in a rival factory that is forced to close – the wages lost	Jobs created in supplier firms in the community – the wages earned
Loss of profit by owners of the rival factory that closes, and loss of taxes by the government	Rise in tax revenue for the government of Thailand from profits of the company
Increased traffic and noise pollution created by the new factory	

Activities should only be carried out if the social benefits are greater than the social costs. It is not always easy to calculate social costs and benefits and give a monetary value to factors such as noise pollution or the benefit of reduced journey times.

> **STUDY TIP**
>
> There is sometimes confusion about the precise meaning of 'social costs' and 'social benefits'. Make sure that you fully understand that social costs are equal to the sum of private costs and external costs. Social benefits are equal to the sum of private benefits and external benefits.

> **ACTIVITY**
>
> Imagine that a large retail outlet or factory is to be built close to your school. New access roads will need to be built. Who is likely to be affected? In each case, outline one external benefit and one external cost to each of these groups. Have a class debate, with some students pointing out the benefits and others pointing out the costs.

> **KEY POINTS**
>
> 1. Private costs and benefits are monetary calculations of the effect of economic activity for individuals or businesses.
> 2. Private costs and benefits are only part of wider social costs and benefits.
> 3. To find out the true net benefits of economic activity, both private and external costs and benefits should be considered.

> **SUMMARY QUESTIONS**
>
> 1. What is the difference between the private cost of an activity and the external cost of that activity?
> 2. Give an example of an activity that involves private costs and benefits and external costs and benefits. Suggest examples of these costs and benefits.
> 3. Why might it be difficult to measure costs and benefits?

2.10.3 Causes of market failure

> **TOPIC GUIDANCE**
>
> Students should be able to:
> - outline the main causes of market failure
> - explain the main consequences of market failure.

Market failure occurs when markets fail to:
- produce goods that customers want
- use resources efficiently
- produce the quantities of goods required
- produce goods at acceptably low prices
- avoid negative externalities.

Causes of market failure

The following are the most common causes of market failure.

- **Monopoly:** a monopoly exists when a single firm dominates a market, pushing up prices or restricting output. The monopolist will take this action in order to increase profits. The market thus fails some consumers who are not able to pay the monopolist's prices. For example, some airline routes between smaller Caribbean islands are controlled by a monopoly airline. Prices are often too high for many people. Another example of a monopoly is the Malaysian power company Tenaga Nasional Berhad, which is the only supplier of electricity in Malaysia and the largest power supplier in South East Asia. It is the only organisation in the area with sufficient funds to purchase power stations, enabling it to control the price at which it supplies electricity to consumers. By using large-scale production, the company can keep prices low. However, the lack of a competitor may also serve to keep prices higher than they would be if the company had rivals to compete with.

- **Public goods and merit goods:** the market system will often fail to supply public goods. Similarly, the market might not provide merit goods (see section 2.10.1), e.g. inoculations, which benefit society as a whole, because drug companies might not be able to sell these goods at the prices they want in countries with higher proportions of people on low incomes.

- **Factor immobility:** because factors of production are sometimes immobile, they do not move into the areas where they will be most effectively used. For example, skilled workers may not be willing to move from one area of the country (where they may be unemployed) to another area where jobs are more plentiful (geographical immobility). Similarly, workers may be reluctant to change from one type of job to another (occupational immobility).

- **Positive/negative externalities:** The market often ignores or hides the negative costs to society (such as pollution or wasted resource use) of economic activities.

Large banana plantations can create negative externalities so that the low price of bananas is not a true reflection of the social cost of using resources to produce bananas

> **DID YOU KNOW?**
>
> Externalities are the spillover effects of economic activity that are often not accounted for by those responsible for them. Negative externalities are a cost to society that are not accounted for by the creator of the spillover, e.g. a company. Positive externalities benefit others in addition to the creator of the externality.

> **CASE STUDY** | Banana growing in Central America
>
> Bananas grown on large scale banana plantations in Central America use large quantities of agrochemicals to increase crop yields. Wages are very low, and this enables producers to undercut rivals such as smallholders in the Caribbean. Ecuador, Costa Rica, Colombia and other exporting countries in Central America are known as 'dollar banana' countries because they are traditionally exported to North America and produced by US multinational companies such as Dole, Chiquita and Del Monte. These companies control about 60 per cent of banana production in Central America.
>
> Employees living in housing on plantations in Central America are exposed to chemicals, as spraying often takes place while they are working in the fields. The result is air and water pollution and long-term damage to the land. When the land can no longer support banana production, new plantations are developed, often destroying tropical rainforest. The market thus supports inefficient and harmful production, and fails to take account of the positive externalities (see section 2.10.2) of many alternative activities. By contrast, small-scale organic agricultural production encourages biodiversity, which benefits both local people and ecotourism.
>
> **Questions**
>
> 1 How does society:
>   a benefit from intensive banana production in Central America
>   b lose out from this banana production?
> 2 How might society benefit from a reduction in banana production on large plantations and an increase in smallholding agriculture?
> 3 How can the market be seen as failing in the context of large-scale banana production?

Consequences of market failure

The result of market failure is that resources are misallocated – that is, they are not used in the best way, causing the following problems.

1 **There will be overproduction and consumption of demerit goods:** a **demerit** good is one which is considered to be unhealthy or damaging to individuals or groups and society as a whole. A good example is tobacco, which is physically harmful in the direct impact it has on smokers' lungs and the spillover impact of non-smokers who inhale cigarette smoke. Cigarette smoking costs health services in extra care burdens. Unhealthy food can also be seen as a demerit good, as can alcohol.
2 **Overconsumption of goods with external costs:** activities that have spillover effects such as pollution will be overconsumed in a market economy, leading to a misallocation of resources – unless a way is found to penalise generators of pollution and make them pay the true cost of the externality.
3 **Underproduction and consumption of merit goods and goods with external benefits:** the market may fail to provide sufficient quantities of merit goods – that is, those with substantial external benefits – because it cannot capture those external benefits by charging for them.

> **ACTIVITY**
>
> Identify positive and negative externalities resulting from a road-building or road-maintenance project near you.

> **KEY POINTS**
>
> 1 Market failure occurs when free markets fail to allocate resources in the most efficient way.
> 2 Market failure arises as a result of monopoly practices, immobility of factors, the creation of externalities and failure to provide public and merit goods.
> 3 Market failure leads to both underproduction and overproduction.

> **SUMMARY QUESTIONS**
>
> 1 Give three examples of ways in which market failure leads to an inefficient use of resources in society.
> 2 How can market failure impact negatively on:
>   a businesses
>   b consumers?
> 3 How can the existence of monopoly lead to an inefficient use of resources?

2.11 Mixed economic systems

2.11.1 The nature of a mixed economy

> **TOPIC GUIDANCE**
>
> Students should be able to:
> - define mixed economy
> - illustrate effects of microeconomic policy measures (pricing)
> - define the terms 'privatisation', 'nationalisation' and 'direct provision of services'.

A **mixed economy** combines elements of the market economy with some government interference, such as some ownership of businesses. Most economies today have strong market sectors combined with government intervention, which may help markets to work more effectively to allocate scarce resources.

Government policy to address market failure

Making a failing market more efficient will make society better off. Market failure therefore provides a justification for government intervention. Governments may intervene to break up monopolies by encouraging competitors to enter a market. Governments can also use taxes to penalise businesses that abuse the market, e.g. by taxing companies that create pollution.

Illustrating government microeconomic policies in the market

The following illustrates two situations in which the government interferes in the micro-economy to influence prices. You will see that it is not easy to predict the impact of such interventions.

Maximum prices

The government may believe that the market price for a product is too high, and therefore consumers are losing out. For example, it may believe that the price of electricity provided by a private company is harmful to poorer households. This is illustrated in Figure 2.11.1. The equilibrium price is Pe where a quantity of Qe is supplied to the market. However, setting a maximum price below the market price will reduce supply to Q1, whereas consumers would wish to purchase Q2, leading to shortages (represented by the distance from Q1 to Q2). However, if the government can exert pressure on suppliers, e.g. by only allowing them to have a licence if they charge government-capped prices, this is less likely to occur.

> **DID YOU KNOW?**
>
> There may be too much government interference in the market. Economists identify this as **government failure**. An example might be government taxes that are so high they discourage business activity that could be beneficial to society.

Minimum prices

The government can also intervene to create a minimum price, e.g. for agricultural produce (to help ensure that more of a crop is planted), or by imposing a minimum price for a factor of production (such as a minimum wage). However, this too can lead to problems. Figure 2.11.2 shows the impact of setting a minimum wage above the market rate.

The market wage is W0. If the government imposes a minimum wage above this rate, this might lead to an excess supply of labour as Q2 workers make themselves available for work at the minimum wage but employers are only prepared to employ Q1 workers. The excess supply is the distance from Q1 to Q2.

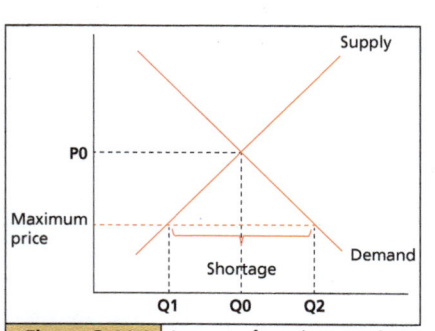

Figure 2.11.1 Impact of maximum prices

Nationalisation, privatisation and direct provision

In section 2.9.1 we saw that the economy is divided into two sectors: the private sector and the public sector.

Nationalisation occurs when the government of a country takes on the ownership and running of industries that were previously in the private sector. The government usually sets up a body known as a **public corporation** to run the industry on behalf of the nation. The chair and managers of that industry will be accountable to a government minister, but day-to-day management lies with the corporation.

Privatisation is the reverse process, and involves the government selling off industries and activities that were previously run by public corporations and **statutory boards** to private entrepreneurs and companies.

Direct provision is where the government provides public and merit goods directly to users free of charge. For example, in the UK the government provides national road networks and free primary and secondary school education directly to users.

The effectiveness of government intervention

To what extent does government intervention help the market to work better? The examples given in this section suggest ways in which intervention can address market failure. The government can provide public and merit goods where the market fails to do so, e.g. through nationalisation and direct provision.

The government can also help to secure supplies by imposing minimum prices or seek to prevent prices from being too high by imposing maximum prices. However, there is a danger that there can be too much government interference, leading to government failure. In this case privatisation may be required to create more competition and enterprise within the economy.

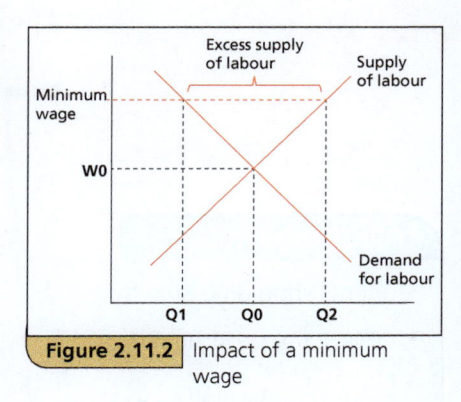

Figure 2.11.2 Impact of a minimum wage

DID YOU KNOW?

In many parts of the world, employers are currently exploiting labour by paying very low rates and making very large profits. Enlightened employers may recognise that they should be paying labourers more so that the demand curve for labour will shift upwards to the right, and more workers will be employed at the minimum wage.

KEY POINTS

1. A mixed economy enables a government to intervene to make the market work better.
2. The government can intervene in the micro-economy, e.g. by setting minimum and maximum prices.
3. Governments can take control of the micro-economy through nationalisation and direct provision, or reduce interference through privatisation.

SUMMARY QUESTIONS

1. What are the differences between market failure and government failure?
2. How might government efforts to set prices not always achieve the desired results?
3. How does direct provision differ from nationalisation?

2.11.2 Government influence on micro-economy: regulation

TOPIC GUIDANCE

Students should be able to:
- discuss the government's influence on private producers through regulation.

Environmental regulations are very important. For example, there are rules about what type of waste can enter water systems. Firms can be fined for failing to comply with these regulations

DID YOU KNOW?

Some economists are in favour of more regulation to limit the externalities (social costs of business activity) and other market failures. Others believe that there is too much regulation, limiting the ability of the free market to supply goods that meet customers' needs. These economists think that too much regulation raises costs and leads to inefficiency.

Regulation

Regulations are rules. They can be rules imposed by a government, backed up by penalties. In the world of business, the purpose of regulations is to influence the behaviour of firms and individuals in the private sector. For example, government regulations cover who can set up a bank, how much the bank is allowed to lend and even the amount of interest the bank is allowed to charge for loans. The table shows some of the areas covered by regulations.

Area covered by regulation	Examples
Methods of production	Management of waste and pollution, rules protecting the health and safety of production workers, e.g. wearing of safety protection equipment
Setting up a new business	Paperwork to be filled in to register the business, rules protecting shareholders, filing of tax returns
Rules about prices	Prices that can be charged for supplying certain products, e.g. agricultural products, minimum wage rules
Product standards	Quality of food products, labelling of contents of a product
Disclosure of information	Information that companies must produce in reports to shareholders, information about how certain products can be used
Providing goods on credit	Information that must be given about the cost of the credit to the borrower, rules setting out the possibility of the borrower pulling out of a credit agreement
Providers of certain products and services	Who can supply certain products, such as repairs to gas pipes, building construction
Supply of harmful products	Health warnings on cigarettes

Regulations can be in the form of laws governing the actions of private firms and individuals. They can also be created by granting licences and permits to firms that meet certain conditions. Inspection by qualified inspectors can then make sure that the businesses are complying with the regulations. Failure to do so can mean fines or loss of the licence.

The advantages of regulation

Governments use regulation to improve efficiency. Regulations are also used to redistribute income.

Governments regulate firms and industry where there are monopoly powers. Monopolists may restrict output and/or artificially raise prices. There are many regulations covering anti-competitive practices by firms, such as a group of suppliers jointly fixing prices. Governments also use regulations to limit the effect of externalities, such as where pollution is created in production, e.g. regulations covering carbon emissions by vehicles, and production processes.

Some industries involve a high level of regulation, e.g. the banking sector, the oil industry, and pharmaceuticals. These industries need to be carefully controlled in the public interest.

Regulation makes it possible to reach a balance between private firms seeking to make a profit and the interests of the people who use their services and the wider public.

The disadvantages of regulations

Regulations usually raise business costs and can affect productivity. To comply with regulations a business must:

- learn the regulations that relate to it
- fill in all the paperwork relating to the regulations
- create systems and methods that fit with the regulations.

Some business people complain that they are over-regulated. They mean that they have to spend so much time and money complying with the regulations that they cannot concentrate on running their business.

Countries with a greater number and complexity of regulations lose competitiveness because of the cost of complying with the regulations. However, these countries also gain a competitive advantage because their standards, e.g. product standards, may be higher than those of competitors.

DID YOU KNOW?

Some economists believe that governments regulate too much. They believe that every regulation imposes a cost of compliance and that these costs are greater than the benefits they create.

SUMMARY QUESTIONS

1. Identify three different business activities that are regulated by governments. In each case give an example of a regulation.
2. Who benefits from government regulation? Illustrate your answer by focusing on a specific regulation.
3. What are some of the disadvantages of high levels of regulation?

STUDY TIP

When discussing regulations, make sure that you are able to refer to both their advantages and disadvantages and can give a balanced perspective on their importance.

ACTIVITY

Study the World Bank's Doing Business database (www.doingbusiness.org). The World Bank collects data from most countries, setting out the costs of regulation in certain areas, such as setting up a business and getting credit. Where does your country rank in terms of the number of regulations that it has? How does this compare with a neighbouring country?

KEY POINTS

1. Regulations are rules imposed by government backed up by penalties.
2. Regulations are designed to modify the behaviour of businesses and individuals in ways that benefit society.
3. Regulations can impose costs and time burdens on private businesses.

2.11.3 Government influence on micro-economy: subsidies

The government has given smallholders in Malawi subsidies in the form of vouchers to buy seeds and fertiliser, and they have been able to raise production of agricultural products

TOPIC GUIDANCE

Students should be able to:
- discuss the government's influence on private producers through subsidies.

DID YOU KNOW?

In recent years governments in many countries have given subsidies to householders to introduce energy-efficient products in their houses, e.g. part payments to install loft insulation, solar panels and energy-efficient light bulbs.

STUDY TIP

You should be able to discuss the potential usefulness of subsidies. This means that you need to be aware of the potential advantages and disadvantages.

Subsidies

Most subsidies are sums of money provided by a government to a producer or supplier for a specific purpose. They may be provided for several reasons.

- **To encourage the production of goods of national importance**. For example, the government may provide subsidies to farmers to produce essential food supplies. The subsidy guarantees an income to the farmer.

- **To encourage the development of new products and industries**. In the short term these products and industries may be uncompetitive, resulting in losses being made by private producers. For example, in many countries the government provides subsidies to encourage the development of new forms of energy, such as wind and solar power.

- **To provide support for industries that are in decline and that are major employers of labour**. If the industry did not receive a subsidy it might not make a profit. Closing the industry could have negative externalities, such as unemployment, which would have a very significant impact on the wider society. For example, an increase in the number unemployed would reduce the revenue received from taxes on income and also result in a government having to make unemployment payments to those out of work. If fewer people were in employment, there would also likely be a negative effect on spending, affecting the revenue received from indirect taxes on expenditure. It is also possible that other jobs in the community could be lost as a result of this original increase in unemployment. The subsidy is thus socially desirable and economically sound from a government's point of view.

- **To protect domestic industries against foreign competition.** The subsidy has the same effect as lowering the cost to the supplier.

In addition to the subsidies listed above there are some additional subsidies to consumers to enable them to make purchases.

Illustrating the effect of subsidising a supplier

When a supplier receives a subsidy it will be encouraged to produce more for the market. This leads to a shift to the right of the supply curve. When the supply curve shifts to the right this leads to an increased supply at lower prices. Figure 2.11.3.1 shows that a subsidy of 10 cents per unit supplied has led to an increase in supply from S to S1. The quantity supplied has increased from Q to Q1.

Of course, a subsidy does not always lead to an increase in supply. For example, in a loss-making industry the more likely effect will be to stop supply from falling, rather than lead to its increase.

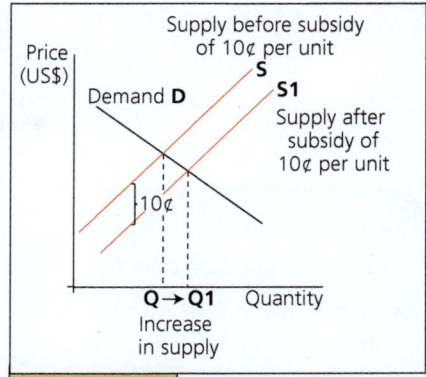

Figure 2.11.3.1 Increase in supply resulting from a 10 cent subsidy

ACTIVITY

Carry out research using a national newspaper to find examples of subsidies provided in your country. Who receives the subsidies, and why?

CASE STUDY | Subsidies to smallholder farmers in Malawi

Farmers in Malawi have been supported by the provision of subsidies by the government, in particular helping in the purchase of seeds and fertiliser.

Eighty per cent of all Malawians are smallholder farmers. The farmers were given vouchers by the government enabling them to buy fertiliser and seeds at a third of the market cost. The farmers have to make a contribution to the cost of the fertiliser and seed rather than being given it. The results have been excellent, with the yield per hectare increasing from an average of about 1.2 tonnes per hectare to 2.2 tonnes per hectare. The government has also started to distribute vouchers for pesticides.

Questions

1 Explain how the subsidies to Malawian farmers will have affected production of crops.

2 Why might it be better to give farmers vouchers rather than cash subsidies?

3 Draw a diagram to show the impact of the subsidy on the supply curve and market quantity of crops produced on the smallholdings.

KEY POINTS

1 Subsidies are incentives provided by the government to individuals and households in order to carry out desired activities.

2 Subsidies are granted to support declining industries, to produce essential products and to protect domestic industries.

3 The effect of a subsidy is to push the supply curve to the right.

SUMMARY QUESTIONS

1 What would be the effect of subsiding producers in a declining industry?

2 What would be the effect of subsidising producers in a new and growing industry?

3 Why are subsidies sometimes given to consumers?

2.11.4 Government influence on micro-economy: indirect taxes

TOPIC GUIDANCE

Students should be able to:
- discuss the government's influence on private producers through taxes.

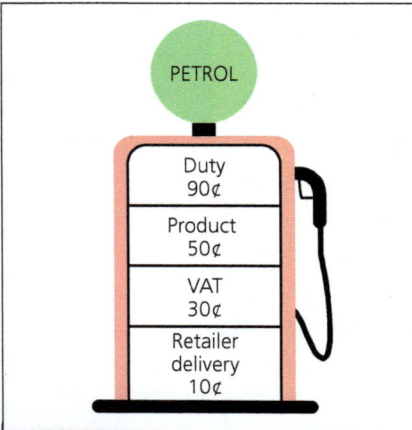

Figure 2.11.4.1 Taxes on fuel in many countries are high. The incidence of the tax falls mainly on motorists

(Petrol pump showing: Duty 90¢, Product 50¢, VAT 30¢, Retailer delivery 10¢)

DID YOU KNOW?

In India and many other countries, two important types of indirect tax are excise duties, which are charged on all goods made in India and passed substantially on to customers, and import duties charged on goods coming into India from overseas. These taxes will in part be passed on to consumers.

Indirect taxes

Indirect taxes work in the opposite direction to subsidies and are a key instrument for influencing the micro-economy. An **indirect tax** is one that is paid by an intermediary (usually a business) to the government. The intermediary then passes the tax on to the person or organisation that buys from it. The intermediary therefore collects the tax on behalf of the government. Two examples are the sales tax on goods bought, and **value added tax** (known as **VAT**), which is a tax on the value added by producers at each stage in the manufacture of a product. The government uses indirect taxes:

- to raise revenue
- to discourage some activities and encourage others, e.g. by imposing a low sales tax on children's clothes and toys, and a high sales tax on luxury consumer items
- give consumers greater choice about how they use their income – a consumer can choose whether or not to buy a good that has an indirect tax component in its pricing.

The incidence of sales taxes and price elasticity of demand

The price elasticity of demand for a product determines how much revenue the government is able to collect from **indirect sales taxes**. When a sales tax is increased, the supply curve of a good shifts to the left. The sales tax acts as a cost to a business. The supply curve shifts upwards by the amount of the tax.

Figure 2.11.4.2 compares an increase in a sales tax by the same amount for a good with an elastic demand curve, and for one with an inelastic demand curve.

Figure 2.11.4.2a (product with relatively elastic demand) shows that the increase in the sales tax leads to a relatively large fall in the quantity

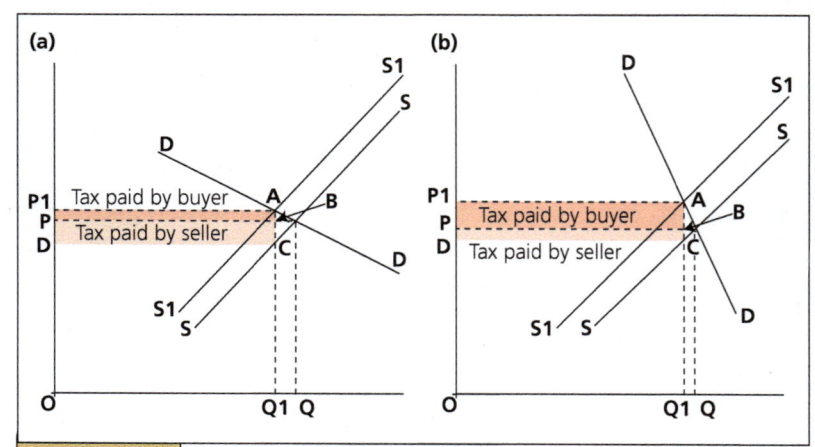

Figure 2.11.4.2 The incidence of a sales tax with (a) elastic demand (b) inelastic demand

demanded (Q to Q1), compared with the impact of the sales tax shown in Figure 2.11.4.2b (product with relatively inelastic demand).

The diagrams also show how much of the tax will be paid by the seller and how much by the customer. **Incidence of tax** refers to who pays the major part of the tax. In Figure 2.11.4.2a the incidence of the tax falls mainly on the seller. This is because the total amount of tax that will have to be paid is P1ACD. Out of this the consumer pays PP1AB – that is, the increase in price from P to P1 multiplied by the quantity now traded in the market 0Q1. The seller has to pay the rest of the tax DPBC.

If demand is elastic, sellers will of course be able to raise their prices only a little.

In contrast, in Figure 2.11.4.2b, with inelastic demand the size of the rectangle DPBC (the incidence of the tax to the seller) is much smaller than PP1AB (the incidence of the tax to the buyer). If demand is inelastic, sellers are of course much better placed to shift the incidence of the tax to the buyer.

Where knowledge of elasticity is useful

Knowledge of elasticity and the impact on indirect taxes helps the government to set tax rates for VAT and other sales taxes. It also helps governments to decide how much they can charge in import taxes to discourage imports.

The government should also consider elasticity in tax levels for licences, e.g. car licences, waste and pollution charges, and local business taxes.

Imposing taxes that are too high can lead to:

- falling sales and falling incomes – and hence rising unemployment as workers are laid off and businesses close
- an incentive for businesses and individuals to avoid paying taxes, leading to an 'undercover' economy involving tax evasion.

Effective taxes

Effective taxes should focus on producing desirable goods and services and discourage businesses from carrying out undesirable activities. They should not discourage effort and initiative. They should also provide suitable revenues for the government. Effectively designed tax systems should create a good relationship between government and private producers. They should be simple to operate and understand, and not need excessive form-filling by taxpayers.

SUMMARY QUESTIONS

1. Give three reasons why the government taxes private producers.
2. When the government imposes a sales tax on a good with an inelastic demand, who does the bulk of the incidence of the tax fall upon? Explain why.
3. What are the dangers of making taxes on private producers too high?

STUDY TIP

Make sure that you understand incidence of tax. This indicates precisely who is paying particular parts of a tax.

STUDY TIP

Price elasticity of demand is a very important concept in economics. Its role in relation to indirect taxation is a good example of how it can be usefully applied.

DID YOU KNOW?

Goods with inelastic demand, which many governments tax at quite a high rate, include cigarettes and petrol. The incidence of these taxes then falls largely on consumers.

KEY POINTS

1. Taxes should be designed to support government objectives without discouraging effort and initiative.
2. Taxes are seen as a cost to business.
3. The incidence of sales taxes depends on the price elasticity of demand for the product being sold.

Unit 2 — Test yourself

SECTION 1: Multiple-choice questions

Each question has ONE correct answer.

1. Which of the following describes a country with a mixed economy?
   a. Goods and services are provided by private companies
   b. Goods and services are provided by the government
   c. Goods and services are provided by private companies and by the government
   d. Goods and services are provided by individuals and by companies

2. Which of the following describes the economic aim of sellers of goods and services?
   a. A wide range of goods on offer
   b. A product made from best-quality materials
   c. A high-cost advertising campaign
   d. A high price to provide profit for the business

3. What is *effective demand* for a good or service?
   a. A want, backed up by money to purchase the item
   b. A need, by all consumers desiring the item
   c. A demand depending on level of income
   d. A demand by one group of consumers

4. What does a typical supply curve show about the relationship between the amount supplied of a product and its price?
   a. Firms will supply more at a lower price
   b. Consumers will buy more at a higher price
   c. Firms will supply more at a higher price
   d. Consumers will buy more at a lower price

5. Which one of the following pairs of products are in joint supply?
   a. Potatoes and maize
   b. Beef and leather
   c. CDs and CD players
   d. Cars and tyres

6. What does the *equilibrium price* in a market show?
   a. The price at which a company will get the highest number of sales
   b. The price at which quantity supplied is equal to quantity demanded
   c. The price at which the most profit will be made
   d. The price at which all production costs will be covered

7. Which of the following would cause the demand curve for chocolate bars to shift to the right?
   a. A decrease in the price of the chocolate bars
   b. A decrease in the price of cocoa beans
   c. A 'chocolate is good for your health' advertising campaign
   d. A health scare about the dangers of eating too much sweet food

8. The price elasticity of demand for a product is estimated at –1.5. The current level of sales is 1,000 per week. If the price elasticity of demand estimate is correct and the price of the product increases from £2 to £2.40, what will be the new weekly level of sales?
   a. 700
   b. 1,300
   c. 800
   d. 900

9. Which of the following is NOT an example of a merit good?
   a. Literacy education
   b. Mobile telephone
   c. Family planning advice
   d. Mosquito net

10. Which of the following is an example of a social cost?
    a. Provision of essential medicines
    b. Recycling plastic bottles
    c. Building community facilities
    d. Pollution from a factory

SECTION 2

Sui Toys is a major manufacturing company with five factories, based in a large developing country. It is a public limited company (PLC), with shares quoted on stock markets worldwide, including London, Hong Kong and New York. Sui Toys manufactures for many of the major toy companies throughout the world and its product range is very diverse, from traditional toys and games to computer games and consoles. With a share of around 30 per cent of this highly competitive market, the company enjoys considerable monopoly power and other toy manufacturers keep a close watch on Sui's prices and product range.

The worldwide recession has hit the company hard, with demand in many countries decreasing. Consumers are still buying the lower-priced products, but demand at the luxury end has declined considerably. Sui's share price has declined from US$10 to US$8 and the company's managing director is concerned that the dividend this year may be low.

Sui also needs to make a major investment in the business, both on the manufacturing side and to improve communication between different parts of the company. As the company has grown, raw materials have become cheaper due to buying in bulk, but communication between the factories and management is very poor, leading to mistakes and delays on orders.

1 a Explain the difference between a *public limited company* and a *public sector organisation*. (2)

  b Explain what is meant by 'monopoly power' in the case of Sui Toys. (2)

  c The management team of Sui Toys has set *profit maximisation* as a major business objective. Explain what this means. (2)

  d Discuss the extent to which Sui Toys may be able to charge high prices for its toys in this market situation. (6)

  e Calculate the percentage fall in the share price of Sui Toys. (2)

  f If Sui Toys decides to pay a low dividend this year in order to invest in the business, discuss the possible effects on the share price, using an appropriate diagram. (6)

  g Using the extract above and the concept of economies and diseconomies of scale, explain and give examples of both within Sui Toys. (4)

  h Using all the information given, discuss how Sui Toys may increase efficiency and profitability. (6)

Total: 30 marks

SECTION 3

Country A is a developing country, with a growing market for consumer products. The political environment has changed recently and the economy is in the process of moving away from a planned system, where all production was controlled by the government. The economy is now moving towards a mixed system, where an increasing number of goods and services are produced by private companies, which have the aim of making as much profit as possible.

The consumers in Country A now have the opportunity to choose from a much wider range of products and services. This choice means that the sellers now need to be much more aware of what consumers are looking for. Many of the older companies, which relied on their products being the only ones available, have gone out of business.

However, it is not all good news for the population, as the decline of many of the older companies has led to unemployment for workers who had relied on a 'job for life'. There is talk of a widening gap between rich and poor under the new system.

1. **a** Explain what is meant by a *mixed economy*. (4)
   b Identify and explain TWO reasons why 'a growing market for consumer products' will lead to more choice for individuals. (6)
   c Using the information given, identify and explain why sellers need to be more aware of the needs and wants of consumers. (4)
   d Discuss what may be the advantages and disadvantages of the changing economic environment for the population of Country A. (6)

2. One of the new retailers in Country A is importing clothing and shoes from the US and selling these products in big new shops in the larger towns. This retailer also stocks traditional styles that are made in local factories.
   a Draw and label a demand and supply diagram for traditional-style clothing before the new products arrived from the US. (4)
   b Draw a new demand and supply diagram illustrating the likely changes in this market following the introduction of imported goods. Explain what your diagram shows. (6)
   c Analyse the impact that the change in demand will have on how the retailer uses its resources. (4)
   d Discuss how the increase in imported products may affect local consumers and workers in Country A. (6)

3. Large wheat farms are major suppliers of food in Country A. Traditionally, they have received large subsidies from the government to produce basic foodstuffs, for sale at low prices to the population. Now these subsidies are being taken away and the market opened to competition.
   a Explain ONE reason why the government in Country A might have chosen to subsidise wheat production. (4)
   b Draw a supply and demand diagram that illustrates the removal of subsidies to wheat farmers in Country A. (4)
   c Using your diagram, explain the likely effects of the removal of the subsidy and opening the market to competition. (6)
   d With reference to the 'widening gap between rich and poor', discuss whether the removal of these subsidies and opening the market to competition will benefit the population and economy of Country A in the long term. (6)

4. Under the new economic system, the government of Country A is continuing to provide education, health and public transport services by bus and rail. However, air services are being provided by a new low-cost airline, which is offering very low fares between the major cities and to major overseas destinations.
   a Explain why the government of Country A may have decided to continue education provision. (4)
   b Explain the view that free health services lead to a more productive population. (4)
   c Explain why vaccination programmes and family planning services may increase social benefits to the population of Country A. (4)
   d Discuss whether the increased use of air services of the new low-cost airline may lead to market failure. (8)

Total: 80 marks

3 Microeconomic decision-makers: banks, households, workers, trade unions, firms

This unit outlines the key micro-economic decision making groups in the economy, and the economic decisions that they make.

The unit considers the parts played by money in the modern world, beginning with the evolution of currency systems from early exchange and barter systems. The role of commercial and central banks, and their importance to individuals and businesses, is discussed.

The unit explores the influences on household spending, saving and borrowing. Further topics focus on workers and their choice of occupations and how wages and earnings are determined. The nature of trade unions and their role in the economy is explored.

Types of firms, and how firms grow from a small to a large scale is examined. The unit then looks at the contribution of factors of production to producing goods.

The following sections shows how costs and revenues are calculated as well as providing definitions of different types of costs.

Finally, the unit identifies market structures including competitive markets and monopoly markets. The characteristics, advantages and disadvantages of different markets are set out.

TOPIC COVERAGE

Students will study the following topics:

- Money and banking including commercial and central banks
- The influences on household spending, saving and borrowing
- Factors affecting a worker's choice of occupation
- Wage determination and reasons for differences in earnings.
- Division of labour and specialization
- Trade unions and their benefits/drawbacks
- Different types of firms and how firms can grow
- Economies and diseconomies of scale
- Influences on the demand for factors of production
- Influences on production and productivity
- Nature and types of costs of production (including calculation)
- How revenue is defined and calculated
- Objectives of firms including profit maximization and growth
- The structure of monopoly and competitive markets
- Benefits and drawbacks of different market structures

3.1 Money and banking

3.1.1 Money

TOPIC GUIDANCE

Students should be able to:
- outline the form, functions and characteristics of money.

What is money?

Money is anything that is widely accepted or used to exchange for goods. Today when we think about money we are typically referring to notes and coins. However, households and businesses also use many other ways of making payments, such as credit cards and debit cards.

Before money was used, people would **barter** – that is, exchange goods, say a goat for several chickens. This requires the two people who make the trade to want what the other has to offer (a **double coincidence of wants**). The obvious disadvantage is that one partner may not have enough goods to make the exchange fair, or they might not want a whole goat, for example. People realised that small but valuable items, such as cowrie shells, could be used instead.

DID YOU KNOW?

Cowrie shells were valued highly because they were rare. They were widely used as money for several hundred years in parts of China, India and Africa. They were also used as jewellery.

For centuries cowrie shells were used as money in many areas of the world

Why were cowrie shells used as money so widely? Look at this list of characteristics of the shells.

- Scarcity – shells were valuable because they were relatively scarce.
- Acceptability – people were prepared to accept shells as payment because they knew that they could use them for future trading.
- Portability – the shells could easily be carried for long distances.
- Durability – the shells were hard-wearing and long-lasting.
- Divisible – shells could be supplied in various quantities, to buy purchases of different sizes. Purchases would be possible using a few or, for the wealthy, hundreds of shells. In modern terms, a car can be priced at thousands or millions of dollars. Dollars can be divided into cents for small items such as a packet of chewing gum or a piece of fruit.

STUDY TIP

You should be able to explain why money is preferable to barter as a means of exchange.

ACTIVITY

Do some research on the history of money in your country. Write a report of your findings or make a poster to display in the classroom.

The functions of money

The functions of money are as follows.

- As a **medium of exchange** – money is generally accepted as a means of payment for most goods.
- As a **unit of account** – the price of an item can be measured in terms of how many units of currency it is worth. For example, whereas a low-quality top may cost US$10, a high-quality one may be valued at US$100 or more.
- As a **store of value** – you can save money because it keeps its value. Saving enables use of the money in the future.
- As a **standard for deferred payments** – borrowers are able to borrow money and pay it back at a later date.

> **STUDY TIP**
>
> Make sure that you can explain these four functions of money.

CASE STUDY | The yuan

The yuan is the money in use in China today. The smallest units of currency are the jiao and fen (10 fen = 1 jiao, 10 jiao = 1 yuan). You can buy goods with the yuan in any shop in China. The notes are easy to carry around and store. Individuals can save yuan in their own homes. Alternatively, they can deposit their savings at a bank such as China's Industrial and Commercial Bank. The yuan maintains its value over time. As a result, a bank can lend yuan to a business knowing that when the time comes for repayment, the value of the currency will be at least as much as when the bank lent the money.

Questions

1. Explain some of the properties of the yuan that make it such a good currency.
2. Show how the yuan acts as a medium of exchange, a standard for deferred payments and a store of value.

> **DID YOU KNOW?**
>
> The characteristics of all forms of money are: scarcity, acceptability, portability, durability and divisibility. Should the official currency of a country lose one or more of these characteristics, then it will become less effective as money.

SUMMARY QUESTIONS

1. Are the functions of money today the same as when cowrie shells were used?
2. How useful would the following be in performing the functions of money today: a gold bar, a chocolate bar, paper currency notes produced by the government, gold coins, an antique table, cowrie shells?
3. What is the smallest unit of currency in your country? How useful is it as a medium of exchange?

> **KEY POINTS**
>
> 1. Money is anything that is generally accepted for payment.
> 2. Today money consists of notes and coins, and also bank cards.
> 3. The main function of money is as a means of making exchange (payment for goods and services).

3.1.2 Commercial banks

> **TOPIC GUIDANCE**
>
> Students should be able to:
> - describe the role and importance of commercial banks for governments, firms and consumers.

The role of commercial banks

Commercial banks provide a safe place to keep money and will also lend money. Sometimes they are called retail banks because their lending to businesses and households is relatively small compared with some investment banks which provide large sums of capital to businesses.

The main activities of commercial banks

The basic functions of a bank are as follows.

- **Keeping money safe**: a bank's vaults are more secure than a safe deposit box in a private house. Individuals and businesses can open bank accounts. They deposit money in the account. **Savings accounts** pay the depositor a set rate of interest on sums saved. **Current accounts** are for keeping money safe, but sums can be withdrawn to make payments. A current account may pay some interest, but this will be lower than on a savings account. Banks also keep documents and other valuable items in safe deposit boxes.

- **Lending**: many people and businesses need to borrow money, e.g. for expensive purchases such as a car. Businesses may borrow from banks when they want to grow. Borrowing methods include the following.
  - **Loans** – borrowing a fixed sum, e.g. US$1,000, for a set period of time, e.g. one year. The business will need to pay back the sum borrowed plus the agreed rate of interest. For example, if the interest rate is 10 per cent per annum, then over one year the borrower will pay back US$1,100 (US$1,000 + US$100 interest).
  - An **overdraft** – that is, taking out more than has been put into the account. The borrower has an agreed overdraft limit, and will pay interest to the bank if the account is overdrawn.
  - Banks offer customers a **credit card**. This enables users to buy goods and pay for them later. Every month users receive a **statement** showing how much they owe the bank. If they pay the bill by a given date, they will not have to pay interest. However, if they do not pay the bill in full, they are charged a high rate of interest. Many businesses use credit cards to finance short-term cash flow needs. A **debit card** is a means of payment using funds in your own bank account rather than through borrowing.
  - **Mortgages** – banks lend to firms and households to buy office buildings and factories. The legal deeds of ownership of the property are kept by the bank until the mortgage has been repaid. Mortgages are usually for long periods of time, such as 25 years.

Commercial banks look after the money of depositors, lend money and make it possible to make payments

> **DID YOU KNOW?**
>
> **Interest** is paid by the bank as a reward to savers. It is calculated as a percentage of the sum saved. The bank also charges interest for lending money.

Commercial banks act as financial intermediaries in the way shown in Figure 3.1.2.1

Other banking services

Commercial banks also perform a number of other important services that benefit the economy.

- They provide **means of making payment**, such as cheques and banker's drafts. These are slips of paper, printed with the name, address and logo of the bank, and customers write in the name of the person and the amount they wish to pay. The bank then transfers money to the recipients. Banks can also make regular payments in the form of standing orders (set payments of regular sums) into a named account. Banks process payments through automatic electronic payments as well as internet banking.
- They provide **foreign currency**. If you visit another country that uses different currency, your local bank may be able to provide you with the currency. However, ATMs (automated teller machines) make it easy for a customer to withdraw money in most urban areas worldwide.

Governments and commercial banks

Governments benefit from commercial banks because current accounts and credit card payments provide a means of making payments in the economy, and are thus 'money'. The government can then control the level of bank lending through its central bank (see section 3.1.3), working closely with commercial banks to ensure that the supply of money in the economy is in line with the level of economic activity.

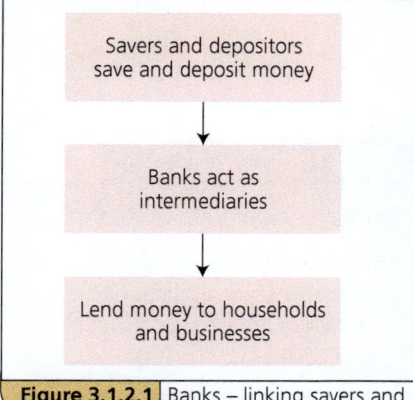

Figure 3.1.2.1 Banks – linking savers and borrowers

DID YOU KNOW?

There is a highly competitive commercial banking structure in Pakistan with many different banks. Some banks meet the general needs of business and household customers. Others target specific types of customers, such as First Women Bank, which sets out 'to be the lead bank for women'.

KEY POINTS

1. Commercial banks provide banking services to businesses and households.
2. Their main functions are to lend money, facilitate payment systems and keep money safe.
3. Banks act as intermediaries between borrowers and lenders.

ACTIVITY

Identify a commercial bank in your country and produce a poster to show how the services it provides help individuals and businesses.

SUMMARY QUESTIONS

1. Why might a customer prefer to have a deposit rather than a current account?
2. How do commercial banks play an intermediary role in the economy?
3. Describe three ways in which commercial banks provide credit for customers.

STUDY TIP

You should be able to explain why people might prefer to keep their money in a commercial bank rather than hide it somewhere in their house.

3.1.3 Central banks

Central banks

Every country has a **central bank** which is responsible for supervising the banking system in the domestic economy. In the UK the central bank is the Bank of England; in Germany it is the Deutsche Bundesbank; in Mauritius it is the Bank of Mauritius.

The central bank influences the economy in the following way. The head of the central bank holds regular meetings with senior officials from the other banks to outline policy for lending. If there is too much spending in an economy leading to rising prices, the head of the central bank may request that banks reduce lending. If there is too little spending in the economy, leading to **recession** (see section 4.6.2), banks will be requested to lend more. The central bank also creates rules (**financial regulations**) that affect how other banks can be set up, and, for example, how much they can safely lend.

As well as supervising the financial system, the central bank has additional functions.

- It prints the notes and mints the coins that are **legal tender** (notes and coins that should be accepted as payment). It also destroys torn notes and worn-out coins.
- The central bank plays a major role in setting **interest rates**. The interest rate is the price paid for borrowing money. Setting interest rates gives the central bank considerable power in the economy. Changing interest rates helps the central bank to control lending by other banks.

Reduction in interest rates	Borrowers find borrowing cheaper, borrow more, increase spending
Increase in interest rates	Savers save more, borrowers borrow less, spending falls

- The central bank acts as a lender of last resort. If another bank needs cash in a hurry (perhaps because depositors are withdrawing unusually large sums of money), it can borrow from the central bank. In this situation, the central bank may decide to penalise other banks for lending too much and charge them a high rate of interest. Other banks set their interest rates at levels just above the central bank's base rate – that is, the rate set by the central bank on which all other interest rates are based.
- The central bank supervises **monetary policy**: this determines the quantity of money in the economy and the interest rate. The central bank helps the government to create and manage monetary policy.
- The central bank acts as banker for the commercial banks and for the government. By acting as the banker's bank, debts between the commercial banks can be settled through their accounts at the central bank.

TOPIC GUIDANCE

Students should be able to:
- outline the role and importance of central banks for governments, producers and consumers.

The Central Bank of Bahrain is responsible for regulating banking in Bahrain, issuing notes and coins and other functions

DID YOU KNOW?

The central bank plays a key role in carrying out the government's monetary policy, determining the quantity and price of money in the economy. Firms and households feel the impact of monetary policy in the form of money to spend when more money is provided by the central bank, and when interest rates fall, making borrowing cheaper. Rising interest rates discourage borrowing, as the cost of money rises. However, they mean good news for savers.

ACTIVITY

Find out the current base rate charged by the central bank in your country and compare it with the rates charged in each of the previous 12 months. Discuss with your classmates why the central bank may have raised or lowered its base rate over this period.

- Government tax revenue and major spending is carried out through accounts with the central bank.
- The central bank helps the government to borrow money by issuing government bills and **bonds**. The total amount the government owes to lenders is called the **national debt**. The bonds are official promises to repay money in the future with interest in return for the loan. Rich investors and other financial institutions are happy to lend governments money because in many countries it is a very safe investment.
- The central bank helps to manage the international financial system. On a world scale there needs to be generally acceptable methods of making payment for international transactions. This requires confidence in the international financial system. The **International Monetary Fund** (**IMF**) was set up to provide supervision for the world's banking system. One of its functions is to lend money to governments to help them in times of financial crisis when investors may have lost confidence in the banking systems of those countries. Central banks work closely with the IMF to create financial stability. Countries deposit gold and their own currency with the IMF. This can then be lent to countries in crisis. Leading central bankers will meet regularly with important government officials and members of the IMF to create better systems of international financial management.

DID YOU KNOW?

The central bank manages the national debt. This involves repaying investors who have lent the government money and paying the interest on this debt. In the UK, the Bank of England was established in 1694 to manage the national debt.

KEY POINTS

1. The central bank supervises the other banks and has a close link with government monetary policy.
2. The central bank issues notes and coins.
3. The central bank is the government's bank and the bankers' bank.

SUMMARY QUESTIONS

1. Explain the terms 'central bank', 'lender of last resort' and 'national debt'.
2. Describe what you consider to be the two main functions of a central bank.
3. The Central Bank of Sri Lanka is responsible for the conduct of monetary policy in the country. What do you think this would involve?

DID YOU KNOW?

The size of national debt is a major concern to governments. If the debt becomes too large, lenders will become reluctant to make further loans and demand higher rates of interest. The higher rates of interest lead to a greater burden of future debt repayments.

In 2010, the government of Greece found that it was difficult to finance the national debt. As the amount of debt was so large, lenders insisted on much higher rates of interest to lend Greece money. Since 2010 the Greek government has had to apply to the European Central Bank for three bailouts (most recently in 2017) to stop the country from going bankrupt. By 2017 national debt was 179 per cent of Greece's national input.

ACTIVITY

Create a poster showing the name of the central bank in your country and setting out some of its main functions.

STUDY TIP

Make sure that you can discuss the role of the central bank in a country's economic and financial system.

3.2 Households

3.2.1 Influences on spending, saving and borrowing

TOPIC GUIDANCE

Students should be able to:

- outline the main influences on spending, saving and borrowing, including income, the rate of interest and confidence.

Spending money enables you to enjoy goods and services now; saving enables you to have the money to spend later

DID YOU KNOW?

The rate of interest is an important influence on how much people are willing to save or borrow. A reduction in interest rates makes saving less attractive and borrowing more attractive, which stimulates spending. A rise in interest rates has the reverse effect.

STUDY TIP

You need to be able to refer to a country's savings ratio, which is the proportion of a country's income that is not spent.

Spending, saving and borrowing defined

- **Spending** is exchanging money for goods. The goods may be for immediate **consumption** (use), or they may be consumer durables. 'Durable' means lasting. **Consumer durables** are items such as radios, bicycles and furniture.
- **Saving** is setting money aside instead of spending it. Savings can be kept in a money box or in a safe place in your house, but it is safer to put money in a bank account or in a savings club.
- Borrowing is when an individual receives money from another individual or financial institution, with the intention of paying it back.

Motives for spending, saving and borrowing

The reason that people behave in a certain way is their motive.

Spending

The main motive for spending money is to buy goods and services that you can consume now: a packet of sweets, a bottle of water, a visit to the cinema. Some spending is on necessities (see Unit 1), such as basic foodstuffs and fuel to cook your food. Other spending is on non-essential goods, such as a new DVD or a computer game.

Spending on consumer durables builds up a stock of wealth that can be enjoyed for a longer period of time (although they lose value each year), e.g. a car, washing machine or television.

When there is a general rise in prices – that is, inflation (see Unit 4) – consumers may put off making expensive purchases and keep consumer durables for longer periods. People spend proportionately more on essentials in a period of inflation as they go up in price, leaving less to spend on other things.

Saving

The main motive for saving is to put money aside in order to make a purchase at a later date. This might be to pay for something relatively expensive or that does not occur regularly, e.g. a visit to a relative, a holiday, or school or college fees. Older people might save for their retirement when they are no longer earning.

The **savings ratio** refers to the proportion of income that consumers save. Attitudes to savings vary with culture. For example, people in Asia tend to save more than in the West. In recent years consumers in the US and UK have borrowed a lot to finance spending on consumer goods so that savings ratios are low. In contrast, in rapidly growing economies such as India and China many people have been saving more money than spending it.

Country	Approximate savings ratios (%)
UK, US	under 5
Germany	7
India	25

Savings ratios in selected countries 2016–7

In periods of inflation the savings ratio tends to fall. People may feel that if prices go up, the money saved will only buy less.

The savings ratio may increase during a recession. People save more for the future because they fear that they may lose their jobs.

Borrowing

A major motive for borrowing is to be able to spend more than you receive in income in order to meet your wants and needs. Another motive is to buy an expensive item such as a house or car.

People also borrow money if they anticipate being able to repay it in the future. Borrowing thus becomes a way of raising present income, knowing that the repayment will eat into future income.

When interest rates are low, people will be encouraged to borrow because the cost of future repayment has been lowered.

If prices are expected to rise in the future, people may borrow more now and spend the money, rather than having to pay more at a later date.

KEY POINTS

1. Economists use the term 'consumption' to refer to spending on goods that are used up either immediately or over a period of time.
2. Incomes can either be spent (consumption) or saved.
3. Incomes can be supplemented by borrowing, to purchase an expensive item such as a house.

SUMMARY QUESTIONS

1. If consumers spend a smaller proportion of their income as income rises, what will be the impact on:
   a saving
   b borrowing?
2. What is likely to be the effect of rising inflation on spending and borrowing? Explain your answer.
3. What are the main motives for:
   a borrowing
   b spending?

DID YOU KNOW?

As income rises, consumers may spend a smaller proportion of each additional unit earned. So a consumer may spend all of the first US$100 earned in a month, but only spend US$50 of an increase from US$900 to US$1,000. The fraction of additional income spent is known as the **propensity to consume**.

ACTIVITY

Find out what has been happening to interest rates in your country over the last year. Plot the base rate charged by the central bank on to a graph. Label the graph to show months in which rises or falls in interest rates are likely to have led to increased saving or decreased saving. Do the same for borrowing.

STUDY TIP

As incomes in a country rise to a higher level, households will spend more, but will save a higher proportion of their income. This is particularly true in a stable economy such as Germany, where there is little uncertainty about employment (which is high) and inflation (which is low and stable).

By contrast, in a low-income country such as Romania, people will have less money to spend and actually spend more than they earn (negative savings ratio). In Romania, there is also greater uncertainty (higher unemployment and inflation rates).

3.2.2 Income and expenditure patterns

> **TOPIC GUIDANCE**
>
> Students should be able to:
> - discuss how and why different income groups have different expenditure patterns.

Increasing incomes in China have seen rapid rises in consumer spending, particularly among the 20–30 years age group

> **DID YOU KNOW?**
>
> Household savings are an important source of funds for business expansion. As households become wealthier they are able to save more. They will deposit their savings in financial institutions such as banks. The banks then lend the money to business and other borrowers.

Patterns of income and expenditure

Studies in different countries have shown that the proportion of income that people spend depends on the size of their income. The table shows the broad findings of these studies.

Size of income	Spending	Saving	Borrowing
High-income household	Not likely to spend all of their income	Will be able to save some of their income	Unlikely to need to borrow
Middle-income household	May spend most of their income	May be able to save a little	Probably borrowing to buy at least some consumer-durable items
Low-income household	Will most probably spend all of their income and this may not cover all their needs	Most low-income households will not be able to save	Many low-income households will have to borrow to meet their needs; however, a problem for low-income households is that they will find it more difficult to borrow – because lenders are less sure about being repaid

As people become richer they are likely to spend more. However, they are likely to spend a smaller proportion of additional income than they earn.

Rising consumption is typically associated with rapid industrialisation. For example, Japan's **household consumption** grew by 9.2 per cent a year in the 1970s. South Korea's grew by over 8 per cent a year in the 1980s. Currently China's household consumption grew at about 12 per cent in the first decade of the 21st century.

> **CASE STUDY** | Rising consumption in China
>
> One of the major reasons for rising consumption in China is the very fast growth of the economy. Each year during the first decade of the 21st century, China was able to produce 9–10 per cent more goods than in the previous year. Many young people benefited from a rise in income because they had the skills to take up new jobs, e.g. in information technology or in the energy industries, as well as in other expanding areas of business. In

China currently about 200 million people are entering their 20 and 30. This group is earning more money in the rapidly growing economy. They are able to spend more, and save more.

Young Chinese people are spending more on their homes and their families. Often they are provided with financial support by their parents. All these factors have led to rapid consumption growth in China.

Questions

1 Why has consumption risen so rapidly in China in recent years?
2 How are young Chinese people able to spend an increasing amount?
3 How are young Chinese people also able to save more?

DID YOU KNOW?

In recent years the rate of growth in China has fallen below 10 per cent, partly as a deliberate policy of the government to focus on economic growth while at the same time giving more emphasis to environmental controls. So while income continues to grow there is more of an emphasis on combining growth of income and spending with a healthier quality of life.

DID YOU KNOW?

The generation of people up to the age of 29 in China makes up a considerable part of the population (almost 600 million people). This group is likely to spend a higher proportion of income than their parents. There are over 3 million university graduates with relatively high incomes (many continue to live at home). They are more likely to buy brands and modern products.

STUDY TIP

Most people would like to save, but it is not always easy to do so. Make sure that you can discuss the various factors that can influence decisions to save money rather than spend it.

KEY POINTS

1 The amount a person spends, saves and borrows is influenced by the size of his or her income.
2 The proportion of income spent, saved or borrowed is influenced by the size of income.
3 Rapid industrialisation gives individuals more money to spend and also more money to save.

ACTIVITY

What is happening to consumption and saving in your country? What factors encourage young people to spend more? What factors encourage them to save more? Discuss this in class and see if there is general agreement.

SUMMARY QUESTIONS

1 How are richer people able to spend more and save more than those who are poorer?
2 Why are poorer people more likely to borrow than richer people?
3 Why is rising consumption associated with rapid industrialisation of countries?

3.3 Workers

3.3.1 Factors affecting choice of occupation

> **TOPIC GUIDANCE**
>
> Students should be able to:
> - identify the factors affecting an individual's choice of occupation, including wage and non-wage factors.

Different types of occupation

There are thousands of different occupations, each with its own conditions of work. Employees are expected to work under a variety of arrangements, including full-time, part-time and shift work. Some people work indoors and others outdoors, some for large companies and others for **micro-businesses**, some work at night and others during the day. Some people are self-employed and work for themselves. There are many factors that help to determine a person's choice of occupation. Particularly important among these are wage factors and non-wage factors.

Wage factors

An important consideration in choosing a career is the wages paid. For example, doctors and accountants typically earn more than electricians and drivers.

Wages are payments for carrying out work. The higher the wage, the more attractive a job may seem. However, highly paid jobs typically require a lot of training and skill development, which can reduce the supply of qualified applicants. Some dangerous jobs, e.g. working on an offshore oil rig, will only attract applicants if wages are relatively high.

In choosing an occupation a potential employee will consider the amount paid, including basic pay and additional incentives such as bonuses and overtime opportunities.

- **Basic pay** is the amount of money that will be received by an employee before any additional increments or deductions are made. For example, the basic pay may be set at US$200 for a 40-hour week.
- **Earnings** relates to the total amount an individual receives when additional payments are added, including overtime, bonuses and commission.
- **Overtime** is hours worked in addition to the basic contracted number of hours. It will be paid at a higher rate, e.g. time and a half (150 per cent of the wage rate). The higher rate is often required to encourage people to work 'unsocial' hours.
- A **bonus** is used as an incentive – that is, to persuade employees to work harder (or longer), e.g. to meet targets such as given production or sales figures.
- **Commission** is a payment made as a percentage of the sales a salesperson makes. In a retail store an employee might receive 10 per cent of each sale made, or may be paid an hourly rate plus 5 per cent commission on each sale.

An offshore oil platform: high wages can encourage people to work in hard and dangerous occupations

> **STUDY TIP**
>
> A key factor affecting choice of occupation is wages. Higher wages attract more applicants. However, remember that other non-wage factors are also important, including opportunities for training and development and fringe benefits.

Non-wage factors

Non-wage factors can be highly influential in the choice of occupation. They include the following.

- **Job satisfaction**: many people are prepared to work for less if they enjoy the work. Job satisfaction is personal to the individual; a person with the skills to be a successful business executive may choose manual work, e.g. making beautiful objects. Some people prefer to work for a business with regular income; others prefer the freedom of working for themselves.
- **Career prospects**: many people want to work in occupations where there is opportunity for promotion, e.g. from junior salesperson to sales supervisor, sales manager, area sales manager, and so on.
- **Fringe benefits**: these are non-financial incentives given to employees. For example:

Type of fringe benefit	Benefits
Subsidised housing	Subsidised or free housing is a strong incentive in city areas where accommodation is expensive and there are long waiting lists
Payment of school fees	Scholarships for education to the children of company employees
Company car or subsidised transport	Provides the benefit of a first car or second car or cheap rail and/or bus transport passes for families of workers
Subsidised company products	Reduced prices for company products

- Other non-wage incentives include length of holidays, e.g. for teachers, and good pension schemes (particularly for public sector workers) and job security (again, often in the public sector). Another influencing factor is the location of the job, such as being close to family and friends or in a desirable area.

DID YOU KNOW?

Employees may be paid by time, or according to a piece rate, performance rate or through profit-sharing. Piece rates are sometimes used in the textile and electronics industries: payment is made for each item that meets a given quality standard. Performance rates are related to meeting given targets. Profit-related pay is an additional reward related to the company's profit.

ACTIVITY

Think of a job that you would like to do when you leave school or college. List the three most important influences that would make the job attractive to you.

SUMMARY QUESTIONS

1 Divide the following rewards into wage and non-wage factors:

  basic pay   overtime   subsidised meals   company car
       bonus   reduced price company products

2 Explain the difference between basic pay and earnings. Which figure will be higher?

3 Explain how the following will have an important part to play in influencing a person's choice of occupation:
  a   one wage factor
  b   one non-wage factor.

KEY POINTS

1 The higher the reward, the bigger the incentive to work in a particular occupation.

2 Rewards consist of wage rewards and non-wage rewards.

3 An individual's choice of occupation is determined by a combination of wage and non-wage factors.

3.3.2 Wage determination

TOPIC GUIDANCE

Students should be able to:

- show how demand for and supply of workers affects wages
- explain how bargaining power of unions affects wages
- illustrate ways in which government policy can affect wages.

Sir Arthur Lewis developed the idea of the wages tipping point, beyond which wages would increase quickly in the manufacturing sectors of developing economies

ACTIVITY

Find reports in a local or national newspaper about shortages of labour in a particular sector. See if you can relate these shortages to wages in that sector.

DID YOU KNOW?

Improved skills can secure higher wages for workers because of increased demand for their scarce skills.

Demand and supply, and wages

Labour is a factor of production. A **derived demand** for labour stems from the demand for the products that workers produce.

The supply of labour consists of workers looking for work, the hours they will work and the wage rates they will accept.

The demand for labour comes from employers seeking workers to produce goods in combination with other factors of production. The lower the wage rate, the more workers an employer will demand. A typical labour market brings together these two forces – the supply of labour and the demand for labour (as illustrated in Figure 3.3.2.1).

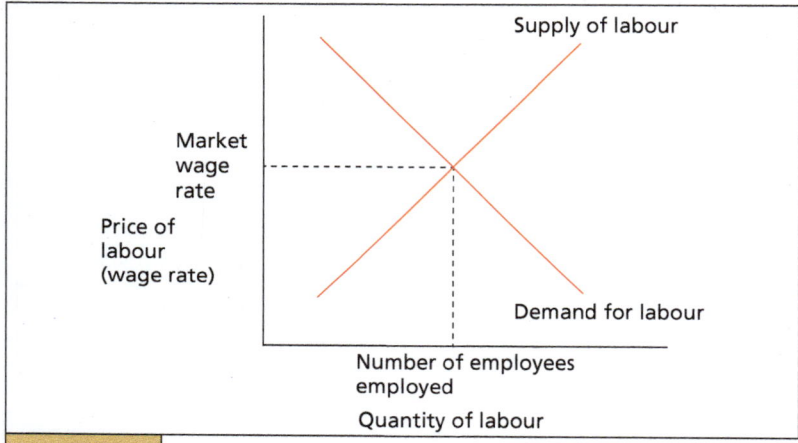

Figure 3.3.2.1 The forces of demand and supply in a labour market

The price of labour is determined by the relative strength of the following factors.

- **The demand for particular types of workers:** this is largely determined by the price of the products that these workers produce. For example, workers in a salt-producing plant will receive far lower wages than those producing high-end fashion garments. Workers producing goods for which demand is inelastic, e.g items made from gold, will receive higher wages than those producing goods for which demand is elastic, e.g. brands of margarine.

- **The supply of particular types of workers:** for example, workers with scarce engineering skills will be more plentiful than those with basic mechanics qualifications. The more elastic the supply of labour for a particular type of work, the lower wages will be: unskilled work that many people can do is unlikely to be highly paid. Where supply is inelastic because it takes a long time to train, e.g. to become a doctor, wages will be higher.

The strength of bargaining power

The elasticity of supply and demand for labour helps to determine the relative bargaining power of employers and workers, as shown below.

Elasticity of demand for labour	Elasticity of supply for labour	Wage outcome
relatively inelastic	relatively inelastic	high wages
relatively elastic	relatively elastic	low wages

Where a particular type of labour is in scarce supply and contributes to the production of goods for which there is inelastic demand, the bargaining power of labour will be strong.

CASE STUDY: The Lewis tipping point

Nobel Prize-winning St Lucian economist Sir Arthur Lewis developed the concept of the tipping point at which wages are likely to increase in the most productive sectors, in developing economies. In economies with two key sectors, e.g. low-productivity agriculture and high-productivity manufacturing, it will initially be easy for manufacturing to recruit labour from agriculture (keeping wages down).

As more labour is employed in manufacturing, shortages of labour (particularly skilled labour) develop, leading to wage rises. This is the case in China: surplus workers from rural areas have moved to higher-paid manufacturing jobs in cities. However, since 2010 increasing shortages of labour have occurred, so manufacturing wages in China are increasing at a much higher rate (as we move beyond the tipping point).

Questions

1. What has happened to the elasticity of supply of labour for Chinese manufacturing?
2. How is this impacting on wages in Chinese manufacturing?
3. What does this tell us about the changing relative power of business owners and workers?

Government policy and wages

Governments can intervene in labour markets by setting maximum and minimum wages in some or all sectors. In a country with significant government interference it might be possible to establish maximum wages in some sectors in order to make these industries more competitive, e.g. to keep the price of exports down. The danger is that this might lead to a reduction in the supply of labour to those industries.

In 2.11.2 we illustrated a situation where a government imposes minimum wages to guarantee a 'fair wage' for employees. However, when the wage set is above the market rate this may lead to increased unemployment.

DID YOU KNOW?

'**Derived demand**' defines a situation where something (usually a factor of production) is demanded not for its own sake but because it goes into producing an output valued by consumers.

KEY POINTS

1. Demand and supply interact to create a market wage.
2. The wage rate and relative bargaining power of employers and workers is determined by the relative strength of demand and supply for labour.
3. Demand for labour is derived from the demand for the end products workers produce; this substantially determines wages.

SUMMARY QUESTIONS

1. In which of the following situations will labour have the greatest bargaining power (and highest wages) and why?
   a. labour is unskilled
   b. demand for the goods produced is elastic
   c. supply and demand for labour are both inelastic
2. In a two-sector economy consisting of a low-productivity sector and a high-productivity sector, at what point will wages in the high-productivity sector start to increase?

3.3.3 Differences in earnings

TOPIC GUIDANCE

Students should be able to:

- explain the differences in earnings between different groups of workers.

In this unit we explain why earnings vary between different groups of workers:

- skilled/unskilled
- private sector/public sector
- male/female
- agricultural/manufacturing/services.

A major cause of differences results from demand and supply. However, there is also an element of discrimination that may lead to inequalities.

CASE STUDY | The relative earnings of doctors and hospital porters

Why does a doctor earn more than a hospital porter?

- To reflect the time and skill invested in gaining medical qualifications.
- To reflect the responsibility the doctor carries.
- Because of the greater demand for and limited supply of doctors.

The demand curve for doctors has a steep shape (relatively inelastic demand, see Unit 2.7). The supply of doctors is also steep (relatively inelastic supply) because of the time and expense that it takes to train them. In contrast, the supply and demand curves for hospital porters are relatively more elastic. A rise in wages of porters will lead to a much more rapid increase in the numbers making themselves available to work in hospitals.

a Doctors' wage — Wage rate (US$) 40 000, Relatively inelastic supply, Quantity of doctors (Q)

b Porters' wage — Wage rate (US$) 20 000, Relatively elastic supply, Quantity of hospital porters (Q)

Questions

1. Explain why the supply curve for hospital doctors is steeper than that for hospital porters.
2. Explain why the wage rate of doctors is US$40 000, whereas it is only US$20 000 for hospital porters.

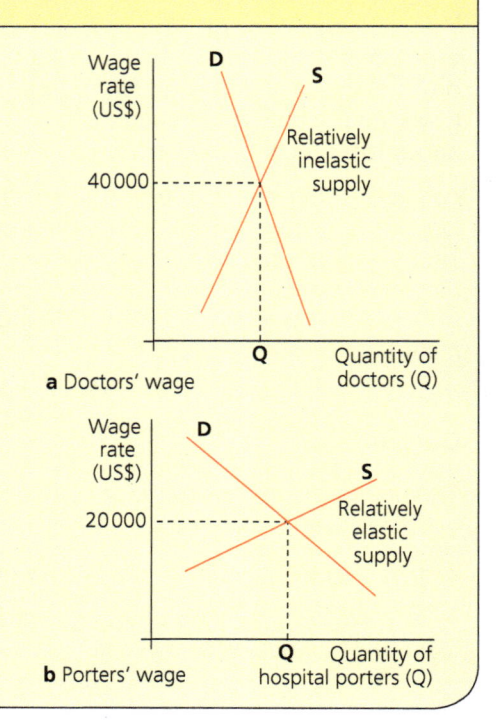

In most countries a large proportion of teachers work in the public sector. High levels of job security and relatively good pensions are non-wage factors encouraging people to work in this sector, as well as the love of the job

Skilled and unskilled workers

If labour is in short supply and the demand for that particular type of labour is strong, employers will be prepared to pay higher wages to engage suitable workers.

Another reason for skilled labour being paid more than unskilled is that it is highly productive. A skilled worker contributes far more value to production than an unskilled worker. For example, if a skilled furniture maker can produce five high-quality chairs in a day and an unskilled apprentice only one, the skilled worker is five times more productive than the unskilled one and merits a higher rate of pay.

The public and private sectors

In many countries, workers in the **public sector** earn more than those in the **private sector**. This is the case in the UK, Ireland, the US and India, for example.

This difference is sometimes described as the public sector premium.

> **CASE STUDY** — Public and private sector pay, UK
>
> The Office for National Statistics in the UK published data in 2017 which showed that public sector employees were paid an average of 3 per cent more than private sector staff, compared with a gap of 5.3 per cent in 2007.
>
> Key factors influencing this difference included the average age of public sector workers (older), and their qualifications (on average better qualified). However, the pay figures do not take into account some other factors such as bonuses and perks such as company cars and health insurance in the private sector.
>
> **Questions**
>
> 1. See if you can access some data from national statistics comparing public and private sector pay in your country.
> 2. Why do you think pay is higher in the public sector?
> 3. What possible reasons could be put forward for the growing difference in pay in the UK?

Differences in pay

There are many economic reasons for the relative differences in pay. Important reasons include the high level of education and professional training required to work in many public sector occupations, such as the civil service and teaching. Other reasons might include the strong bargaining power of **trade unions** in the public sector. Public sector workers may carry out work that is regarded as essential, such as providing medical care.

Some economists argue that in fact public sector workers' wages would be higher if it were not for the job security and relatively high pensions associated with such work.

Male and female workers: the wage gap

In most countries average wages for men are higher than for women.

The term '**gender wage gap**' refers to the comparison between the wages of men and women. The wage gap is expressed as a percentage. For example, women earn 81 per cent as much as men.

In the US, statistics are collected on the wage gap by the US Census Bureau (Current Population Survey). This compares pay for full-time year round (FTYR) employees. It compares median (average) earnings.

> **DID YOU KNOW?**
>
> Private sector wages can give a distorted picture – they may appear lower because non-wage factors, such as a company car, are not considered.

> **ACTIVITY**
>
> Compare a job carried out by two workers in your economy who have similar education and skills, one of whom works in the private sector and the other in the public sector. Which worker receives the greatest range of non-wage benefits?

> **DID YOU KNOW?**
>
> In some countries the **average earnings** of women are broadly similar to those of men, e.g in Bolivia and Guatemala in South America. In Bahrain, however, women earn 40 per cent more than men, but there are far fewer female than male workers in the labour force.

In India wages of agricultural labourers using little capital are low. They are much higher for those in the new industries, such as engineers in wind energy

For example, in 2017 the median earning of FTYR male employees was US$51 212, and for females US$40 742, leaving a gender wage gap of 0.80:

$$\frac{40\,742}{51\,212} \times 100 = 79.55 \text{ per cent}$$

There are various explanations for the gap. One is that on average women spend a shorter period as part of the full-time labour force. As a result they are less likely to be skilled, leading to lower wage rates. Women are also more likely to be doing part-time jobs, as illustrated in the figures below from the Northern Ireland Labour Force Survey.

	Males	Females
% of employees of working age in full-time employment	89.2	60.8
% of employees of working age in part-time employment	10.8	39.2

Source: Department of Finance and Personnel

Another reason for inequalities in wages results from **discrimination**. In the US the Equal Pay Act was signed in 1963, making it illegal for employers to pay unequal wages to men and women who hold the same job and do the same work. This has led to some reductions in inequality. In 1963 the wage gap was 58 per cent; in 2017 it was nearer to 80 per cent. However, in the US and elsewhere, the wage gap still persists and part of this may be the result of discrimination. Figure 3.3.3.1 shows the demand for labour resulting from discrimination leading to a lower wage for a group that is discriminated against.

DID YOU KNOW?

Discrimination at work involves treating one group less favourably than others. The discrimination may be in the form of providing poorer working conditions and lower wages.

DID YOU KNOW?

Over the last 20 years the percentage of female to male workers in the UK has been steadily increasing. Today roughly half the workforce is female. However, average wages for men are higher, in part because a greater percentage of men are in full-time (rather than part-time) work.

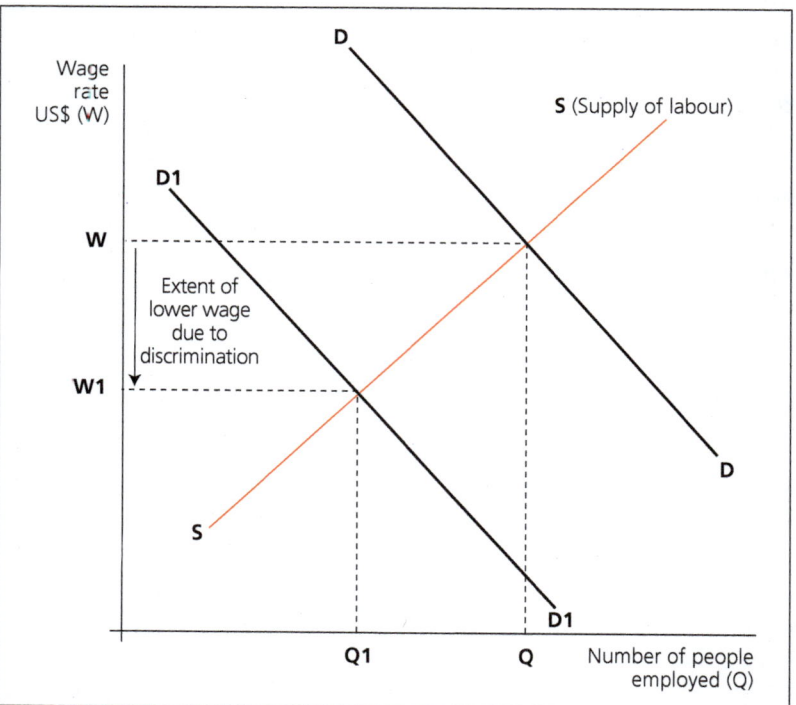

Figure 3.3.3.1 The impact of discrimination

Agriculture and manufacturing/services

Wages vary between different industries. In economics we describe the demand for labour as a **derived demand**. Labour is wanted not for its own sake but to produce end products desired by customers. The demand for a farm worker may therefore be derived from the demand for sugar cane, tea or butter. The demand for a manufacturing worker may be derived from the demand for chocolate bars, cars or radios. The demand for a service sector worker may be derived from the demand for transport services, bank accounts and so on.

Many theories of development show how low wages in agriculture lead to a migration of populations from poor rural areas to higher-wage occupations in cities where people can get jobs in manufacturing. In many countries much more capital (machinery and equipment) is used in manufacturing. Employers in manufacturing are therefore able to tempt workers to transfer from agriculture into manufacturing.

Today it is the new service industries such as insurance, health and education where there is the biggest demand for workers. As a result service sector jobs offer some of the highest wages. In addition, the new information technology sector of the economy has seen booming wages in areas such as computer games design and robotics.

As new industries develop, wages will increase in these industries. For example, there is an increasing demand worldwide for wind energy. Companies in this area, such as the Danish company Vestas, which has 20 per cent of the global wind power market, are thriving, and are thus able to pay higher wages to their engineers.

STUDY TIP

When discussing wage differences, make sure that you put the differences in a theoretical context. You should refer to demand and supply.

KEY POINTS

1. There are several factors leading to differences in wages.
2. These include the level of skill, the nature of the industry (e.g. agriculture/manufacturing/services), public or private sector and male/female differences.
3. Sometimes discrimination may distort wages determined by market forces of demand and supply.

DID YOU KNOW?

The Indian agriculture sector is one of the lowest paid in the world. Unskilled labourers producing a variety of agricultural products including new hybrid seeds for multinational companies receive very poor rewards. Production may be highly labour intensive using little capital and machinery. Although the Indian government has sought to raise wages through the National Rural Employment Guarantee Act (NREGA), this is ignored by many employers.

SUMMARY QUESTIONS

1. What is meant by derived demand? Using an example of a particular job, show how the demand for it, and hence the wage paid, is derived.
2. Are the differences in pay between males and females simply a result of discrimination?
3. What is meant by the wage gap? How is it measured? Is there an obvious wage gap in your country?

3.3.4 Division of labour/specialisation

TOPIC GUIDANCE

Students should be able to:
- describe the benefits and disadvantages of specialisation for the individual.

What is specialisation?

Specialisation involves concentrating on a particular task. Employees specialise in given occupations, e.g. teachers, doctors, shop workers. Managers specialise in given activities, such as managing production or managing the accounts of a business.

If people and resources concentrate on things that they can do relatively well, then usually everyone benefits. Specialisation results in an increase in production.

A specialist occupation such as shoemaking enables an individual to produce goods of a very high quality. The shoemaker can concentrate on his work while buying in products and services from other specialists

It benefits individuals to concentrate on what they do best. For example, if an author can earn US$10 an hour from writing a book and it only costs US$5 an hour to have someone paint his house, it will make sense for the author to sit and write while the decorator paints. However, things cannot just be weighed up in money terms – you also need to consider the satisfaction or dissatisfaction you get from a particular activity.

In the modern economy many employees play specialist roles. However, because the economy is changing so rapidly it is important for employees to be flexible by learning new skills. This enables them to adapt to take advantage of new opportunities. Flexibility enables employees to secure higher lifetime earnings.

Division of labour

The principle of specialisation is easily illustrated in relation to the division of labour (specialisation by job task). Figure 3.3.4.1 shows some of the specialist occupations involved in a factory that makes chocolates.

ACTIVITY

Create a poster to show some specialist workers. With their permission, photograph three specialists in your locality and the type of work they specialise in. How does specialism enable them to earn more than non-specialists? How has specialism enabled them to develop particular skills?

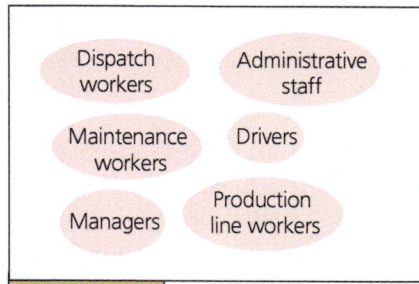

- Dispatch workers
- Administrative staff
- Maintenance workers
- Drivers
- Managers
- Production line workers

Figure 3.3.4.1 Each of these specialists develops skills from concentrating on one thing

Advantages and disadvantages of division of labour

The table shows some of the advantages and disadvantages of division of labour.

Advantages of division of labour	Disadvantages of division of labour
Increase in skill: by doing something repeatedly the employee becomes more skilled. The skilled employee becomes more productive, producing higher or more valuable output per hour worked.	Dependency: because of specialisation many individuals, groups and processes become dependent on each other. If the person or machine at the previous stage to you is slow, unreliable or inefficient in some other way, your own work will suffer.
Time saving: it takes time to change from one task to another. Specialisation helps to eliminate this.	Unemployment: specialisation in a specific task or job can be harmful if the economy no longer requires that specialism. The individual may find it difficult to find work elsewhere.
Specialisation in 'best lines': division of labour makes it possible for people to concentrate on what they do best. Some people like working with their hands, others enjoy selling things. As employees become more skilled at a set task they often take great pride in what they are able to achieve.	Frustration and boredom: if the work that people have to do is unimaginative and repetitive they may not enjoy work. Accidents are more likely to happen and people will be less motivated to work hard.
Use of supporting technology: specialists can draw on technologies that make their work easier and enhance their skills. Most specialist work is supported by applications such as databases of relevant information, spreadsheet tools for making calculations, applications that enable designers to work on screen and accountancy packages.	Over-concentration: by concentrating on specialist skills individuals may not develop other abilities. Their work may require so much focus on particular skills that they may not be able, or have the time, to develop other useful general skills.
Higher earnings: an individual who becomes good at their specialism should be in a stronger position to secure higher earnings.	

KEY POINTS

1. Specialisation of individuals at work is called the division of labour.
2. Division of labour enables individuals to become more skilled and productive.
3. Division of labour increases earnings, but individuals also need to be flexible.

SUMMARY QUESTIONS

1. What are the advantages and disadvantages of the division of labour?
2. What other resources can specialise as well as labour?
3. Give two examples of specialist workers in (a) agriculture (b) manufacturing and (c) service industries.

STUDY TIP

There are a number of advantages and disadvantages to division of labour. Make sure that you can discuss this topic and remember to consider both sides.

3.4 Trade unions

3.4.1 Nature and purpose of trade unions

TOPIC GUIDANCE

Students should be able to:
- describe trade unions and analyse their role in an economy.

Workers in Bangladesh demanding better conditions in textile factories: an important function of trade unions is to negotiate better conditions for all their members

STUDY TIP

Some trade unions are more powerful than others. You should understand the various factors that could lead to this.

DID YOU KNOW?

Trade unions are more powerful when they have a large number of members, where most of the workers in an industry or trade belong to the union, and where industrial action can seriously weaken business profits and disrupt large areas of the economy.

What is a trade union?

A trade union is an association of employees formed to protect and promote the interests of its members. Trade unions are formed, financed and run by their members, who pay an annual subscription. The unions try to influence some of the decisions made by the owners and managers of businesses. Public sector unions bargain with government-appointed public sector employers.

In Bangladesh the National Garment Workers Federation, with about 25 000 members, represents textile workers. In some countries, such as Germany, there are very large trade unions that represent all the workers in the same industry. In New Zealand, the Council of Trade Unions (CTU) consists of 19 unions with over 200 000 members, ranging from professional footballers and nurses to building tradesmen and dairy workers.

Figure 3.4.1.1 shows some of the aims of trade unions. You can see that the main aim is to secure the best possible conditions of work for members. Unions know that the decisions a firm makes will affect the livelihoods of workers and their families.

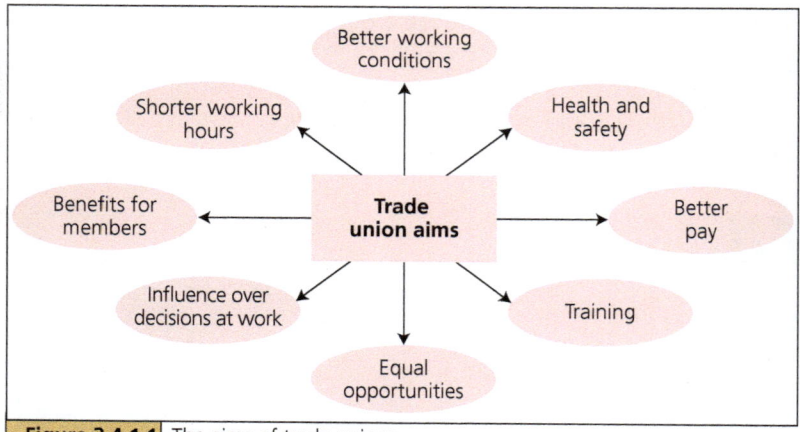

Figure 3.4.1.1 The aims of trade unions

- Better working conditions
- Shorter working hours
- Health and safety
- Benefits for members
- Trade union aims
- Better pay
- Influence over decisions at work
- Training
- Equal opportunities

Negotiation

One of the purposes of a trade union is to negotiate – that is, discuss with employers. Talks take place between the representatives of the employees (union officials) and representatives of the employer. Both sides try to reach agreement on issues such as conditions of employment (e.g. hours worked, safety of the workplace) or wage levels. This negotiation takes place at a local level (e.g. within a factory) or at national level, where the union represents all the members of the trade union in the country.

Figure 3.4.1.2 illustrates the bargaining range.

Figure 3.4.1.2 The bargaining range

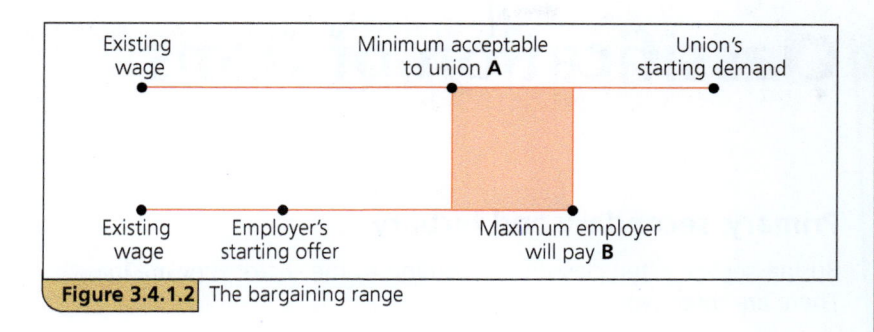

Trade union membership: the benefit to individuals

Typical benefits of belonging to a trade union include:

- knowing that you are part of a group that represents you and fellow workers
- belonging to a body that negotiates better terms and conditions for you, e.g. increased pay or improved conditions
- direct benefits, e.g. sickness benefit
- support for members if there is a **grievance** (e.g. if a member of a trade union feels that he or she has been treated badly at work) or disciplinary procedure (e.g. when a union member has been disciplined, perhaps for poor timekeeping)
- direct action to support members (e.g. if negotiations over pay break down with employees, union officials may call a strike; this means that union members stop work).

The ability to strike gives unions considerable power: if airline or railway workers go on strike, their companies lose money, profit and their reputation for reliability. Other actions that unions can take include working more slowly (a go-slow) and working to rule – only doing things that fit strictly with the rules set out in a contract of employment.

Trade unions: the impact on the economy

Trade unions may play an important part in determining wages. Where unions are strong they have power to push up wages, increasing costs. In some countries workers' representatives are part of company decision-making. In Germany elected works councils make suggestions about the running of the business. In contrast, unions may call frequent strikes, which can lead to unemployment and disruption.

SUMMARY QUESTIONS

1. Who are the members of trade unions? What benefits can they receive from union membership?
2. With which other bodies do trade unions interact, and for what purposes?
3. What impact might strong trade unions have on the economy?

ACTIVITY

Find out whether trade unions, or similar associations of workers, exist in your country. If so, how many are there and in which industries can they be found? What do they set out to achieve? Compare your findings with those for New Zealand – you can find information on the internet by searching for 'Union Database NZCTU'.

STUDY TIP

When discussing the role of trade unions in an economy, be prepared to give advantages and disadvantages; avoid giving a one-sided argument. For example, an advantage of trade unions is that employees are able to communicate demands collectively. A disadvantage is that collective action can disrupt output and other sectors of the economy.

KEY POINTS

1. Trade unions are set up to protect the interests of their members.
2. Trade unions negotiate with employers and try to secure better working conditions.
3. Trade unions protect the interests of workers within the wider economy. Their leaders meet regularly with government officials and employer representatives.

3.5 Firms

3.5.1 Classification of firms

TOPIC GUIDANCE

Students should be able to:
- classify firms as being in the primary/secondary and tertiary sectors
- classify firms as private or public sector
- classify firms by size.

Indian Railways employs 1.4 million people. It is a tertiary sector industry, in the public sector and classified as a large firm

STUDY TIP

Most countries today are going through a de-industrialisation process as the service sector grows and more workers are employed in this sector at the expense of manufacturing. For example, in Brazil 30 per cent of people are employed in agriculture and 14 per cent in manufacturing, but the remaining 66 per cent work in services.

Primary, secondary and tertiary

Businesses are often classified according to the sector they are in. There are three types:
- extractive (**primary industry**)
- manufacturing and construction (**secondary industry**)
- services (**tertiary sector**).

Extractive industries

Brazil is the world's second-largest ethanol supplier after the US. Figure 3.5.1 shows the three stages involved in producing ethanol fuel for cars in Brazil.

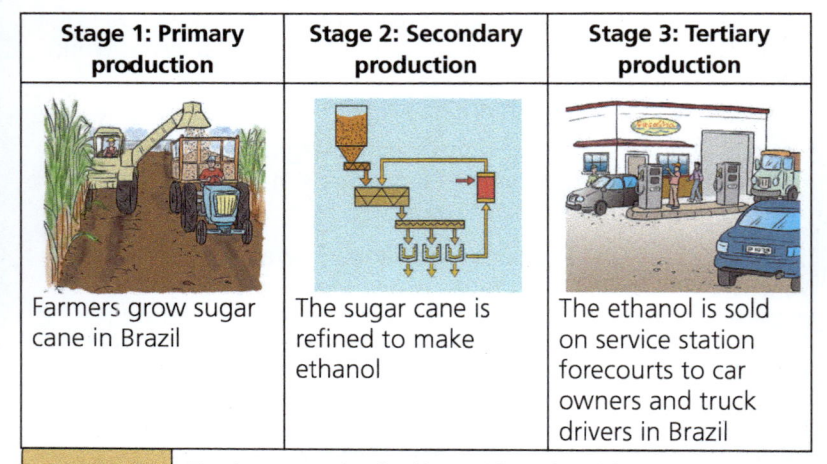

Stage 1: Primary production	Stage 2: Secondary production	Stage 3: Tertiary production
Farmers grow sugar cane in Brazil	The sugar cane is refined to make ethanol	The ethanol is sold on service station forecourts to car owners and truck drivers in Brazil

Figure 3.5.1 The three stages involved in providing ethanol fuel for cars in Brazil

Extractive, or primary, industries are concerned with using natural resources. They include framing, mining and oil drilling. Farmers grow and harvest crops and farm livestock; miners take fuel and minerals from the ground. Primary industries produce raw materials such as iron ore and oil; they also produce finished products such as fish and oranges.

Manufacturing and construction industries

Manufacturing and construction industries are concerned with making and assembling products. Manufacturers use raw materials and parts from other industries. Most products go through several stages of production; when the good is only partly made, it is a semi-manufactured good, e.g. the body of a car. Examples of manufactured goods are chocolate, oil rigs and cars.

Service industries

Service or tertiary industries give something of value to people, but are not physical goods. You cannot touch or hold a visit to the cinema or a lesson given to you in school; these are both services. Other services include banking services and public transport.

Private and public sector

In section 2.9.1 we looked at the classification of sectors in modern economies. A business may be owned by individuals for personal profit (the private sector) or by the government (through direct ownership or through a government-owned public corporation). The private sector consists of sole traders (one owner), partnerships (two or more owners) and private companies and public companies owned by shareholders. Shareholders elect a board to represent their interests, and the board chooses managers.

The goal of a public-sector enterprise such as Indian Railways is to provide essential transport for goods and for hundreds of millions of people.

The ratio of private/public sector jobs varies widely across the world. For example, in Cuba 80 per cent of the population works in the public sector, although this number is falling. In the UK there were 5.4 million public sector jobs and 26.7 million private sector jobs in 2017.

By size

Businesses can be classified by size using one of the methods shown below:

Method	How it is done
Number of employees	A small business might be one employing fewer than 50 people
Value of output	Determined by value of sales in a year, e.g. a small business might be one selling up to US$6.5 million of goods
Market share	Determined by the percentage of the market the business is responsible for. A small business might have less than 5% of the market
Value of capital employed	Determined by the value of what the business owns

Classifying by number of employees is straightforward. For example, in South Africa a micro-enterprise is one with fewer than five employees, very small up to 10, small 11–50, and medium 51–120. Anything over 120 employees is classified as a large firm.

Classifying businesses into sectors helps to develop a picture of how an economy changes over time and helps government to make decisions, e.g. about differential rates of tax to encourage small and micro-enterprises, and to help them grow.

ACTIVITY

Building, Cinema Attendant, Electrician, Sign Writing, Cloth Making, Coal Mining, Laundry, Fire Fighting, Book Publishing, Civil Service, Selling Lottery Tickets, Banking, Oil Drilling, Food Manufacture, Key Cutting, Public Transport, Fishing, Retailing, Food Selling

Figure 3.5.2 Classify these industries as primary, secondary, or tertiary.

KEY POINTS

1. Industrial sectors can be defined as primary, secondary and tertiary, and public and private.
2. Firms can also be classified as being small, medium or large.
3. Classifying businesses helps the government to target support at different sectors to encourage growth in the economy.

SUMMARY QUESTIONS

1. Which is the largest sector of the economy in your country: primary, secondary or tertiary? What are the main types of industries involved in your largest sector?
2. From the list below, what do you think would be the best way of classifying the size of retail businesses, and why?
   a number of employees
   b market share
   c value of output
   d value of capital employed.

3.5.2 Small firms

> **TOPIC GUIDANCE**
>
> Students should be able to:
> - explain the advantages and disadvantages of small firms
> - identify challenges facing small firms.

In section 3.5.1 we saw that a firm can be defined as small through a number of forms of classification, e.g. size of output and number of employees. Small firms are essential to the economy because:

- they are major employers
- they provide many of the raw materials and components for larger companies
- they provide goods and services to the local economy, e.g. small local shops, sometimes in areas where larger businesses will not supply
- they provide new enterprise and dynamism in the economy – all large companies were originally small companies.

> **CASE STUDY** | **Small enterprises and micro-enterprises in India**
>
> Official definitions of small enterprises and micro-enterprises in India are based on the amount of investment and machinery in manufacturing businesses, and on investment in equipment in service businesses.
>
> In 2015 there were 48 million small businesses in India – more than twice as many as in the US. Of these, 40 per cent were in retail and 8.8 per cent in clothing manufacture.
>
> **Questions**
>
> 1. Why do you think there are so many small enterprises in India and why are so many of these retailers?
> 2. What would be the benefits and drawbacks of being a small enterprise in retailing?

Retailling provides a clear opportunity for small business, in India 40% of small businesses are retailers ranging from street vendors to corner shops.

The advantages of small businesses

There are several reasons for the existence of small firms, many of which are important for their country's economy.

- Some are new businesses that have just set up. In the early days it pays to be small, as owners learn how to: run and manage a business, make decisions, access capital; and know what products to supply.
- Small businesses can supply a local market e.g. a local corner shop, restaurant or hairdresser. A small business finds out what local customers want and the level of service they require.
- Small businesses provide essential components and supplies for larger businesses. This enables the larger businesses to focus on what they do best. For example, small businesses might provide advertising, marketing and packaging support for larger businesses, or make sub-assemblies for a larger company.

> **STUDY TIP**
>
> *You should be able to describe the main reasons for the different sizes of firms, such as the size of the market, the amount of capital raised or the type of business organisation of the firm.*

- There may only be limited demand for a small firm's product. An example might be a supplier of specialist medical supplies for patients with rare diseases.
- Small enterprises provide an opportunity for people who want to work for themselves. They are more likely to be satisfied and work harder when working for themselves. A small enterprise might also involve family members.
- Small firms are also particularly good when personal service and attention to detail is required, e.g. in hairdressing or wedding planning.

The small firms sector may benefit from government policies such as low tax rates for start-up profits and grants for small businesses to develop new ideas and technologies.

The disadvantages of small businesses

- Small enterprises are not able to meet very large demand for products. A small firm has a limited production capacity and will be unlikely to compete with larger firms around the world.
- Small enterprises are not able to benefit from the cost advantages (known as **economies of scale**) that large-scale producers benefit from (see section 3.5.5). While a small, local company might be able to supply local customers with lemonade, it won't be able to compete nationally or internationally with a huge manufacturer.
- Small firms have less access to the quantity and quality of capital that is available to larger firms. Small firms may find it difficult to raise finance because they are less well known than larger firms. Small firms may not have the funds to buy or hire advanced technological equipment, and they may not have the expertise to use it.
- Small firms do not have access to the research and development facilities that large firms have. Research and development is crucial to modern industries such as pharmaceuticals and IT applications. This research and development enables many breakthroughs in technology and product innovation.
- Small firms are less well known than larger firms because they have smaller advertising and marketing budgets.

KEY POINTS

1. Small firms are an important part of the economy, and there are a number of reasons why small firms continue to exist.
2. Most firms start out as small enterprises benefiting from flexibility, good relationships with local customers, government grants, being able to supply larger firms and being able to satisfy customers where demand is limited.
3. Small firms face the challenges of lack of capital, inability to supply on a large scale and failure to acquire the benefits of large-scale production (economies of scale). Consumers may also be less aware of small firms.

ACTIVITY

Using the example of two firms operating locally in the same industrial and business sector, e.g. a small clothing retailer and a clothing retailer that is part of a large retail chain, identify the advantages that each firm will have.

DID YOU KNOW?

Dr Arokiaswamy Velumani founded Thyrocare – the world's largest thyroid testing company in the world. He started work as a shift chemist in a small pharmacy. When it closed down, he set up his own testing laboratory for thyroid issues and based on his initial knowledge in this area he has been able to create one of the biggest companies in India.

SUMMARY QUESTIONS

1. Explain whether the following types of industrial production are more suitable for large-scale or small-scale businesses:
   a television broadcasting
   b baking bread
   c coffee shops
   d computer manufacture
   e wind energy turbines
   f selling fruit
   g postal services

   Give reasons for your answers.

2. Why are small firms so important for the economy?

3. Give examples of situations and markets where small firms are likely to be more effective than large companies.

3.5.3 Growth of firms

Business growth

Businesses may be able to gain advantages over competitors by growing: they may be able to cut costs and win a greater share of the market. By growing they may also be able to develop new products or sell to new markets. Growth may be internal (inside the business) or external (joining together with existing businesses).

> **TOPIC GUIDANCE**
>
> Students should be able to:
> - understand the different methods by which a business can grow
> - discuss the advantages and disadvantages of methods of growth.

CASE STUDY | Notey

Notey is a good example of a growing company. It was started up by husband-and-wife team Catherine Tan and Kevin Lipsoe in Hong Kong in 2015. The company provides an online service. The members of the company continually read and review original content and blogs on the internet to select the most helpful information that can then be accessed by signing up for Notey information and services. Notey helps users to research topics. The founders reviewed 20 million blogs to narrow down to the most useful sources of information. They currently focus on the best 500 000 blogs on selected topics, e.g. tourism in remote destinations, weddings, football, 3D printers. Users can quickly access high-quality information on specific topics. The business was originally built using the personal capital of the founders but more recently $11.6 million has been ploughed into the business by **angel investors**. These are people that put funds into businesses that are seen as being useful for only a very small return on their investment. Like other internet-based businesses Notey may grow in the future by taking over similar businesses (external growth) or simply by expanding the scale of its operations.

Questions

1. Why might a business like Notey benefit from growth?
2. Why is external capital required for growth as well as owners' funds?
3. What are the potential drawbacks of taking over a similar business?

Notey is a start-up business with good growth prospects

> **STUDY TIP**
>
> When a business grows as a result of internal change, it is called 'organic' change. You should be able to discuss possible reasons for such growth.

Internal growth

'Organic' growth takes place within a business. Money to finance the expansion can come from ploughing back profits or asking the owners to put in more capital. Many small businesses grow organically in their early years. This is because the owners will not want to risk borrowing money from outside the business. However, growing organically may be a slow process. Internal growth can then take place by investing in new products or selling more of existing products.

Other forms of internal growth include the following.

- Franchising: allowing others (for a share of profits) to use a business idea or format created by the franchisor.
- Opening new stores or other outlets: most well-known restaurant chains and **retail** outlets started out from a single premise, for the idea is then 'rolled out' (introduced) to multiple outlets under single ownership.
- E-commerce: creating an online trading platform such as a website enables small businesses to expand organically to a potential worldwide market.
- Outsourcing: this involves contracting out some of your work to an outside supplier who will then make goods or provide a service on your behalf. Outsourcing makes it possible for a business to grow quickly at low cost, partly because managing tasks is done by people external to the business.

External growth

External growth involves the takeover of another business, or merger with another business.

An important way of raising finance in a large company is to sell shares. One share represents one unit of ownership in the business. (A **shareholder** is someone who is a part-owner of the business; the shareholder will typically have many shares.)

A merger occurs when two businesses combine to form a single company. The existing shareholders of both businesses retain a shared interest in the new business.

To take over another company one business will buy up a majority shareholding or all the shares in the business it wants to take over. It may offer shareholders in the company being acquired shares in the new business.

An acquisition occurs when one business gains control of part of another business. A business may be prepared to sell off one of its divisions that it no longer wishes to keep.

Businesses carry out external growth in order to:

- buy new and exciting brands where sales are likely to be high
- acquire new inventions and new technologies
- break into new markets, perhaps in other countries.

The key benefit of internal growth is that it enables owners to keep control of their own business. However, internal growth can be slow and can put a lot of pressure on the existing owners.

The key benefit of external growth is that it enables more rapid expansion and enables a business to gain skills and knowledge that it may not possess internally. However, it is risky in that the existing business may be joining with others that it has little knowledge of.

DID YOU KNOW?

If a business wishes to take over another business, it will set out to purchase more than 50 per cent of the shares. As soon as the investing business has one share over 50 per cent of the shares, it is in control of the company it has taken over. It can make all the decisions as it cannot be outvoted by other shareholders. The business that has acquired over 50 per cent of the shares in another is known as the holding company. The business that has had its shares bought is known as the subsidiary.

KEY POINTS

1. Business can grow internally through ploughing funds into expansion, through franchising, e-commerce and outsourcing.
2. External growth takes place through takeover, merger and acquisition.
3. External growth is a quicker form of expansion but involves more risk.

SUMMARY QUESTIONS

1. What methods of growth would you suggest to the owner of a small successful family hotel that has accumulated profits for several years?
2. A business selling confectionery from retail outlets in India is considering internal growth as a means of expansion. Why should external growth also be considered? The company also hopes to set up new retail outlets in Europe and the US.

3.5.4 Mergers and integration

TOPIC GUIDANCE

Students should be able to:
- describe and evaluate horizontal, vertical and conglomerate integration.

Vertical integration in tea manufacture involves businesses joining together at different stages of production, e.g. a tea processor taking over tea estates that grow tea

DID YOU KNOW?

Information in the media about integration is often described as 'M & A' activity. 'M & A' stands for mergers and acquisitions.

DID YOU KNOW?

In order to expand, many firms will try to merge with or take over others. If a business wishes to take over another business it will set out to purchase more than 50 per cent of the shares. As soon as it has a 50 per cent share plus one share, it is in control. It can then make all the decisions as it cannot be outvoted by other shareholders.

Integration

To integrate means to join together. In business, **integration** may be in the form of a **takeover** or a **merger**.

A merger occurs when two businesses combine to form a single company. It is similar to a takeover except that the existing shareholders of both businesses retain a share in the new business.

A takeover occurs when one business gains control of, or acquires, part of another business. A business may be prepared to sell off one of its divisions which it no longer wishes to keep.

Mergers and takeovers take place for the following reasons.

- There is too much supply in the market, relative to demand. A firm may take over part of a rival in order to control supply to the market.
- A business wants to get access to new markets, perhaps in other countries.
- A firm wants to acquire new technologies from other businesses.
- A firm wants to acquire dynamic products.

CASE STUDY — Tata Tea takes over Tetley

Tata Tea is part of India's giant conglomerate, Tata, which has a range of divisions, each focusing on a specific area, such as steel, motor vehicles or tea. Each of these divisions operates as a separate company with its own board of directors. Tata Tea has taken over the British tea company, Tetley. There were many advantages to be gained from doing this, one of which was the internationally respected brand names belonging to Tetley, the company's expertise in producing flavoured and herbal teas, and its access to international markets in Europe and North America. Tata has a strong base in growing tea and owns a range of tea estates. It has access to a huge market in India, with over 1 billion potential customers. Tata has now been able to build a strong brand image of providing quality tea across the world, with increased sales and profits in most countries.

Questions

1. Why do you think that Tata wanted to take over Tetley?
2. Why do you think the takeover has been successful?
3. What type of integration was involved in the takeover?
4. What are the benefits of this type of integration?

Types of integration

The table sets out different ways in which businesses can merge, or integrate.

Horizontal integration	Firms join together at the same stage of production. They can learn from best practice in each company and concentrate on processing activities in the most efficient plants. The increased size of the business provides economies of scale.
Vertical integration	It may be *forward* – that is, taking over a firm at a later stage of production, e.g. a business with tea estates taking over a company that processes tea – or *backward* – that is, taking over a firm at an earlier stage of production, e.g. a firm that advertises and markets tea taking over one that processes it. The advantage of this sort of integration is that the firm gains control over its supply chain.
Lateral integration	Occurs when there is a merger of firms that use the same distribution channels. For example, a company selling tea may join with a firm selling coffee, so that the goods can be distributed together to supermarket chains.
Conglomerate integration	One example is Tata Industries, which is able to spread interests and risks over many industries. Profits from one established business can be used to develop a new business area. So, for example, Tata Steel and Tata Tea profits could be channelled into the growing Tata IT company. A large conglomerate also builds up a high profile, enabling it to raise finance more easily.
International integration	Global companies like Tata buy up other companies worldwide. In China, for example, Tata Tea has invested in Chinese tea companies producing green tea. A **joint venture** is a good way of entering a new international market. In this case a new company is set up, owned by Tata and a Chinese company.

DID YOU KNOW?
A conglomerate business is made up of a range of companies or divisions producing products that are not necessarily related. The conglomerate looks for opportunities for growth and profits in a range of unrelated fields.

STUDY TIP
You should be able to discuss both the advantages and disadvantages of a firm merging with, or being taken over by another.

ACTIVITY
Study the newspapers to find examples of takeovers and mergers. What type of integration is involved? What are the advantages of the integration? Compare your findings with those of others in your group.

KEY POINTS
1. Businesses can grow through takeovers, acquisitions and mergers.
2. Integration involves the joining together of businesses.
3. Integration gives access to new markets, technologies and large-scale production.

SUMMARY QUESTIONS
1. Why might two steel manufacturers at the same stage of production join together?
2. What is lateral integration? What would be the benefits?
3. What is the advantage of conglomerate integration?

3.5.5 Economies and diseconomies of scale

TOPIC GUIDANCE

Students should be able to:
- describe and explain economies and diseconomies of scale.

Shenzhen, China: the concentration of many leading-edge electronics factories provides external economies of scale to all firms in the industry, including a pool of highly skilled workers

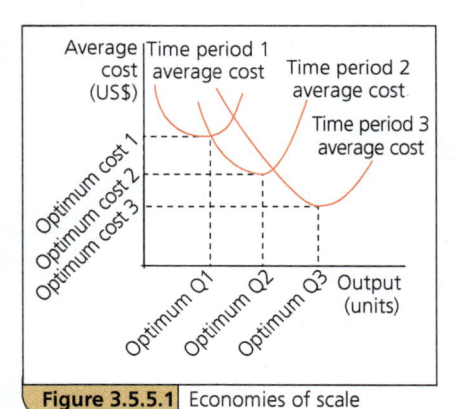

Figure 3.5.5.1 Economies of scale

Economies of scale

Economies of scale are the advantages of producing on a scale large enough for a business to be able to cut the cost of individual units of production. Economies of scale enable a business to reduce its average cost curve. Figure 3.5.5.1 illustrates the average cost curve for a growing business in three successive time periods. In period 2 it can produce a larger output at a lower average cost than in period 1. In period 3 it can produce a large output at a lower average cost than in period 2.

Businesses can benefit from two main types of economies of scale:

- **internal economies**: the advantages that a firm gains from its own growth
- **external economies**: the advantages gained from the growth and improvement of a firm's industry and locality.

Internal economies of scale

Technical advantages

Large firms can benefit from better techniques of production. Automated plant and equipment, e.g. in a confectionery manufacturing company, may be so expensive to install that only large companies can afford it. Automated production lines enable very high production at low unit cost and can be run 24 hours a day, 7 days a week.

Financial advantages

Large firms usually find it easier and cheaper to borrow money because they have more assets than small firms. Assets such as machinery and factories can be offered to the financial lenders of money in case the firm cannot repay the loan. A huge multinational like Tata Tea was able to raise extra capital for the takeover of Tetley by issuing new shares to existing shareholders. Tata can borrow money at a low rate of interest because the bank is confident that the loan will be repaid.

Managerial advantages

Large companies are able to attract the best managers worldwide because of the high salaries these companies can pay.

Commercial advantages

Large firms are able to buy and sell in bulk. They obtain discount for bulk purchases. The cost of creating a global advertising campaign can be spread over billions of people who will watch the television advert across the globe.

Risk-spreading advantages

Large firms can spread their risks in various ways, such as:

- product diversification – producing and selling lots of different products
- market diversification – producing and selling in many different countries and regions
- supplier diversification – using several different suppliers in case one is unable to supply on time
- production diversification – having several different production plants.

Internal diseconomies of scale

If an organisation is too large, managers may not be able to manage it effectively. There may be technical problems with complicated equipment. If a firm is producing more than it can sell, the proportion of advertising costs may increase. If the business produces too many products for too many markets and a number of them fail, the losses may have a damaging effect on the development of the company's other products. It is possible that strikes and various kinds of disruption could occur if the workers believe that they are not being treated fairly.

External economies of scale

External economies arise from the growth of the industry rather than a particular firm in that industry. All firms benefit from external economies of scale, such as:

- improved communications and transport links, such as a new railway line that cuts distribution costs
- improved educational facilities, such as a new college or university training people in the skills needed by local businesses
- the development of suppliers, supplying components to all the firms in an industry
- improved housing and social amenities that encourage workers to move to an area
- the development of banking and insurance services in an area.

External diseconomies of scale

There can be problems arising from the growth of an industry. Labour and other costs can increase as more competitors hire more labour and buy more land and machinery. There may also be congestion and pollution from the business activities.

KEY POINTS

1. Internal economies of scale enable larger businesses to produce with lower unit costs.
2. Economies arise from better technology, management and marketing, as well as diversification.
3. External economies result from the growth of an industry or improved services in a region reducing costs for a range of businesses.

DID YOU KNOW?

Over a quarter of a million people now live in the Chinese city of Shenzhen. The city has grown rapidly to become a centre for high-technology industries – particularly multinational electronic companies such as China Mobile, Apple and Nokia. There is a large, young and highly skilled labour force, and a university specialising in science, engineering and technology.

STUDY TIP

You should be able to demonstrate that you understand there are both advantages and disadvantages of a firm growing in size.

SUMMARY QUESTIONS

1. Explain the difference between an internal and an external economy of scale.
2. What benefits can a firm gain from being larger than its rivals?
3. How can external economies help more than one firm?

3.6 Firms and production

3.6.1 Demand for factors of production

TOPIC GUIDANCE

Students should be able to:
- describe what determines the demand for factors of production.

Uranium miners in Niger. The demand for miners and their equipment is derived from the demand for the uranium they mine

DID YOU KNOW?

The rewards to the factors of production are:

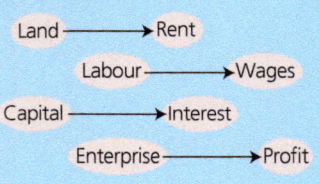

- Land → Rent
- Labour → Wages
- Capital → Interest
- Enterprise → Profit

STUDY TIP

It is important that you understand what is meant by 'derived' (see section 3.3.3). Factors of production are not demanded for their own sake, but for what they can contribute to the production process.

Factors of production

Factors of production are the elements needed by a business to produce goods and services. Examples are land (and the raw materials it contains), labour, capital and enterprise. The **demand** for factors of production is derived in turn from the demand for the products that these factors are used to produce. For example, the demand for agricultural land, labour and machinery is derived from the demand for lentils, maize, rice and other crops which these factors contribute to producing.

CASE STUDY | Uranium production

Many governments and scientists, e.g. in India, Pakistan, China, the UK, France and the US, believe that nuclear power is an important source of energy. (In France nuclear energy is the principal source of energy.) To produce nuclear energy you have to process uranium. It can be mined in only a few countries, and the price of uranium has therefore increased from US$10 a pound in 2000 to US$48 in 2013. This has led to an increase in the cost of producing nuclear energy and hence the prices charged for nuclear energy. The demand for uranium is *derived from* the demand for nuclear energy.

This derived demand creates further demands. There is a demand for land, to mine the uranium. Then building the mine involves a huge increase in demand for mining equipment (capital), and working the mine involves a demand for thousands of workers.

Questions

1. Why do you think the demand for nuclear energy has increased in the world in recent years?
2. What has happened to the price of nuclear energy?
3. What has been the resulting effect on the demand for land, labour and capital to mine uranium?

Illustrating the demand for factors of production

As the demand for factors of production is a **derived demand**, an increase in demand for the end products will lead to an increase in demand for the factors themselves.

Figure 3.6.1 shows that the rise in demand for uranium to produce nuclear energy leads to a rise in the price of uranium from US$10 to US$42. Note that as the demand for uranium increases, more of it is supplied to the market.

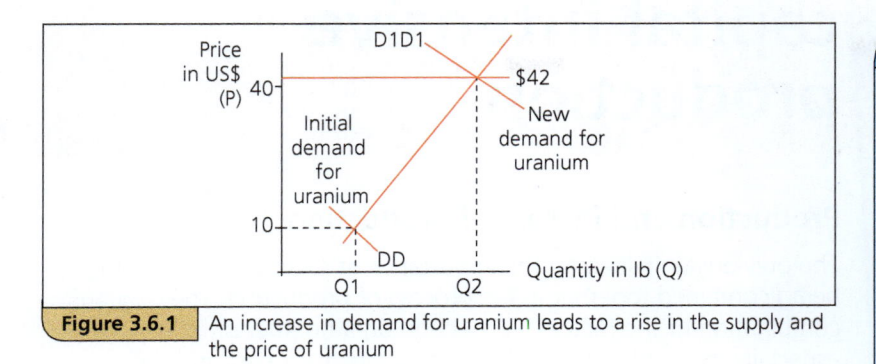

Figure 3.6.1 An increase in demand for uranium leads to a rise in the supply and the price of uranium

Figure 3.6.2 shows that as the price of uranium increases this also leads to an increase in demand for miners to mine uranium in countries like Niger. Note the increase in the miners' wages in Niger. In response, more people are willing to make themselves available and to train to be miners of uranium.

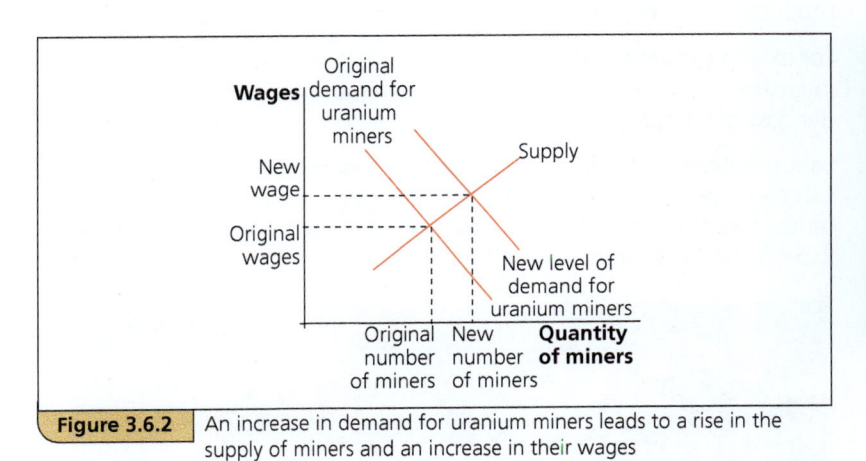

Figure 3.6.2 An increase in demand for uranium miners leads to a rise in the supply of miners and an increase in their wages

Combining factors of production

Factors of production are demanded as a combination because they are required to work together. In buying factors of production, buyers will consider the relative prices of factors in order to choose the best combinations.

Important production decisions involve combining factors of production. The chosen combination depends on the relative productivity of these factors compared with their cost.

DID YOU KNOW?

Uranium is mined in Canada, the US, Brazil, Namibia, South Africa, Niger, Ukraine, Russia, Kazakhstan and Australia. The huge publicly-owned French nuclear power company Areva has invested more than US$1 billion in a giant mine in Niger in West Africa. This will provide the French company with large quantities of uranium to sell to the nuclear industry in South Korea, France and elsewhere.

DID YOU KNOW?

When factors of production become more productive, the demand for them is likely to increase. For example, when machinery becomes more technologically efficient, the demand for it is likely to increase.

KEY POINTS

1. The demand for factors of production is derived from the demand for the products they make.
2. Rewards to factors are related to the demand for the products they make.

SUMMARY QUESTIONS

1. What is the demand for machinery derived from?
2. What do the relative rewards to different factors of production depend on?

3.6.2 Labour-intensive and capital-intensive production

TOPIC GUIDANCE

Students should be able to:
- distinguish between labour-intensive and capital-intensive production.

STUDY TIP

Make sure that you are able to clearly distinguish between labour-intensive production and capital-intensive production.

DID YOU KNOW?

It is not only in developed economies that great use is made of capital equipment, such as robots. In India, an economy often associated with labour-intensive production, given its large population (the second largest in the world), increasing use is being made of machinery. For example, the car company, Tata Motors, is reducing the size of its workforce and increasing the number of robots that it uses in the production process.

Production and factors of production

The previous unit stressed the importance of factors of production being combined together in the process of production. The combination of the factors will depend on a number of influences, especially the availability of different factors, their cost and their relative efficiency or productivity. The objective will be to maximise output and to minimise cost and how this is actually done may vary from one industry to another.

Labour-intensive production

A labour-intensive industry employs a high proportion of labour in the production process compared with the amount of capital employed.

For example, much of the textile industry in Bangladesh is labour-intensive. This is largely because there is an abundance of labour and so the cost of labour is relatively cheap. The labour may be highly skilled.

Labour-intensive production can be very flexible because production can be increased through the use of overtime and/or employing temporary staff. If production has to be decreased, workers can be laid off for a certain period of time.

Labour-intensive production in the textile industry

Labour-intensive production is particularly associated with countries which have a large population, such as China (1.4 billion), India (1.2 billion), Indonesia (230 million), Brazil (200 million), Pakistan (190 million), Bangladesh (170 million) and Nigeria (160 million). However, this does not mean that all industries in, say, China or India, are labour-intensive. Although these countries have a large population, and therefore an abundance of labour, some industries may well be capital-intensive, such as the car industry.

Capital-intensive production

A capital-intensive industry employs a high proportion of equipment and machinery in the production process compared with the amount of labour employed. There is likely to be a high level of automation, with production on a relatively large scale.

This is usually a sign of the development of an economy, with labour being replaced to some extent by machinery and equipment, leading to a more efficient and productive process of production. Machines are able to work 24 hours a day, 7 days a week, unlike labour, although it is necessary to take into account the initial cost of obtaining the equipment and the continual cost of maintaining and repairing it. Capital machinery and equipment is generally seen as a long-term investment, but over a period of time the machinery and equipment will wear out and will need replacing. This wearing out of capital is known as depreciation.

The Japanese car industry is an example of a highly capital-intensive production process. Automated factory machines are able to produce a large output at a lower unit cost.

The use of robots in car production

DID YOU KNOW?

In 1963, nearly 30 000 workers worked at the car factory in Cowley, Oxford. Fifty years later, in 2013, only 6,000 workers were employed at the factory by BMW, and yet the 6,000 workers were able to produce more in 2013 than the 30 000 workers in 1963. This is largely due to the very capital-intensive nature of the production process, such as the use of robotic welders.

STUDY TIP

Make sure that you are able to demonstrate an understanding of the reasons why one industry may be labour-intensive and another capital-intensive.

KEY POINTS

1. Labour-intensive industries use a high proportion of labour relative to capital and other factors of production.
2. Labour-intensive production occurs because in a particular country there is an abundance of labour and so it is relatively cheap compared to the relative cost of other factors of production.

SUMMARY QUESTIONS

1. Why are some industries more capital-intensive than others?
2. What is likely to make one industry more labour-intensive than another?

3.6.3 Production and productivity

TOPIC GUIDANCE

Students should be able to:
- define productivity and recognise the difference between productivity and production.

DID YOU KNOW?

When taxi drivers buy a new car they are buying a good. When they use the car as a taxi they are providing a service for the passengers who pay to travel with them.

Producing goods and services

One of the major functions of an economy is to produce goods and services. A good typically means a physical item such as a bag of sugar, a pencil or a laptop computer. Some goods are referred to as 'consumer goods' because they are used by consumers, e.g. food items such as a bag of rice. Other goods are referred to as producer goods, e.g. a machine in a factory used by the producers of goods.

In contrast, services are intangible items that meet consumer and producer needs. 'Intangible' means that you cannot physically touch the service. Examples of services include banking, insurance and transportation services. In each of these examples, customers are paying the producer to provide a service for them – to look after their money, to cover their insurance risks or to transport something for them. Services are bought both by individuals and by businesses.

Production and productivity

Production

Production consists of the processes involved in providing goods and services. Each stage in production adds value to the good or service being produced. This process of producing a good can be illustrated in the production of fresh orange juice (Figure 3.6.3.1).

Stage of production:	How value is added	Stage of production:	How value is added
1 Growing the oranges 	Farmers look after the orange trees for several years before the trees give fruit. Each year the trees must be treated against pests.	**3** Preparing the oranges 	The juice is squeezed from the oranges and ice is added.
2 Transporting the oranges 	Fresh ripe oranges are transported closer to market.	**4** Serving the customer 	The juice is presented to the end consumer in a polite and friendly way.

Figure 3.6.3.1 Adding value to a product: the customer benefits from value being added at each stage of production

Productivity

Productivity is a measure of the output that can be obtained from using productive resources. For example, if 10 employees can produce 100 units of output in an hour, the productivity is 10 units per employee hour. Productivity can be increased by the employees working harder or by working with improved resources. For example, if the 10 employees work with new, more advanced machinery they may be able to produce 200 units in an hour, as shown in the below table.

Productivity at different output levels		
	Working with old machinery	Working with new machinery
Number of employees	10	10
Hourly output	100	200
Productivity per employee (per hour)	10	20

Productivity can be measured either in real terms, that is units of output produced per unit of input, or in money terms, that is the money value of output per unit of input. For example, if we wanted to measure the productivity of a machine, we could record this in the following ways (in our example we are assuming that each physical unit is sold for US$5):

- the physical output method, e.g. 200 units per machine hour
- the revenue output method, e.g. US$1,000 per machine hour.

KEY POINTS

1. A good is a physical item: a service is intangible.
2. Production consists of processes used to produce goods and services.
3. Productivity is a measure of the output per factor of production used over a given period of time, e.g. output per person per week.

SUMMARY QUESTIONS

1. Explain the difference between goods and services. Give examples of each.
2. How would you raise production and productivity in a business?
3. Ten workers can produce 120 units of a product in an hour. If the output of the workers increases to 150 units per hour, what will be the impact on productivity?

DID YOU KNOW?

The term 'productivity' can be related to any of the factors of production. For example, the productivity of land could be increased by adding fertiliser on a field.

DID YOU KNOW?

The productivity of labour refers to the output that can be obtained from a given quantity of labour. The productivity of land is the output that can be obtained from a set quantity of land. The productivity of capital is the quantity of output that can be obtained from a set quantity of capital.

STUDY TIP

The terms 'production' and 'productivity' are often confused. Make sure you understand that production is concerned with output and productivity is concerned with the efficiency with which that output is produced.

3.7 Firms' costs revenue and objectives

3.7.1 Fixed and variable costs

TOPIC GUIDANCE

Students should be able to:
- define fixed and variable cost and perform simple calculations.

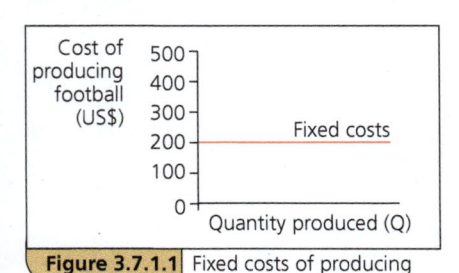

Costs

Producing goods costs money. A business enterprise, for example, needs to buy raw materials, pay wages and spend money on marketing the finished product. Economists divide the cost of production into two main types: fixed cost and variable cost.

- **Fixed costs (FC)** do not alter with the quantity of output.
- **Variable costs (VC)** increase directly as output increases.

Fixed costs

Fixed costs are costs that have to be paid whether the business is producing nothing or thousands of units. They depend on the type of business, but often include items such as rent, rates and interest on money borrowed, which are not related to how much is produced. Fixed costs can be illustrated as a horizontal straight line: Figure 3.7.1.1 shows that the costs of a small firm producing footballs are US$200 a week, whether it produces no balls, 5 balls or 25 balls.

Figure 3.7.1.1 Fixed costs of producing footballs

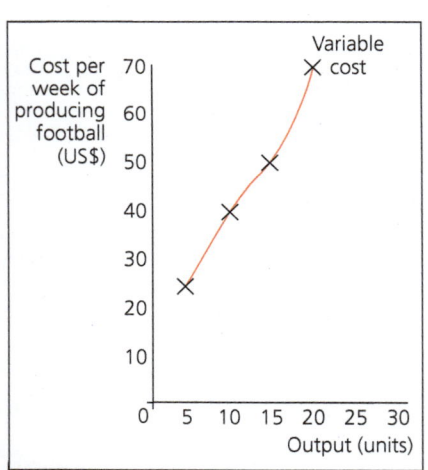

Variable costs

Variable costs, such as the cost of raw materials, are zero when output is zero and rise directly with output. The table shows the variable costs of the football-manufacturing company.

Output per week	Variable cost (US$)
0	0
5	25
10	40
15	50
20	70

Figure 3.7.1.2 shows the variable costs of producing different quantities of footballs as a graph.

Figure 3.7.1.2 The variable cost to a firm producing different quantities of footballs

Average fixed cost

The greater the number of goods produced, the more the fixed costs will be spread over the output. If a bottling plant produces only 100 bottles a week, each bottle produced would involve a very high fixed cost element. In practice, bottling plants produce tens of thousands of bottles a week and the total fixed cost is spread over a large output (resulting in a low average cost per unit).

Figure 3.7.1.3 shows the **average fixed cost (AFC)** as output increases. As the level of output increases, the fixed cost per unit falls.

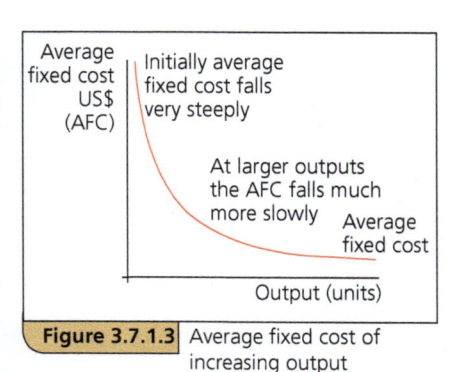

Figure 3.7.1.3 Average fixed cost of increasing output

Average variable cost

Variable costs of production usually include the raw materials and increases in labour to produce more goods, and **average variable costs (AVC)** alter as output increases. For example, a business with a small output will not be able to make good use of variable resources. Two or three workers in a bottling factory would not be enough to handle the machinery efficiently, but a higher number would mean that they could be organised so that each additional worker added to production at an increasing rate. For example, each worker could specialise in one or a small number of tasks.

However, the increase in production cannot keep accelerating (because the equipment and factory floor capacity is limited). Additional labourers would start to get in each other's way and thus work less efficiently, and the average variable cost of producing more would start to rise.

Figure 3.7.1.4 shows the average variable cost as a curve that falls at first and later starts to rise.

CASE STUDY | Costs at different levels of output

A business has fixed costs of US$1,000 a week. Variable costs at different levels of output are shown in the table.

Output	Average variable cost per unit
100	10 cents
200	8 cents
300	6 cents
400	8 cents
500	10 cents

Questions

1. Illustrate the average variable cost curve on a graph.
2. Explain why it has the shape that it does.
3. Calculate the average fixed cost at each of the levels of output shown in the table.
4. Draw and then explain the shape of the average fixed cost curve.

SUMMARY QUESTIONS

1. Define:
   a fixed cost
   b variable cost.
2. Why do average fixed costs fall as output increases, even though the overall fixed cost stays the same?
3. Explain why the average variable cost initially falls and then rises with higher output.

DID YOU KNOW?

Giant manufacturing companies like Coca-Cola have billions of dollars of fixed costs, including advertising and the construction costs of plants and buildings. Spread over many billion units of production, however, the fixed cost element of each can of Coca-Cola produced is only a few cents.

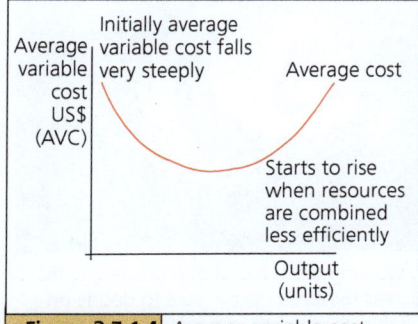

Figure 3.7.1.4 Average variable cost

KEY POINTS

1. Fixed costs are the same whatever quantity is produced.
2. Variable costs increase as output increases.
3. Average fixed costs fall as they are spread over larger quantities of output.
4. Average variable costs initially fall with more efficient use of factors of production. Once resources are combined less well, they start to rise again.

3.7.2 Total and average costs

TOPIC GUIDANCE

Students should be able to:
- define total and average cost and perform simple calculations.

By working out the cost of producing items such as footballs, Nike is able to decide on suitable prices to charge to cover costs and make a profit

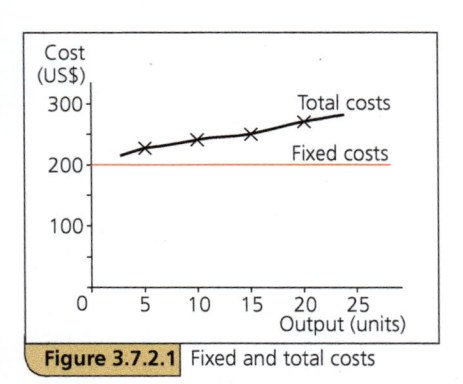

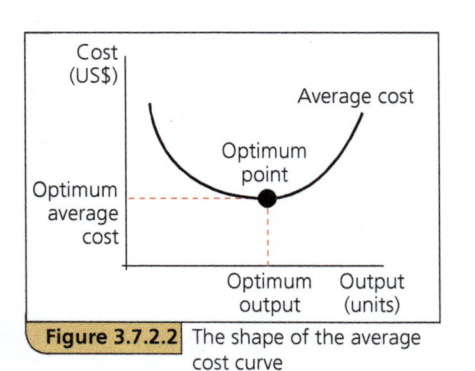

Total cost

Total cost (TC) can be calculated by adding the fixed and variable costs at different levels of output. Figure 3.7.2.1 shows in graph form the total, fixed and variable costs given in the table below. The shape of the total cost curve makes sense if you think that the more goods produced, the higher the overall cost of producing them.

Output per week	Fixed cost (US$)	Variable cost (US$)	Total cost (US$)
0	200	0	200
5	200	25	225
10	200	40	240
15	200	50	250
20	200	70	270

Average cost

Average cost is the cost of producing a unit of product at a particular output.

To calculate average cost, use the following formula:

$$\text{Average cost} = \frac{\text{Total cost}}{\text{Output}}$$

For example, in the table above, the average cost of producing 10 products would be US$24 (240 ÷ 10). The average cost of producing 20 products would be US$13.50 (270 ÷ 20).

The shape of the average cost curve

It is important to know and understand the shape of a typical average cost curve. Figure 3.7.2.2 shows its characteristic U-shape.

It has this shape for the following reasons.

- Average fixed cost is falling as output levels increase. This effect pulls the curve down at a slower and slower rate. So if fixed costs are US$1,000, producing two units rather than one will lower the curve from US$1,000 to produce 1 unit, to US$500 to produce 2 units. However, at much higher levels of output, e.g. producing 1000 units rather than 999, you will only be reducing the average fixed cost from US$1.11 to US$1.00 – that is, by just a few cents.
- Average variable cost falls initially as the firm is able to combine its factors of production more efficiently. However, there comes a point at which inefficiencies creep into the production plant (see section 3.7.1).

Figure 3.7.2.1 Fixed and total costs

Figure 3.7.2.2 The shape of the average cost curve

The lowest point on the average cost curve shows the point at which the business is combining its resources most efficiently. We call this lowest point the **optimum output** level.

CASE STUDY | Calculating average cost

A firm has calculated that its total costs (fixed + variable costs) at different levels of daily output are as follows:

Output per day	Total cost (US$)	Average cost (US$)
0	10.00	
1	15.00	
2	18.00	
3	20.00	
4	21.00	
5	23.00	
6	26.00	
7	30.00	
8	35.00	
9	41.00	

Questions

1 Copy the table. Using the data given, calculate the average cost of production for a firm at different output levels, and complete the final column for each level.
2 At what point does average cost start to rise?
3 Explain why average cost starts to rise at this point.

ACTIVITY

Working in groups of three or four, prepare a presentation for the rest of the class. Choose one of the following topics: an explanation of fixed costs and how they are illustrated; variable costs (explained and how they are illustrated); total costs; average costs; average fixed and average variable costs.

DID YOU KNOW?

Businesses need to be able to calculate the cost of producing individual units. If a company such as Nike can establish the cost of producing a soccer ball or a pair of trainers, it will be able to price its products to ensure that it makes a profit.

KEY POINTS

1 Total cost measures all the costs at given levels of output.
2 Average cost is calculated by dividing the total cost by the units produced.
3 Average cost shows the cost of producing a typical unit at a particular level of output.

SUMMARY QUESTIONS

1 How would you calculate the average cost of producing a given level of output?
2 Why does the average cost curve have a U-shape?
3 Compare the shape of the total cost curve with that of the average cost curve.

3.7.3 Output and costs

TOPIC GUIDANCE

Students should be able to:

- analyse situations to show changes in total and average cost as output changes.

Variable costs of manufacturing paint include the raw materials that are mixed into the paint, and the tins. Fixed costs include costs such as interest on money borrowed by the manufacturer and the lighting and heating of the factory

ACTIVITY

Working in groups of three or four, identify five products that your families buy regularly. Set out a list of the likely fixed costs and variable costs of producing these products. Explain how the costs of producing one of these items would vary with output.

Costs and output

We are now in a position to examine the relationship between the various types of costs and output levels.

Total and average cost

CASE STUDY — Manufacturing paint

A paint manufacturer has calculated that fixed costs for the business are US$1,000 per week. These are made up of the costs of advertising, transporting paint to the store, lighting and heating, as well as the rent and rates of running the business. The variable costs of manufacturing the paint consist of the materials that go into the paint, and the labour required to manufacture it – the more that is produced, the greater the number of people employed (so their wages vary with the quantity produced).

The fixed and variable costs are set out in the following table.

Number of tins produced	Total fixed cost (US$)	Total variable cost (US$)	Total cost (US$)	Average cost (US$)
0	1,000	0		
100	1,000	1,000		
200	1,000	1,800		
300	1,000	2,300		
400	1,000	3,200		

Questions

1. Copy the table and complete the columns for total cost and average cost.
2. What is the optimum output? Explain your answer.
3. Explain the changes in the average cost curve as output increases.

Fixed, variable and total cost

CASE STUDY — Canning tomatoes

The total costs for a canning plant that specialises in canning tomatoes are:

- the fixed costs – interest paid on a loan, rent and rates, and the cost of energy to run the plant

- the variable costs – the tomatoes, the cans and the labels.

Output (units)	Total fixed cost (US$)	Total variable cost (US$)	Total cost (US$)
0			
100		1,200	
200			3,800
300		2,400	
400	2,000		4,700
500			5,400

Questions

1. Some of the figures are missing from the table. Copy the table and fill in the missing numbers.
2. Now calculate the average fixed cost, the average variable cost and the average total cost at each of the levels of output shown in the table.

The following table summarises some key terms and their meanings.

Total fixed cost	The sum of all of the different types of fixed costs at different outputs
Total variable cost	The sum of all of the variable costs at different outputs
Total cost	The sum of total fixed cost and total variable cost at different outputs
Average fixed cost	The total fixed cost divided by the level of output
Average variable cost	The total variable cost divided by the level of output
Average total cost	The total cost divided by the level of output

DID YOU KNOW?
A tax paid per unit sold or produced is a variable cost, e.g. an output tax charged on the number of a particular good produced, such as US$1 per pair of trainers. A lump sum tax, such as a vehicle tax or rates on property and land, is a fixed cost.

DID YOU KNOW?
It is not always easy to decide which costs are fixed and which are variable. For example, wages for full-time workers are a fixed cost for a business, whereas when a firm pays piece rates these would count as variable costs.

KEY POINTS

1. Business costs consist of fixed and variable costs.
2. Total cost is calculated by adding together all the costs at each level of output.
3. Total cost rises with output.
4. Average cost is the total cost divided by the level of output or sales.

SUMMARY QUESTIONS

1. How would you calculate average fixed costs of production?
2. What is the relationship between total costs and the level of production?
3. How does average cost change as a result of changes in the level of output of a manufactured good?

3.7.4 Revenue

> **TOPIC GUIDANCE**
>
> Students should be able to:
> - define total and average revenue and perform simple calculations.

Revenue

Revenue is the sum of money that a business receives from making sales. Obviously sales revenue increases with the quantity of goods sold. Mars earns revenues from its sales of chocolate bars to supermarkets and other shops. Tata Tea earns revenue from its sales of different types of tea. Shell earns revenue from selling oil and petrol.

To calculate the total revenue from selling tea, multiply the number of packets sold by the price per packet. The average revenue is the price charged for each packet

Total revenue

To calculate **total revenue** (in order to calculate the value of sales made by a business), multiply the quantity of goods sold by the price they are sold for:

Total revenue = Quantity of goods sold × Price

$$TR = Q \times P$$

Average revenue

The **average revenue (AR)** is the price received for selling a given quantity of goods. It is helpful for a business to know its average revenue because this can be compared with the average cost of making and/or selling that item.

The best way of illustrating this is to show the market price – that is, where demand and supply meet. Take the example of footballs produced by a major sports good producer. The market price (where demand cuts supply) is US$10. At this price the business is prepared to supply 1,000 footballs a week to sports shops. Sports shops are happy to buy 1,000 footballs a week.

So what is the total revenue?

1,000 (Q) × US$10 (P) = US$10 000

> **STUDY TIP**
>
> Make sure that you understand the differences between the various types of cost and revenue.

> **DID YOU KNOW?**
>
> At low levels of output total revenue will always be below total cost. This is because total revenue starts at zero, whereas total cost nearly always has a fixed cost element. Businesses therefore make a loss if they only produce a small output. As output increases and the product is sold, total revenue should start to catch up with, and then overtake, total cost.

On Figure 3.7.4.1 this is illustrated by the shaded area OPAQ.

So what is the average revenue?

The average revenue is simply the price: US$10.

This is because every ball will be sold to shops for US$10 each.

Total and average revenue

The total revenue is the sum of all of the revenues received by a supplier. The table below shows the weekly average and total revenue of a company that supplies footballs to shops in a particular country for a price of US$10 each.

Sales	Average revenue (= price) (US$)	Total revenue (total value of all sales) (US$)
100	10	1,000
200	10	2,000
300	10	3,000
400	10	4,000
500	10	5,000
600	10	6,000
700	10	7,000
800	10	8,000
900	10	9,000

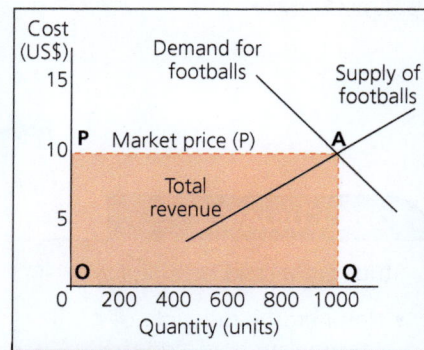

Figure 3.7.4.1 The market price (average revenue) for a supplier of footballs

Figure 3.7.4.2 shows this data in graph form. Notice the straight line starting at zero and then rising by US$10 for each sale made.

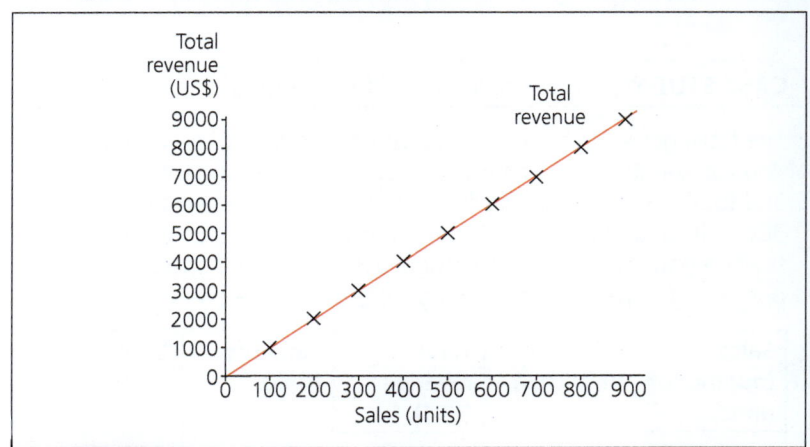

Figure 3.7.4.2 Total revenue rises in proportion to the number of sales made

ACTIVITY

Working as a group, propose an idea for a business that sells a product or service. Decide on a price that you would charge for your chosen product or service. Calculate how many units of the product or service you could sell each week. Then calculate what your weekly total revenue would be.

KEY POINTS

1. Revenues are receipts from sales.
2. Total revenue is calculated from adding the value of all sales made.
3. Average revenue is the total revenue divided by the quantity sold.

SUMMARY QUESTIONS

1. How would you calculate the average revenue from the sales of a product?
2. What is the relationship between average revenue and price?
3. How does total revenue alter with the volume of sales made?

113

3.7.5 Objectives of firms

TOPIC GUIDANCE

Students should be able to:

- describe the principle of profit maximisation as a goal
- recognise that business organisations may have different goals.

Shareholders in businesses such as Tata Tea expect to receive a large dividend – their share of the profit of the company

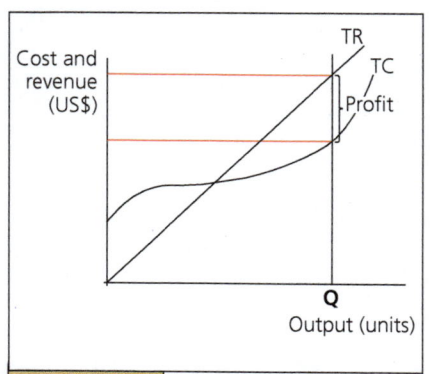

Figure 3.7.5.1 The profit maximising point: the greatest difference between total revenue (TR) and total cost (TC)

Making a profit

The main aim of a business is to make a **profit**. There may be wider goals, such as building a reputation for quality or helping to build a stronger community, but most businesses will place an emphasis on profit. Many businesses set targets, one of which will be to meet, or exceed, given levels of profit. The directors who control the business will be responsible for seeing that these targets are met – they may have large salaries to reflect the responsibility that they carry for achieving this.

One group that is very interested in the profits is the shareholders. They risk their money when they buy shares but, as their name suggests, they receive their share of the profits, called dividends. Good profits, and so good dividends, are important in order to convince the shareholders that the company is strong and that they should continue to invest their money in it.

To *maximise* is to make something as large as possible, and a business will want to maximise its profits. Analysis of costs and revenues helps us to find out how much businesses should produce, and what prices they should charge, in order to maximise their profits. The **profit maximising point** of a business is the point at which there is the greatest difference between total revenue (TR) and total cost (TC). Figure 3.7.5.1 shows this as a graph.

CASE STUDY: An example of profit maximising

The table gives the figures for a business producing men's suits. You can see that the greatest difference between the total revenue and total cost occurs in the fourth row, when there are sales of 300 units at a price of US$15. In other words, the best profit that the company can make is to produce 300 units and charge US$15 per item. The **profit maximising output** is therefore 300 sales.

Sales (number of units)	Price per unit (US$)	Total revenue (US$)	Total cost (US$)	Total profit (US$)
0	30	0	1,000	−1,000
100	25	2,500	2,000	500
200	20	4,000	2,800	1,200
300	15	4,500	3,200	1,300
400	10	4,000	3,700	300
500	5	2,500	4,300	−1,800

At very low outputs the business would make a loss because it has fixed costs of US$1,000 to cover. A lower price would mean a greater number of sales, but at prices below US$20 the business would find total revenue falling, because sales are rising less proportionately than the fall in price (demand is relatively more inelastic). Another problem for the business is that as it produces more to sell initially, its costs rise only slowly, but above 200 units of output costs rise at an increasing rate, as resources are combined less efficiently.

Questions

1 Why would the firm prefer to sell 300 units than 200 units?
2 Why would the firm prefer to sell 300 units than 400 units?
3 How does:
   a total cost change with higher levels of output
   b total revenue change with higher levels of output
   c total profit change with higher levels of output?
4 What is the profit maximising point?

Other goals of business organisations

Businesses have goals other than just profit maximisation. **Survival** is another important goal. When a business first sets up, it may just want to survive while it builds up a customer base. This might mean making initial losses, running down the capital of owners. Later, in hard times such as recession, the business may simply seek to survive, hoping for better prospects ahead.

Another goal for some organisations is **social welfare**. Owners may want to make a positive contribution to society, e.g. by making socially useful products such as health care and educational books. Some not-for-profit organisations such as charities have purely social objectives.

Growth is another powerful objective. Firms will often forego distributing profits today in order to build the company for tomorrow, e.g. through capital investment.

> **STUDY TIP**
>
> Profit maximisation is a very important concept in relation to a private firm. You should be able to discuss why this is the case.

> **STUDY TIP**
>
> Although the principle of profit maximisation is a very important goal of a business, you need to recognise that business organisations may have a variety of different goals.

> **ACTIVITY**
>
> Study the national newspapers in your country to find stories about businesses making higher than average profits. In what industries do these firms operate? How do you think they are able to make such large profits?

KEY POINTS

1 Profit maximisation is achieved when the difference between total cost and total revenue is greatest.
2 Studying total costs and total revenues helps a business to identify the output at which it will maximise profit.
3 Businesses may have goals other than profit maximisation.

SUMMARY QUESTIONS

1 How can shareholders share in business profits?
2 What is profit maximisation?
3 How can a business maximise its profits?

3.8 Market structure
3.8.1 Competitive markets

TOPIC GUIDANCE

Students should be able to:
- describe the characteristics of perfect competition
- describe pricing and output policies in perfect competition.

Price competition

Businesses compete with each other to make sales. The greater the competition, the closer the prices charged by rivals. Take the example of three petrol stations that are located close together. They display their prices on signs that are clearly visible so that motorists can choose which petrol station to buy from. The motorists know that the petrol in the pumps is almost identical. If one petrol station charges more than its rivals it will lose sales. In this situation the prices charged are likely to be identical. Even a 1 cent difference in fuel prices per litre will lead to motorists choosing the cheaper petrol.

Competition can also be intense when there are lots of producers of identical agricultural products, e.g. the same grade of grain.

Perfect competition

As a way of analysing how businesses compete with each other, economists have developed a theory of **perfect competition**. Perfect competition does not exist in a pure form because there are always differences between sellers, e.g. the cashier in one petrol station may be friendlier and more helpful than the cashier in a rival station.

The idea of perfect competition that economists have modelled is based on the following assumptions.

- There would be a large number of firms competing with each other.
- Each firm would produce an identical or homogeneous product.
- Each firm would know exactly what the others were producing and the prices they were charging.
- There would be no barriers to new firms entering the market, and no barriers to existing firms leaving the market, so that firms could enter or leave the industry easily.
- Each firm would only produce a very small percentage of the overall production in the industry, because consumers could immediately switch to a cheaper supplier.
- There would be a large number of buyers, each of whom would know the prices charged by different sellers.

Given these conditions, economists believe that the following would apply.

- Businesses would all charge the same price.
- This price would be the minimum they could charge without going out of business.
- The price would be equivalent to the lowest average cost of producing goods.
- At the market price, the average cost of production would be the same as the average revenue received for selling.
- No firm would risk charging more than the market price, because it would make no sales if it did so.

Some grades of grain, such as this in Nebraska, are almost identical. The produce therefore creates a competitive market for grain – particularly if there are many producers

DID YOU KNOW?

Within markets that have near perfect competition, there are lots of buyers and sellers of an almost identical product, such as varieties of rice or corn. However, in these cases, some suppliers will still have advantages over competitors, e.g. close proximity to customers.

Price takers

Under perfect competition a business would be a **price taker**: it would take its price from the market. The alternative would be a **price maker** – that is, a business that chooses at what price to sell its products. You will read about this in section 3.8.2.

Illustrating average cost and average revenue in perfect competition

Figure 3.8.1.1 shows the price a firm would receive under perfect competition and how many products it would supply to the market.

The diagram indicates the following points.

- The business would produce OQ of output. This is the point at which the average revenue line is equal to the average cost curve.
- The average revenue line is a horizontal straight line. It is at the market price, which the firm takes from the market.
- The market price is OP.
- Total revenue is exactly equal to total cost. The area OQAP (total revenue) = the area OQAP (total cost).

> **STUDY TIP**
> The horizontal average revenue line for a firm in perfect competition is also the demand curve.

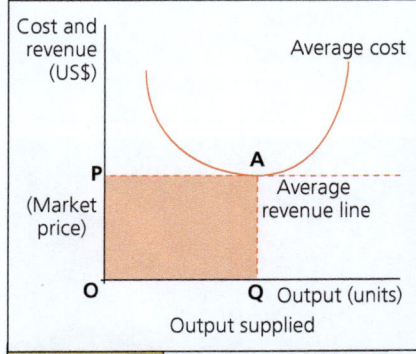

Figure 3.8.1.1 A price-taking firm under perfect competition

> **DID YOU KNOW?**
> The theory of perfect competition is based on economists' idea that something they call normal profit should be included as a fixed cost for a business. As a fixed cost it is part of the average cost curve. The normal profit is the reward that a business person would need to keep the business running (rather than close down).

> **STUDY TIP**
> Economists understand that perfect competition may not exist in practice, but they still regard it as a very important concept. You should be able to demonstrate that you know why this is.

KEY POINTS

1. The idea of perfect competition helps economists to understand what an absolutely competitive market would be like.
2. In perfect competition suppliers would be price takers.
3. Businesses would produce at the point where:
   output × average revenue = output × average cost.

SUMMARY QUESTIONS

1. Why have economists created a model of perfect competition?
2. How are prices determined under perfect competition?
3. Why would a business not raise its prices if it was operating in a perfectly competitive market?

ACTIVITY

Identify markets in which the market largely determines the price at which a producer can sell its product. Compare the prices charged by different producers in this market. How similar are they? Compare your findings with those of classmates.

3.8.2 Monopoly markets

TOPIC GUIDANCE

Students should be able to:
- describe the characteristics of monopoly
- describe pricing and output policies in monopoly.

Branding products helps to differentiate them and give the producers some elements of monopoly powers. This in turn enables them to charge higher prices

STUDY TIP

The downward-sloping average revenue curve for a firm in monopoly is also the demand curve.

DID YOU KNOW?

In some countries, e.g. the UK, the government defines a monopoly as existing in law if it has 25 per cent or more of the market. This is because when it has a substantial share of the market, it has power to influence price and other aspects of competition.

What is a monopoly?

Monopoly is the opposite of perfect competition. In a pure monopoly there is only one firm in an industry, so there is no competition. There are very few pure monopolies in the real world, but there are local examples in, say, the only shop or petrol station in a remote area. There are businesses that are so large that they can benefit from the same advantages as monopolies, e.g. Microsoft, which provides the operating system for most computers. Microsoft is able to use its virtual monopoly position to create exclusive deals with computer manufacturers.

In some countries, government-owned public corporations have monopoly powers. For example, state-owned oil companies sometimes manage all of the oil reserves in a particular country. This unit looks at how the lack of competition enables companies to benefit from monopoly-like powers.

Price makers

One of the main features of a monopoly is that it acts as a price maker. A price maker chooses what price to charge rather than having to charge a price that is identical or very similar to the prices charged by rivals. Microsoft, mentioned above, is able to choose the price it charges to computer manufacturers. Of course it would not want to make this price unaffordable to computer manufacturers.

The demand curve under monopoly

A downward-sloping demand curve occurs when more of a product is demanded at lower than at higher prices. Monopolists are faced with a downward-sloping demand curve for their products. The monopolist will want to set prices at the profit-maximising output. Figure 3.8.2.1 shows the demand curve for the output of a monopolist. It also shows the average cost of producing goods.

The monopolist will choose a price where the difference between cost and revenue is maximised.

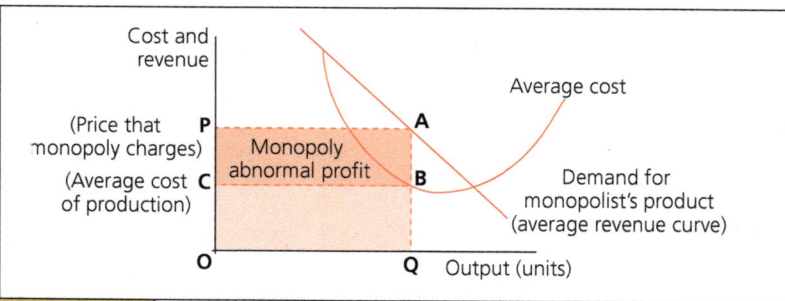

Figure 3.8.2.1 The demand curve for the output of a monopolist

In Figure 3.8.2.1, you can see that the monopolist is charging a price (P) that is higher than the average cost (C) of making that output of goods. Sales revenue for the monopolist is OPAQ (price × quantity produced). Total cost for the monopolist is OCBQ (average cost × quantity produced). The monopolist is therefore making profit over and above normal profit.

Note that the monopolist's demand curve is the same as the industry demand curve because he is the only supplier. He can choose price or output, but not both.

The features of a monopoly

The key features of a monopoly are as follows.

- There is only one firm in the industry and it controls the market.
- It is very difficult for new firms to enter the industry.
- The monopolist is the price maker – that is, the setter of prices.
- Monopolists make profits over and above normal profit.

Examples of virtual monopolies include Microsoft Internet Explorer®, for accessing the internet, and Google, for carrying out an internet search (although in China, Baidu is the leading search engine).

Advantages and disadvantages of monopolies

These are the **advantages** of monopolies.

- Where there is a government monopoly, the industry or firm can be run in the national interest, ensuring steady supplies to all or most citizens, e.g. water supply.
- By using economies of scale a monopoly, e.g. Microsoft, can produce a high-quality product at relatively low cost to consumers.
- Some businesses are 'natural monopolies', where resources are located in a small geographical area, e.g. some mined minerals, so that it makes sense for one firm to manage production.
- Having one firm cuts out duplication and waste, e.g. having two railway companies operating on the same route.

Where monopolies exist, there are also **disadvantages**:

- The monopolist may restrict output or raise prices (through lack of competition).
- The quality of the product or service offered may be limited because the monopolist does not compete with rival firms.
- Monopolists make abnormal profits (over and above the profit that would be made in a competitive market).

ACTIVITY

Identify some of the products that you consume where the business appears to have monopoly powers. Are the prices of these products relatively high compared with other products that you buy, where there appears to be more competition between producers and sellers?

KEY POINTS

1. A pure monopoly exists when there is only one firm in the industry.
2. Firms have monopoly powers when they control a large percentage of a particular market. In the UK this is more than 25 per cent of market share.
3. Monopolists are price makers.
4. Monopolists maximise profits when there is the greatest difference between their total costs and total revenues.

SUMMARY QUESTIONS

1. What is the difference between *monopoly* and monopoly powers?
2. How can businesses develop monopoly powers?
3. What are the key features of monopoly?

Unit 3   Test yourself

SECTION 1: Multiple-choice questions

Each question has ONE correct answer.

1. What does the phrase *a medium of exchange* mean when describing a function of money?
   a. Price of an item can be measured in terms of money units
   b. Money is a generally accepted means of payment
   c. You can save money because it keeps its value
   d. Borrowers know how much they need to pay back on a loan

2. Which of the following is NOT a function of a commercial or retail bank?
   a. Acting as banker to the government
   b. Keeping money and valuable items safe
   c. Lending money to people and businesses
   d. Paying interest to savers

3. What is the *base rate* as set by a country's central bank?
   a. The smallest amount of money that can be loaned
   b. The shortest amount of time over which loans can be taken
   c. The interest percentage from which all other loan rates are taken
   d. The length of time it takes to get a loan

4. An external economy of scale may be:
   a. Low costs due to bulk buying
   b. Lower interest on bank loans
   c. Training courses at local colleges
   d. product diversification

5. Which of the following is a feature of *division of labour*?
   a. Shorter production times
   b. Specialisation by workers
   c. Lower cost of products
   d. Use of unskilled workers

6. Which of the following is NOT true in the economic model of perfect competition?
   a. Companies produce identical products
   b. Companies charge different prices to different consumers
   c. There are many buyers and sellers of the product
   d. Companies make normal profit in the long term

7. According to economic theory, why might a lawyer get paid more than a shopkeeper?
   a. A low demand for and a high supply of labour
   b. A high demand for and high supply of labour
   c. A high demand for and a low supply of labour
   d. A low demand for and low supply of labour

8. Which of the following is a disadvantage of monopoly power to consumers?
   a. Advertising expenditure is high
   b. Economics of scale are unlikely
   c. There are barriers of entry into the industry
   d. Prices may be higher

9. Which of the following is NOT a difference between the spending and saving habits of high-income and low-income families?
   a. High-income earners spend more than low-income earners
   b. High-income earners spend a bigger proportion of their income on essentials
   c. Low-income earners save less than high-income earners
   d. Low-income earners suffer more when prices are rising

10. Which of the following is a benefit to an employee of trade union membership?
    a. Union may strike and halt production
    b. Rising wages leading to rising prices
    c. Ease of negotiation with one union official
    d. Support in the case of a grievance at work

SECTION 2

Country B is a large developing nation, with a young, growing population. The government controls a large percentage of the economy, including public transport, health and education provision, as well as the offices that deal with taxation and government statistics. This means that many people are employed in these public sector organisations, which have a reputation for inefficiency and very slow service. Some government employees also receive subsidised housing and public transport.

Trade union membership is encouraged and is widespread in businesses, as it makes negotiations over pay and conditions easier and gives workers the chance to take part in collective bargaining. Of the country's workforce of 232 million, 174 million are members of trade unions. However, public sector workers have only received pay increases in line with inflation (around 1 per cent) for the last few years. Most employees receive their wages weekly, paid in cash, and only 10 per cent of the population has a bank account.

Economic growth is slow, around 1.5 per cent per year, but privately owned companies are becoming more widespread as public demand for imported consumer goods increases. The government has recently relaxed import controls, which has given the population access to goods from abroad for the first time. Wages in the private companies are increasing at a much faster rate than in the public sector and the gap is widening.

1 a Explain what is meant by a *public sector organisation* and give ONE example from the extract. (2)

b Why might the government of Country B be concerned about *slow economic growth*? (2)

c Some public sector workers receive *overtime* payments. Explain what this means and give a possible example for a railway worker. (2)

d Discuss the likely long-term benefits and drawbacks to workers in the public sector in Country B. (6)

e Calculate the proportion of the workforce that is in trade unions. (2)

f Some women teachers in Country B are paid less than men. Discuss whether this may be *gender discrimination*. (6)

g Using the concept of *derived demand*, including a diagram and written explanation, show how falling demand for public transport may affect the number of people employed as bus drivers, and their wages. (4)

h The government of Country B would like to encourage the population to make more use of banking services. Discuss the best ways to achieve this aim. (6)

Total: 30 marks

SECTION 3

Penelope is a sole trader who has recently set up a small pizza takeaway shop in a popular tourist town. At present she runs the shop on her own, but the hours are long and she has not taken a break for the last 18 months. The business is seasonal to some extent, but the town attracts visitors all year round, so she does not want to close the shop for a holiday period, as she feels she may lose business to one of her many competitors. Penelope is considering going into partnership with a friend who has recently lost her job as a chef and is willing to put money into the pizza business. Penelope would like to expand and open another takeaway shop or a restaurant. Penelope has spoken to a business adviser, who has suggested that she also considers the option of forming a private limited company.

Her business costs and revenues are as follows:

Rent of shop	US$250 per week
Penelope's wage	US$150 per week
Business rates	US$140 per week
Electricity bills	US$30 per week
Marketing leaflets	US$10 per week
Pizza ingredients (average)	US$2.50 per pizza
Pizza boxes	US$0.30 each
Selling price of pizzas	US$7.50 (average)

1. a Define *fixed costs* and give two examples from Penelope's business. (4)
   b Define *variable costs* and give two examples from Penelope's business. (4)
   c Identify and explain TWO advantages to Penelope of operating her business as a sole trader. (6)
   d As a sole trader, Penelope has unlimited liability. Explain what this means and how it may affect Penelope's future plans for her business. (6)

2. a Calculate total fixed costs for Penelope's business for one week. (4)
   b Calculate Penelope's total variable costs if she produces 50 pizzas. (4)
   c Calculate Penelope's profit or loss if she produces and sells (i) 120 pizzas and (ii) 175 pizzas in a week. (6)
   d Calculate and comment on Penelope's average fixed costs for the output levels. (6)

3. Penelope is trying to decide whether to expand her business by forming a partnership with her friend, or to start a private limited company. She needs to consider the advantages and disadvantages of both options.
   a Explain ONE advantage and ONE disadvantage to Penelope of expanding her business by taking on a partner. (4)
   b Explain ONE advantage and ONE disadvantage to Penelope of expanding her business by starting a private limited company. (4)
   c Penelope needs to measure the size of her business in order to give information to prospective investors. Identify and explain TWO possible ways she could do this and decide which would be the best. Justify your decision. (6)
   d Referring to the information in the case study, and your answers to **3a** and **3b**, discuss the best way for Penelope to expand her business. Justify your decision. (6)

4. Penelope's major competitor in town is the branch of a major multinational pizza takeaway and delivery company. This company sells pizzas at an average price of US$6.50, due to economies of scale in the production and marketing costs achieved by the large company.
   a Explain what is meant by *economies of scale* and *multinational company*. (4)
   b Identify and explain TWO likely examples of economies of scale in this type of business. (4)
   c If Penelope reduces the price to US$6.50 in order to compete with the multinational company, explain what may be the implications for her sales, profits and future plans. (5)
   d Evaluate the view that 'local businesses like Penelope's are likely to remain small'. (7)

Total: 80 marks

4 Government and the macroeconomy

This unit starts out by identifying the role of government locally, nationally and internationally. It then goes on to examine the key macroeconomic aims of government relating to economic growth, high employment, low inflation, balance of payments stability, and a fair distribution of income. A number of conflicts between these aims are identified.

The unit then explores the nature of fiscal policy including types and reasons for taxation and government spending. It explores how spending and tax totals can be adjusted to seek to achieve macroeconomic aims (for example, by raising or lowering government spending totals). Next monetary policy is identified as the deliberate manipulation of the price and quantity of money (for example, by raising or lowering interest rates in order to secure economic objectives). Supply side policy is identified as a means of making the supply of goods in the wider economy more efficient.

Economic growth is identified as a key government objective. Different measures are identified to calculate growth rates and the causes and consequences of growth are explored. The unit then defines employment and unemployment before going on to examine causes and consequences of unemployment. Finally the unit investigates inflation which is defined as a general rise in the level of prices. Causes and consequences of inflation and deflation are explored.

TOPIC COVERAGE

Students will study the following topics
- The role of government, macro-economic aims and conflicts between aims
- Fiscal policy, the budget and government spending
- Reasons for taxation, principles of taxation, types of tax and the impact of taxation. The effects of fiscal policy.
- Definitions of monetary policy, monetary policy measures and how the government uses monetary policy
- The nature and impact of supply side measures and how the government uses supply side policy
- Economic growth, causes and consequences of growth and recession
- Definitions of employment and unemployment
- Patterns, measures, causes and consequences of unemployment
- Policies to reduce unemployment
- Definition and measurements of inflation and deflation
- Causes and consequences of inflation
- Policies to control inflation and deflation

4.1 The role of government

4.1.1 Government roles

TOPIC GUIDANCE

Students should be able to:
- describe government roles at local, national and international level.

The Malaysian houses of Parliament in Kuala Lumpur hosts the country's central government, responsible for national policy-making

DID YOU KNOW?

Generally speaking, central government across the globe has reduced the amount of direct interference in the economy from the 1980s onwards, reducing the overall level of direct government control of a number of sectors of national economies. A key reason for this has been to encourage industries to become more competitive.

Government roles

The **government** is a group that that oversees a community, establishing rules and administering public policy. Governments can exert power and create many of the arrangements around how business disputes are resolved and the framework in which business is carried out.

Some governments intervene significantly in the business sphere, making key decisions about what will be produced, how it will be produced and who will receive the outputs supplied by business. A high level of intervention is characteristic of a centrally planned economy, such as that of North Korea and to a lesser extent Cuba.

Other governments are far less hands-on (e.g. those of the US, Mauritius and Barbados), leaving the business sector to make most of its own decisions – although within a framework of laws established and administered by the courts of law.

Governments are involved in the life of the local, national and international economy in many ways. Government involvement ranges from providing local roads and street lighting in urban areas, to taxing businesses both at local and national levels and subsidising some firms and industries. At the international level, national governments work together to create frameworks for joint collaboration, such as the General Agreement on Tariffs and Trade (GATT) which seeks to create rules of fair play in international trading, and to reduce tariff (tax) barriers on trade between countries.

Government is thus involved in the macro-economy at three levels.

1. **Locally**: local government will establish local business taxes and provide a number of local services for business (as well as for citizens). Local government:
   - establishes regulations (rules) governing what takes place in local regions, e.g. providing permits and licences to trade or carry out specific business activities
   - invests in local infrastructure, e.g. building business parks for rent
   - taxes local businesses and provides tax incentives, e.g. low tax rates for start-up firms
   - carries out marketing activities to encourage new firms to set up in the area, and to promote the area, e.g. as a tourist destination.
2. **Nationally**: central governments establish national business taxes and provide a number of services nationally for businesses and citizens. Governments are responsible for the overall management of their economies through a range of fiscal and monetary policies.

One of the most important roles of a national government is as manager of the national economy. A government minister has overall responsibility for economic policy, and he or she will work closely with the central bank and treasury. The central bank will manage monetary policy and the treasury will manage fiscal policy.

Monetary policy and fiscal policy are the government's economic instruments for managing the economy. Monetary policy is the control of the quantity (supply) of money and the price of money (interest rate). Fiscal policy is the control of the relationship between the level of taxes and government spending.

3 **Internationally**: governments engage interactions of an economic nature that are bilateral (between two countries) and multilateral (between several countries). Typically these interactions involve working together through international groupings including the following.

- Trading interactions: countries form trading groups such as the European Union and the North American Free Trade Area (NAFTA), to enable freer trade to take place within a given group of countries.
- Borrowing and financing interactions: countries form international groups including the International Monetary Fund and the World Bank to provide means of making international payments, and to enable countries to borrow from a central pool to finance short and longer term debts.
- Sustainability interactions: countries work together at inter-governmental level to create treaties and agreements that support sustainable growth, e.g. the Kyoto Protocol governing poisonous emissions into the environment.

> **DID YOU KNOW?**
> Businesses are likely to pay business taxes both to local and national government, e.g. in the form of profit taxes. Businesses will benefit from government spending both by local government, e.g. on local roads, and by national government, e.g. on motorways.

> **STUDY TIP**
> Make sure that you can give examples of situations in which economic decisions are made at local, national and international levels. List examples of recent decisions you have read about.

SUMMARY QUESTIONS

1 Which of the following decisions most strongly involves local, national or international government?
   a imposition of local business taxes
   b raising subsidies to exporters by the UK government
   c licensing arrangements for new business premises within a city
   d agreeing with other countries to allow more goods to be traded free of import duties
   e establishing a free trade zone within the European Union
   f raising interest rates in Germany
   g local road maintenance.

2 Do all national governments intervene to the same degree in the business life of a country? Explain your answer.

3 Describe one situation where national governments have cooperated with other governments to create a better running international economy.

> **KEY POINTS**
> 1 The role of government is to create and administer policy at local, national and international levels.
> 2 Central government is responsible for national economic policy-making.
> 3 National governments interact at international level to create agreements and frameworks to support national and international economic development.

4.2 Macroeconomic aims of government

4.2.1 Macroeconomic aims

TOPIC GUIDANCE

Students should be able to:

- outline government macroeconomic aims.

Government responsibility

Nearly all governments take some responsibility for the smooth running of the overall system – the macro-economy.

Intervention can be likened to a pilot flying a plane. The pilot watches an instrument panel showing variables, such as speed and altitude. The pilot can make adjustments to make sure the plane flies smoothly and on course to its destination.

Similarly, through their central statistical office, governments receive data about the growth of the economy, the level of inflation (general price changes) and the level of exports and imports. Government ministers in charge of the economy assesses the information provided and will decide whether changes to economic policy are necessary.

Macroeconomic aims

All governments have a number of economic aims which they need to balance. The government will develop policies and plans related to the areas below.

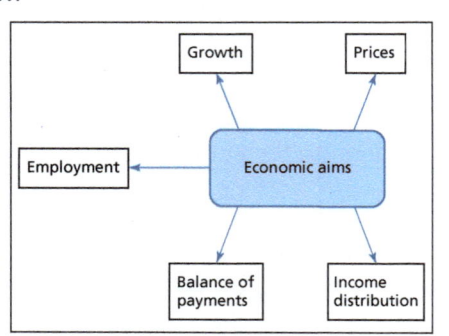

Diagram: Economic aims — Growth, Prices, Employment, Balance of payments, Income distribution

Economic growth

The government will want the economy to grow. Economic growth will be measured in part by the overall level of activity and output of a nation. It will be important to ensure that growth is steady and not characterised by periods of rapid growth and sudden slowdowns. Growth also needs to be sustainable.

Government can encourage growth through helping private business to grow, e.g. through low business taxes or through government involvement in growth sectors such as new high-tech industries.

Prices

The government will want to make sure that the general level of prices in the economy is effectively managed. It is helpful for prices to rise a little, because this encourages firms to produce more goods. However, prices need to rise in a relatively slow and predictable way so that future contracts can be made where both sides know the value of what they pay or receive. Government (through the central

DID YOU KNOW?

Economic growth involves increases in output and earnings. As people that make up the economy receive income in the form of wages, profits, interest and rent in exchange for their contribution to national output, they will be able to use this to buy a share of the national output.

bank) will want to manage inflation so that it does not distort the economy. You will learn more about inflation in Unit 4.8.

Government policies to control inflation might include reducing spending or raising taxes when prices start to rise.

Income distribution

All economies are characterised by inequalities in income. The government needs to manage inequality and poverty in a way that is acceptable to society. In Unit 4.3 you will look at ways in which the government seeks to redistribute incomes through taxation and other policies. There are different views as to what constitutes a fair distribution of income, so the government needs to weigh up the interests of different stakeholders and interest groups.

Balance of payments

The government will want to make sure that trade with other countries helps its country to prosper. The balance of payments on current accounts compares values of exports (bringing revenues into a country from overseas) with values of imports (leading to outflows of expenditure from a country). Exports need to be competitive and imports need to be at levels the country can afford.

Government policies to tackle balance of payments issues might involve encouraging exporters and discouraging imports.

Employment

A key indicator of the effectiveness of economic policy is the level of employment and unemployment in a country. Employment needs to rise in line with increases in population. At the same time, unemployment needs to be minimised so that those seeking work can gain suitable employment.

Policies to increase employment might include the government increasing the number of workers it directly employs, or reducing business taxes to encourage private firms to take on more labour. The government will seek to stimulate the aggregate supply (national output) in the economy, while at the same time seeking where appropriate to stimulate and manage aggregate demand.

> **DID YOU KNOW?**
>
> There are different views as to what makes up a fair distribution of income. Some people believe that inequality of income reflects how hard people work, and is thus fair: those who work the hardest should receive the highest rewards. Other people believe that this is unjust and that there should be a lot more similarity between incomes in a sharing society.

> **KEY POINTS**
>
> 1 The macro-economy is the overall economic system, such as the national economy producing the national output.
>
> 2 Macroeconomic policies are those concerned with controlling inflation, creating growth, managing employment and the balance of payments, and ensuring a fair distribution of income between citizens and households.
>
> 3 Macroeconomic policy seeks to manage the level of aggregate demand and supply in the economy.

> **SUMMARY QUESTIONS**
>
> 1 What do you understand by the term 'macroeconomic aim'? Identify one policy designed to achieve or work towards a specific macroeconomic aim of government.
>
> 2 Identify one likely macroeconomic aim of government in relation to:
>   a employment
>   b inflation
>   c growth
>   d redistribution of income.
>
> 3 What is the difference between monetary and fiscal policy?

4.2.2 Conflicts between government aims

TOPIC GUIDANCE

Students should be able to:
- discuss the possible conflicts between government aims.

Oil and gas fields provide Norway with a healthy balance of payments position. The surplus is invested in a sovereign wealth fund for the future

STUDY TIP

You should be able to discuss the possible conflicts between different government aims.

STUDY TIP

You can include appropriate examples from your own country, or any other country you are interested in, unless specified otherwise.

Conflicting aims

Governments managing their economies often face conflicting policy aims. Here are some examples:

- Spending more money to stimulate economic growth can lead to rising prices, resulting from increased demand. If, however, spending is reduced to cut back the demand that is causing inflation, this will lead to a fall in growth.
- If the government tries to create full employment, labour becomes increasingly scarce. Employers have to compete more strongly to attract labour. They raise wages, which in turn leads to rising wage inflation.
- If the government tries to redistribute income, this may involve taxing richer people at higher rates. Richer workers may feel that they are unfairly penalised for working hard and may decide to migrate: this is the '**brain drain**'. This in turn might slow down economic growth.

Trade-offs

The government has to balance its various policy aims. For example, it may have to **trade off**, or accept, a little more unemployment for a little less inflation. Economists may need to fine-tune the economy, creating the best possible balance between policy objectives. **NAIRU** is an example of this. This is the Non-Accelerating Inflation Rate of Unemployment and involves allowing just enough unemployment in the economy to prevent inflation rising above a given target figure. Prices are allowed to increase gradually and some unemployment is tolerated. NAIRU involves living with manageable inflation and acceptable unemployment.

A suitable mix

The government should be trying to achieve:

- a state of almost full employment
- inflation held at a manageable rate, e.g. about 2 per cent
- year-by-year sustainable growth of the economy
- the reduction in inequality of income over time
- international payments balanced so that deficits in some years are balanced by surpluses in others.

Economies need to be quite strong to achieve this. They will probably have a strong resource base that makes them competitive in the world, and a government able to manage the economy carefully.

Successful economies

Many economies experiencing high rates of growth in gross domestic product (GDP) and those that are rich in resources often have quite high levels of inequality. This is not the case in Norway!

CASE STUDY | Norway

Norway's natural resources include petroleum, hydro power, fish, forests and minerals. The oil and gas industry accounts for over 30 per cent of exports and Norway runs a surplus in most years on its balance of payments. The government controls the petroleum sector through large-scale enterprises, owning the majority of shares. As oil and gas reserves will eventually run out, the government saves almost all state revenue from this sector in a sovereign wealth fund (a reserve owned by the government for the nation). The government used some of the sovereign wealth fund to increase spending to get the economy growing again. Norway has averaged an annual growth in real GDP of 1–4 per cent during the last 10 years. Norway uses the 'Nordic economic and social model': taxes are high, to pay for a large welfare state, spending on schools, hospitals and care for the elderly. There is almost full employment, and there is a strong emphasis on redistribution to create gender and other forms of equality. In 2017 inflation was 1.9 per cent.

Questions

1 Describe the Norwegian economy in terms of:
   a the level of employment
   b the rate of growth
   c redistribution of income
   d inflation.
2 What is the importance of the oil industry, and of the sovereign wealth fund, to Norway's prosperity?
3 See if you can find out, e.g. in the *World Factbook* these figures relating to Norway: the most recent annual figure for GDP annual growth, the inflation rate; the balance of payments on current account.

See section 4.6.1 for more on measuring GDP.

SUMMARY QUESTIONS

1 Explain how the policy objectives of full employment and low inflation may clash.
2 Do high growth rates always lead to the increased redistribution of income?
3 What is NAIRU and why is it desirable?

> **STUDY TIP**
>
> Make sure you understand that it would be very difficult, if not impossible, to achieve success in all of these policy objectives at the same time. There will, therefore, be an opportunity cost of taking one set of decisions rather than another.

DID YOU KNOW?

The Nordic model, used by Norway, Sweden, Denmark and Finland, is made up of a mixed market economy with a generous welfare state. This model may be difficult to finance in periods of recession: the economy of Finland suffered badly in the crisis of 2008–09, leading to rapidly growing unemployment and rising government debt.

KEY POINTS

1 There is often a clash between policy aims, e.g. between full employment and low inflation.
2 The government needs to trade off and balance its five main economic policy objectives.

4.3 Fiscal policy

4.3.1 Elements of fiscal policy

TOPIC GUIDANCE

Students should be able to:
- define fiscal policy
- explain the role of the budget in fiscal policy
- outline the nature of budget surplus, deficit and balanced budget
- give key reasons for government spending and taxation.

Sri Mulyani Indrawati, the Indonesian Minister of Finance, has overall responsibility for creating the national budget and formulating fiscal policy

DID YOU KNOW?

Public investment is investment by central and local government in capital projects, e.g. building roads, hospitals and schools.

ACTIVITY

In your country: when is the national budget published? Who is responsible for presenting the annual budget? What are the main areas of government expenditure set out in the most recent annual budget? What are the main forms of taxation used?

What is fiscal policy?

Fiscal policy is government policy designed to deliberately alter the amount of government spending or taxation to help achieve 'desirable' macroeconomic objectives by changing the level and composition of aggregate demand.

Fiscal policy involves two elements.

- It involves changing the relationship between the relative size of spending and taxes. For example, this might involve raising government spending while maintaining the rate of taxation.
- Structural changes in government spending and taxes will be needed. For example, the government may alter the emphasis in its taxation and spending patterns, e.g. spending more on public investment in infrastructure and less on welfare.

The budget

The **budget** is the principal tool of fiscal policy. A budget is a statement setting out financial income and expenditure of a given person or entity, e.g. a business. The national budget is the government's statement of its expected expenditure and revenue in a given year (and often in the following years).

CASE STUDY | The UK budget

In the UK, the Chancellor of the Exchequer is responsible for the preparation of the government's budget. The chancellor presents the budget for the coming year to parliament in a speech in the spring, and then presents an autumn statement, giving details of government expenditures and revenues to date. The budget sets out:

- the total amount the government expects to spend in the coming period
- a breakdown of different types of expenditure, e.g. social protection, health, education, debt interest, foreign aid.
- changes in emphasis in expenditure, such as which areas it will invest in, coupled with an explanation of its reasons for changing emphasis
- the total amount the government expects to raise in revenue in the coming period
- different types of taxes and other means of raising revenue
- changes in emphasis in taxation, e.g. why some taxes are being raised and others lowered.

In the budget speech, the chancellor will want to show how revenues can be raised to finance government expenditure. If government expenditure is rising it will be essential to show how extra taxes and other means of raising revenue will be increased (if the government wants to balance additional spending). The budget speech will provide a good indicator of broad fiscal policy – whether spending is rising or falling relative to taxes.

Since 2010 the UK has had an Office of Budget Responsibility, which has been set up to provide semi-independent support to the chancellor in creating budgets that are appropriate to the economic situation of the UK economy. The idea is to create economically sound budgets rather than ones that are politically driven.

Questions

1 What are the main components of fiscal policy as set out in the case study?

2 Why is it important to set out the relationship between taxes and spending in the budget?

3 Why is it important to create economically responsible budgets?

Reasons for government spending

Government spending enables a government to make direct interventions in the economy by investing in infrastructure, providing social welfare, investing in new technologies and investing in state-run industry. Key areas of government spending are social welfare, education, health, defence and public transport.

Reasons for taxation

Taxes enable a government to raise revenue for its spending programmes. In addition, taxes have other purposes e.g. to discourage certain activities and outputs, like smoking and pollution.

Budget possibilities

There are three possible outcomes of a budget:

1 A **budget deficit**: this is where public expenditure is greater than the revenue received. Governments may employ budget deficits in order to pump additional spending into the economy, for example when unemployment is high and the economy has stagnated. Budget deficits may also be indicators of weak and greedy governing.

2 A **budget surplus**: this is where public revenues are greater than public expenditure. The government might run a surplus in order to reduce excess spending in the economy.

3 A **balanced budget**: this is where taxes and spending are equal. A government may employ this policy as a sign of government prudence (being careful with the public purse). Political parties who believe in less government interference may seek to apply balanced budgets.

DID YOU KNOW?

A fiscal stimulus is an injection of government spending designed to encourage spending and growth in the economy.

STUDY TIP

Government spending decisions can be discussed in the context of the concept of opportunity cost.

KEY POINTS

1 Fiscal policy is concerned with: the relationship between government spending and taxes: the emphasis on different types of tax and spending.

2 A budget is a plan setting out future spending and income at a national level.

3 The government can: spend more than it receives in taxes (a deficit budget); or balance spending with taxes (a balanced budget); or apply a surplus budget.

SUMMARY QUESTIONS

1 Who is responsible for creating a nation's budget? How does the budget relate to fiscal policy?

2 What is the relationship between government taxes and spending when a surplus budget is employed? How might this impact on an economy?

3 Give two reasons for government spending and two reasons for government taxation.

4.3.2 Classification of taxes

> **TOPIC GUIDANCE**
>
> Students should be able to:
> - describe the types of taxation and their impact.

> **STUDY TIP**
>
> Make sure that you can clearly distinguish between direct and indirect taxes.

Reasons for taxing

A tax is a payment made by individuals or businesses to the government. The government imposes taxes for various reasons.

- **To raise revenue** – the earliest taxes were raised by governments to pay for the expenses of the rulers of a country and to finance wars. Today, taxes are levied to raise money to cover a range of government expenditures, e.g. on building schools, hospitals and roads, paying for defence and a police force.
- **To discourage certain activities** – such as those seen as antisocial in terms of the damage to health and pollution that they cause, such as smoking or driving; so cigarettes, cars and fuel may be heavily taxed.
- **To discourage the import of goods** – import taxes are referred to as **tariffs**. They can be levied as a percentage of the value of imports (an **ad valorem** tax) or a set tax on each item imported (a **specific tax**).
- **To redistribute income from the rich to the poor**.

Direct and indirect taxes

Economists make a distinction between:

- **direct taxes**, for which the burden falls on the person paying it – for example, when you pay income tax it is taken directly from your wages or salaries and paid to the government
- **indirect taxes**, which are imposed by the government on goods and services, but are usually paid by consumers rather than by the businesses that collect the tax for the government in the first instance.

> **DID YOU KNOW?**
>
> Payers of direct taxes have no choice about whether they pay the tax. In contrast, consumers can choose to buy a good with a tax on it or not. Some people believe that because of this element of choice the government should rely more on indirect than direct taxes.

Progressive, regressive and proportional taxes

If income is going to be redistributed then the rich need to pay more in tax than the poor.

Progressive tax takes a greater proportion of income from a wealthy person than from a poor person. Someone earning US$5,000 a year

Progressive taxes are ones that redistribute income from the rich to the poor

might pay 5 per cent of this in tax, a person earning US$10 000 might pay 15 per cent and a person earning US$20 000 might pay 30 per cent.

A **regressive tax** is one where the poor pay a higher percentage of their income in tax than the rich. This happens when the government imposes a tax at a set rate. For example, a person may pay US$20 for a licence to fish in a river, and US$100 a year to tax a car, or pay some other set rate tax. You can see that US$20 would be a higher percentage for a poor person to pay than a wealthy person.

Progressive taxes redistribute income in favour of the poor. Regressive taxes redistribute income in favour of the rich.

Proportional tax refers to a situation in which tax rises in proportion to the income of the taxpayer.

Figure 4.3.2.1 shows the relationship between income and the percentage of tax taken.

Common taxes

Taxes that are common to most countries include the following.

- **A tax on incomes**: this is often a progressive tax. Higher-income earners pay a larger percentage of income in tax. It is a direct tax.
- **A tax on purchasing**: examples are value added tax and goods and services tax. Producers and sellers of goods pay the tax to the government as a percentage of the value they add in the production of an item. The shop then makes the customer pay the tax. The tax is thus indirect. If the government taxes goods that are bought by the rich more than those bought by the poor, the purchase tax system would be progressive.
- **A tax on company profits**: this is a direct tax. The government can make it progressive by increasing the rate as profits increase.
- **Taxes on imports**: these are indirect, as they are passed on to consumers.
- **Taxes on specific products**: such as cigarettes, and petrol – are indirect. They may be regressive if they hit the poor harder than the rich.

> **STUDY TIP**
>
> You should be able to discuss the various reasons why governments impose taxes.

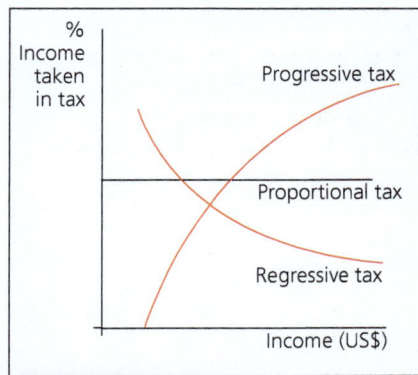

Figure 4.3.2.1 The relationship between income and the percentage of tax taken

> **STUDY TIP**
>
> When discussing different types of taxation, make sure that you are able to include appropriate examples of particular taxes.

SUMMARY QUESTIONS

1. Identify three types of indirect tax. Who pays indirect taxes? Who collects them?
2. Why might progressive taxes be fairer than regressive taxes?
3. What is the difference between an *ad valorem* (percentage) tax and a specific tax? Give an example of an *ad valorem* tax.

KEY POINTS

1. Direct taxes are levied directly on households and/or firms and are paid directly by them to the government. Indirect taxes are paid through an intermediary rather than the person on whom the burden of the tax falls.
2. Progressive taxes are designed to place a greater burden on the rich than on the poor.

4.3.3 Principles and impact of taxation

> **TOPIC GUIDANCE**
>
> Students should be able to:
> - outline the qualities of a good tax
> - show how taxes impact on consumers, producers and the government.

The qualities of a good tax

There are a number of qualities that economists recognise in a 'good' tax.

- It should be **economical** to collect. The cost of administering a tax should be low in relation to the revenues gained from levying it. For example, if a tax involves a lot of paperwork, can easily be avoided by payers, and raises relatively little revenue for the government, there would be a strong case for scrapping it.
- It should be **fit for purpose**. It should achieve the desired result. For example, if a tax on pollution leads to dramatic decreases in pollution levels, then the tax can be said to be 'fit for purpose'.
- The principle of **equity** should exist. The burden of the tax should fall fairly on those in similar circumstances, e.g. two businesses of a similar size, in the same sector, making similar profits should pay broadly similar taxes.
- The tax should be **simple** to understand and pay. It should be easy for taxpayers to understand the tax forms they fill in, and they should know how they are expected to pay.
- The tax should be **predictable**. Taxpayers and governments should be able to predict with ease how much tax will be paid, and the government should be able to make sound calculations about how much revenue will be received from particular taxes.
- Taxes should be **compatible** with each other so that the whole pattern of taxes fits together in a clear and coherent way.
- Taxes should be **convenient** to pay. Ease of payment by the taxpayer should be a priority.
- Taxes should be **broad-based**. They should fall widely across the community, (including among businesses) so that everyone pays (or most people pay) a contribution to the government.

Direct taxes

Direct taxes can act as a disincentive to hard work, enterprise and saving. Some people may be discouraged from working overtime or seeking promotion because of the disincentive effect of higher tax rates. Similarly, entrepreneurs may be discouraged from setting up businesses because they feel that rates of tax on profits are too high. Taxes on saving reduce the incentive to save. Where these effects occur, the government will lose some of its potential tax revenue and the economy may suffer.

Higher tax rates may encourage some people to work harder in order to maintain their income. Direct taxes often help to redistribute income and wealth. Direct taxes are a good way for governments to raise revenue in economies where productivity and incomes are high.

> **ACTIVITY**
>
> Using the example of a sales tax in your country, find out the rate of the tax and who is responsible for paying it. Then evaluate the tax in terms of the extent to which it meets the principles of a good tax.

> **DID YOU KNOW?**
>
> Rising income taxes provide consumers with less disposable income, meaning they are likely to spend less. Businesses will be faced by falling demand and hence make fewer sales. This can lead to a downturn in economic activity, which impacts on the overall level of government tax receipts.

Indirect taxes

Indirect taxes tend to be regressive so that they hit the poor harder than the rich. For example, in the case of sales taxes, poorer households are more likely to spend their income rather than save it. Increasing indirect taxes also has an inflationary impact, as they are likely to raise prices. Sales taxes tend to involve a lot of paperwork, which can be a burden.

Indirect taxes are easy and cheap to collect (for the government), as firms do some of the work in collecting them. They are believed to create less of a disincentive to work hard and be entrepreneurial. They can be used selectively for specific purposes, e.g. to target smoking or alcohol use, and are harder to avoid. They are relatively easy to adjust, e.g. by altering the VAT rate from 17.5 per cent to 20 per cent. The main benefit of indirect taxes is that they give greater choice to the taxpayer about whether to buy goods on which indirect taxes are levied.

Elasticity and impact of indirect taxes

In 2.11.4 we saw how the elasticity of demand and the supply of goods influences the impact of indirect taxes. Knowledge of the impact of indirect taxes helps the government to set rates for VAT and other sales taxes. Elasticity of demand and supply determines the extent to which sellers can pass on indirect taxes to consumers. For example, the more inelastic demand is, the greater the proportion of tax that can be passed on to consumers.

The government should also consider elasticity in tax levels for licences (e.g. driving licences), waste and pollution charges, and local business taxes.

Imposing taxes that are too high can lead to:

- falling sales and falling incomes – and rising unemployment as workers are laid off and businesses close
- an incentive for business and individuals to avoid paying taxes, leading to an 'undercover' economy involving tax evasion.

SUMMARY QUESTIONS

1. Identify a tax that you feel demonstrates the principles of good taxation and explain why.
2. How might raising sales tax impact on consumers, producers, government and the economy as a whole?
3. How might raising income tax rates – that is, the percentage of income paid in income tax – impact on consumers, producers, government and the economy as a whole?

CASE STUDY | How effective is this tax system?

In Goldland, businesses were expected to fill in a complicated 34-page tax form that asked for a lot of detail.

The tax system was designed to make businesses with the highest profits pay the largest burden of taxes. However, a number of businesses claimed that profits made overseas should not be counted. Large companies were therefore paying much lower overall taxes than smaller firms. There were a lot of queries about how to fill in the forms. As a result the government's tax department had been forced to double the number of tax officials administering the system.

Questions

1. Identify ways in which Goldland's tax system worked against the principles of good taxation.
2. Suggest ways in which Goldland's tax system could be modified in line with the principles of good taxation.

KEY POINTS

1. A good tax follows the principles of being simple, clear, easy to calculate, easy to collect, convenient to payers, economic, equitable and fit for purpose.
2. Direct taxes are a good way for governments to raise revenue in high income countries.
3. Indirect taxes give consumers greater choice about whether or not to pay them. Indirect taxes may also raise prices, making it more difficult for business to sell goods and creating an inflationary impact in the economy.

4.3.4 Fiscal policy and government aims

> **TOPIC GUIDANCE**
>
> Students should be able to:
> - explain fiscal policy and fiscal policy measures
> - show how fiscal policy helps government to achieve its aims
> - show the impact of balanced, deficit and surplus budgets.

Fiscal policies

A government can deliberately use fiscal policy to achieve certain economic objectives. During the recession that followed the 2008 financial crisis, the US government engaged in deficit financing. It pumped large sums of money into the national economy to try and turn around the recession that was leading to a fall in economic activity. For example, it gave large subsidies to US car companies to prevent them from going bankrupt. The policy was largely successful in regenerating demand in the US, and in saving jobs. The reduction of unemployment is the main reason a government decides to spend a lot of money even if it results in a budget deficit.

A government can also cut back on taxes to encourage consumers to spend more money; the US government also did this after the 2008 financial crisis. If taxes are reduced, consumers will have a greater disposable income to spend.

The main issue with deficit financing – that is, where a government spends more money than it receives – is that it can lead to inflation because, unless government spending leads to more goods being produced, the only thing that will change is that prices will go up, as more money chases the same amount of goods.

Impact of different budget positions

Budget position	Impacts
Balanced	A neutral impact on the economy. The balanced budget will have little impact on the general level of prices (inflation), enabling businesses and consumers to make decisions based on predictable information. The size of the government sector remains the same.
Deficit	More money is pumped into the economy, with the aim of providing stimulus for job creation, which it is hoped will stimulate more output overall. However, potentially inflationary impacts may only push up prices, rather than creating more output and jobs.
Surplus	Taxes are higher than government spending. Reducing the overall level of demand in the economy can lead to a reduction in supply and a downward spiral of reducing spending and output.

After the 2008 recession the US government stepped in, using fiscal policy to subsidise large US car companies such as General Motors

> **DID YOU KNOW?**
>
> Economic policy is government action designed to affect economies or help to achieve desired goals, such as an increase in economic growth.

Types of fiscal policy

In addition to distinguishing between balanced, surplus and deficit budgets, it is helpful to differentiate between discretionary fiscal policies and automatic stabilisers.

Discretionary fiscal policies are one-off policy changes designed to achieve a specific objective. For example, business taxes may be lowered for the purpose of stimulating business enterprise. This is a one-off adjustment for this specific purpose.

Automatic stabilisers are fiscal mechanisms designed to enable the economy to remain on an even keel. For example, when the economy moves into a recession, the proportion of taxes paid by taxpayers (particularly those on low incomes) should fall so that their disposable income is maintained. Similarly, in a period of boom when inflations is looming, an automatic stabiliser would ensure that a larger proportion of income is taken in taxes than previously, in order to limit the growth of disposable income.

In designing tax structures, the government should seek to combine discretionary fiscal policies to achieve specific objectives with long-term stabilisers to achieve the objective of steady and sustained economic growth.

DID YOU KNOW?
Fiscal policy involves the government altering the relationship between the amount of money it spends and the amount it receives in taxation, to achieve economic objectives. For example, deficit funding would involve spending more than is received in taxes. Surplus funding would involve taking more in taxes than the government spends.

STUDY TIP
When discussing this topic, it might be useful to contrast the advantages and disadvantages of fiscal policy in terms of a possible trade-off, e.g. a policy to reduce unemployment could end up increasing inflation.

KEY POINTS
1. The government employs balanced, deficit or surplus budgets depending on whether it is seeking to maintain a neutral role in the economy, seeking to stimulate the economy, or to remove excess spending from the economy.
2. Fiscal policy enables government to make major interventions in the economy, as for example with the deficit spending of the US government following the 2008 financial crisis.
3. Discretionary fiscal policies are one-off, whereas automatic stabilisers are designed to smooth out cycles of economic activity over a longer period.

SUMMARY QUESTIONS
1. How might deficit funding be used to meet government aims of unemployment reduction and economic growth?
2. How might a surplus budget enable a government to achieve its aim of reducing inflation?
3. How might income tax act as an automatic stabiliser?

4.4 Monetary policy
4.4.1 Monetary policy measures

> **TOPIC GUIDANCE**
>
> Students should be able to:
> - define monetary policy
> - explain how monetary policy includes changes in interest rates, money supply and foreign exchange rates
> - outline the effects of monetary policy on macroeconomic aims
> - show how monetary policy may help a government to achieve economic aims.

Monetary policies

Monetary policy is concerned with a government's decisions about the amount of money in an economy and the price of that money.

Monetary policy operates in the following two ways.

- It alters the quantity or stock of money in an economy – that is, the notes and coins that can be accessed through withdrawals from bank accounts. This can also be known as the money supply in an economy.
- It alters the price of money in an economy. The more usual way to describe the price of money is to refer to the rate of interest that lenders or borrowers of money pay.

A group of economists, referred to as 'monetarists', believe that a key part of controlling the economy revolves around the management of the money supply in an economy. They believe that the quantity of money should be increased only very gradually as the economy grows to enable more transactions to take place. However, if the government resorts to printing too much money too quickly (often because a government wants to spend more) this can destabilise the economy, resulting in inflation.

Effective monetary policy involves controlling any increases in the quantity of money to support economic growth. At the same time, interest rates can be altered by a government in line with changes in the economy. In addition to managing the money supply and the interest rate, the monetary authority of a country may seek to manage the exchange rate between the country's currency and those of other countries as a means of achieving monetary policy targets such as low inflation.

The Monetary Authority of Singapore is responsible for managing monetary policy, and it focuses on managing the exchange rate, because the country is an open economy relying on international trade

> **STUDY TIP**
>
> It is important that you are able to clearly distinguish between the money supply in an economy and the price of money – that is, the interest rate.

> **CASE STUDY** Singapore's use of the exchange rate as a monetary policy tool
>
> Singapore is a small country with a very open economy. Its port and airport are at the centre of one of the world's most important trade routes.
>
> The Singapore Monetary Authority has been very successful in using the management of the exchange rate (between the Singapore dollar and currencies of the countries with which it trades and competes) as a means of securing sustainable economic growth and low levels of inflation. The government manages the exchange rate by establishing its level between an upper and lower limit for the upcoming six months. The currency then fluctuates depending on the demand and supply of the Singapore dollar.
>
> A review is carried out to determine an exchange rate for the next six months which will enable the country to be competitive while controlling inflation. This is then set out in a monetary policy statement. The domestic interest rate has little significance in

monetary policy, because it is determined largely by foreign interest rates. Singapore thus uses the management of its exchange rate as a key tool of monetary policy.

Questions

1 What factors particular to Singapore's economy make the exchange rate a suitable monetary policy tool?

2 What aims does management of Singapore's exchange rate seek to achieve?

3 Why does the exchange rate need to be reviewed on a regular basis?

> **DID YOU KNOW?**
> The US central bank – the Federal Reserve – sets out to achieve three policy goals set by Congress in its monetary policy:
> - maximum employment
> - stable prices
> - moderate long-term interest rates.

Use of monetary policies

Monetary policies can also be used to manage an economy. For example, in recent years a number of governments, including those of the UK and the US, have deliberately increased the money supply through a process known as '**quantitative easing**'. The idea is that if there is more money available in an economy, this should encourage spending, which will help avoid a recession.

The other possible monetary policy is to change the rate of interest. For example, at a time of recession, interest rates should be lowered to encourage borrowing by businesses and consumers. In the UK, the government maintained the main interest rate in the country at a historically low figure of 0.5 per cent for a number of years after March 2009; in late 2017, the figure was the same. In contrast, if the main economic concern is a high rate of inflation, interest rates could be increased to discourage spending and borrowing.

Monetary policy helps a government to achieve economic aims

Monetary policy is of great importance in helping a government to achieve its economic aims. Keeping the money supply in line with the growth of national output helps to ensure steady growth of the economy while holding prices stable so that they rise only in a slow and predictable way. This is the best way to create new jobs.

Interest rates should be managed in such a way as to choke off any rises in prices that threaten to get out of control. Interest rates would be raised in such a situation, to discourage spending and encourage saving.

Keeping exchange rates stable and predictable (as in the example of Singapore) creates a good environment for international trade and helps exporters to create jobs.

> **KEY POINTS**
> 1 Monetary policy is the deliberate management of the quantity and price of money in order to achieve government macroeconomic aims. Exchange rate management is another important element of monetary policy.
>
> 2 Raising interest rates and/or restricting the supply of money helps to choke off inflationary pressures.
>
> 3 Managing the quantity of money in line with the growth of the national economy helps to stimulate growth and holds back prices at a suitable level.

SUMMARY QUESTIONS

1 Identify suitable monetary policies to
   a encourage the growth of the economy
   b reduce inflationary pressures.

2 Who is responsible for monetary policy in a country? How might monetary policy be used to encourage employment?

3 How might effective management of the exchange rate support other monetary policy measures in an open economy?

4.5 Supply-side policy

4.5.1 The effects of supply-side policy

TOPIC GUIDANCE

Students should be able to:
- define supply-side policy and outline supply-side measures
- outline the effect of supply-side measures on government macroeconomic aims.

For all countries, creating an educated workforce enables workers to make better contributions in the workplace

STUDY TIP

You should be able to distinguish between: demand-led macroeconomic measures, such as increases in government spending; and supply-led measures, such as government investment in education, training and infrastructure.

DID YOU KNOW?

Any policy measure that improves an economy's ability to produce is a supply-side policy. One example is when the government introduces performance-related pay for public sector workers.

What are supply side measures?

Supply-side measures consist of a range of policies designed to make the economy more efficient, and create sustainable economic growth. Examples of these measures are: in the private sector, investing in production facilities; in the public sector, spending to make factors of production more productive, e.g. investment in training.

CASE STUDY | Human capital and economic growth

Each year, the World Economic Forum assesses human capital across the globe. Human capital is a key indicator of supply-side effectiveness. Human capital endowments are people's skills and capabilities that are put to productive use. Human capital is measured in four areas:

- **Education**: indicators relating to aspects of education across primary, secondary and tertiary levels; information on the present and future workforce. Early childhood is seen as the most important phase for overall development.
- **Health and wellness**: indicators relating to physical and mental wellbeing, from childhood to adulthood.
- **Work force and employment**: quantifies experience, talent, knowledge and training in a working-age population.
- **Enabling environment**: the legal framework, infrastructure and other factors enabling returns on human capital.

Human capital improvement is seen as a key part of driving economic growth. In a 2017 report by the World Economic Forum the top five countries in terms of human capital were:

1. Switzerland
2. Finland
3. Singapore
4. The Netherlands
5. Sweden

Questions

1. What is the relationship between human capital and improving the supply side of the economy?
2. Carry out some internet research to find out where your country stands in comparison with other countries in terms of human capital. You could use the figures set out in the World Economic Forum report on human capital.
3. What might policy-makers do to improve human capital?

Examples of supply-side measures

- **Education and training**: public investment in primary, secondary and university education – as well as in apprenticeship schemes for industry – helps to make workers more productive. Well-educated and trained employees can make much more significant contributions to national output than poorly trained ones. Examples of countries that invest above average expenditures on education and training include Saudi Arabia, Ireland and Germany. Investment in training has a direct impact on the supply side, whereas investment in education will have more long-term impacts.

- **Labour market reforms**: the labour market needs to be highly efficient. Workers need to: move quickly into areas of the economy that are growing and are most productive, develop new skills required and train and retrain to be effective in growing sectors. This might involve reducing the power of trade unions to limit the supply of workers or to keep wages above market rate.

- **Deregulation**: this involves relaxing restrictions that may affect business by: adding to costs, slowing down decision-making or preventing entrance to markets. Some rules (e.g. those relating to health and safety) are essential, but some are overly restrictive.

- **Incentives to work and invest**. Government can provide a range of incentives. For example, a reduction in income taxes can encourage people to work longer hours. Similarly, government subsidies on children's nursery provision encourages parents of young children to work. Incentives to invest include tax breaks for firms that invest in capital and reduced corporation tax on profits resulting directly from investment.

Effects of supply-side measures on macroeconomic aims

Supply-side policies and their affects include:

- lowering taxes – to encourage businesses to invest more
- privatisation – to increase efficiency and maximise profit
- reducing barriers to business – allowing greater competition
- reducing trade union power – leading to a more flexible labour market
- training and retraining: to gain a more skilled workforce and increase occupational and geographical mobility of labour.

KEY POINTS

1. Supply-side measures are policies designed to make the economy more productive and hence increase national output.
2. Key supply-side measures include increasing workers' productivity through education, training and performance-related pay.
3. Anything that makes the economy run more smoothly, e.g. deregulation of markets, labour market reforms, helps to increase productivity.

ACTIVITY

Identify supply-side measures recently used by your government. How are they designed to increase national output?

STUDY TIP

You should be able to distinguish between government 'supply side measures', designed to make production more efficient in the economy, and 'demand side measures', designed to increase or reduce spending in the economy e.g running a deficit budget.

SUMMARY QUESTIONS

1. How might reductions in income and corporation tax help to increase the supply side of the economy?
2. What will be the effect of increasing the supply side of the economy on:
   a economic growth
   b national output
   c productivity of firms
   d productivity of employees?
3. What is human capital? How can government investment in human capital enhance output and growth?

4.6 Economic growth

4.6.1 Measuring gross domestic product

TOPIC GUIDANCE

Students should be able to:
- define gross domestic product (GDP) in relation to output.

Growth and gross domestic product (GDP)

Gross domestic product (GDP) is a measure of the total value of goods produced in an economy in a particular period, such as a year or quarter of a year. It is the most common measure of national income and indicates how an economy is growing. Rises in GDP indicate that the value of goods being produced is increasing.

Comparisons of GDP can be made over a period of time. The following statistics, based on the *World Factbook*, compare GDP in Nigeria in 2016 with earlier years.

	2012	2013	2014	2015	2016
GDP (US$ billions)	455	515	568	481	405

Measuring GDP

There are several ways of measuring GDP. It is important to use a method that yields accurate results.

The output method

This involves adding up the output produced by the various industries in the economy. The details for Nigeria are listed here:

- agriculture makes up about 21 per cent of GDP
- the service sector makes up about 43 per cent of GDP
- the manufacturing industry makes up 26 per cent of GDP
- the oil industry alone is responsible for over 11 per cent of GDP.

It is important not to double-count outputs. For example, oil output will be used for manufacturing.

To avoid double-counting, statisticians only count the value added by each industry (and not inputs that have already been counted once).

The expenditure method

This involves adding together the final spending on outputs produced by a country. There are four types of spending:

- consumer spending (by households on goods and services)
- investment spending (by businesses on premises, machinery and equipment)
- government spending (on goods, services and investment)
- net exports (the difference between exports and imports).

Nigeria's GDP is the output of the Nigerian economy, including exports to other countries. Spending by Nigerians on imports is deducted from GDP because the spending leaves Nigeria, to be spent on the output of foreign countries.

Street vendors, Nigeria. All countries have an element of unreported income from these types of businesses, whether market traders in Rome or street traders in Mumbai or Lagos. If they do not provide detailed statistics of their sales to the tax authorities, this can lead to extensive under-reporting of the country's GDP

STUDY TIP

Don't incorrectly state that GDP per head is calculated by dividing a country's GDP by its labour force.

DID YOU KNOW?

An International Monetary Fund study, titled *Comprehensive Measures of GDP and the Unrecorded Economy*, has defined hidden economic activities as 'legal production deliberately concealed from the public authorities to avoid payment of taxes'.

The income method

This involves adding together the incomes earned for producing all the goods that year. Only incomes earned for producing outputs are included. Therefore, 'transfer payments', such as pensions and unemployment benefits, are not included because no work was produced to earn those incomes.

GDP per head

The figure for GDP per capita (or per head) of population is probably more informative than the total value of GDP, but it does not take account of the way income is spread out or distributed between the different income groups in the population.

Nigeria has Africa's largest population, with about 150 million people. The GDP in 2012 was 455 000 million (US$ equivalent). This gives an income per head of about US$3,000 (which is very low on a global scale).

To calculate GDP per head we simply divide GDP by the population of the country.

$$\frac{US\$455\,000 \text{ million}}{150 \text{ million}} = US\$3{,}033$$

Real GDP

When calculating GDP, it is important to take account of the effect of inflation – this usually means taking it out. Rising inflation can distort increases in GDP. Economists, therefore, make a distinction between **nominal** GDP and **real** GDP.

- Nominal GDP figures are ones that have not been adjusted for inflation.
- Real GDP figures are ones that have been adjusted for inflation.

This involves calculating the value of the GDP produced in a particular year in terms of the prices of a base year.

For example, if the nominal GDP and inflation both double between 2005 and 2013 real GDP will stay the same. For example, if 2005 was given an index of 100 as the base year:

Nominal GDP = US$10 000 in 2005 and US$20 000 in 2013.

The prices index would be 200 in 2013 (prices doubled). US$20 000/2 = US$10 000. Therefore, real income stays the same.

Problems in measuring GDP

It is not always easy to measure GDP. One difficulty is that some economic activity is simply not recorded. For example, Italy and Nigeria both have a substantial 'underground' or 'unrecorded' or 'hidden' economy. For instance, there are many roadside businesses selling farm products, where tax is not declared. In Nigeria, there is also a substantial local film production and distribution industry (known colloquially as Nollywood) where films are sold through hidden channels. It is estimated that this unrecorded economy in Nigeria could account for up to 40 per cent of all trades made, leading to a substantial under-reporting of Nigeria's GDP.

ACTIVITY

Using national newspapers or by carrying out an internet search using 'GDP' and the name of your country, find details of:

- the most recent GDP figure for your country
- the figure for GDP per head
- the growth rate for GDP in your country over the last year
- the inflation rate in your country.

What would be the effect of the inflation rate on real GDP in your country?

KEY POINTS

1. GDP is a measure of the value of output produced in an economy in a period of time, used to measure economic growth.
2. GDP can be calculated by adding together the outputs of the various industries, total expenditures in the economy or incomes earned.
3. Real GDP is a measure that takes inflation into account.
4. GDP per head calculates GDP per person in the economy.

SUMMARY QUESTIONS

1. Define GDP, GDP per head and real GDP.
2. Why might comparisons of the GDP of two countries provide an inaccurate picture of the relative size of output in those countries?
3. Why is GDP such an important indicator for economists?

4.6.2 Economic growth and recession

TOPIC GUIDANCE

Students should be able to:
- describe and have a general understanding of the causes and consequences of economic growth in relation to output
- define the term 'recession' in relation to output.

What is economic growth?

There are considerable differences of opinion about what constitutes economic growth. In this topic we focus on traditional definitions of economic growth while in section 5.1.1 we will look at a broader definition of what it means for an economy to develop and for people to be better off.

An economy grows in a traditional sense if over a period of time it is progressively able to produce more outputs of goods. The conventional way of examining economic growth and making comparisons is through the measurement of GDP.

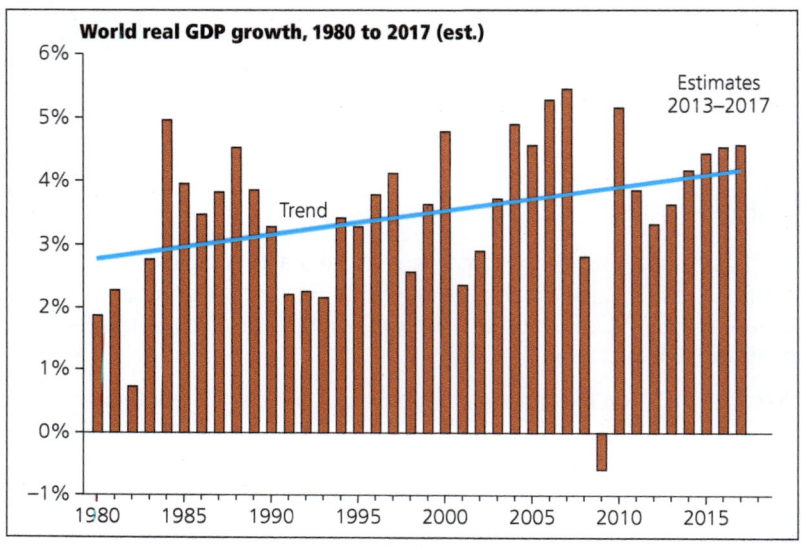

World real GDP growth, 1980 to 2017 (est.)

Source: IMF and http://mjperry.blogspot.co.uk

The graph above, based on International Monetary Fund figures, illustrates the growth of world GDP over time. You can see that the trend (shown by the blue line) is in an upward direction but that growth has been uneven. In some years global GDP has been rising quickly and in some years less quickly, with a brief fall at the end of the first decade of this century as a result of the banking crisis in the US.

The table to the left shows that measuring GDP makes it possible to contrast the relative growth rates of different economies.

Relative GDP growth rates

Country	2011	2012	2013
Eritrea	17%	7.5%	8.5%
Ethiopia	7.5%	5.0%	5.5%
Djibouti	4.5%	4.8%	5.0%
Sudan	−3.9%	−7.3%	3.6%

The table shows that rates of growth in Eritrea, for example, have been considerably faster than in Sudan. In 2011 and 2012 Sudan experienced negative growth.
Sources: EIU, IMF, RB

Causes of economic growth

In seeking causes of economic growth, economists typically look at two sets of factors: those relating to supply and those relating to demand.

Supply-side growth

In recent years there have been increasing rates of economic growth in a number of parts of the world, particularly in Africa, e.g. in Ghana and Ethiopia, and in Asia, e.g. in China, India, Vietnam and Thailand.

DID YOU KNOW?

Some of the key factors that slow down economic growth through the supply side are corruption, including bribery and fraud, and poor infrastructure, such as bad road and rail links, and lack of air transport to key areas.

Typically these are economies with substantial populations that have benefited from rapid industrial and service sector growth. There are a number of factors that contribute to supply-side growth, including:

- the development of markets for the buying and selling of goods, and in which enterprise can flourish
- government enforcement of commercial contracts that enable business people to make deals with confidence
- the development of the business sector of the economy including small, medium and large enterprises
- improvements in infrastructure, including gas, electricity, water and fuel distribution
- the development of primary, secondary and higher education sectors
- the focus on training and skills development supported by both the government and private sectors
- the use of new technologies as an engine for growth in the economy
- the growth of a sophisticated financial sector made up of stock exchanges, banks and insurance companies – the development of the financial infrastructure encourages foreign investment in economies.

Where government and the private sector have worked closely together to develop the supply side, this has resulted in the rapid growth of economies.

Demand-side growth

Demand-side growth involves increases in consumer spending power acting as an incentive for businesses to increase their output. Rising urban populations in many emerging economies, including large numbers of people in the substantial middle-class consumer group, have fuelled demand-side growth in many countries in Africa, Asia and Latin America, as well as in the US and parts of Europe, Australia and elsewhere. Countries such as China are characterised by huge cities with highly skilled workers operating both in the industrial and services sectors of the economy. As these economies grow increasingly wealthy, citizens seek to spend more on consumer goods, leading to demand-stimulated growth.

Consequences of economic growth

Economic growth has both positive and negative impacts. For example, it can lead to improvements in social welfare services, rising living standards and less reliance on aid from foreign governments. However, it can also bring with it increased levels of pollution, a growing gap between rich and poor and growth in opportunities for fraud and corruption. Use the activity at the top of this page to find out about the different consequences.

The nature of recession

Economies typically do not grow in a smooth and sustainable pattern. They also suffer from downturns in economic activity and from recession. A recession is defined as a period in which for two successive quarters (periods of three months) there is negative economic growth – that is, GDP falls. Recession leads to a waste of resources in that during a recession GDP falls, some people lose jobs, and fewer goods are produced.

ACTIVITY

Research the various possible consequences of economic growth for a country, including both benefits and costs. Present your findings as a wallchart.

KEY POINTS

1. Economic growth is traditionally associated with rising GDP.
2. Supply-side growth occurs when an economy becomes more efficient at producing output, e.g. through more efficient markets, use of better technology and improved education and training.
3. Demand-side growth stems from consumers having more money which they spend on goods, hence encouraging suppliers to bring more goods to the market.
4. A recession involves two successive quarters of declining economic activity.

SUMMARY QUESTIONS

1. What supply-side factors can you identify in your own economy that are likely to:
   a encourage growth
   b discourage growth?
2. How might the demand side of the economy help to stimulate the economy of your region and the country in which you live?
3. How might a recession hold back the long-term growth of a country?

4.6.3 Illustrating growth and recession

TOPIC GUIDANCE

Students should be able to:
- illustrate growth and recession on production possibility curves.

Illustrating economic growth

Economic growth can be illustrated in a diagram showing GDP growth over time. For example, the Russian economy has experienced much higher growth than most European economies since 2000 as it has increasingly freed its markets to competition. In addition, it no longer has to support weaker economies in the former Soviet bloc. The Russian economy has been growing steadily from a base of 100 in the year 2000. The only period of recession was when the world economy struggled in a period following the global financial crisis in 2008.

Illustrating economic growth using production possibility curves

Economists use production possibility curves (PPCs) to illustrate economic growth. A PPC, sometimes referred to as a production possibility frontier (PPF), shows combinations of goods that can be produced using the available production resources in a country. As a result of economic growth, an economy is able to produce more goods.

For example, in Figure 4.6.3.1 we can see this in a situation where a country focuses on two products: computers and cars. As a result of economic growth, the PPC shifts upwards and to the right, from PPF1 to PPF2. If it used all of its resources to produce computers, then it would be able to produce 5 550 000 cars rather than 5 000 000. Alternatively, if it just focused on automobiles, it could produce 4 500 000, rather than 4 000 000. Any combination of automobiles and computers will be at a higher output level (on PPF2) than previously (PPF1).

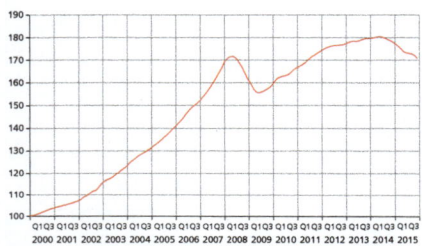

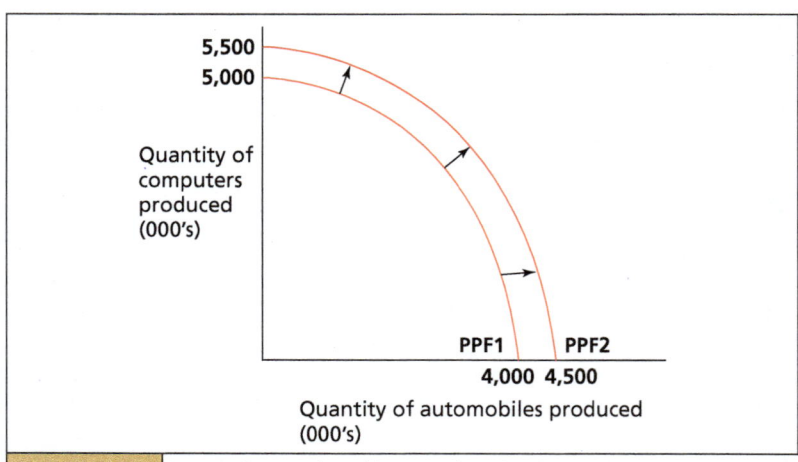

The chart illustrates Russia's recent economic growth, with just one period of recession (in 2008–09). An index of economic growth is set out using 2000 as the base year

DID YOU KNOW?

An index is an indicator or measure of something, e.g. economic growth.

DID YOU KNOW?

A base year is the first in a series of years in an economic index. It is usually set at a level of 100. From time to time, the base year will be changed to keep the index up to date. Any year can act as a base year, but economists typically choose a recent year.

Figure 4.6.3.1 Economic growth and increased production

The key benefit of economic growth is that it provides an economy with more productive resources so that it is possible to move the PPC further upwards and to the right.

Illustrating recession using production possibility curves

The illustration below shows the impact of recession on the PPF of a country. Initially the economy can either produce 5 000 000 cars or 5 000 000 computers, or a combination of the two. However, as a result of recession the frontier falls downwards and to the left so that a combination of only 5 000 0000 computers or 4 000 000 automobiles can be produced (or a combination of the two).

The curve shows that as a result of recession the economy is able to produce less with a given combination of resources than before. The diagram illustrates the waste associated with recession. In a period of recession some key resources such as industrial buildings, machinery, equipment and labour are unused. The buildings may go into disrepair and machines may not be effectively maintained or repaired. Employees' skills may become outdated, and workers may become demoralised as a result of being out of work.

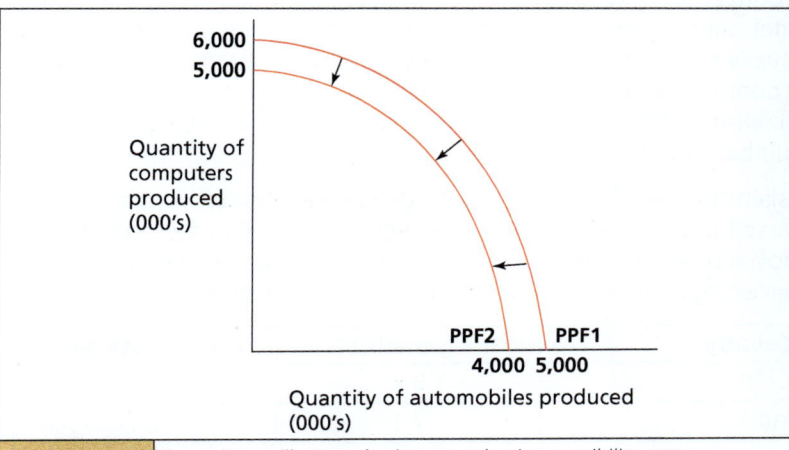

Figure 4.6.3.2 Recession as illustrated using a production possibility curve

DID YOU KNOW?
Economic growth can be illustrated either in a chart showing rising GDP from one period to another, or in the form of a production possibility frontier moving outwards and to the right.

ACTIVITY
Carry out some research to find out how economic growth has occurred in your country. Find out (using an internet search) what the base year currently is for measuring economic growth in your country. Then set out a diagram showing GDP over time, from the base year to the most recent year for which there is published information.

KEY POINTS
1. Production possibility curves (frontiers) can be used to illustrate the impact of growth and recession.
2. When the economy grows, the production possibility curve will move upwards and to the right.
3. In a period of recession, the production possibility curve will move downwards and to the left.

STUDY TIP
Make sure that you can illustrate how economic growth leads to an outwards and upwards move in the production possibility curve, and recession leads to a downwards and inwards move.

SUMMARY QUESTIONS
1. Draw a series of production possibility curves to show three successive years of growth followed by one of recession. Label the curves PPF1, PPF2, PPF3 and PPF4. What does the series of curves tell us about the combination of goods that can be produced with given baskets of resources in each of the years shown?
2. How does economic growth make it easier to move the PPF curve further outwards and to the right in successive years?
3. How does a production possibility diagram for a period of recession illustrate the waste of resources in an economy?

DID YOU KNOW?
The terms 'production possibility frontier (PPF)' and 'production possibility curve (PPC)' are interchangeable.

4.6.4 Government policies for economic growth

TOPIC GUIDANCE

Students should be able to:
- describe the aims of the government polices for economic growth.

The hydroelectric power scheme at Three Gorges Dam, China, is an example of government investment to support economic growth

ACTIVITY

Find out from newspapers and the internet the most recent figures for economic growth in the following countries: India, China, Brazil, Russia, the US, Pakistan, Japan, the UK and your own country. Set out these figures in the form of a table.

Economic growth

An essential part of government policy is to grow an economy. Over time an economy needs to be able to provide better living standards, so that people have more goods to consume, more leisure time and better environmental and other living conditions. This is most likely to take place if there is a growth in gross domestic product (GDP). As you learned in section 4.6.1, GDP measures the total value of goods produced in the economy in a given period – usually one year or a quarter of a year. It is important for a country's economy that the GDP per capita or per head of population is increasing. It is calculated by dividing the country's GDP by the number of people.

Asia has some of the most rapidly growing economies in the early part of the 21st century. The table below, which is based on figures provided by the International Monetary Fund, shows the year-on-year percentage change in GDP growth in selected economies:

Country	GDP growth 2011	GDP growth 2016
China	9.2	6.7
India	7.1	7.1
Indonesia	6.5	5.0
Malaysia	5.1	4.2
Vietnam	5.9	6.2

While these countries have significant differences, key factors they have in common are large populations (hence large markets), availability of capital for investment and many large strong domestic businesses.

The government and economic growth

Governments place a very high priority on **economic growth**. Tables are often drawn up ranking countries by GDP per head, and by how fast their economy is growing. Rising GDP per head means that:

- incomes within a country are rising
- the standard of living of people within a country is rising
- the government is able to raise more in taxes and to use this money to meet its objectives, such as providing public goods for citizens.

Government investment in major projects that improve an economy helps to support growth, such as the Three Gorges Dam project in China which supplies huge quantities of electricity.

Sustainable economic growth

Sustainable economic growth occurs when the growth is maintained over a period of time. An important aspect of sustained growth is that there is investment for future generations. Investment can be in roads, ports, railway lines and other parts of the economic infrastructure to make the economy more productive. It can also be social and welfare investment, e.g. in schools, hospitals and clinics, providing a healthier and more educated population. Both of these types of investment improve the productive capacity of the economy over time.

The trade cycle

The nature of economic growth is that it does not take place in a steady way. Economies experience periods in which the rate of growth is rising, followed by periods in which the rate of growth falls. In some periods there is even negative growth. The cycle of growth and recession is termed the **trade cycle**. It can also be known as the business cycle or the economic cycle.

Most advanced economies have experienced periods of growth and recession in recent years, including an international recession in 2008–09. In a period of recession, spending in the economy falls, as does the output of goods. This leads to reductions in employment. Figure 4.6.4.1 shows the UK recession, which started in the second quarter of 2008 and ended in the first quarter of 2010 and then turned into what is called a 'double dip' recession at the end of 2011 and start of 2012. There were fears that it might even become a 'triple dip' recession in 2013, but this was narrowly avoided.

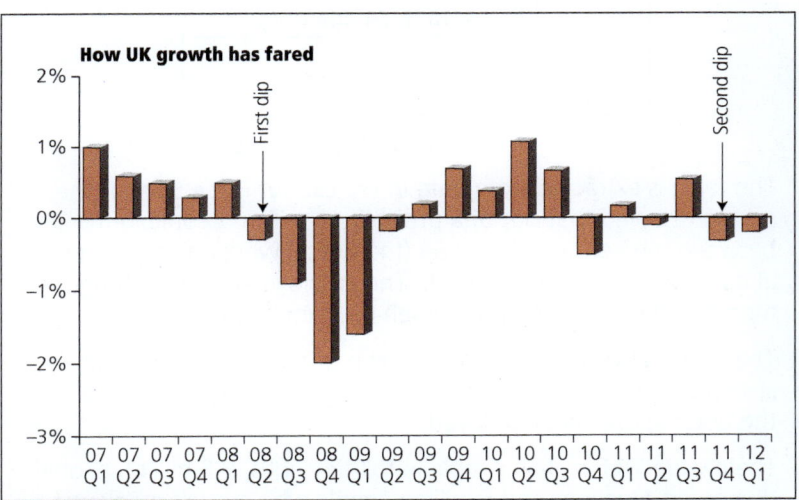

Figure 4.6.4.1 The UK recession 2008–12. The arrows show the start of periods of recession. Source: Office for National Statistics

Government policy is to try to prevent recession, or at least minimise the effects, and to stimulate economic growth. Growth can be encouraged by:

- making it easier to conduct business, e.g. by lowering taxes
- providing incentives for businesses to set up in growing industries, e.g., wind power energy
- employing people in productive activities in the public sector
- encouraging investment by both the private and public sectors.

STUDY TIP

When discussing economic growth, you should be able to contrast its potential advantages and disadvantages.

DID YOU KNOW?

The reverse of a recession is a period of economic growth known as a recovery. Recovery can then lead to a boom, as experienced in India and China in 2010.

KEY POINTS

1. Economic growth is measured by changes in GDP over time.
2. Improving growth increases production, living standards and government revenues.
3. Sustainable growth involves maintaining growth over time.

SUMMARY QUESTIONS

1. Why does a government place importance on economic growth?
2. How does investment help to sustain economic growth?
3. How can a government encourage economic growth?

4.7 Employment and unemployment

4.7.1 Patterns and levels of employment

TOPIC GUIDANCE

Students should be able to:
- describe the changing patterns and levels of employment.

Skilled full-time workers producing modern products are best placed to earn high wages and to help an economy to grow

DID YOU KNOW?

Core workers are at the heart of an organisation. They have full-time well-paid jobs. Their work is supported by a more flexible labour force of part-time and temporary contract workers. Terms of employment, such as wage rates and job security, are less good for contract workers.

STUDY TIP

You should be able to demonstrate that you understand the difference between the private sector and the public sector.

Employment

Employment is the work that people do in an economy. Over a period of time, patterns of employment change: some industries go into decline and jobs disappear while new types of industries and jobs develop.

Government statistics provide indicators showing what jobs people do and how many are employed. These are important for governments. (Ideally everyone who wants a job should be able to find work that meets their own needs, as well as the needs of the economy as a whole.)

Case study | Labour force indicators in the UK

The table below presents a picture of employment in the UK for June 2017.

	Employment rate (%) in the 16 to 64 age range
Men	79.6
Women	70.7

Source: Labour Force Survey

The table is extracted from data in the Labour Force Survey. The survey showed that out of a possible 43 million people in the UK between the ages of 16 and 64 (the typical working age range), almost 32.1 million are at work. The employment rate among men is higher than among women (but not by much).

The survey also shows the breakdown of employment by age structure. For example, in the 35–49 age range 93 per cent of the population were employed.

There were 18.5 million people in full-time jobs, 8.5 million people doing part time jobs and 5 million people who are self-employed (working for themselves, perhaps running a small enterprise).

There are 27 million people working in the private sector, while just over 5.4 million people work in the public sector.

Questions

1. What reasons would you put forward to explain why only 32.1 million out of the 43 million people in the age category 16–64 are in work?

2. What is meant by the employment rate? Why do you think that the employment rate is higher among men than among women?

The table (right) shows the different status of employees in a workforce.

Participation rates

The number of people available to work in an economy depends on:

- the number within the working age range
- the number within that age range who are prepared to participate in work. This is the **participation** rate.

$$\text{Participation rate} = \frac{\text{Number who are prepared to work}}{\text{Number within working age range}}$$

Participation rates vary from country to country, depending on various factors, such as:

- social attitudes, e.g. in some countries it is acceptable for women to go out to work; in others they may be expected to stay at home and focus on looking after their children and the home
- number going to school and university
- age at which people stop work and **retire**
- facilities available to enable groups to work, e.g. in some countries, shops, offices and industrial premises are adapted to enable people with disabilities to participate in work.

The industrial structure

Another way of examining patterns of employment is to look at the industrial structure of an economy.

The table below gives some recent statistics from the UK: jobs are divided into 14 categories (A–O), using a classification known as the Standard Industrial Classification.

By studying the table on the previous page, you should be able to see that most jobs in the UK are in service occupations.

Job	Category	Number of employees (thousands)
All jobs	(A–O)	30 997
Agriculture, forestry and fishing	A–B	488
Mining, energy and water supply	C–E	191
Manufacturing	D	2,885
Construction	F	2,170
Distribution, hotels and restaurants	G–H	6,816
Transport and communications	I	1,854
Finance and business services	J–K	6,409
Education, health and public administration	L–N	8,193
Other services	O	1,991
Total services	G–O	25 263

Type of employee	
Full-time (core workers)	Very important to the economy. They may work for the same employer for a number of years and develop increased knowledge and skills, enabling them to produce high-quality products for the economy.
Part-time	Able to combine work with other commitments, such as bringing up a family.
Self-employed	Work for themselves. The businesses they set up may take on others and grow to become major employers in the future.
Employed workers	Work for someone else, e.g. large businesses or the government.
Private sector workers	Work for businesses. Most employees in developed economies, such as the US, UK or Germany, work for large companies, some of which employ thousands of workers.
Public sector workers	Employed by the government, for example, in the Civil Service. In India the biggest employer is the government-run Indian Railways.
Skilled employees	Have developed skills through training and practice. Typically, they are relatively well paid compared with **unskilled** workers.

> **DID YOU KNOW?**
> In many countries, tourism is a major provider of employment that swells the size of the tertiary industry. Hotel work, excursions and trips are all 'services'.

> **STUDY TIP**
> You should be able to show that you can clearly distinguish between the primary, the secondary and the service sector.

As you saw in section 3.5.1, the industrial structure is split into three main areas:

- extractive (primary industry)
- manufacturing and construction (secondary industry)
- services (tertiary industry)

As a reminder, these areas are outlined below.

Extractive industries

Extractive industries use natural resources. Examples include farming, mining and drilling for sources of oil. Farmers grow and harvest crops and farm livestock, miners take out, or extract, fuel and minerals from the ground. Extractive industries sometimes produce raw materials such as iron ore (for making steel) and oil (for making petrol, plastics, fibres, and so on). Some primary products can be sold direct to consumers, e.g. fish and oranges sold by a grower at the farm gate.

Manufacturing and construction industries

Manufacturing and construction industries use raw materials and parts from other industries to make and assemble new products, such as chocolate, furniture, cars and oil rigs. House, factory and bridge building are examples of construction industries. **Semi-manufactured** refers to goods that are partly made and will need further processing by manufacturing industries.

Service industries

Service industries are particularly important in the modern world. **Services** give something of value to people, but are not physical goods. Examples of services are being served in a restaurant, or having a bank look after your money for you. Society has gone through three waves of development. In modern third-wave societies services dominate employment in advanced economies.

In the **first stage**, countries are dominated by agriculture and farming. This is still the case for many developing countries, such as Côte D'Ivoire and Ghana in West Africa, where over 90 per cent of the population live in rural areas.

In the **second stage**, countries are dominated by manufacturing, when industries such as coal, steel, car manufacture and engineering become important.

In the **third stage**, services become the most important sector of the economy, with many people working in insurance, banking, leisure, entertainment, tourism and hotels. This can lead to countries being highly developed in some areas, while still having districts where people live in considerable poverty.

In modern, third-wave societies, computers and robotised machinery have replaced many manufacturing jobs.

The data shown for the US is very different from **newly industrialised countries (NICs)**. Brazil is a NIC and roughly 20 per cent of the working population there is still engaged in agriculture and other

| CASE STUDY | Employment by major industry sector in the US |

The US is frequently given as an example of a third-wave society. The following data is drawn from information provided by the US Bureau of Labour Statistics. It shows percentages of people employed in the three sectors. The table includes a prediction for the future.

	1996 (%)	2006 (%)	2016 (%)
Primary industry	2.4	1.8	1.6
Secondary industry	16.9	14.5	12.7
Tertiary industry	81.7	83.7	85.7

Source: US Bureau of Labour Statistics

Questions

1. Describe the key trends that are taking place in the data.
2. Why do you think the figures for primary and secondary industries show a decrease?
3. Do you think that the patterns of change from 1996 to 2016 are likely to continue?

ACTIVITY

Find statistics for your own economy to find out how the working population – that is, people who are of working age – is distributed between primary, secondary and tertiary occupations. You will need to examine statistics from the government department responsible for collecting employment statistics. Obtain some information from the past five years so that you can see the trends in the three sectors.

primary industries, and a further 15 per cent in manufacturing, with the remainder working in services. In Ghana in West Africa, over half the working population still works in primary industries, including cocoa growing and other forms of small-scale agriculture. About 25 per cent of Ghana's population is engaged in services.

In all countries, the percentage of people employed in tertiary industries tends to be higher in urban than in rural areas.

KEY POINTS

1. The structure of employment refers to the employment rate, proportions of men and women working, differences between public and private sector employment and other structural differences.
2. The structure of employment in an economy changes over time.
3. As economies develop, the main change is an increasing proportion of jobs in the service sector.

SUMMARY QUESTIONS

1. Explain the difference between the primary, secondary and tertiary sectors of an economy. Give examples of industries that would fit into each sector.
2. What is meant by the 'participation rate'? What are the key factors influencing rates of participation?
3. Between 2003 and 2013 the employee percentage working in manufacturing fell in these countries: Australia, Barbados, China, Colombia, Finland, France, Iceland, Ireland, Japan, Poland, the Republic of Korea and the UK. Give four reasons why you think this may have happened.

4.7.2 Full employment

> **TOPIC GUIDANCE**
>
> Students should be able to:
> - describe the aims of the government policy of full employment.

Villagers in Bihar, India working on a flood protection scheme. The scheme provides work in areas of unemployment while improving the agricultural infrastructure

> **STUDY TIP**
>
> Make sure that you can define the term 'full employment' very clearly.

> **STUDY TIP**
>
> Make sure that you can discuss unemployment and how to deal with it. You should understand the various actions that could be taken by a government to reduce the rate of unemployment in a country.

Full employment

It might seem that full employment means that everyone has a job. However, at any time people are moving jobs, so there will be an element of temporary unemployment. If everyone was in employment, wages would start to rise and employers would have to compete to attract new employees. Economists therefore define full employment as a situation where most people are in work, but there are enough people out of work to prevent wages from starting to rise at an increasing rate. Employers seeking to recruit new workers can attract them without this leading to a surge in wages in the economy.

The **rate of unemployment** in an economy can be measured as follows:

$$\text{Unemployment rate} = \frac{\text{Number of unemployed}}{\text{Labour force}} \times 100$$

where labour force is the number of people making themselves available for work.

Every month government statistical offices calculate unemployment rate figures. In most countries unemployment rates are higher among younger workers, people with the lowest educational qualifications, minority groups and people in rural areas.

Why the government seeks to achieve full employment

Unemployment wastes resources that could be used to make goods. High levels of unemployment are costly to the government: tax revenues fall and spending on the unemployed increases. Rising levels of unemployment and falling incomes for poorer people can lead to social unrest and rising crime figures.

Labour is the most important resource in an economy. When people are in employment that they enjoy, they feel happier, are able to feed themselves and their families and do not have to rely on the government for handouts. Most people regard full employment as a desirable state.

> **ACTIVITY**
>
> How close to full employment is the economy in which you live? Find out the latest statistics for the unemployment rate. Look at recent newspapers for stories about national, or regional and local, employment. What actions (if any) is the government taking to bring about full employment? Set out your findings in a newspaper report called *Employment Supplement*. This should include facts and figures that would interest employers and general readers of a national newspaper.

Dealing with unemployment

Governments need to identify cures – that is, policies to deal with the different causes of unemployment. These are shown in the table below.

Cause	Possible cures
Temporary	Publicise job vacancies
Seasonal	Not necessarily a problem if employees can find a second job in addition to their seasonal work
Technological	Provide educational and training opportunities focusing on new technical skills required for new jobs
Frictional	Training in job areas where there are shortages of supply; providing more information through government and private labour recruitment agencies about job opportunities – to reduce the period of 'search unemployment'
Structural	Encourage people and businesses to move into growth areas of the economy – regions and occupations
Cyclical, demand-deficient	Government increase in its own spending in times of recession; lower business taxes to reduce costs and encourage employment of more labour

The more serious the type of unemployment, the more it will cost the government to provide a cure. The job-creation scheme in Bihar, India (see photo opposite) shows how unemployed people can be given a purpose and earn an income while carrying out work of national importance, in this case a scheme to protect valuable agricultural land from flooding. A similar scheme in Trinidad in the West Indies ensures that roads and verges are kept clean.

Governments need to identify the cause of unemployment (see section 4.7.3) in order to deal with it effectively. If it is a result of job seekers not having enough information about job opportunities, the government can create job centres and job noticeboards, maybe online. If it results from too few workers with the right skills, the government can subsidise or run job-creation schemes.

KEY POINTS

1 Full employment occurs when almost everyone who wants a job has one.
2 Economists feel that a small amount of unemployment may be helpful to an economy.
3 The government can use a range of policies to try to create full employment, depending on the type of unemployment.

SUMMARY QUESTIONS

1 How would you define:
   a full employment
   b the unemployment rate?
2 Outline three major problems of not being at the point of full employment.
3 Describe three policy measures that the government can employ to deal with long-term unemployment.

DID YOU KNOW?

Structural unemployment involves major changes in the industrial structure of a country – some industries decline and others grow. Cyclical unemployment occurs when there is a general decline in demand across the economy. Seasonal unemployment reflects the change in demand for workers in response to seasonal changes, especially in agriculture and tourism. Technological unemployment refers to a situation where workers lose their jobs as a result of technological progress and development. Frictional unemployment refers to a situation where workers are temporarily out of work while they are searching for another job.

DID YOU KNOW?

The government's main aims in seeking to secure full employment are to:
- maximise the use of resources in the economy
- minimise human suffering, poverty and potential social unrest arising from people being out of work.

4.7.3 Causes of unemployment

> **TOPIC GUIDANCE**
>
> Students should be able to:
> - discuss the causes of unemployment.

Machines taking jobs away from humans is an example of technological unemployment

> **STUDY TIP**
>
> It is important you understand that the unemployed are included in the working population.

> **ACTIVITY**
>
> Identify the current rate of unemployment in your country. How does this compare with figures for your region and for the world? Study news reports to get the figures for your country. Do newspaper reports suggest any of the causes for unemployment? As a group, collect monthly statistics for unemployment in your country and display these on a poster in your classroom.

What is unemployment?

As we have seen, employment usually refers to the use and payment of labour. Unemployment typically occurs when people who want to work are not able to find jobs.

Measuring unemployment

The International Labour Organization (ILO), an agency of the United Nations, defines unemployed people as those who are:

- without a job, but who want a job and have actively sought work in the last four weeks and are available to start work in the next two weeks
- out of work, have found a job and are waiting to start it in the next two weeks.

There are two major statistics to look at when examining unemployment:

- The total number of unemployed people in an economy: is this rising or falling over time?
- The unemployment rate: this rate measures the percentage of the working population who are unemployed. Note that the 'working population' consists of those with jobs as well as those who are unemployed. A key question is whether this rate is rising or falling over time.

What causes unemployment?

Unemployment and inflation are two of the most serious economic problems. It is not surprising that governments pay so much attention to indicators that measure unemployment.

Unemployment is caused by a range of factors, some of which are more harmful than others in that they affect more people and have a longer-term impact on the economy. Figure 4.7.3.1 shows the range of unemployment types: the factors that cause them are explained below.

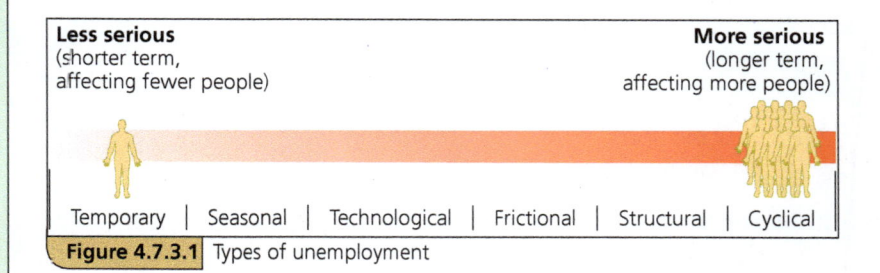

Less serious (shorter term, affecting fewer people) — **More serious** (longer term, affecting more people)

Temporary | Seasonal | Technological | Frictional | Structural | Cyclical

Figure 4.7.3.1 Types of unemployment

Temporary unemployment

Temporary unemployment is short-term, occurring usually while people are leaving one job to go to another, or perhaps when they are leaving school or university before going on to work.

Seasonal unemployment

Seasonal unemployment occurs in countries where there are distinct seasons and harvest times. For part of the year there will be plenty of jobs, such as harvesting sugar cane or picking fruit and vegetables. In the rainy season or winter, fewer jobs will be available.

Technological unemployment

New technology frequently replaces older methods that might have required more labour. For example, the use of tractors and giant harvesting equipment on modern farms has reduced the demand for agricultural labour. Automatic bottling, canning and packaging equipment has reduced the need for factory labour. However, new technology also helps to create new jobs by leading to economic growth. Computer technology has taken away the need for many factory workers, but it has created new opportunities for office workers and people setting up small businesses from home.

Frictional unemployment

Frictional unemployment occurs when the market system does not work as smoothly as it should – as its name suggests, there are **frictions** in it. This sort of unemployment occurs when there is a mismatch between the demand for, and the supply of, labour. This might occur when employers are trying to recruit highly skilled construction workers but too few workers have been trained with the skills required.

Another cause of frictional unemployment might be **search** unemployment. This occurs when workers who have lost their previous jobs are searching for new ones, but are unable to find them because there is too little information about availability.

Structural unemployment

Structural unemployment arises when there are longer-term changes in the economy, affecting specific industries, regions and occupations. In section 4.7.1 we saw that one of the main structural changes in economies has been the move away from primary and secondary industry to services. This has led to rural and urban poverty in areas where agriculture and the manufacturing industry are in decline.

Cyclical unemployment

On a larger scale, a major cause of unemployment across the globe is cyclical unemployment, also called **demand-deficient** unemployment. This is unemployment resulting from a substantial fall in aggregate demand that affects the economy as a whole.

Dealing with unemployment

Because there are many causes of unemployment, as shown in Figure 4.7.3.1 on the different types of unemployment, governments need to identify cures – that is, policies to deal with them. The table in section 4.7.2 suggests some possible cures. The more serious the type of unemployment, the more it will cost the government to provide a cure.

DID YOU KNOW?

In Mauritius the sugar cane harvest depends on weather conditions. Once the hurricane season starts (usually in December) there are fewer available jobs in this industry.

KEY POINTS

1 'Unemployment' refers to the situation of people seeking work who are unable to find a job.

2 Some of the causes of unemployment are more serious and long term than others.

3 Structural and cyclical unemployment are the most deep-seated causes of long-term unemployment.

SUMMARY QUESTIONS

1 What type of unemployment is caused by:
   a the decline of an industry
   b the end of the agricultural harvest?

2 What is the difference between the level of unemployment and the rate of unemployment?

3 Why is structural unemployment likely to have long-term consequences?

4.7.4 Consequences of unemployment

TOPIC GUIDANCE

Students should be able to:
- discuss the consequences of unemployment.

Unemployed people queuing for work in the US. Recent studies in the US link unemployment with increased levels of stress, crime and people losing a sense of self-worth

DID YOU KNOW?

The International Labour Organization classifies some workers as 'vulnerable'. They are poorly paid and often work for employers who do not apply employment laws. They are particularly at risk in periods of economic recession or when they try to press for their employment rights.

STUDY TIP

Make sure that you are able to discuss the various consequences of unemployment.

Who suffers from unemployment?

High or rising levels of unemployment create consequences for:
- people who are unemployed
- the communities in which they live
- businesses
- the government
- the economy.

People who are unemployed

The United Nations Convention on Human Rights lists the right to work as an essential human right:

> Everyone has the right to work, to free choice of employment, to just and favourable conditions of work and to protection against unemployment.

As well as providing income for a wage earner and his or her family, work brings a sense of self-worth from playing a role in society, and a sense of satisfaction and achievement, particularly when the work is enjoyable and challenging.

Unemployment means that people losing their job have all the privileges and benefits of being part of the workforce taken away. In some countries, it is possible to claim unemployment pay based on contributions made during the time at work. However, in many countries, this right does not exist.

Large numbers of people losing work through **cyclical unemployment** can lead to widespread poverty and hardship (unemployed people are more likely to suffer from stress and illness and have lower life expectancy). Cyclical unemployment was a particular feature of the 1920s and 1930s and, more recently, occurred in the global recession of 2007–09.

CASE STUDY | The impact of unemployment on individuals in the US

Studies in the US show some of the harmful effects of unemployment. The most obvious effect is the inability to pay bills and meet financial commitments, such as mortgage payments on a house. In the US, health insurance is often tied to having a job, so without a job medical bills can build up rapidly. Unemployment insurance in the US is unlikely to pay more than half of what a worker would have earned in wages.

Without a job, individuals lose contact with fellow workers and lack a sense of purpose for many hours a day. A further damaging effect is a lack of self-esteem. Studies show that unemployment leads to rising crime, suicide and bad health.

Questions

1. What impact is unemployment likely to have on a person's savings?
2. What are the consequences of being unemployed for someone who becomes ill in the US?
3. Why might unemployment lower a person's self-esteem?
4. How are the problems of being unemployed in the US likely to be similar for unemployed people in your own country?

ACTIVITY

Carry out some personal research using older relatives and friends to find out what impact unemployment has had in your area, either today or in the past. Find out what impact this had on local people and the local community. Write a report to present to the class.

The communities in which they live

Areas of high unemployment often have poorer facilities, e.g. there are fewer shops and recreational facilities. There is an increased likelihood of social problems, such as higher crime rates and drug abuse. Businesses often play a major part in supporting community activities. For example, the US car manufacturer, General Motors, plays a prominent part in supporting local orchestras, sponsoring sports teams and providing educational scholarships for needy students in the areas in which it operates.

Businesses

Increased unemployment has an effect on business known as a **ripple** or **multiplier effect**. This means that as unemployment increases, people have less income to spend and so businesses make less money from sales. Some businesses close down, others reduce the size of their labour force. In 2009, General Motors closed down many of its car plants in the US because of falling demand for cars during a major recession. The multiplier effect was that other factories supplying General Motors with engine systems and other components had in turn to lay off workers or shut down completely.

The government

When unemployment is rising, ideally the government should increase its spending. It can set up job-creation projects, perhaps to reduce youth and long-term unemployment. Unfortunately, however, government revenues fall in periods of recession. More unemployed people mean that fewer people are paying taxes and more are claiming benefits. As businesses start to close down or make reduced profits, they pay less in corporation tax (profits tax) to the government. Tax revenue then falls, spending rises and there is a greater likelihood of a budget deficit.

The economy

All the above problems are likely to damage an economy. Rising unemployment has a downward effect on the trade cycle. This in turn creates cyclical unemployment. When major businesses start to lay off workers there is a much wider multiplier effect on the economy. Initially, the local economy is affected, but this quickly spreads to the regional economy, where component suppliers lose steady orders, and then further to the national and even the international economy.

KEY POINTS

1. High and rising unemployment has a negative effect on many groups within the economy, e.g. the unemployed and the communities in which they live.
2. The government loses revenue in times of rising unemployment, making it more difficult for it to combat the effects of unemployment.
3. Rising unemployment on a large scale has a negative effect on the trade cycle.

SUMMARY QUESTIONS

1. Who else suffers from unemployment in addition to the unemployed?
2. Describe two ways in which governments can lose revenue when unemployment is rising.
3. What effect does rising unemployment have on the wider economy?

4.8 Inflation and deflation

4.8.1 The retail prices index and inflation

> **TOPIC GUIDANCE**
>
> Students should be able to:
>
> - describe how a retail prices index (RPI) and consumer prices index (CPI) are calculated.

Average prices are measured by governments using a **retail prices index (RPI)** or the **consumer prices index (CPI)**. These indices measure changes in average prices over a year. Measurements are made by recording the prices of goods and services that most people will be expected to buy, or put in an imaginary shopping basket. Government statisticians decide what goods to include in this basket. This list should be updated to take account of changing spending patterns.

Most governments measure prices in similar ways. This section uses the example of Kenya. The examples show some of the difficulties involved in accurately measuring average price changes.

A basket of goods

The imaginary shopping basket for a typical family in Kenya contains, for example, milk, bottled water, sugar, tea, meat, cooking fuel, school books and mobile phone charges. The contents included in the basket are fixed in the short term, but the prices of individual goods change.

Shopping in a supermarket in Kenya. A CPI measures general increases in the prices of a basket of goods. Changes in food prices are particularly important in Kenya as this is the largest item of household expenditure

> **DID YOU KNOW?**
>
> Food prices (especially for rice, maize, flour and coffee) have a prominent weighting in the prices index in Kenya. When they rise, this will have a major impact on inflation as measured by the prices index.

Figure 4.8.1.1 A helpful way of thinking about the prices index is to imagine the contents of a shopping basket bought by a typical household

A prices index uses a single number to indicate changes in prices of a number of different goods. This is calculated by comparing the price of buying the basket of goods with a starting period, called the **base year**. The base year is given a figure of 100. So if the average price of goods in the basket today is 10 per cent higher than the base year, the prices index will be 110. Changes in average prices (the cost of the basket of goods) can be measured on a monthly, quarterly or annual basis.

Inflation

Inflation is a persistent or sustained rise in the general level of prices over a period of time. So not every price will rise, but average prices will. The effect of this rise on ordinary people will vary, depending on what they buy.

Price inflation in Kenya is measured by the Kenya National Bureau of Statistics (KNBS). One of its responsibilities is to decide on the 216 goods and services to be included in the prices index, or 'basket'. The selection is made after carrying out a survey of spending patterns – that is, what most people in Kenya are buying. From time to time the items in the basket will change: in 2013 the basket was 'widened' to include airtime, cellular phones, parking charges and boda boda (bicycle taxi) fares.

Statistics covering the prices of all items in the CPI are gathered each month in 10 areas of the capital, Nairobi, and 15 other price collection zones across Kenya selected for their high expenditure levels.

Weighting

The weighting is a figure given to a category of goods according to the percentage of a typical household's income that is spent on it. Statisticians have found that typical families in Kenya spend 36 per cent of their income on food, so this is given a weighting of 36 per cent in the prices index.

> **CASE STUDY** | Changing inflation in Kenya
>
> In 2013, the Kenya National Bureau of Statistics reduced the weighting attached to food in the national retail prices index to reflect the fact that food plays a less significant part in household budgets than in recent years. The immediate impact was to lower the recorded level of consumer price inflation at a time when the price of a number of food products such as maize, flour and sugar had been rising, partly as a result of poor harvests in Northern Kenya and because of rising world food prices.
>
> #### Questions
>
> 1. Why do you think that reducing the weighting of food in the prices index would have the impact of lowering recorded inflation rates?
> 2. Why do you think that changes in food prices are so important to people living in Kenya?
> 3. Are some Kenyans likely to have been more affected than others by the high inflation figure? Explain how.

> **STUDY TIP**
>
> Make sure that are able to give a full and accurate definition of inflation.

> **DID YOU KNOW?**
>
> The 'average annual' rate of inflation is computed as a percentage change of a 12-month average of the CPI. The 'year-on-year' inflation rate is calculated as a percentage change of the CPI between the current month, e.g. April 2018, and the same month a year ago, e.g. April 2017.

> **STUDY TIP**
>
> Remember that the proportion of income spent on different goods or services will vary a great deal. This is why goods and services are given different 'weights' in a basket to reflect the proportions of income spent on the various products.

> **DID YOU KNOW?**
>
> From time to time, weighting of items in the basket needs to be adjusted. For example, in most (if not all) countries the more frequent use of mobile phones and cellular phones has meant that the weight attached to spending on mobile phone and cellular phone use has increased significantly.

Calculating average price changes

Calculating average price changes will give the rate of inflation. The calculation involves two sets of data:

- the prices data (collected each month)
- the weights (representing patterns of spending, updated each year).

With this data it is possible to construct a weighted prices index. A consumer spending survey has been carried out that shows the percentage spend of typical households in an imaginary country. The table on the left shows how the percentage spend forms the basis of the weighting given to the categories.

Category	Percentage spend	Weight
Food	40	4
Clothing	20	2
Transport	10	1
Other household goods	30	3
Total	100	10

The weighting for food is twice that for clothing, because typical households spend twice as much on food as on clothes

The next stage is to identify price changes in each of these product categories. Let us suppose that surveys carried out in supermarkets, shops and other retail outlets across the country show the following changes since the base year.

- Food prices have increased by 20 per cent.
- Clothing has increased by 10 per cent.
- Transport has fallen by 10 per cent.
- Other household goods have increased by 30 per cent.

To find out the **average change in prices** we need to take account of each of these price changes in terms of how much consumers spend on that item (the weight). For example, the increase in food prices of 20 per cent will have a major impact on average prices because 40 per cent of household income is spent on food. In contrast, even though transport prices have fallen by 10 per cent, this will have a smaller impact on average prices because consumers only spend a tenth of their income on transport.

To create a **weighted price index** we need to multiply the weight for each item by the prices index for that item. This is shown in the table below.

Product category	Weight price index	Weighted price index
Food	4 × 120	480
Clothing	2 × 110	220
Transport	1 × 90	90
Other goods	3 × 130	390
Total		1,180

Finally, divide the weighted price index by the total number of weights:

$$\frac{1180}{10} = 118$$

This shows that prices have risen on average by 18 per cent – that is, from the base year figure of 100 to 118 in the new year.

> **STUDY TIP**
>
> Make sure that you understand this difference: the prices index shows how much the price of that item has risen by compared with a base year of 100; the weighted price index shows the prices index times the weight attached to the product category.

Problems involved in using a prices index

The prices index is designed to show general increases in prices and how they affect consumers. There can be some problems, however, with its use as an indicator.

- The index does not necessarily show how price changes affect typical consumers. For example, in Kenya the weighting attached to food in the index was reduced from 40 per cent to 36 per cent in 2013. However, food purchases for a poor person in Kenya may make up 80 per cent or more of their spending.
- The index makes comparisons with a base year. However, if prices were low at the base year, the comparison may exaggerate the price rise. If prices were high at the base year, the index comparison may suggest that subsequent price changes have been low (especially if the base year is at the top or bottom of the trade cycle fluctuation).
- Some items, e.g. fuel and food, are subject to quite a lot of variation.

For indicators to provide useful information, it is essential that the statistics gathered are accurate.

> **DID YOU KNOW?**
> In Kenya separate indices are calculated for low-income households and medium- to high-income households in recognition of the way that they purchase different baskets of goods each week.

> **STUDY TIP**
> Make sure that you are able to discuss both the benefits and the limitations of using a price index.

ACTIVITY

Working in a group, find out the monthly inflation rate of your country, or a large country in your part of the world. You should find this information published each month by your national statistical office. With your teacher's help, try to find the rate on the internet or in a national newspaper. Plot the current rate on a large chart and display this in your classroom to monitor ongoing changes. Then try to find the inflation rate of another country and compare it with your country's rate.

SUMMARY QUESTIONS

1 What items are likely to be included in a basket of goods bought by a typical consumer in your country? Which categories of items should be given the greatest weights?

2 What two sets of data are required to calculate a CPI?

3 Why is it necessary periodically to alter the list of items included in a country's 'shopping basket' of items included in the CPI?

KEY POINTS

1 Inflation is a persistent or sustained rise in the general level of prices over a period of time.

2 A prices index can be used to measure price increases by reducing prices to a single number starting at 100 in a base year.

3 A prices index measures changes in an average basket of goods bought by a typical consumer or family.

4 Weighting items in the basket makes it possible to take account of the relative importance of spending on different items when measuring average price changes.

4.8.2 Causes of inflation

> **TOPIC GUIDANCE**
>
> Students should be able to:
> - discuss the causes of inflation and how it can be caused by changes in pricing.

Rising oil and energy costs are a major cause of cost-push inflation that affects many businesses across an economy

> **STUDY TIP**
>
> Make sure you understand that inflation can be the result of more than one cause.

> **DID YOU KNOW?**
>
> If wage increases are not matched by higher labour productivity – in other words, if the workers do not produce more goods to sell – production costs will rise.

Causes of inflation

A cause is a factor that has an effect on something else. For example, a cause of inflation might be that people increase the amount of money they spend. The effect might be an increase in prices.

Inflation is usually the result of a number of causes. It may occur when a number of prices rise at the same time, say for oil, food and housing or rented accommodation.

In examining inflation, economists distinguish between **cost-push** and **demand-pull** factors. These are explained below.

Cost-push factors

Cost-push refers to the costs that a business has to meet, such as wages and raw materials. As costs rise, the business will often pass these on to consumers by increasing the prices for the product they are selling.

Food costs

In section 4.8.1 we saw that 36 per cent of the weighting in Kenya's consumer prices index (CPI) is allocated to food. In the years 2000–13 the food supply in Kenya has been badly affected by droughts in the north of the country.

At the same time, the price of basic foodstuffs, including the price of cereal crops on global markets, has been increasing. There is increased competition for cereal crops as a result of the growth of huge economies such as China and India, and also as a result of cereals being used as alternative **biofuels**. Whatever the cause, high food prices lead to higher costs for other businesses.

Raw material costs

As the pace of development picks up in the world economy, with more and more countries picking up their long-term average growth rates, the costs of raw materials such as steel, copper, oil and gas have risen. These raw materials are at the centre of modern economies, so as their prices rise, there is an effect on many other prices.

Wage costs

Wage costs are another major cause of cost-push inflation. If food and fuel prices rise for workers in Kenya, they will press their employers for higher wages. If, however, the wage increase is not matched by higher labour productivity – in other words, if the workers do not produce more goods to sell – production costs will rise.

Land costs

Land prices in many countries have risen as land is used more intensively. For example, the Ethiopian government has granted long-term leases to overseas companies to use land for large-scale agricultural production of grain and other crops. Land is also increasingly being used for housing as the world population increases. This leads to land price inflation.

Exchange rate costs

Changes in the exchange rate between currencies can have a major impact on business costs. For example, if the Kenyan Shilling (KES) loses value against the South African Rand (ZAR), people in Kenya will have to pay more for imported goods, oil and food from South Africa.

Demand-pull inflation

Demand-pull inflation occurs when rising demand pushes up the prices of goods. This happens when people have more to spend. This is most likely when an economy is near to full employment. Businesses compete for resources and this will lead to a rise in prices.

> **CASE STUDY** | **Monetary inflation**
>
> Monetary inflation provides a good explanation of demand-pull inflation. It illustrates clearly the impact of economic indicators on the economy.
>
> The idea of monetary inflation is not new. One of the best explanations was provided by the American economists Milton Friedman and Anna Schwartz, *A Monetary History of the United States, 1867–1960*.
>
> Friedman and Schwartz argued that if governments increase the quantity of money, there is more to spend on new goods. If, however, there are not enough goods being produced for the people who want to buy them, manufacturers will be able to put up prices. The authors concluded that price levels are linked to the quantity of money available. In their words, 'inflation is always and everywhere a monetary phenomenon'.
>
> This work was published in 1971 and became a model of good practice in using detailed statistical analysis over a long period (in this case in the US) to make the link between prices and the quantity of money.
>
> **Questions**
>
> 1 What connection did Friedman and Schwartz identify between the quantity of money and the level of prices?
>
> 2 What statistics did the authors study and use to make their claim?
>
> 3 How can monetary inflation also be described as demand-pull inflation?
>
> 4 With what economic indicators were Friedman and Schwartz primarily concerned?

> **DID YOU KNOW?**
>
> Demand-pull inflation can result from an increase in the money supply (monetary inflation) if the government increases the quantity of money available in the economy, e.g. to finance increased government expenditure. When the money supply increases at a faster rate than the supply of goods in the economy this will lead to a rise in prices (after a time lag). See the case study below to understand how monetary inflation results from an increase in the quantity of money in circulation relative to the volume of goods available for purchase.

> **KEY POINTS**
>
> 1 Causes of inflation can be split into cost-push and demand-pull factors.
>
> 2 Rising costs include agricultural prices, raw material costs, labour costs and weakening exchange rates.
>
> 3 Demand-pull occurs when demand increases and is usually associated with monetary inflation.

> **SUMMARY QUESTIONS**
>
> 1 Define cost-push inflation, explaining one type of cost-push inflation.
>
> 2 How is an increase in the quantity of money in the economy likely to affect price levels?
>
> 3 When the exchange value of a country's currency falls, how is this likely to impact on import prices?

4.8.3 Consequences of inflation

> **TOPIC GUIDANCE**
>
> Students should be able to:
> - discuss the consequences of inflation and its effect on pricing.

> **DID YOU KNOW?**
>
> The reverse of inflation is **deflation**, when prices start to fall. Deflation (negative inflation) discourages businesses, who may restrict supply to markets (see section 4.8.4).

Maize grain is a major staple food in many countries. An increase in the price of maize and other food staples can have a major impact on the livelihoods of the poorer members of society

> **STUDY TIP**
>
> Remember that inflation can have varying effects on different groups of people in an economy.

Inflation is a sustained rise in the general level of prices over a period of time. Mild inflation of 1–2 per cent is not particularly harmful because it encourages producers to supply more to the market. When inflation rises more quickly it can disrupt economic decision-making because it becomes difficult for businesses, governments and even ordinary people to make plans. For example, unpredictable rises in prices make it difficult for businesses to plan ahead when making contracts because the real value of what they receive, e.g. when they supply goods on credit, will fall.

The impact of inflation on the wider economy is that as prices rise the goods produced within the economy become less competitive on an international scale, resulting in a deterioration of the balance of trade (particularly as a result of a rise in imports which are now cheaper and a fall in exports which are now more expensive on international markets). Inflation therefore results in a loss of value of units of currency.

There are many historical examples of rapid inflation. When prices rise rapidly governments are often tempted to print more money. Where the quantity of money increases, people lose confidence in it and businesses push up prices because they see money as being less valuable. The government is forced to print more money, but it becomes worthless. In the first decade of the 21st century, the government of Zimbabwe printed so much money that citizens started exchanging goods and services rather than using money to make payments.

Who loses out in a period of inflation?

Those members of the economy who have the greatest ability (power) to raise their own prices and incomes, such as producers of goods who have monopoly powers or labour that is in short supply, are likely to suffer least in a period of inflation. In contrast, other members of society are less able to raise their prices and incomes, e.g. employees in occupations that are not represented by trade unions, or small producers of goods where there is a lot of competition from rival producers. The following table and paragraphs show how inflation affects people in different circumstances.

Income level	Effect of inflation
Low income	People can afford fewer goods, including basic necessities. People resort to buying the lowest-priced products available.
Fixed income	There is a fall in real income (what can be afforded with money coming in). Money loses value, so people on fixed incomes save less and spend more.
High income	There is less income to spend on some luxury items. People may, therefore, switch to cheaper alternatives and cut back on some extravagant purchases. They may save less and spend more.

The poor

Poor people are the first to suffer in times of inflation. For example, in Kenya, an important part of people's diet is maize grain. In recent years there have been several droughts, reducing the supply, and so raising the price, of maize. Drought has hit Kenya every two or three years and this has forced the country to buy expensive imports to meet its people's needs. This has pushed up the rate of inflation.

People on fixed incomes

People on fixed incomes are those whose incomes remain the same, or nearly the same, during periods of inflation. They may be poorly paid workers who are not in a trade union, or pensioners. Workers who are unskilled and so have less bargaining power, such as office cleaners and car park attendants, also suffer in times of inflation. Skilled workers in well-paid jobs may be able to bargain with their employers to receive wage increases. This is often the case for people who work for the government: civil servants, teachers, the police and armed forces.

Savers

Many people like to save some money each month for future needs. Their savings may be deposited in a financial institution or kept in a safe place. However, during a period of inflation, savings lose their value. When the money comes to be spent it is not worth as much as when it was first saved. Similarly, money saved in a pension scheme can lose value by the time the saver becomes old enough to draw on it.

Businesses

A lot of business activity involves supplying goods on credit, perhaps to other businesses. Payment may be required one month, three months or six months later. When money starts to lose value quickly, businesses become reluctant to supply on credit. Therefore, inflation is very harmful to business activity.

In contrast, people who borrow money in a period of inflation are likely to gain. When they come to pay back the sum they have borrowed, the value of their repayment will have fallen.

Mild inflation

As mentioned above, a small level of inflation is not necessarily a bad thing. Gently rising prices encourage businesses to supply more to the market and help to increase profits. In fact Milton Friedman argued that the government should increase the quantity of money. However, this should be done in a planned way that anticipates growth in production in the economy.

Hyperinflation

The term 'hyperinflation' refers to periods of high and accelerating inflation which can have a dramatic effect on destabilising an economy. When prices rise at accelerating rates people lose confidence in money. Hyperinflation is often caused by war, or natural disasters such as famine, when the government resorts to printing more money. As the quantity of money rises while the availability of goods falls, then prices can only rise.

> **ACTIVITY**
>
> Argentina and Turkey have both experienced rapid inflation. Carry out some internet research to find out when these periods of inflation occurred and how the governments in the two countries managed to stabilise prices. Try to find out what caused the inflation in these countries.

> **KEY POINTS**
>
> 1 In a period of inflation the economy becomes less stable. Groups such as the poor and those on fixed incomes suffer most.
>
> 2 Rapidly rising prices can quickly destroy business confidence and the willingness of business people to supply goods on credit.
>
> 3 A mild level of inflation can have a positive effect on business confidence.

> **SUMMARY QUESTIONS**
>
> 1 Which two of the following groups would suffer least in a period of high inflation: savers pensioners, poor households, employees whose skills are in great demand, borrowers, or the government? Explain your answers.
>
> 2 Explain why a period of very mild inflation may not be harmful for an economy.
>
> 3 Explain why high inflation can be damaging for long-term business planning.

4.8.4 Causes and consequences of deflation

TOPIC GUIDANCE

Students should be able to:
- discuss the causes of deflation in relation to pricing
- discuss the consequences of deflation in relation to pricing.

DID YOU KNOW?

A distinction is sometimes made between benign and malign deflation. Benign deflation, resulting from increased output of goods, brings with it the benefits of more goods at cheaper prices. Malign deflation in contrast is associated with falling demand, falling production, and rising social problems e.g. resulting from poverty and unemployment.

DID YOU KNOW?

Deflation can be as harmful as rapidly rising prices. When prices are falling business income from sales falls. Businesses become reluctant to invest and they reduce the number of employees.

Deflation

Deflation refers to a general fall in the level of prices over a period of time. Typically, this will occur when there is a general fall in demand for goods, e.g. when people are spending less through uncertainties over rising unemployment. This is likely to be harmful to the economy as businesses will start to lay off workers and reduce levels of production.

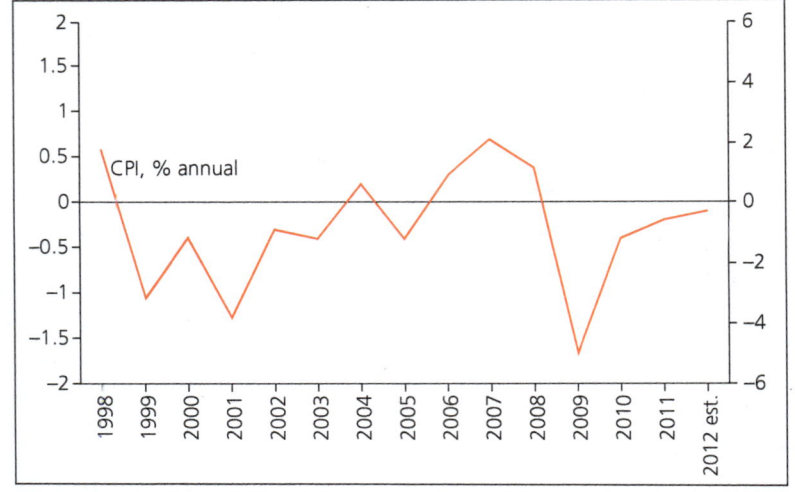

Consumer prices index (CPI) deflation in Japan over a 15-year period. Source: www.mauldineconomics.com

Causes of deflation

There are four main causes of deflation.

- It occurs as a result of a decrease in the money supply in an economy. If the quantity of money in an economy falls while the quantity of goods stays the same or increases common sense tells us that there would be a fall in price. For each good that is for sale there is a smaller quantity of money available to purchase the goods.

- It occurs as a result of an increase in the supply of goods in the economy (at a faster rate than the increase in the quantity of money). With improvements in technology more goods can be produced. If the money supply in the economy doesn't increase in line with the availability of goods then this will also lead to deflation – that is, falling prices.

- It occurs as a result of a fall in the demand for goods. Our demand and supply analysis in Unit 2 showed that when the demand for a good shifts to the left while supply remains constant then prices will fall. The same logic can be applied to the demand and supply for goods in general. A general fall in the demand for goods, e.g. as a result of a recession, can lead to deflation.

- It occurs as a result of an increase in the demand for money. If people become more cautious and decide to save for the future they will prefer to hold money rather than spend it. The impact is to increase the demand for money and reduce the demand for goods – so prices may fall.

The consequences of deflation

Whether deflation is a problem for the economy, and for people, depends in some measure on the cause. For example, if it results from an increase in the supply of goods this will typically have beneficial effects as there will be more goods available at cheaper prices.

However, deflation can be damaging for the economy, for individual businesses and for members of the economy, for the following reasons.

- Consumers cut back on spending. They might do this because they have lost their jobs or are worried this will happen, or they anticipate prices will be lower in the future (so for example postpone purchasing an expensive consumer good).
- Profit margins fall. With falling demand, sales revenues and profits will fall, so that firms make cutbacks.
- Debts increase. People have less money so they are not able to pay back their debts, and their debts increase.
- Savings increase. People will save more and spend less, leading to an increasing spiral of deflation.

> **STUDY TIP**
>
> Make sure that you are able to distinguish clearly between inflation, which refers to rising prices, and deflation, which refers to falling prices.

CASE STUDY | Deflation in Japan

The Japanese deflation of the late 1990s illustrates some of the causes and consequences of deflation. This followed almost half a century of growth of the Japanese economy. However, by the late 1990s, Japanese exporters were faced with increased competition from low-wage-cost producers in South East Asia. As demand for Japanese products fell, companies were faced with falling prices, reduced sales and falling profits. They responded by laying off workers and making pay cuts. By 2000 unemployment in Japan had risen to 5 per cent (from 2 per cent 10 years earlier).

Up to that time many Japanese companies had offered their workers jobs for life but they now had to change this policy. As unemployment increased, so did the suicide rate, particularly among middle-aged men who were no longer able to support their families. The Japanese government reduced interest rates to almost zero to encourage people to borrow and spend with little success. They even made a handout of money to every one in Japan – but rather than spend, most people chose to save this extra income.

The Japanese economy has still not recovered fully from this period of deflation and economic growth continues to be slow. Interest rates are relatively low, and unemployment continues to be an issue.

Questions

1. Identify some of the causes of deflation in this case study.
2. Identify some of the consequences of deflation in this case study.

KEY POINTS

1. Deflation is a fall in the general level of prices.
2. The four main causes of deflation are: a decrease in money supply; an increase in the supply of goods; a fall in the demand for goods; an increase in the demand for money.
3. Consequences of deflation are falling demand for goods, falling sales, falling profits, increased layoff of labour, increased unemployment, reduced spending and rising debt.

SUMMARY QUESTIONS

1. What is the impact of a period of deflation on the prices of goods in an economy, the production of goods in an economy, and the general economic outlook in the economy?
2. In what circumstances is deflation desirable and in what circumstances is it undesirable for people and for the economy?
3. What similarities are there between some of the consequences of inflation and the consequences of deflation?

4.8.5 Policies to control inflation and deflation

TOPIC GUIDANCE

Students should be able to:
- describe the aims of the government policy of price stability.

Rising prices over time are a worry to the government – particularly when there is a general rise in prices, referred to as inflation

Price stability

When prices are stable it is easier for households, businesses and governments to make economic decisions. For example, if savers invest US$100 for a year expecting an interest rate of 5 per cent, they can expect to receive US$105 at the end of the year. If prices remain stable, US$105 at the end of the year should buy more than US$100 at the start of the year.

Inflation can be a major cause of concern for economists. It occurs when there is a general rise in the price of goods and services in the whole economy. Of course, not every price will rise, but average prices will. In many countries, average prices are measured by the government using the **consumer prices index** (**CPI**). (This is explained in section 4.8.1.)

Small increases in general prices are not a bad thing. Slowly rising prices encourage producers to supply more goods to the market. However, problems arise if prices start to rise more quickly, e.g. above 2 per cent per year, and when the changes in prices are unpredictable. It is in situations like this that prices become unstable.

The unpredictable nature of inflation makes life very difficult for government and business planning. Most businesses sell goods on credit. They supply now, expecting to be paid a given sum at a future date. However, inflation may reduce the value of the sum that is eventually paid. This makes businesses reluctant to supply goods on credit. In a similar way, each year governments set out a **national budget** showing the taxes to be raised for government spending. Inflation will reduce the value of some of the taxes received. A further problem caused by inflation is that when prices of domestic products rise they become less competitive when compared with imports.

The main reason that governments want price stability is to enable accurate planning. Price stability enables businesses to carry out their activity with more certainty.

DID YOU KNOW?

General increases in prices within an economy are worrying, particularly if changes are sudden and unpredictable. Economists agree that small and predictable rises can be a good thing because they encourage firms to produce more. For example, in 2018 the UK government target for inflation was 2 per cent. Rises above this would be unsettling for the economy.

STUDY TIP

You should understand why the government tries to create price stability, such as the types of policies it would use to deal with excessive inflation.

ACTIVITY

What is the current level of inflation in your country? Is it rising or falling? Can prices be described as stable or are they changing in an unpredictable way? Create a short report to present to the class, setting out the implications of price changes in your country. The report should show the impact of price changes for consumers, businesses and the government.

Government policy to create price stability

A **prices and incomes policy** is a set of measures by which the government sets prices and wages to create stability. There are a number of policies that can be implemented.

- **Direct control** of prices. The government can set prices for goods and impose limits on wage increases for public sector employees. The problems with doing this are as follows:
  - The price system no longer operates as an efficient system for signalling the preferences of consumers.
  - There may be conflict between the government and businesses that want to raise prices, and trade unions that want increases in wages.
- The government could reduce its own spending and raise taxes in a period of inflation. This would work in the following way:
  - Reduced government spending lowers the demand for goods in the economy, leading to falls in prices.
  - Increased taxes mean that taxpayers' incomes fall. They have less to spend, leading to a fall in demand, and a fall in prices.
- Controlling the **quantity of money** available for spending in the economy. In section 3.1.3 we saw how the central bank controls the supply of money in the economy, and the interest rate. By printing less money, and raising the cost of borrowing money (raising the interest rate), it is possible to discourage people from borrowing and spending.

The central bank can also impose restrictions on other banks, requiring them to reduce their lending. This then reduces the quantity of money available for spending, which can also reduce price inflation.

KEY POINTS

1. Quickly rising and unpredictable changes in prices unsettle an economy.
2. In periods of inflation, government and businesses find it more difficult to calculate how much they will receive at future dates from creditors.
3. Inflation makes an economy's goods less competitive.
4. Governments can create price stability through implementing a range of policies.

STUDY TIP

Make sure you understand that there may be conflicts between different government objectives. For example, policies to reduce the rate of unemployment in a country could lead to a rise in the rate of inflation.

DID YOU KNOW?

Government policies for deflation (a general fall in prices and spending) are the reverse of measures to control inflation. In a period of deflation the government will seek to stimulate demand in the economy through fiscal policies (increasing government spending relative to taxes), monetary policy (lowering interest rates and increasing the money supply), and supply-side measures, such as providing incentives for businesses to invest and creating more competitive markets through deregulation.

SUMMARY QUESTIONS

1. What is inflation and how can it make prices unstable?
2. What direct actions can the government take to control prices?
3. How can the government reduce demand in an economy in order to manage prices?

Unit 4 — Test yourself

SECTION 1: Multiple-choice questions

Each question has ONE correct answer.

1. Why might a government take responsibility for production in an economy?
   a. To make a profit
   b. To widen consumer choice
   c. To supply merit goods
   d. To supply demerit goods

2. Which of the following is a public sector employee?
   a. A bank cashier
   b. A taxi driver
   c. A private school teacher
   d. A tax collector

3. What may be a disadvantage of a high rate of economic growth for a government?
   a. Increasing rate of employment
   b. Increasing tax revenues
   c. Increasing risk of inflation
   d. Increasing wages

4. Which of the following is NOT a method governments may use to decrease unemployment?
   a. Increase unemployment benefit
   b. Reduce the rate of interest
   c. Introduce worker training schemes
   d. Reduce corporation tax

5. Which of the following policies might be used to control inflation?
   a. Increase government spending
   b. Increase interest rates
   c. Increase the money supply
   d. Decrease direct taxation

6. Which of the following is NOT an example of fiscal policy?
   a. Provision of merit goods
   b. Taxation on polluting businesses
   c. Lowering interest rates
   d. Progressive income tax

7. What might be a government method of income redistribution?
   a. Environmental taxation
   b. Control of the supply of money
   c. Regressive sales tax
   d. Progressive direct taxation

8. Which of the following would indicate a balance of payments deficit on a current account?
   a. Revenue from taxation greater than government spending
   b. Value of imports greater than value of exports
   c. Government spending greater than revenue from taxation
   d. Value of exports greater than value of imports

9. Which of the following is NOT an example of a government regulation on business?
   a. Display of health warnings on cigarettes
   b. Payment of minimum wage
   c. Display of information on food labels
   d. Payment of income tax

10. A government may seek to limit monopoly power of a big company because:
    a. They benefit from economies of scale
    b. They use up many resources
    c. They may exploit consumers
    d. They pay higher wages to workers

SECTION 2

Country B is a medium-sized developed nation, whose economic and business environment is dominated by tertiary businesses, many in banking and insurance. The public sector in the country is also very important, as tax rates are high and welfare benefits very generous. The government provides a wide range of health and education services and promotes high public awareness of healthy eating and environmental issues. Taxation on products such as cigarettes is high, leading to high prices, but this has not reduced demand to any great extent.

- The population is fairly static, only growing at approximately 0.2 per cent a year; there is a net emigration to other countries of young professional workers seeking high-paying jobs elsewhere.
- The unemployment rate is low; there are 2.6 million unemployed out of a labour force of 30 million. There are unfilled job vacancies for low-skilled workers in the public sector.
- Consumers are increasingly demanding healthy food products and there is an increasing interest in energy-saving products, such as light bulbs.
- The government of Country B has recently decided to subsidise IT training for older workers, via a public sector training agency.
- Energy is becoming a major issue as the country is reliant on an unreliable neighbouring nation. The government is considering a plan to build a nuclear power station, with the potential capacity to supply the entire country's needs.

1 a Explain what is meant by *public sector* and give an example from the text. (2)

  b Explain why 'net migration' may lead to a 'static population'. (2)

2 Calculate the unemployment rate for the country. (2)

3 Discuss whether government provision of essential services will always lead to the best-quality service for the population of Country B. (6)

4 a Explain, using a diagram, why high taxes should lead to a decrease in quantity demanded for a product or service. (2)

  b Discuss the possible reasons why high taxation may not have led to a decrease in the consumption of alcohol and cigarettes. (6)

5 Using the example of government provision of training and education in Country B, explain why this is an example of intervention to correct market failure. (4)

6 Using information from the text and the concept of social costs and benefits, discuss the development plans for the nuclear power station in Country B. (6)

Total: 30 marks

SECTION 3

Country A is a medium-sized nation, whose economy has been growing at an average rate of 5 per cent per year for the last five years. The population is growing at around 3 per cent per year and unemployment is low, and falling. Out of a total workforce of 12 million citizens, only 600 000 people are currently recorded as unemployed and seeking work. Incomes and prices are rising and the consumers of Country B are increasingly demanding imported products. The government of Country B has the following economic objectives for the next few years:

- Inflation to be low, at a maximum of 3 per cent per year
- Economic growth steady at 4 per cent
- Maintain a balance of payments current account surplus
- Redistribute income in order to help the poorest families

1 a Explain why the government of Country B may have set the objective of low inflation. (4)

b Explain, with the use of a diagram, why inflation in Country A may increase due to higher wages. (6)

c Suggest ONE policy the government of Country A may implement to control inflation. (4)

d Discuss whether measures to control inflation may have other negative consequences for the economy of Country A. (6)

2 a Using information in the text, calculate the unemployment rate for Country A. (4)

b Why might rising GDP lead to falling unemployment in Country A? (4)

c With the help of a diagram, explain why falling unemployment may lead to increasing inflation in Country A. (6)

d Discuss the extent to which 'full employment' may be a major objective for the government of Country A. (6)

3 a The government of Country A would like to redistribute income to help those on lower incomes. Explain why a government may have this objective. (4)

b Explain how a *progressive* tax system may help to redistribute income. Give an example. (6)

c The government of Country A subsidises the production of basic foodstuffs, such as milk and bread. Using a diagram, show how this may affect production levels and prices. (4)

d Discuss the ADVANTAGES and DISADVANTAGES of taxing higher-income earners at a higher rate to help pay for benefits for unemployed people in Country A. (6)

4 a Explain what is meant by a *balance of payments current account surplus*. (3)

b Explain why rising incomes may lead to higher demand for imported goods. (3)

c Describe TWO ways in which the government of Country A may protect domestic firms from foreign competition. (6)

d Considering the case study information and economic objectives of Country A, discuss the extent to which these aims may conflict with each other in the short term. (8)

Total: 80 marks

5 Economic development

This unit examines the nature of economic development. There are different perspectives about what constitutes development. Traditionally, in economics, development was seen as involving improvements in incomes and rising standards of living within a nation. However, today it is recognized that more sophisticated thinking is required, as being better off not only involves having more income but also better educational opportunities, improved healthcare and protection and improvement of the environment.

The unit therefore starts out by examining what is meant by living standards and different ways of measuring living standards. Next, the unit examines different definitions of poverty, what causes poverty and measures that can be taken to reduce poverty.

The size of the population globally, within nations and within regions, is a key determinant of living standards. The unit thus explores population growth, reasons for population growth and the differences between countries in demographic characteristics such as the age structure.

Finally the unit seeks to chart differences in development between countries including the causes and impacts of these differences. A key element of the unit is to use wider indicators such as the Human Development Indicators (HDIs) to contrast development in different countries.

TOPIC COVERAGE

Students will study the following topics:
- Indicators of living standards, e.g. Gross Domestic Product and Human Development Indicators
- Comparing living standards and income distribution
- Definition of absolute and relative poverty
- The causes of poverty
- Policies to alleviate policy and redistribute income
- The factors that affect population, e.g. birth rate, death rate, net migration
- Reasons for different rates of population growth in different countries
- Effects of changes in the size and structure of the population in different countries
- Differences in economic development in different countries. Causes and impacts of differences in income, e.g. productivity, investment, education and healthcare.

5.1 Living standards

5.1.1 Indicators of living standards

TOPIC GUIDANCE

Students should be able to:
- compare and contrast indicators of living standards, including real GDP per head and the Human Development Index (HDI).

Barbados ranks as 'high' in the Human Development Index (HDI) because of high income per head, long life expectancy and high rates of enrolment in schools coupled with high literacy rates

DID YOU KNOW?

An international dollar would in any given country pay for the same quantity of goods and services as in the US.

Standard of living

A person's standard of living refers to the level of material comfort that they are able to enjoy in terms of the goods and services which they can buy or use.

Making comparisons using GDP

In Unit 4 we saw that GDP measures the total value of goods produced in an economy in a given period of time. Until the 1970s, GDP per head was widely regarded to be a good measure of living standards.

The argument was that if an economy produced more goods, people in that country would become better off. GDP and GDP per head were regarded as good ways of measuring the economic growth of a country.

It might be claimed, therefore, that the economic indicator GDP would be a good way of:

- measuring the growth of economies over time
- making comparisons between levels of production, income and spending between countries.

CASE STUDY | Comparing countries

In 2017, the International Monetary Fund estimated the following ranking of the world's top 10 economies in terms of GDP.

Ranking	Economy	International $ millions
1	China	23 122 027
2	US	19 362 129
3	India	9 446 789
4	Japan	5 405 072
5	Germany	4 149 573
6	Russia	4 000 096
7	Indonesia	3 242 966
8	Brazil	3 219 129
9	UK	2 880 254
10	France	2 826 456

Questions

1. Why is China top of the world GDP indicators table?
2. What would a country need to do to move up the GDP indicators table?
3. Why might the GDP indicators table not give a clear picture of how well off individual people are in the countries listed?
4. Is measuring GDP a good way of measuring economic growth and comparing standards of living in different countries? Give reasons for your answer.

Criticisms of using GDP as an economic indicator

Since the 1970s there has been a lot of criticism of linking GDP with standards of living. These criticisms are explained below.

- It does not take into account the degree of inequality in a society. For example, the Brazilian economy grew rapidly in the first decade of the 21st century compared with other smaller countries. However, Brazil has among the highest income inequality in the world. The richest 10 per cent of Brazilians receive 50 per cent of GDP, while the poorest 10 per cent receive less than 1 per cent. Most countries around the world have not been very successful in reducing inequality. For example, in the UK in recent years, the percentage of national income going to the richest 20 per cent of households has actually risen from 40.9 per cent to 42.6 per cent. During this time, the share taken by the poorest 20 per cent of families fell from 7.7 per cent to 7.2 per cent. So although GDP per head in a country might rise over time, prosperity does not necessarily make much difference to the living standards of poorer people.
- GDP simply measures the value of goods produced. GDP calculations do not take into account the harmful effects of growth, such as pollution and waste. A country that produces more food does not necessarily produce healthy food. Cigarettes are counted as 'goods' even though they might create lung cancer and other illnesses.
- GDP calculations are not very good at making comparisons between countries. This is because GDP is usually calculated within a country using the currency of that country. For example, GDP in South Africa is measured using the South African rand (ZAR), but the value of the rand may change over time against other currencies. For example, on 29 July 2013 the exchange rate between the South African rand and the US dollar was about 10 rands to one dollar. At the time, the GDP of South Africa was worth about 400 billion US dollars. However, the value of the rand was falling against the dollar. This means that the value of South Africa's GDP, as measured in dollars, might change quite dramatically on a day-to-day basis.

ACTIVITY

Find out the most recent published figure for GDP in your country. Compare this with the GDP of another country with a similar-sized population.

What factors might explain the difference in your country from that of the country you have chosen to compare it with?

STUDY TIP

You will need to be able to discuss both the benefits and the limitations of GDP as an economic indicator.

ACTIVITY

By 6 November 2017 the exchange rate of the South African rand to the US dollar had fallen to 14.21.

Explain the implications of this change for calculations of South Africa's GDP when compared with 2013.

Average years of schooling are an important ingredient of HDI calculations, where they are compared with an ideal figure of 15 years

> **STUDY TIP**
>
> Although GDP is still a very important indicator, the gross national income (GNI) is now becoming increasingly important and has replaced GDP in the HDI.

> **DID YOU KNOW?**
>
> Countries with an HDI of more than 0.8 are classified as very high, those between 0.71 and 0.799 as high, those between 0.535 and 0.71 as medium and under 0.555 as low.

> **DID YOU KNOW?**
>
> Education measurements for HDI compare the mean (average) number of years of schooling in a country to an ideal of 15, and expected years of schooling with an ideal of 18 (including time spent in higher education, e.g. university).

- Standard of living is not the same thing as quality of life. People may have more goods, but they are not necessarily better off or happier. In recent years, economists have suggested that a person's quality of life depends on a range of factors, including being healthy, being free from stress and worry or living in a pleasant climate – all factors that are not measured by GDP calculations.

Human Development Index

The Human Development Index (HDI) is a broader method of measuring the quality of life. The well-known economists Mahbub ul Haq and Amartya Sen led a team that developed this for the United Nations Development Programme in 1990.

The HDI contains three elements:

1. Standard of living, as measured by GNI (gross national income) per head at purchasing power parity (this takes into account what money can buy in various countries).
2. Life expectancy at birth.
3. Education as measured by:
   a mean years of schooling
   b expected years of schooling.

Achievement in each of these three areas is measured by how far a country has gone in attaining the following goals:

- real GNI per head of US$75 000 (real GNI is the value of goods produced in a given period when we have taken out the effect of price rises caused by inflation)
- life expectancy of 85 years
- targets for years of enrolment in school.

These goals have not yet been fully attained by any country, so the actual indicators are expressed as decimal shares of the ideal. Therefore, 0.5 represents halfway towards the goal. The HDI score for any country is measured between 0 and 1. The highest possible score is 1. In 2013, Norway had the highest score at 0.955.

Using HDI indicators, countries are ranked into four categories: very high, high, medium and low. Here are some of the countries in the very high, high, medium and low categories, with their ranking in brackets and the HDI score as a decimal.

Very high	HDI	High	HDI	Medium	HDI	Low	HDI
Norway (1)	0.949	Barbados (54)	0.795	Botswana (108)	0.698	Swaziland (148)	0.541
Australia (2)	0.939	Bahamas (58)	0.792	Gabon (109)	0.697	Angola (150)	0.533
Switzerland (2)	0.939	Sri Lanka (73)	0.766	Philippines (116)	0.632	Uganda (163)	0.493
Malta (33)	0.856	Jordan (86)	0.741	India (131)	0.624	Chad (186)	0.396
Bahrain (47)	0.824	Jamaica (94)	0.730	Pakistan (147)	0.550	Niger (187)	0.353

Source: United Nations, Human Development Indicators, 2016

> **ACTIVITY**
>
> Do some research to find where these countries are ranked and their HDI score: Greece, Argentina, Cuba, Zambia, Senegal, Brazil, Sri Lanka, Singapore, Kuwait and Mexico.

Criticisms of the HDI are that it fails to take into account the impact of economic growth on the environment. The economist Bryan Caplan has criticised the HDI as concentrating on too narrow a range of indicators. He says that the HDI is a measure of how *Scandinavian* your economy is because it focuses on areas such as education and health care, which countries such as Norway and Sweden do particularly well in.

In some countries HDI is also measured in areas of the country. In India HDI is measured for each of the country's states, and even for different districts within the states. This enables national and regional governments to identify areas of great hardship and to use this as a basis for providing support. The Indian government also places particular emphasis on measuring infant mortality and this, rather than life expectancy at birth, is sometimes used as an indicator.

An alternative way of looking at development is the Human Poverty Index (HPI). This was created by the United Nations, which regards it as a useful way of measuring human deprivation. It includes indicators such as the proportion of the population living below the poverty line and the rate of unemployment.

The HPI is often regarded as a more accurate measure of deprivation than the HDI in highly developed countries because it takes account of those living below the poverty line. For the purpose of the index, these are people whose incomes fall below half the average (median) disposable income in the country.

Since 2010, the HPI has been replaced by the Multidimensional Poverty Index (see the 'Did you know?' above).

> **ACTIVITY**
>
> Find out where your country ranks in the HDI ranking this year. Is this higher or lower than each of the following: Australia, Barbados, Bahrain, Kenya, Syria, Peru, Nigeria and the US?

> **SUMMARY QUESTIONS**
>
> 1 Why does GDP only give a very rough measure of how well off people are in different countries?
> 2 What is the HDI and what does it measure?
> 3 If a country scores very high in the HDI, what does this tell you about the country?

> **DID YOU KNOW?**
>
> Another important index is the United Nations Multidimensional Poverty Index developed in 2010 to take account of three key ingredients – standard of living, knowledge (education), and longevity (life expectancy). It is seen as a good way of measuring deprivation. Not surprisingly, the top two countries – that is, those with least poverty – are Sweden and Norway.

> **STUDY TIP**
>
> Don't incorrectly state that the quality of water is included in the HDI. It is not included in the HDI, but it is included in the Multidimensional Poverty Index.

> **KEY POINTS**
>
> 1 The standard of living measures access to levels of material comfort.
> 2 GDP is criticised as being too narrow a measure of the broader quality of life.
> 3 The HDI has been developed as an alternative measure.
> 4 The HDI takes account of the standard of living, life expectancy and education.
> 5 The Multidimensional Poverty Index is an even broader measure than HDI.

> **DID YOU KNOW?**
>
> The infant mortality rate measures the number of deaths per 1,000 live births in one year of infants under one year old.

5.1.2 Comparing living standards and income distribution

Standards of living

The **standard of living** is the level of material comfort that is available to individuals or groups, as measured by the goods, services and luxuries that they have. Individuals' standard of living can be thought of as a basket of goods and services they need in order to live their day-to-day lives. The imaginary basket does not just contain goods that you can buy in shops, but also access to clean water supplies, health services, education and other requirements for a good life. Some people have access to more goods and better services than others.

Differences in standards of living within countries

Within countries there are considerable differences in standards of living. These differences arise for the following economic reasons.

- Some people have inherited wealth which is handed down from family and friends.
- Some people earn a higher income because of the type of work they do. Those with scarce skills, such as doctors and lawyers, will receive a much higher income than unskilled workers.
- Some people own their own business, or have a shareholding in businesses. These people take a risk whether they run a business or simply own shares. The rewards in the form of profit may be high.
- Some people prosper because they work harder than others (or because they are lucky to be doing the right job at the right time).

> **TOPIC GUIDANCE**
>
> Students should be able to:
> - discuss differences in standards of living within countries and between countries.

Some members of an economy have access to a large basket of goods (their standard of living), while others have access to a much smaller basket

> **DID YOU KNOW?**
>
> Mexico has the second highest income per head in Latin America after Brazil. Wages for farm workers may, however, be very low (particularly when people are working illegally). HDI scores show 0.80 for northern states and 0.70 for some southern states. Wages for factory workers are higher than for other workers.

Figure 5.1.2.1 Different standards of living are enjoyed by people within the same society

Differences in standards of living between countries

There are many indicators that can be considered in comparing standards of living between countries.

Standards of living depend on how effective an economy is in producing goods and services – that is, the productivity of its industries. Productive industries enable employees to achieve high standards of living and they also contribute benefits to everyone in the economy, e.g., through higher taxes. Standards of living also depend on the provision of health and educational facilities within countries. For example, Norway, Sweden and Denmark invest heavily in education and healthcare.

Typically, citizens of more developed countries have access to bigger baskets of goods and welfare services. However, the relationship between development and well being is not a straightforward one – for example, some countries with relatively high GDP per head do not always come out on top in terms of other indicators of well being.

Standards of living and quality of life

What is 'beneficial' depends on personal judgement. For example, while some people may want to own a car, others may consider cars to be harmful in terms of the pollution they create, road accidents and other negative impacts. Access to the internet may be regarded by some as beneficial, while others may see it as an intrusion on privacy.

While standards of living may be useful for making comparisons in terms of access to goods and services, they may not be so useful at measuring **quality of life**. For example, the greater the volume of goods that a society creates, the greater the potential to create pollution and negative externalities. Quality of life is difficult to measure, but it is more concerned with providing individuals with what they value – this might include access to fresh water and clear unpolluted air. When we look at other indices of well being, it is possible to question how closely standards of living represent quality of life. For example, indicators of life expectancy give a different perspective on the growth of a society.

You might expect the US to feature higher in such a table. However, just as poor countries have illnesses associated with poverty, rich countries such as the US have illnesses associated with wealth, e.g. obesity and its links to diabetes and heart disease. Also, as we saw on the last two pages, national indicators for GDP per head often hide inequalities within a society.

Australian citizens benefit from high-quality health care and schooling. GDP per head (US$49 928 in 2016) was lower than that of Qatar (US$59 331), but on the HDI Australia scored 0.939 compared with Qatar's 0.856

ACTIVITY

Carry out some research to find out the HDI, GDP per head and car ownership per 1,000 people in one other country in each of the seven continents. How similar are the figures to those of the countries shown in the table below? Set out your findings in a chart.

Country	Life expectancy at birth (years) 2013
Spain	83.3
New Zealand	82.0
US	79.5
Saudi Arabia	74.7
Seychelles	73.8
India	68.8
Uganda	60.2

KEY POINTS

1. Standards of living vary between rural and urban areas, regions of a country and different income earners.
2. Inequalities exist within countries and between countries.
3. Some people feel that living standards fail to measure quality of life.

SUMMARY QUESTIONS

1. What are the main differences in living standards within a country? Use your country as an example.
2. What are the main differences in living standards between countries? Compare your country with another country.

5.2 Poverty

5.2.1 Causes of poverty

TOPIC GUIDANCE

Students should be able to:
- define poverty
- outline the major causes of poverty.

Public distribution system shops in India provide the poor with basic food supplies at subsidised prices

STUDY TIP

Make sure that you are able to clearly distinguish between absolute poverty and relative poverty.

DID YOU KNOW?

A report by Oxfam in 2013 ('Europe: For the many, not for the few') showed that between 2009 and 2013 the number of Europeans living without enough money to heat their homes or cope with unforeseen expenses – known as 'severe material deprivation' – rose by 7.5 million to 50 million people.

Inequality and poverty

In all economies there are people with fewer goods and services than others (in **relative poverty**), with some not receiving enough to meet even basic needs (in **absolute poverty**). This **inequality** between rich and poor can mean, for some, high levels of infant mortality, malnutrition, starvation, ill health and low life expectancy. A key government policy in all countries is to redistribute income more equally through society.

However, a study published in 2010 by the European Anti-Poverty Network showed that inequality in Europe is growing in that nearly 1 in 7 people are at risk of poverty. Poverty was defined as having an income below 60 per cent of the median (average) income. People whose income is below 60 per cent of the average are in danger of falling into 'poverty'. People in this group are likely to be disadvantaged with less access to a good education and are more likely to suffer health risks and to be in debt.

ACTIVITY

Find figures that show the extent of inequality and poverty in your country. How does this compare with the figure of 1 in 7 in Europe?

CASE STUDY | Redistribution in India

About a quarter of the population of India is estimated to live in poverty and the Indian government has created a range of measures to redistribute income to the poorest groups. This includes the provision of food subsidies and public goods to rural areas. In the 1950s the Indian government created a public distribution system (PDS) and set up supply depots to provide everyone with basic foods. This system was changed in 1997 to target the poor, so that from that time they were able to buy basic foods at half their actual cost. Since 2000 the poorest 15 per cent receive even cheaper food. They are entitled to a maximum of 35 kg of wheat and rice at very low prices (about 2 rupees per kg) per month.

The second government redistribution scheme is in the provision of merit goods. From the 1970s a Minimum Needs Plan was introduced to provide clean water, schools, health facilities, electricity and roads to rural areas. By 2013 most villages had a primary school and access to electricity and piped water. Over half of Indian villages can now be approached by a paved road. However, there is still a substantial lack of publicly funded health facilities, and in a number of states publicly provided goods are of poor quality, e.g. irregular electricity supply or water supplies that dry up. As a general rule, the greater the GDP of a particular state, the better and more extensive the merit goods provision.

Questions

1. In what ways do the two schemes described above illustrate redistribution of income?
2. Who are the principal beneficiaries of these schemes and who will pay for the schemes?
3. Can you identify similar redistribution schemes in your own country? Explain how they work.

> **STUDY TIP**
>
> Make sure that you can identify the major causes of poverty as being unemployment, low wages, illness and old age. In addition, you may be able to identify specific causes in your own country, e.g. discrimination against certain groups.

What is poverty?

Poverty is usually assessed by a person's income: individuals are considered poor if their income falls below the minimum level necessary to meet basic needs. This minimum level is called the **poverty line**, which countries identify in different ways. Information about income is collected by surveying a sample of the population. The World Bank identifies the poverty line as having US$1.90 or less to live on per day. In 2017, this was the situation for 10.7 per cent of the world's population (768.5 million people), although the numbers are falling.

Causes of poverty

The following are among the underlying causes of poverty.

- **Unemployment** (lack of work) or **underemployment** (not doing enough work to earn a wage – in the case of Haiti, the poorest country in the western hemisphere, unemployment is over 13 per cent, but over half the population (of 10 million) is classified as living in extreme poverty, because of insufficient work and low wages.
- **Old age** – citizens who are too old to work slip into poverty. The Oxfam report referred to earlier in this section found that most of those below the poverty line in Europe are old people or children.
- **Ill health** – people who suffer from mental and physical health problems are most likely to be poor and to hold down full time jobs. A recent report by the World Health Organization stated that: 'An overwhelming majority of people with mental and psychosocial disabilities are living in poverty, poor physical health, and are subject to human rights violations'.
- **Lack of social welfare payments** – these may include old age pension or sick pay provided by the government. The lack of these payments can compound the other causes of poverty.

> **DID YOU KNOW?**
>
> Another country committed to reducing poverty is Pakistan, from 26 per cent of the population in 1990 to 13 per cent by 2015. There are many initiatives, such as a food support programme for poor families – the initiative includes the provision of cheap *roti* (bread), free medicines and educational support for deserving students.

> **SUMMARY QUESTIONS**
>
> 1. Explain two ways in which the government can redistribute income from the rich to the poor.
> 2. Define poverty.
> 3. What are public goods? How can the provision of public goods help to reduce inequalities?

> **KEY POINTS**
>
> 1. Redistribution of income involves transferring income or benefits from the rich to the poor.
> 2. Redistribution can be achieved through taxation, subsidies and spending by the government on public goods.

183

5.2.2 Policies to alleviate poverty

TOPIC GUIDANCE

Students should be able to:
- describe the difference between absolute and relative poverty
- recognise and discuss policies to alleviate poverty.

Brazil is a rapidly developing economy: 13.6 per cent of adults are still unable to read, so providing literacy classes is now a priority in the poorest communities

DID YOU KNOW?

Since 2010 the United Nations have used a new measure of poverty – the Multidimensional Poverty Index (MPI). The MPI assesses a range of 'deprivations' at household level: child mortality, nutrition, years of schooling, school attendance, availability of electricity, quality of sanitation, quality of drinking water, standard of floor surface, use of particular cooking fuel and ownership of specific assets. These provide a fuller picture of poverty than simple income measures.

Defining poverty

Poverty can be defined as absolute or relative.

- **Absolute poverty** defines someone as poor by a particular standard. It usually refers to a lack of basic human needs, including water, food, sanitation, shelter, clothing and education. It is in this sense that absolute poverty really means extreme poverty. In India, a recent official report produced by the economist S.D. Tendulkar, defined absolute poverty as not having enough to meet the basic needs of people, including an adequate diet and sufficient access to education and health services. The report estimated that about 38 per cent of India's population (400 million) were in a state of absolute poverty. In 1990, the World Bank introduced an absolute poverty line of US$1 a day to live on. This figure has since been increased and in 2017 the World Bank defines absolute or extreme poverty as having to live on less than US$1.90 per day.

- **Relative poverty** involves making comparisons between poor and rich people in a particular society. It is defined as economic inequality in a given society. Being poor usually means being deprived in certain ways. Issues include a high rate of infant death, low levels of literacy (reading and writing), poor health conditions and a lack of job opportunities. In the UK, for example, someone in relative poverty is defined as a person trying to live on less than 60 per cent of average income. In 2013, the average income in the UK was £436 a week (down from £461 the previous year) or £22 672 a year. Relative poverty in the UK, therefore, would be a person having to live on 60 per cent or less of that income – that is, £261 a week or £13 603 a year.

Dealing with poverty

Policies that can help to reduce poverty include the economic growth of a society (this can lead to benefits for the poor), redistribution of income, e.g. by taxation and benefits, or targeted policy measures designed to help poorer people, e.g., by providing employment opportunities in rural and urban areas.

Sustained economic growth

Economic growth maintained over time leads to a rise in GDP (see section 4.6.1). In an ideal world everyone benefits. However, there is no guarantee that this will happen – the rich may simply become richer. Economic growth can be achieved if the government helps markets to work more smoothly by cutting out unnecessary regulation, or by providing subsidies and tax incentives to new growing industries. The government could also invest in new training and employment-creation schemes.

Redistribution of income

Income can be redistributed through raising taxes so that the rich pay more than the poor (**progressive taxes**). **Regressive taxes**, where the poor pay the highest percentage, can be lowered. However, critics of such a scheme argue that high taxes discourage effort. Businesses might also get around this by raising wages for better-paid workers and cutting wages for those on lower pay.

Measures to help poorer people

There are many measures that a government can use to help poorer people directly: public distribution schemes for subsidised food, means-tested benefits such as cash payments to low-income families, and subsidised or zero-cost housing and education. Minimum-wage legislation can also be implemented for low-paid workers.

In Brazil, the Alfasol programme has been created to increase literacy rates for young people and adults. The programme concentrates on the poorest rural and urban communities.

> **STUDY TIP**
>
> When discussing policies to reduce poverty, you should be able to explain which policies you think will be more likely to be effective, and why. For example, focusing on education and literacy provides both short-term and long-term benefits, enabling better educated people to hold down jobs and work their way out of poverty.

CASE STUDY: Policies to alleviate poverty in India

Professor S. Subramanian, at the Madras Institute of Development Studies in Chennai, India, has suggested that India adopts the following policies:

1. Collect unpaid income and wealth taxes and use the proceeds to tackle poverty.
2. Create an additional element to income tax – a poverty surcharge to redistribute income from rich to poor.
3. Improve the public distribution system.
4. Draw up maps to identify poor districts – for example, those without access to drinking water, fuel for cooking, a school or other basic amenities – and then seek to improve these areas.
5. Extend free adult literacy schemes.
6. Improve social security schemes to provide better pensions for those who have had accidents or who are old.
7. Improve pro-growth policies to grow the whole economy – for example, by encouraging more foreign investment.

Questions

1. Which of the suggestions listed involve:
    a. growing the economy as a whole
    b. redistributing income
    c. targeting initiatives at the poor?
2. Which of the policies do you think are likely to be particularly effective at tackling poverty?
3. Which of the policies are most similar to those that you have read about for your own country?

KEY POINTS

1. Relative poverty involves comparisons between richer and poorer members of society. Absolute poverty measures poverty against set poverty thresholds, e.g. US$1.90 per day to live on.
2. Policies for combating poverty include redistributing income, economic growth and targeting benefits at the poor.

SUMMARY QUESTIONS

1. An individual earns US$10 per day. Why might he or she be classified as poor?
2. An individual earns US$3 per day. Why might he or she be classified as not poor?
3. Identify three policies that might be effective for reducing poverty.
4. How might the redistribution of income through progressive taxes benefit the poor?

5.3 Population

5.3.1 Factors that affect population growth

TOPIC GUIDANCE

Students should be able to:
- describe the factors that affect population growth.

The main factors

The four key factors affecting population growth are the birth rate, death rate, fertility rate and net migration.

- The **birth (natality) rate** is the ratio of total live births to total population in an area in a particular time period. It is often expressed as the number of live births per 1,000 of the population per year.

The birth rate is the number of live births per 1000 people

- The **death (mortality) rate** is the number of deaths per 1,000 of the population per year. Two important indicators in this context are the **infant mortality rate** (the number of children under one year dying divided by the number of live births that year) and the **maternal mortality rate** (the number of deaths of women related to childbearing divided by the total number of live births that year).

- The **general fertility rate** can be measured by the number of live births per 1,000 women between the ages of 15 and 44 years. It can also be measured by the number of children born to the average woman in her lifetime.

- **Net migration** measures the difference between *immigration* (that is, the movement of people into) and *emigration* (that is, the movement of people from) of an area during a year. If the number of emigrants is greater than the number of immigrants, the net migration figure is negative.

DID YOU KNOW?

Every year over half a million women and girls die as a result of complications during pregnancy, childbirth or in the six weeks following delivery; 99 per cent of these deaths occur in developing countries.

STUDY TIP

When discussing population growth, you should be able to refer to the birth rate and the death rate, and be able to mention the impact of the net migration rate on the size of a country's population.

ACTIVITY

Find out the most recent figures available for birth rates, death rates and net migration in your country. What will be the impact on population growth? Make a poster or wall chart that displays your findings.

Population growth

To calculate annual **population growth** (or **fall**), subtract the population figure at the start of the year from the figure at the end. Divide this number by the figure at the start. Multiply this number by 100 to get a percentage figure for population growth (or decline).

Here is the calculation for a population increase from 50 million to 51 million over one year:

51 million − 50 million = 1 million

$$\frac{1}{50} \times \frac{100}{1} = 2 \text{ per cent population growth}$$

Factors affecting population growth

A number of factors affect population growth.

- **The birth rate**: more births per 1,000 lead to an increasing population. Birth rates are highest in developing countries, because people aim to have more children to counteract high infant mortality, and children can add to household earnings once they start work.
- **The death rate**: the under-fives mortality rate per 1,000 live births fell in sub-Saharan Africa between 1990 and 2013, leading to an increasing population. Better medical care, inoculation against diseases and better diet will cause a fall in death rates.
- **The relationship between the birth and the death rate**: in Brazil in 2015 the birth rate was about 14 per 1,000, compared with a death rate of 5.8 per 1,000. Thus there is a **natural increase** here, as is the case in many other developing economies.
- **The net migration rate**: the 2015 net migration rate in Brazil was −0.15. This helped to reduce the impact of the natural increase in population. **Economic migration** occurs when people come to, or leave a country in search of work. Relatively low wages in a country will lead to workers emigrating to areas where wages are higher.
- **The fertility rate** (children born per woman): Brazil had a relatively low 2015 fertility rate of 1.74.

Birth and fertility rates are affected by numbers of women of childbearing age, attitudes to having children and the extent to which contraception and other methods are used to limit the number of children per family (China has used a one-child-per-family policy to control the birth rate). In some countries, increase in female employment and more people marrying later in life can reduce fertility rates. Some people choose a higher standard of living over having children. The death rate is affected by the quantity and quality of food available and medical facilities. Net migration is determined by the ease with which people can move between countries, and whether they want to do so.

> **KEY POINTS**
>
> 1. Falling infant mortality rates result from better medical care and nutrition.
> 2. Net migration also influences population growth, as does the fertility rate.

> **STUDY TIP**
>
> Make sure that you can clearly distinguish between immigration, where people move into a country, and emigration, where people move out of a country.

> **STUDY TIP**
>
> You should be able to discuss the possible reasons for different rates of population growth in various countries. This means that you need to consider which reasons may be more important than others. For example, in Brazil in 2015, population growth was 0.8 per cent as a result of the birth rate being significantly higher than the death rate. Medical advances have helped to bring down the death rate considerably, while the birth rate is falling because of contraception.

> **SUMMARY QUESTIONS**
>
> 1. What would be the effect of a fall in the death rate on population growth?
> 2. Why might a population grow even though the death rate is higher than the birth rate?
> 3. How might a fall in birth rate affect the fertility rate in future years?

5.3.2 Reasons for different rates of population growth

TOPIC GUIDANCE

Students should be able to:
- discuss reasons for the different rates of population growth in different countries.

Young people in Uganda: in some developing countries half the population is under 15

Pyramid A
Typical of developing countries
- high death rate
- high birth rate
- low life expectancy

Pyramid B
Typical of developed countries
- low death rate
- lower birth rate
- longer life expectancy

Figure 5.3.2.1 Population pyramids for a developing and a developed country

STUDY TIP

Although interpretation of a population pyramid is required, you will not be asked to draw one in the exam.

Population growth in developing and developed countries

- **Developing countries** have high death rates and birth rates, and low life expectancy. Higher death rates result from lower incomes, which in turn result in poor nutrition for the poorest. There are fewer doctors, nurses and hospitals per head of the population. There are fewer medicines and a much lower percentage of the population is inoculated against diseases. Malaria and HIV/AIDS are major causes of high mortality rates – the drugs to combat and treat them are very expensive.

- **Developed countries** have a low death rate, lower birth rate, and longer life expectancy. The low death rate results from better health care and relatively high incomes, enabling people to have a more nutritious diet. The average age at which women have their first child is higher. Most families choose to have fewer children so that they can enjoy a higher standard of living.

Population pyramids

A **population pyramid** compares the numbers of males and females in different age categories in a country or territory. Each bar in the pyramid represents five years and the length shows the population in that age category: the age distribution. The structure of the pyramid is determined by births, deaths and migration.

Figure 5.3.2.1 shows that the shape for the developing country is triangular, with a wide base and a narrow top. For the developed country it is more egg-shaped. It also shows that in the developing country a large proportion of the population is under 15 and very few live beyond the age of 65.

Population growth in Uganda and the UK

Figure 5.3.2.2 shows the numbers in the different age bands in the UK population (63.2 million in 2011). There are fairly even numbers of people in each age category up to the age of 60 when, as a result of old age, numbers start to decline. Children aged under 16 represent about one in five of the total population, around the same proportion as those of retirement age. The tapering of the pyramid for people aged 31 to 37 reflects low fertility rates in the 1970s as people chose to have smaller families. Low fertility occurred again in the late 1980s to early 2000s, but increased from 2003 onwards, broadening the base of the pyramid.

In 2013 the UK birth rate was about 10.7 per 1,000 and the death rate 10.1 per 1,000, with net migration +2.0. Net migration increased as a result of migrant coming to the UK, particularly from countries such as Poland which became part of the European Union in 2004 (enabling Polish people to live and work in EU countries).

The table shows how the population in Uganda is rising at a very fast rate.

Population	33 million
Population growth	3.2 per cent per annum
Birth rate	48/1,000
Death rate	12/1,000
Infant mortality rate	65/1,000
Average fertility	6.5 per woman
Age distribution	50 per cent under 15
Population by 2050	100 million

So while Uganda has a rapidly growing population, there is also long-term poverty and poor health, particularly for children. Infant mortality is high because of a lack of trained midwives and medical clinics, particularly in rural areas. The birth rate is high because of a lack of availability of family planning advice, and because children are seen as providing hope for the future. Figure 5.3.2.3 shows the numbers in the different age bands in Uganda's population.

Some developed countries such as Japan have a falling population. The birth rate is lower than the death rate as Japanese families choose to have fewer children. The table below shows birth and death rates in Japan, 2008–16.

	Birth rate (births/1,000)	Death rate (deaths/1,000)
2008	7.87	9.26
2012	8.60	9.80
2016	7.90	10.20

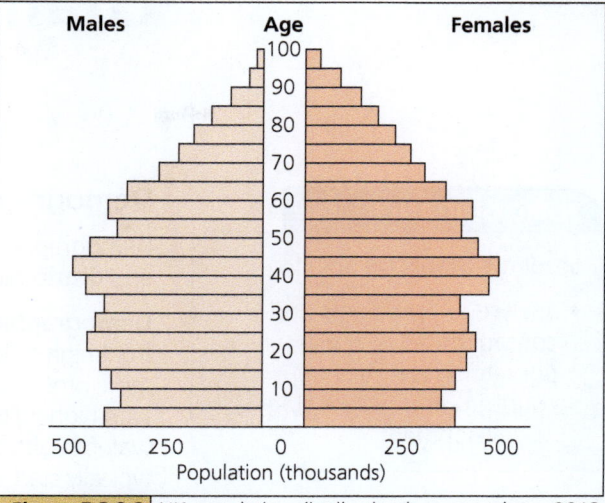

Figure 5.3.2.2 UK population distribution by age and sex, 2012
Source: Office for National Statistics

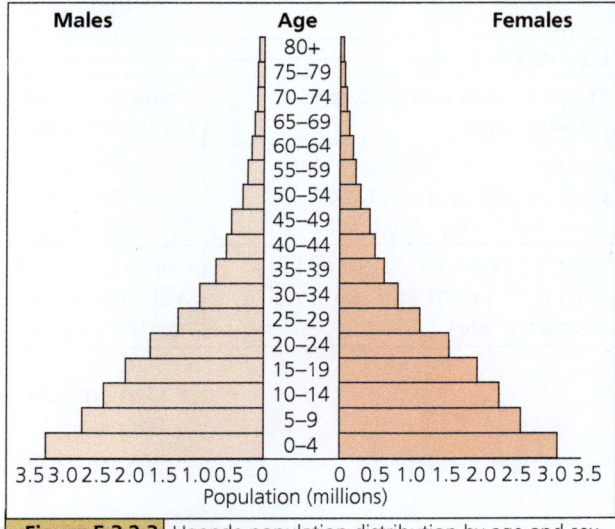

Figure 5.3.2.3 Uganda population distribution by age and sex, 2012

ACTIVITY

Is population rising quickly, slowly or declining in your country? What are the latest figures for birth rate, death rate and net migration? Draw a population pyramid.

KEY POINTS

1. Developed countries have stable or declining populations as a result of low birth and death rates and as a consequence of higher standards of living and better medical facilities.
2. Developing countries have high death rates, including high infant mortality rates. Health facilities are poor, particularly in rural areas.
3. Developing countries have high birth rates, often as a result of a lack of availability of family planning education and resources, and people choosing to have more children.

SUMMARY QUESTIONS

1. Why is the shape of the population pyramid different in developing and developed economies?
2. Why is population rising in many developing countries and falling in some developed countries?
3. Why might the growth of population of a country speed up or slow down?

5.3.3 Problems of population change

> **TOPIC GUIDANCE**
>
> Students should be able to:
>
> - analyse the problems and consequences of these population changes for countries at different stages of development.

Demographic transition

Demography is the study of population features, such as size, growth and distribution in different age groups.

Demographic transition describes the process of a society moving from high to low mortality and fertility rates. As societies become more prosperous – that is, developed – average incomes rise, along with higher literacy rates and improvements in diet, access to clean water, health care and sanitation. As societies develop, mortality rates typically start to fall before birth rates, leading initially to an increase in population. Once the birth rate starts to fall, the rate of increase of population will slow down. The table indicates different stages of demographic transition.

Low development		High development
Stage 1: High mortality and fertility rates	**Stage 2: Falling mortality combined with high fertility rates**	**Stage 3: Low mortality and low fertility rates**
Problems: low life expectancy, poor health and sanitation conditions, high birth rate	Rising life expectancy leads to rapid increases in the population because birth rate is still high	Rising standards of living but problems may arise from falling population
Current example: Afghanistan, with high infant and maternal mortality rates	Current example: Uganda, with high birth rate and falling mortality rate	Current example: Japan, with falling mortality, fertility and birth rates

Demographic transition varies from one part of a country to another. For example, in a number of southern Indian states fertility rates are low, while in northern India the rates, while falling, are still quite high.

Consequences of population change for developing countries

The following table shows recent United Nations population predictions. The figures make it possible to calculate how much population will increase in different countries between 2010 and 2020.

Name of country	Start-date population 2010 (millions)	End-date population 2020 (millions)
Afghanistan	29 117	39 585
Uganda	33 796	46 319

Within 10 years the populations of these countries are estimated to increase by between 30 and 40 per cent.

The following table compares aspects of development in these countries in 2012.

A primary school class in Afghanistan. Improvements in healthcare and a rise in the number of trained midwives are helping the national population figure to rise

Indicator	Afghanistan	Uganda
Average income per head	US$335	US$300
People not meeting daily food needs	40 per cent	31 per cent
Women dying in childbirth	1,800/per 100 000 live births	435/100 000
Children dying before the age of 5	191/per 1000 live births	137/1000
Children receiving primary school education	37 per cent	52 per cent

Rising population growth has a dramatic effect on economies where resources are already stretched. In Uganda problems are made worse by the **HIV/AIDS pandemic** and many children are being brought up in orphanages.

If the population grows in a poor country, there is less to go round. Problems include threats of famine, the rapid spread of disease, overcrowding and lack of employment opportunities. There is unsustainable use of natural resources if forests are cut down for firewood and land is overused for agriculture so the soil quality falls. The movement of people into towns and cities creates further problems of overcrowding and lack of access to basic amenities.

Consequences of population change for developed countries

Developed countries are more likely to face problems of falling population. As shown in section 5.3.2, Japan has a declining population: between 2010 and 2020 the population will fall from about 127 million to about 124 million. Couples are marrying later and more women prefer to work longer before starting a family. Many young couples no longer live with their parents, thus there are fewer people to look after children.

In a number of countries there are not enough people of working age. In parts of Germany migrant workers from Turkey have for many years provided extra labour in car factories and other industries. To counteract a falling population in France, the government provides generous state benefits for parents who have more than two children. This has helped to counteract the fall in the birth rate, and after a time lag is leading to increases in numbers of younger workers.

With longer lifespans in developed countries there is more pressure on those in work to pay taxes to provide the pensions for those who are retired. Lower fertility results in a smaller working population and a larger **dependent population** – the young and the old depend on those in work.

KEY POINTS

1. A feature of many developing countries is rapid population growth.
2. Resources are stretched by population growth, leading to pressures on health, education and other services and an inability to meet the basic needs of people.
3. Developed economies are more likely to suffer from population shortages.

STUDY TIP

Make sure that you can show that you are aware of the problems that can be caused in a country by a rapidly rising population.

ACTIVITY

Search the UN World Population Prospects database (http://esa.un.org/unpd/wpp/index.htm) to find three other countries where population is increasing rapidly. Are these developing or developed countries? Set out a table like the one for Afghanistan and Uganda, comparing these countries.

SUMMARY QUESTIONS

1. What is demographic transition? How might a society benefit from demographic transition?
2. Describe three problems that may be caused by rapid increases in population in developing economies.
3. What problems result from a falling population in developed economies?

5.3.4 The effect of changing size of population on an economy

TOPIC GUIDANCE

Students should be able to:
- describe the effects of changing size of population on an economy.

Uruguay has an ageing population. It has the lowest birth rate in South America and average life expectancy is just under 80

ACTIVITY

Discuss with your classmates how a country could be 'overpopulated' with a relatively small population, and 'underpopulated' with a relatively large population.

STUDY TIP

Whether a country is regarded as underpopulated or overpopulated depends on the availability of its resources to support the population; make sure that you understand this.

The optimum population

Most countries are either **underpopulated** or **overpopulated**: they have too few people to work efficiently with other resources available (or not enough people with the required skills), or they have too many people for the resources available. For economists the **optimum** – that is, the ideal or best – **population** size has the best ratio of people to other resources. The optimum population depends on the availability of other resources. Some countries are underpopulated – they do not have enough people to use existing land, capital and other resources efficiently.

CASE STUDY | Underpopulation in Canada

Canada is one of the largest land masses in the world, with an abundance of raw materials such as coal, iron ore and oil reserves (although many of these are buried beneath ice sheets for much of the year). The table shows changes in the population of Canada in 2012.

a	Births	381 598
b	Deaths	252 242
c	Natural increase (a – b)	129 356
d	Net international migration	1 098 444
e	Total growth (c + d)	1 227 800

Source: based on figures from Statistics Canada, 2012

Canada recruits migrants from a range of countries, but they are required to have the skills needed to support the development of the Canadian economy, e.g. they are IT professionals, doctors and nurses.

Questions

1 How did the population of Canada grow in 2012? What was the major source of growth?
2 Why do you think it makes economic sense for Canada to focus on encouraging certain types of economic immigration?
3 What is likely to be the effect of immigration on productivity in Canada?

Overpopulation

The world's population is growing (in 2017 it was about 7.6 billion and growing by 265 per minute) and this raises questions as to whether the planet as a whole will be able to support growing numbers in the future. The threat of overpopulation is very real.

Some economists suggest that areas of land have a carrying capacity – that is, an optimum number of people for sustainable economic development. If a population is greater than this carrying capacity, the water tables may be lowered, leading eventually to drought, overuse of land so that soil capacity deteriorates, increased pollution from human activity, and other non-sustainable effects.

Areas most in danger of overpopulation include:

- small island economies with large poulations, e.g. Haiti
- landlocked economies with no access to ports, e.g. Chad, Central African Republic
- parts of **megacities** where there are large numbers of people overstretching facilities such as sanitation and water, e.g. the slum area of Dharavi in Mumbai, India, and Kibera in Nairobi, Kenya.

Ageing populations

An **ageing population** occurs when the average age in a region or country increases. This is currently happening in almost every country in the world. For example, in Uruguay improvements in sanitation, quality of drinking water, vaccinations and other merit goods have raised life expectancy so that a newborn girl can now expect to live to 78 years. Now, too, 17.3 per cent of the population is over 60. The economic effects are:

- an increase in the dependency ratio – there are fewer people working and paying taxes, and they must support more older people who may be receiving state pensions, so there is increased government spending on health care and pensions
- higher taxes for those in work, which could discourage them from working so hard
- a shortage of workers, which could push up wages, leading to wage inflation.

In Germany in 2013 there were four workers supporting each retired person. By 2030 the ratio could be down to 2:1.

Ageing populations push an economy towards overpopulation by putting more pressure on the working population. However, older people can be an economic asset because of their greater experience and willingness to work hard and take on more responsibility. Governments can raise the retirement age, making it illegal for employers to discriminate against older workers, and making it compulsory for employees to contribute towards paying part or all of their pension.

KEY POINTS

1. The optimum population is a situation where a population is combined most efficiently with the resources available to that population.
2. Some countries are underpopulated and some are overpopulated.
3. The ageing of the population often pushes an economy away from the optimum position.

DID YOU KNOW?

According to a report by the Worldwide Fund for Nature, in order for all humans to live with a high degree of luxury we would be spending three times more than the planet could supply. However, some people criticise this view, saying that it does not differentiate between sustainable (e.g. spending on bread) and unsustainable (e.g. spending on oil) consumption.

STUDY TIP

You should be able to discuss the effects of an ageing population. For example, you should be able to consider the consequences for a country and what the government might do to reduce the impact of an ageing population.

SUMMARY QUESTIONS

1. How might a small country be underpopulated and a large one overpopulated?
2. What is the relationship between carrying capacity and optimum population?
3. What are the main economic problems associated with an ageing population?

5.3.5 Changes in population structure and their effect on an economy

TOPIC GUIDANCE

Students should be able to:
- describe the effects of changing structure of population on an economy.

Recent years have seen large-scale migration to megacities such as Mumbai (22 million people in 2017)

STUDY TIP

Make sure that you have a clear understanding of the effects of a changing structure of population on an economy.

DID YOU KNOW?

A major change taking place in India is that women are having fewer children and more women are joining the paid labour force for longer periods. How will this be a demographic bonus for India?

The structure of the population

The structure of the population is the way that the total population can be divided into distinct groupings:

- **age structure** – grouping people according to age
- **gender structure** – grouping people according to whether they are male or female
- **urban/rural divide** – grouping people according to where they live – that is, in towns and cities or in villages.

Age structure

Economists make a distinction between the working population and the dependent population. The working population is those people who are old enough to work and under retirement age. Dependants are those who, for various reasons, such as age or condition, are not in paid work.

The table shows the age groups in India. Since the 1970s the fertility rate in India has been falling, leading to fewer dependants in the young age group; this will continue until 2025–30. This decline means that the number in the working population, compared with the dependent population, is increasing. It is expected to peak by 2025.

Young (0–14)	Together with the elderly group, the young are most dependent on the working population for services such as education, healthcare, accommodation, food
Youth (15–24)	Working or studying
Young working age (25–49)	With dependants, will not be able to save much
Mature working age (50–64)	Higher incomes and work experience; group most likely to be able to save
Elderly (65+)	Similar requirements to 0–14 group

The mature working population is currently increasing. There is a great opportunity therefore for India to increase productivity of labour and to save and invest more in the economy. However, after 2025 there will be more people in the elderly age group. This will lead to an increasing burden on health care and social security.

ACTIVITY

Investigate the changing structure of your own population. Set this out in the form of a newspaper article outlining problems resulting from changes in the age structure, occupational structure and rural/urban structure of the population.

Gender structure

The gender structure of a population is an important economic variable. In most countries, more boys than girls are born, but the infant mortality rate is higher among boys, and over time females outstrip males as the larger proportion of the population pyramid.

In cultures where males are seen as the major income earners, males may be valued more. For example, in China in the 1980s, the ratio of male/female births was 108/100. However, when China adopted its 'one-child' policy to slow down population growth, the ratio increased to 120/100.

However, in modern society, with its emphasis on service occupations, there is no valid economic argument for inequality in the labour market. In Japan in recent years, the encouragement of female participation in the workplace is seen as a key driver for economic growth. This was an important platform of Japanese Prime Minister Shinzo Abe's policy – known as 'Abenomics'. Abe's plan was to get 3 million extra women back into work by providing high-quality nurseries and childcare for the children of working women.

In most countries, women are disproportionately represented in lower paid occupations. For example, a 2013 report by the International Centre for Research into Women found that 80 per cent of the world's garment workers are women. Women make up 60 per cent of the world's working poor.

Urban/rural divide

The UN forecasts that by 2030 three out of five people worldwide will live in cities. Poor agricultural workers seek better opportunities in cities so that they can send money home to their families. An important economic effect is that as younger workers leave rural areas, these areas become increasingly dependent on an ageing (less efficient) workforce. Rural incomes fall, leading to a deterioration in rural services.

One effect on cities is to increase overcrowding. Overcrowding makes it difficult to provide suitable sanitation, water and electricity. In the highly populated Dharavi area (with a population of nearly one million) of Mumbai it is estimated that there is only one toilet per 1,500 residents. In other overcrowded cities some areas are characterised by high levels of unemployment and high crime rates.

In other countries underpopulation is the problem in urban areas. For example, Hoyerswerda in eastern Germany has become almost a ghost town as its population has moved to western areas of Germany seeking employment. Depopulation often leads to a deterioration of local services because there are not enough people to pay for them.

KEY POINTS

1. A key feature of the age structure of the population is the relationship between the working and dependent populations.
2. Women make up a disproportionate number of those in low paid occupations in most countries.
3. Large-scale migrations are taking place from rural areas to cities.

DID YOU KNOW?

The US, Germany and Japan have ageing populations. The average age of the population is increasing and there are more people of retirement age. One effect is a 'pension timebomb': it will be increasingly difficult for the working population to pay enough taxes to provide for pensions of retired people.

DID YOU KNOW?

Shinzo Abe is famously quoted as saying 'Abenomics won't work without womenomics'. He borrowed the idea of 'womenomics' (the idea that women should rejoin the workforce after childbirth) from Kathy Mitsui.

SUMMARY QUESTIONS

1. How can a decline in the fertility rate of a population provide an opportunity for economic development?
2. Although women typically make up half of the population, they do more of the low paid jobs. How would you explain this?
3. Describe two problems associated with the rapid growth of cities.

5.4 Differences in development between countries

5.4.1 Different rates of economic development

TOPIC GUIDANCE

Students should be able to:
- discuss the causes and impacts of factors leading to different rates of economic development between countries.

DID YOU KNOW?

A number of economic studies show that higher scores for literacy and numeracy and for educational attainment in school and university impact positively on lifetime earnings of individuals, and on the productivity and development of economies around the globe.

DID YOU KNOW?

At an international level the World Bank plays a prominent role in coordinating development initiatives. It is not a bank in the normal sense of the word, but rather a specialised agency of the United Nations. One of its purposes is to transfer resources from rich countries to poor countries to support economic development. The World Bank has 189 member countries collectively funding development projects.

Economic development

For economists, **development** can mean different things. Most definitions relate to the ongoing raising of living standards (what a person can afford to buy) and the improved ability of a country, through its own efforts, to produce more goods and services over time. Definitions usually include improving medical and education services.

A key aspect of the development of any economy is the education of children. Enrolment in schools is a major development indicator

The World Bank defines countries as **low income**, **middle income** and **high income**. This helps it to make decisions about lending money and supporting development projects in specific countries. Lower-income countries can borrow more finance for development. The World Bank considers low- and middle-income countries to be 'developing'. High-income countries are regarded as 'developed'. Figure 5.4.1.1 shows a range of countries, from developing to developed.

Low GDP/head Developing				High GDP/head Developed		
Afghanistan	Zambia	Bangladesh	Algeria	New Zealand	Italy	Singapore

Figure 5.4.1.1

In Unit 5.1 we explored another view of development, in terms of Human Development Index (HDI) indicators. These included three elements: standard of living, life expectancy at birth and education.

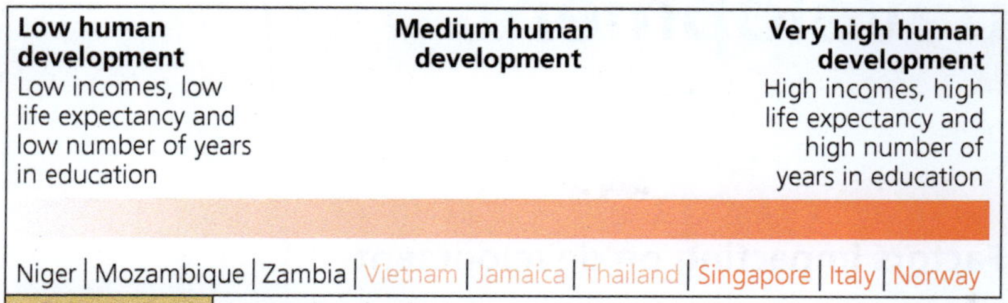

Low human development	Medium human development	Very high human development
Low incomes, low life expectancy and low number of years in education		High incomes, high life expectancy and high number of years in education

Niger | Mozambique | Zambia | Vietnam | Jamaica | Thailand | Singapore | Italy | Norway

Figure 5.4.1.2 Measuring development

Development is then measured by an index that includes each of these indicators (Figure 5.4.1.2).

Some of the other characteristics of developing economies include high infant mortality, high rates of population growth, relatively poor levels of education and healthcare, poor infrastructure (such as roads and water supplies), sanitation and housing, an over-reliance on a small number of export industries, and low productivity in large parts of agriculture.

Development as freedom

Amartya Sen is a famous economist who has won the Nobel Prize for his work. He believes that development should be seen as a process of expanding *freedom*. Freedom (and hence development) requires the removal of poverty, tyranny, lack of economic opportunities, social deprivation and the neglect of public services. In his book *Development as Freedom* he showed that, contrary to accepted views, economic growth on its own does not bring about development. He showed that people in the relatively poor South Indian state of Kerala, in which there are plentiful public services (including a public distribution system providing subsidised food), had a higher **life expectancy** than African Americans living in poverty in the US, a country with a much higher GDP per head. Amartya Sen believes that by providing freedoms – that is, social opportunities, political freedom, economic opportunities and security – development is most likely to occur.

Inequality as uneven development

Differences in income can be measured by the Gini index. Zero represents an imaginary society with absolute income equality between households, 100 represents absolute *in*equality. Scandinavian countries and Japan have the lowest levels of inequality. The US, however, has one of the highest at 41. The poorest 10 per cent of households only receive 1.9 per cent of income, while the richest receive 30 per cent. See if you can find the Gini score for your country and compare this with that of the US. Inequality can be seen as an indicator of uneven shares between the rich and the poor in terms of the rewards of development.

ACTIVITY

Research one country in each of the continents of South America, North America, Asia and Africa. Find out whether these countries are considered by the World Bank to be low income, middle income or high income. Then, using the United Nations Human Development Index, find out whether these countries are defined as having a high, medium or low development index.

STUDY TIP

Make sure that you can show an understanding of what is meant by 'developed'.

KEY POINTS

1 Development occurs when people are better off, not only with higher incomes, but also with access to benefits such as improved education and health.

2 International bodies, including the World Bank and the United Nations, have created classifications of development.

3 Amartya Sen believes that development requires freedom.

SUMMARY QUESTIONS

1 How does the World Bank classify the development of a country?

2 Why might the World Bank's classification not give a true reflection of development?

3 What types of freedom are associated with development?

5.4.2 Factors affecting development

TOPIC GUIDANCE

Students should be able to:

- outline the causes and impacts of factors affecting development.

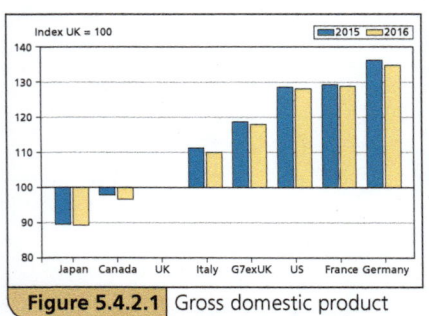

Figure 5.4.2.1 Gross domestic product per hour worked, G7 countries, 2015 and 2016

DID YOU KNOW?

German workers produce more in the same timeframe than workers in the UK, partly because they tend to work with better equipment and invest more in research and development. For example, in Germany in 2016 there were 1,034 research staff per 100 000 of the working population, compared with 883 per 100 000 in the UK. Germany also invests more in education and training.

Factors impacting on development

There are a number of factors that can encourage or inhibit **development** and development processes. These are differences in income within a country, levels of productivity, the growth of the population, the size of different industrial sectors, levels of saving and investment and education and health care.

Differences in income

Some economies are highly unequal, while others are characterised by greater levels of equality. One view is that inequality of income and wealth provide incentives for people to work hard, and that those with more wealth and income can invest their savings to enhance growth.

However, some economists believe the reverse: that greater equality provides an incentive to growth. Research by the Organization for Economic Cooperation and Development (OECD) in 2014 found that countries where income inequality is decreasing grow faster than those with rising inequality. The research found that the single biggest impact on growth is the widening gap between lower-middle class and poorer households. Rising inequality slowed growth by more than 10 percentage points in New Zealand and Mexico. In contrast, falling inequality increased growth rates in Ireland and France. Inequality holds back growth by undermining educational opportunities for children from poor households, reduces social mobility and hampers skills development.

Levels of productivity

Productivity measures how much output can be produced by given quantities of input. The more output that can be derived, the more productive that nation will be. The higher productivity levels are, the greater the opportunity for economic growth. Figure 5.4.2.1 contrasts UK productivity with other G7 (group of seven) countries. Productivity is measured in terms of output per hour worked.

On this basis, productivity in the UK in 2016 was:

- 12 per cent higher than that of Japan
- 3.4 per cent higher than that of Canada
- 9 per cent lower than that of Italy
- 21.8 per cent lower than that of the US
- 22.3 per cent lower than that of France
- 25.6 per cent lower than that of Germany
- 15.1 per cent lower than the average for the rest of the G7.

Population growth

The growth of the population can be seen as both a contributor to development and as a force that holds back economic development.

Rapid increases in population may be seen as having a negative impact on development, as this places more demand on the existing resource base of a country. However, if the country is underpopulated then a rise in population (particularly when this is based on a greater number of younger people) can lead to a more productive use of the resource base. Economists have identified other benefits of increasing populations, including the following:

- as people live longer, they tend to think more about the future and are more likely to take risks and innovate.
- educational attainment and savings rates will rise, leading to increased investment in physical capital, e.g. machinery and human capital (people).

Size of industrial sectors

As economies develop from agricultural societies, they will typically go through a process of industrialisation, with more people being employed in manufacturing, e.g. producing chemicals, textiles, iron and steel.

Further development results in the tertiary sector, e.g. banking, insurance and tourism, becoming predominant. Some smaller economies, such as small island economies in the Caribbean, often move directly from an emphasis on agriculture to services. The relative size of these sectors is a rough indicator of development. Developed nations typically use highly automated equipment in farming and manufacturing, requiring relatively little labour, so that most citizens can be focused on service jobs.

Saving and investment

Savings are a key influence on development. The higher people's incomes, the more money they can save. The World Bank provides statistics for savings as a percentage of GDP around the world. The highest level of savings take place in East Asia and the lowest levels are in Sub-Saharan Africa. For example, in 2016 the savings ratio was −3.7 per cent in the Central African Republic and 29.1 per cent in Vietnam.

Education and health care

In 5.1.1 and 5.1.2 we saw how education levels and health care are key components of wider definitions of development. More developed countries tend to have children and young people in school and university for longer periods of time, and life expectancy is longer through better medical care. Healthier and more educated people then drive further development.

SUMMARY QUESTIONS

1 In what ways might inequality act to hold back economic growth and development?
2 Why are some nations more productive than others? How does productivity help the development process?
3 Why might having a large proportion of people involved in agriculture hamper economic development?

DID YOU KNOW?

Savings are low in economies where citizens do not have enough income to save, where the government has poorly developed state saving schemes, and where financial institutions have poorly developed private saving schemes. Savings ratios in Haiti (2016) were −0.4 per cent, compared to 27.5 per cent in the United Arab Emirates.

ACTIVITY

Access the World Bank database online to find out recent figures for gross domestic savings in your country as a percentage of GDP.

High savings ratios provide businesses with funds to invest by borrowing savings through financial institutions. The level of investment (a key driver of economic growth) is strongly influenced by the level of domestic savings. Developed economies can also access savings more readily from international savers.

KEY POINTS

1 There is a debate as to whether inequality supports development or holds it back.
2 Higher levels of productivity, savings and investment are key drivers of development, with savings being chanelled into productive investment.
3 Standards of education and health care are also important indicators of development.

Unit 5 — Test yourself

SECTION 1: Multiple-choice questions

Each question has ONE correct answer.

1. Which of the following is NOT usually used as an indicator of the overall health of the whole economy?
   a The level of unemployment
   b The level of economic growth
   c The level of retail sales
   d The level of inflation

2. What is inflation?
   a An increase in the population of a country
   b An increase in the value of a country's currency
   c An increase in a country's interest rate
   d An increase in a country's general level of prices

3. If the Retail Prices Index at the start of 2012 is 100 and increases to 130 by the end of 2013, what is the average yearly inflation rate for the time period?
   a 10 per cent
   b 11 per cent
   c 15 per cent
   d 30 per cent

4. Which of the following may be an advantage of an increasing rate of inflation for the population of a country?
   a People who borrow money find that the real value of repayments falls
   b People on fixed incomes find that their spending power decreases
   c Poor people must pay higher prices for basic foodstuffs
   d People who save money find that the real value of their savings has fallen

5. Unemployment may cause a negative 'multiplier effect' because:
   a People spend less so businesses close down
   b People may claim welfare benefits
   c People have out-of-date skills
   d People suffer from low self-esteem

6. What does the participation rate for workers in an economy measure?
   a The total number of people of working age
   b The percentage of people of working age who are prepared to work
   c The percentage of workers who are in full-time jobs
   d The number of retired people who continue working

7. Which of the following works in a secondary industry?
   a A school teacher
   b A restaurant chef
   c A car factory worker
   d A mobile phone salesman

8. Which of the following is a disadvantage of increasing rates of employment for the population of a country?
   a Rising prices for goods and services
   b Rising wage rates
   c Rising levels of income
   d Falling levels of benefit payments

9. Which economic indicator measures the total output of an economy?
   a Gross Domestic Product
   b Human Development Index
   c Gross Domestic Product per head
   d Retail Prices Index

10. Which of the following is a problem with using GDP to measure the total output of a country?
    a Workers' incomes are not equal
    b Prices are different in different areas
    c Some incomes are not reported
    d Higher earners pay more income tax

SECTION 2

Country B is a developed nation, whose working population are mainly employed in jobs in the tertiary sector. The country has been suffering from an economic recession and the government has reported the following indicators for the third quarter (three-month period) of 2013:

- A fall in GDP of 0.2 per cent for this quarter, which is the sixth successive quarter of falling GDP.

- A population which has increased by 400 000 to 60 400 000 from the previous year. This is noted to be due to 'increase in births, decrease in deaths and changing patterns of international migration'.

- An unemployment rate of 7.8 per cent, having increased by 0.1 per cent over the quarter, indicating that unemployment is still increasing but at a slower rate than in previous quarters. However, there are 'over one million employed and self-employed people working part-time, as they are unable to find a full-time job'.

- An inflation rate of 2.3 per cent as measured by the Retail Prices Index, or 1.9 per cent as measured by the Consumer Prices Index, the government's preferred measure. It is noted that the largest upward pressure on inflation is due to the rising price of oil leading to increasing transport costs for businesses and individuals.

1 a Explain what 'A fall in GDP' means. (2)

b Why might the government of Country B be worried by 'six successive quarters of falling GDP'? (2)

c 'Most of the working population in Country B are employed in the tertiary sector'. Give examples of one occupation in each of the three industrial sectors. (3)

d Calculate the percentage increase in the country's population from the previous year. (2)

e Discuss whether 'over one million people working part-time' may benefit the economy of Country B. (6)

f Explain what is measured by the 'HDI' or Human Development Index. (3)

g Discuss the benefits to an economist of using the HDI to compare Country B with another country rather than using GDP per head. (6)

h Using all the information in the text, write an assessment of the health of the economy of Country B. (6)

Total: 30 marks

SECTION 3

Country A is a developing nation, whose population, due to better health care, is now growing at 10 per cent per year. There are two major cities and several large towns, but the majority of the population live in rural areas and farm small areas of land. There is an increasing trend for people to move to the cities, but there are not enough jobs, so many people end up living in poverty. The increasing population is also putting pressure on resources. Gross Domestic Product (GDP) is only increasing at 2 per cent yearly, causing average prices to rise by an average of 12 per cent per year.

1.
   a. Explain why 'better health care' may lead to an increase in population. (4)
   b. Country A's government measures price changes using a Retail Prices Index. Explain how this is constructed. (6)
   c. Using the information given, explain how you would expect the measure of 'GDP per head' to have changed. (4)
   d. Discuss whether GDP might be an accurate way to measure living standards in Country A. (6)

2. The government of Country A is worried about the rising prices. The Minister of Finance is quoted as saying '12 per cent inflation per year is far too high'.
   a. Explain why the increasing population of Country A is causing prices to rise at 12 per cent per year. (4)
   b. Why are some types of products, such as basic foodstuffs, given a 'prominent weighting' in the Retail Prices Index in Country A? (4)
   c. Explain the effects of 12 per cent inflation on the different population groups of Country A. (6)
   d. Discuss why the RPI may not provide an accurate measure of the level of price rises suffered by all citizens in Country A. (6)

3. In the capital city of Country A, 30 per cent of people are estimated as being unemployed. There are increasing numbers of jobs in secondary employment in new factories, but people moving into the city do not have appropriate skills, as they only have experience in primary farming occupations.
   a. Why might it be difficult to measure the unemployment rate in the capital city of Country A? (4)
   b. Explain the economic causes of unemployment of the people moving into the capital city of Country A. (6)
   c. Describe likely changes in the structure of industry and types of occupation that will be available to Country A's population as it becomes more developed. (4)
   d. How might the government of Country A decrease the level of unemployment in its capital city? (6)

4. The President of Country A has been quoted as saying 'this increase in our population can only be good for living standards in the long-run, as we will have more workers'.
   a. Explain what is meant by 'living standards'. (3)
   b. Explain the President's view that 'more workers will lead to better living standards'. (3)
   c. Apart from using GDP to measure output, how might living standards in a country be measured? (6)
   d. Discuss which will be the most important factors that will determine whether the President will be proved correct in his assumption. (8)

   Total: 80 marks

6 International trade and globalisation

This final unit explores the nature of the international economy. It starts out by identifying the reasons for and benefits of specialization at a national level. The unit then introduces globalization and the global economy. Key definitions are provided of terms, including 'globalization' and 'multinational companies'.

The relative benefits of free trade and protection are set out as well as the reasons why countries impose trade restrictions despite the advantages of free trade.

The unit then goes on to explain exchange rates as the value of one country's currency when exchanged with the currencies of other nations. Some countries allow their currency to find its own value on currency exchanges, whereas others fix the value against that of other currencies. The unit introduces the importance of international trade currencies such as the dollar which is widely accepted in international commerce. The unit spells out the significant impact of fluctuations in currencies, e.g. through depreciation and appreciation.

The last section shows the structure of the balance of payments. The most significant component is the current account which shows flows of currency resulting from trade between a country and the rest of the world. The section identifies the problems of running a current account surplus or deficit. Policies to achieve balance of payments stability are outlined.

TOPIC COVERAGE

Students will cover the following topics:
- Specialisation at national level – advantages and disadvantages
- Globalisation and the role of multinationals
- discuss the causes and consequences of deflation.
- Benefits of free trade and methods and reasons for protections
- Consequences of protection
- Definition and determination of exchange rates
- Causes and consequences of exchange rate fluctuations
- Floating and fixed exchange rates
- Structure of the balance of payments
- Consequences of deficits and surpluses
- Policies to achieve balance of payments stability

6.1 International specialisation

6.1.1 Advantages and disadvantages of specialisation

TOPIC GUIDANCE

Students should be able to:
- describe the benefits and disadvantages of specialisation at regional and national levels.

Regional specialisation

Countries and regions concentrate on producing things that they are best at producing rather than wasting resources on products that they make less efficiently.

The climate of a country is obviously a major factor affecting what a country produces. Italy shows how a country can have distinct **regional specialisations**: in the north, the cooler climate is suitable for producing grains, meat and fruits such as pears and apples. The region is also industrialised, with large car factories. In the warmer south, citrus fruits (oranges and lemons), oils and vegetables are produced and there is a stronger focus on agriculture and tourism. This pattern of regional specialisation has led to more skilled workers in the north, and less availability of capital and skilled workers in the south – southern Italy has about 40 per cent of Italy's population, but only earns 25 per cent of the country's GDP.

Southern Italy specialises in producing citrus fruit because its resources, including land and climate, give it an advantage in this line of production

International specialisation

The table shows national specialisation that has resulted from superior factor endowments (the qualities of production factors that make them particularly efficient at doing certain things).

Country	Main product and factor endowment
Saudi Arabia	World's leading producer of oil: it has the most plentiful oil reserves in the world, and the technology to extract it
Japan	World's leading producers of cars: new technologies have been used to develop efficient manufacturing systems
Guinea	Has the world's largest reserves of bauxite lying close to the earth's surface; this is extracted by large earth-movers and then refined to make aluminium
New Zealand	A cool, damp climate and pastures have led to the country becoming a leading producer of lamb and wool
UK	Major publisher of books, based on its history of developing expertise in this industry over time

ACTIVITY

What products does your country specialise in producing? Why does your country specialise in making these products? Keep notes of your findings in order to demonstrate the benefits of specialization in the context of your domestic economy.

How does specialisation occur?

Countries specialise where they have superior factor endowments. There are several reasons for doing this.

- The country has the resources required to produce certain goods. For example, the geology of South Africa has created the rock formations in which diamonds are found.

- The country has abundant resources of the right kind. Some resources, such as oil reserves, occur naturally; others, such as Japan's investment in automated car manufacturing technology, are developed over time.
- By **trading**, countries may be able to acquire certain goods more cheaply than they can produce them domestically. For example, people in the UK can buy t-shirts made in Pakistan for the equivalent of just three or four US dollars. It would cost at least twice as much to make a similar t-shirt in a British factory.

The table shows some of the advantages and disadvantages of specialisation.

Advantages	Disadvantages
Enables increased output: Mexico, for example, uses large areas of land for onion growing; large-scale farming yields large low-cost outputs.	A country can be vulnerable if it has to rely on imports to meet its needs. For example, if a country fails to invest in its own domestic energy industries, it will have to import energy from overseas.
Consumers have access to a greater variety of higher-quality products from across the world.	A country may be vulnerable if the specialised products can be replaced by alternatives. For example, Malaysia produced large quantities of rubber from rubber plantations for the automobile industry – today most of the rubber is produced synthetically.
Specialisation and international trade increase the size of the market, enabling economies of scale to take place.	Jobs in areas such as production may be vulnerable if cheaper labour is available elsewhere. Too much specialisation can result in inflexibility in the economy.
Leads to greater efficiency which in turn leads to production being carried out by the most efficient producers/countries.	A country becomes very vulnerable to changes in exchange rates and also world economic conditions.

KEY POINTS

1. Specialisation involves concentration on what a country does most efficiently.
2. Regional specialisation often results from differences in climate, geography or skills of the local population. People in these areas develop skills based on the specialisation.
3. International specialisation increases world production and provides consumers with greater variety and choice. Resources are used more efficiently, but risks are involved.

SUMMARY QUESTIONS

1. What is international specialisation? Give one example of a country that specialises in a:
   a   primary product
   b   secondary product
   c   tertiary service.
2. Explain the difference between regional and international specialisation.
3. What arguments would you put forward to encourage a country to increase its specialisation in products that it makes well?

STUDY TIP

Specialisation is an important concept in economics. You should be able to explain what it means and how it comes about, and discuss its various advantages and disadvantages. It can be useful to support the points you are making with appropriate examples.

6.2 Globalisation, free trade and protection

6.2.1 Globalisation

TOPIC GUIDANCE

Students should be able to:
- define globalisation
- outline key benefits and drawbacks resulting from globalisation.

The nature of globalisation

Globalisation involves the free movement of goods, services, capital, labour and technology. In a global economy, goods and services can be produced in many different places and transported for sale across the world. This leads to intense competition.

Globalisation involves a number of interrelated concepts. A key feature is that products, people and capital are highly mobile. Shops stock products sourced from overseas, and products and services made near you are exported. People travel to your country as students, managers, workers, researchers and tourists, for example. Enterprises in your country have overseas investors, and people from your country invest overseas.

> **CASE STUDY** | The Caribbean: impact of globalisation
>
> The 25 countries in the Caribbean differ widely, comprising relatively large economies – Jamaica (population around 3 million); Trinidad (around 1.5 million) – and smaller ones – Aruba has around 100 000 inhabitants.
>
> Mass-produced products can be distributed to the Caribbean from much larger countries (such as China and Brazil) at very low cost. Some people are concerned about the disappearance of regional distinctions.
>
> Caribbean countries have opportunities to export to a global market. Instant communication via the internet mean that producers of niche products such as recording, film and art studios can now export worldwide.
>
> The development of air links has made the Caribbean region one of the prime global destinations for tourism.
>
> **Specialisation** enables some Caribbean economies to mass produce for global markets. For example, Trinidad brings revenue into the Caribbean by supplying oil and gas to many countries outside the area.
>
> **Questions**
>
> 1 In what ways does globalisation pose a threat to relatively small countries in the Caribbean?
>
> 2 What are the key benefits of globalisation to businesses and consumers in the Caribbean?

Oil and gas produced in Trinidad is sold within the country, within the wider Caribbean area, in the US South America and beyond

DID YOU KNOW?

Being integrated into the global economy enables national economies to benefit from global pools of capital, the international labour force, technology transfer and selling into international markets. Additionally, the economy will benefit from the import of foreign goods and services.

Benefits of globalisation

Globalisation enables large companies to exploit huge economies of scale. For example, large car companies can produce vehicles in the car plants of Brazil and Mexico where labour is relatively cheap.

Multinational firms are able to make vast sales and profits. For example, in the first quarter of 2017 US technology company Apple posted profits of US$17.8 million on sales of US$78.3 million, which worked out as US$3.36 for every share in the company. Consumers around the world benefit from Apple's high-quality products made by Apple at relatively low cost because of economies of scale. The countries where Apple has manufacturing plants and retail outlets, e.g. Mongolia, China and South Korea, also benefit.

Globalisation also offers opportunities through international joint ventures: businesses owned by a local firm and an overseas partner. The local firm provides specialist knowledge of markets and contacts; the overseas partner provides additional capital and greater access to global markets.

Global companies enable countries to develop faster through technology transfer, through sharing of technological know-how and equipment. The free movement of goods within large trading areas encourages international specialisation.

Disadvantages of globalisation

A major challenge is the scale of competition facing businesses in smaller countries. Muitinationals (e.g in the US Europe, China, Brazil and India) have huge domestic markets, enabling large-scale production and distribution. This drives down their costs.

Global companies spread marketing, advertising and production costs across global sales. Globalisation has a negative impact on economies that rely on a narrow range of products. For example, some Caribbean islands produce copra, sugar, mother of pearl and a small number of other products on a small scale. It is difficult for them to compete with large plantations in Central and South America. The worst hit economies suffer from a lack of productive capital and the export of capital to pay interest on debts.

The decline of agriculture in smaller countries often leads to rising unemployment and falling living standards. Consumers in poorer countries cannot afford global brands. A global economy is also volatile when countries become more interdependent. A crisis in one part of the economic system can spread across many economies, leading to exchange rate volatility and downturns in economic activity.

> **DID YOU KNOW?**
>
> Negative impacts of globalisation for poorer countries include falling living standards, rising unemployment and the inability to purchase goods afforded by richer people (the problem of relative poverty). Governments in poorer countries may resort to borrowing from international lenders (including the International Monetary Fund) to finance debt and fund development. The more indebted the nation becomes, the more conditions lenders can impose – so governments lose control over their domestic economic policy making.

> **KEY POINTS**
>
> 1. Globalisation is an economic process involving increased linking of people, goods, services and capital across international borders.
>
> 2. Firms benefit from economies of scale and access to wider markets. Consumers benefit from a greater choice of goods and lower prices. Workers benefit from access to new and better paid international jobs. Many countries benefit through faster growth.
>
> 3. Smaller, localised businesses may not be able to compete in a global marketplace. Some countries will experience slower growth and increasing debt. The result will be fewer job opportunities and reduced living standards.

> **SUMMARY QUESTIONS**
>
> 1. Using the example of your country's economy, list ways in which the following groups are benefiting from globalisation:
>   a businesses   b the government   c consumers
>
> 2. Using your country's economy, give specific examples of businesses and consumers suffering as a result of globalisation.
>
> 3. Define globalisation in two sentences.

6.2.2 Multinationals

> **TOPIC GUIDANCE**
>
> Students should be able to:
> - describe multinationals
> - outline the benefits and drawbacks of being a multinational, and the impact on host countries.

> **DID YOU KNOW?**
>
> Some multinationals, such as the Ford Motor Company in the US and the Anglo-Dutch oil company Shell, have grown steadily for more than 100 years. Others, such as the mobile phone company China Mobile and Ali Baba (a Chinese website business trading goods between businesses), have grown rapidly in recent years.

> **STUDY TIP**
>
> Make sure you understand that a multinational does not just sell abroad: it is a company that produces abroad – that is, it has factories in a number of different countries.

Multinational companies

Multinational companies, as the name suggests, produce and sell products in many countries. They have their headquarters in one country and may focus on a particular region of the world, but many have shareholders worldwide.

CASE STUDY | Haier

Haier is one of the world's largest manufacturers of white goods, e.g. refrigerators and washing machines. It has grown rapidly to become a multinational selling 'brown' goods as well – televisions, computers, mobile phones and cameras.

The company was set up in 1984. Between 1984 and 1998 the company expanded in China, developing a strong brand reputation for providing excellent goods and service to customers. It exported an increasing number of goods to Malaysia, India, Pakistan and Nigeria.

The Chinese multinational Haier is one of the world's leading producers of white goods manufactured and sold in many countries

Haier then set up its own factories, marketing and research and design centres in other countries: it opened a large factory and research centre in South Carolina in the US from where it sells a range of products to the US market, Canada and Mexico. Haier now has 30 international manufacturing plants worldwide.

Today over 30 per cent of all domestic appliances in China are sold by Haier. One of the reasons for success overseas is that products were adapted to suit local conditions. For example, a Haier fridge can keep food frozen for up to 100 hours after a power cut.

Questions

1. How does Haier fit the definition of being a multinational company?
2. What benefits will Haier receive from operating in different countries?
3. How might consumers in the US benefit from Haier's manufacturing in that country?

Measuring the size of multinationals

The table shows how the size of multinational companies can be measured.

Number of operating countries	The British-Dutch company Unilever has over 300 factories in 90 countries.
Value of all of the shares in the business	By this measure the giant US retailer Wal-Mart, and China's mobile phone company China Mobile, are two of the largest companies.
Number of employees	China's Haier (see opposite) employs 30 000 people across the globe.
Range of products	Tata Industries (India's largest industrial conglomerate) produces a range of products, from steel manufacture to cars and textiles.

Benefits and disadvantages of operating in many countries

These are some of the benefits to multinationals from operating in a range of countries.

- They gain access to natural resources that may be in limited supply in their domestic market. For example, giant steel manufacturers may be able to gain access to new iron ore deposits.
- They can access a source of labour that may be cheaper than in the home country.
- They have the opportunity for a global market – in India and China there are over a billion potential customers. Other huge markets include Brazil, Nigeria, Pakistan and Russia.

The disadvantages to multinationals of operating in many countries are that there may be different tastes, requirements and legal standards in different countries. This could make it more costly to produce different models and varieties of products.

Benefits and disadvantages to host countries

Multinationals bring employment, new products and new technologies to host countries. The presence of multinationals can speed up development. However, multinationals are sometimes criticised for not paying enough for the raw materials, nor to their employees, in poorer countries. They have also been criticised for causing pollution and environmental damage.

SUMMARY QUESTIONS

1. What is a multinational? Give five examples of multinational businesses.
2. Who owns multinational businesses? How do these owners benefit?
3. Give three reasons why a company may become a multinational.

DID YOU KNOW?

Getz Pharma has been one of the fastest-growing companies in Pakistan. It develops a range of molecules for use in pharmaceutical products such as those used to treat cardiovascular diseases, hepatology and infectious diseases. It now markets and sells its products in Asia, the Middle East and Africa.

ACTIVITY

Carry out some research into a multinational that has its home base in your country or operates in your country. Find out how many other countries it operates in. What is the current value of the shares in the company? How many people does it employ? Give examples of the range of its products. Produce a poster or wall chart to display your findings.

KEY POINTS

1. A multinational is a company that operates in several countries.
2. Some multinationals have grown over a long period. Others, such as internet-based businesses and mobile phone companies, have grown rapidly.
3. Multinationals are able to buy labour and raw materials in more countries and can sell to a much larger market.

6.2.3 The benefits of free trade

TOPIC GUIDANCE

Students should be able to:
- discuss the benefits of free trade for consumers, producers and the economy in different countries.

The ASEAN-China free trade area is the largest in the world in terms of population

The case for free trade

Free trade is trading without hindrance in the form of barriers such as import tariffs.

Free trade enables countries to specialise in what they do most efficiently and then trade with others to buy – at less cost than manufacturing itself – what other countries produce.

Free trade can make people more prosperous. If countries specialise, the global output of goods and services is increased. Along with economies of scale, more will be produced at lower cost per unit and of better quality.

Comparative advantage

Brazil is the world's leading exporter of sugar, coffee, beef and orange juice. Soya beans are its most rapidly increasing export, mainly to China. Other major exports include aircraft, vehicles, iron ore, steel, textiles and footwear. If it wished, Brazil could also be self-sufficient in making all its own clothes (using its existing land and labour), but to understand why the country concentrates instead on the other products you need to be familiar with the theory of **comparative advantage**.

An important economic principle is that of **specialisation according to comparative advantage**. This states that a country should concentrate on the lines at which it is relatively most efficient. For example, Pakistan and Bangladesh are both very efficient textile producers. This is because they have access to the raw materials such as silk, cotton and wool. They also have a highly skilled labour force and many factories equipped with modern machinery. It therefore makes sense for these countries to produce textiles.

ACTIVITY

Make a list of all the food and drink that you have consumed today. Discuss with your classmates which of these items are likely to have been produced in your own country or imported. Now list the white goods, e.g. refrigerators, washing machines, that you have in your home. Find out the make of these goods and whether they are likely to be imports.

STUDY TIP

There are clearly a number of potential advantages of free trade: make sure that you are able to discuss these various benefits.

The UK, and other European countries, import textiles from Pakistan and Bangladesh. This does not mean that the UK cannot produce textiles – indeed it has a number of textile manufacturers, particularly of woollen garments. However, many businesses that produced textiles in the UK closed down (particularly between 1970 and 2000) because they could not compete with the textile industry in Eastern Europe, Pakistan, Bangladesh and elsewhere. Instead of producing textiles the UK therefore concentrates on products in which it has a comparative advantage, in this case pharmaceutical products, among others.

Other benefits of free trade

- Free trade enables people to sell their products to those who are willing to pay the highest price for them. This means that the producer is able to capture a larger proportion of the value of the product.
- Free trade increases the range of products available, giving consumers more choice.
- Free trade enables consumers to buy better-quality imports from other countries.
- Free trade enhances the spread of new ideas, new lifestyles and new products.
- New job opportunities result from the growth of production.

The World Trade Organization

The **World Trade Organization (WTO)** was set up in 1995. Its purpose is to open up trade for the benefit of all, achieved by rules and agreements set out for trading between nations. Its main principles are:

- to pursue open borders – that is, free trade
- the most favoured nation principle: if a country reduces tariffs to another country it will do so to all the other members of the WTO.

WTO agreements are followed by most of the world's trading nations. Through the organisation, trade ministers come together to make agreements and to settle trading disputes. The main activities are negotiating a reduction or elimination of import tariffs and other barriers to trade, and agreeing rules on the conduct of trade, e.g. rules relating to dumping of waste.

Areas in which free trade operates

There are a number of **free trade areas**. These include:

- North American Free Trade Area (NAFTA): the US Canada and Mexico
- Asia-Pacific Cooperation, consisting of over 20 countries, including the US, Japan, Russia and China
- Association of South East Asian Nations (ASEAN)
- South American Free Trade Area (SAFTA).

The European Union (EU), currently consisting of 28 countries including Germany, France and Spain, is also an area in which free trade operates.

> **ACTIVITY**
>
> Mexico is a major producer of agricultural products. It is the world's largest producer of avocados, onions, limes, lemons and sunflower seeds. Produce a poster that explains how Mexico benefits from concentrating on these agricultural products.

> **STUDY TIP**
>
> It is proposed that the European Union will reduce in size from 28 to 27 countries as a result of the decision of the UK to withdraw from the group.

> **KEY POINTS**
>
> 1. Free trade leads to specialisation and the possibility of increased production of goods at lower cost.
> 2. With free trade, countries can specialise in lines where they have the greatest comparative advantage.
> 3. There are a number of free trade areas in the world, the largest of which is ASEAN-China.

> **SUMMARY QUESTIONS**
>
> 1. Explain how your country benefits from advantages resulting from free trade.
> 2. Explain why your country imports a particular product that it could produce domestically, but chooses not to.
> 3. How does the WTO contribute to creating free trade?

6.2.4 Methods of protection

TOPIC GUIDANCE

Students should be able to:
- discuss methods of trade protection.

In 2009 Ecuador imposed import tariffs on over 600 goods, including pasta, an important part of the diet for Ecuadoreans

ACTIVITY

Carry out some research to find examples of goods that are protected in your country against foreign imports by the use of:

a import quotas
b import tariffs
c the requirement for importers to have an import licence.

Report your findings to your class and explain how these different methods of protection help domestic industries.

What is protection?

Trade **protection** is restricting the entry of foreign goods into a domestic market, or imposing a tax to raise the price of imports.

Limiting numbers or prices

To protect domestic industries, a government can restrict the number of imports allowed into its country. It can make imports more expensive by taxing them. Another way of restricting imports is to limit the availability of foreign exchange required to purchase them.

Methods of trade protection

The following are the main methods of protection.

- **Import tariffs**: these are taxes on types of imports. For example, the US has imposed a tariff on imported car tyres to protect its own tyre industry from cheaper imports – or from certain groups of countries. Tariffs increase the cost of importing and increase the price of the imported goods in domestic markets. Tariffs can also be imposed on exports. However, they are unlikely to be used, as this would have a negative effect on domestic industries.
- **Import quotas**: quotas set a physical limit on the number of imports, e.g. the number of Japanese cars entering the European Union in a given year. Restricting quantities in this way is also likely to make products more expensive.
- **Import licensing**: governments can grant licences for the import of certain goods. Not granting a licence is a type of protection.
- **Administrative complexity**: the government may require importers to fill in time-consuming paperwork. This creates a burden that can be seen as a cost and therefore a discouragement for importers.
- **Subsidies**: these are payments to a domestic producer. They make domestic goods cheaper to produce, often enabling these goods to be sold at lower prices than imports. Subsidies may take the form of a lump sum or a cheap loan to a domestic business. Export subsidies are the opposite of tariffs. They involve a direct payment to an exporter. The US government provides a number of agricultural subsidies, including those to cotton farmers.
- **Exchange control**: governments preventing or limiting the amount of foreign exchange to which importers have access. For example, if Indian importers are not allowed to buy dollars, they may not be able to buy goods from the US.
- **Exchange rate manipulation**: the government can buy or sell its own currency in order to alter the exchange rate. For example, it could sell its own currency in order to reduce the exchange rate and make exports cheaper.
- **Embargo**: this is a complete ban on the import of certain types of goods, or goods from specified countries.

CASE STUDY | Ecuador's protectionist measures

Ecuador is a small South American economy with a population of 14 million people. Its main export is oil. As a result of the world recession in 2009, the price of oil on world markets fell significantly. Ecuador's currency is the US dollar. With the recession the country was suddenly exposed to very high import costs compared with exports – leading to a huge deficit on the current account. The government imposed tariffs on 627 products, including furniture, phones, shoes and pasta, intended to halve the country's imports. The government argued that without these measures the country would have rapidly run out of money. These measures have succeeded in protecting Ecuadorean industries and in keeping the economy running in difficult times.

Questions

1. Why did Ecuador decide to impose tariffs on so many goods? What criteria might the government have selected in choosing goods to protect?
2. What would be the impact if many other countries decided to act in the same way as Ecuador?
3. Who would have benefited most from Ecuador's actions?

KEY POINTS

1. Protectionism is the means by which a government 'protects' its economy.
2. The main methods of protecting domestic industries are through tariffs and quotas.
3. Countries may use protectionist measures to improve their current account balances.

SUMMARY QUESTIONS

1. Classify the following according to whether they predominantly affect the price or the quantity of imports:
   a tariffs
   b embargoes
   c quotas
   d import licences
2. What would be the impact on the quantity of exports of introducing an export subsidy?
3. How can governments make it more difficult for importers to import goods?

STUDY TIP

You should be able to discuss the various methods of trade protection that can be used. This means that you need to consider their relative advantages and disadvantages.

DID YOU KNOW?

In 2000 Ecuador adopted the US dollar as its currency. Up to that point the country had been characterised by instability and high levels of inflation. Introducing the US dollar (known as dollarisation) was designed to create price stability. A small number of other countries use the US dollar as their currency. See if you can find out which they are.

ACTIVITY

Carry out some research to identify five protectionist measures that have each been used recently by a country to protect its domestic industries. Explain why the country used this measure and outline the advantages and disadvantages of using each one. Produce a leaflet of your findings to compare with others in your group.

6.2.5 Reasons for protection

> **TOPIC GUIDANCE**
>
> Students should be able to:
> - discuss the reasons for and consequences of protection.

> **DID YOU KNOW?**
>
> An infant industry may need some trade protection as it develops in an economy. India and Pakistan have developed their pharmaceutical industries in the last 30 years – initially they needed protection against European and US imports. Today companies from India and Pakistan are world leaders in the industry.

> **STUDY TIP**
>
> When discussing protectionism you should be able to consider both its advantages and disadvantages and come to a reasoned conclusion.

Most countries subsidise wind energy – because it is an infant industry and part of a larger strategic industry

Reasons for protection

In section 6.2.4 we saw how countries can take measures to protect domestic industries. Here we look at the purposes of these measures.

- To help a new industry to grow: for example, a country trying to develop its own biofuels industry might find it difficult to compete with other large countries that have already developed their own large-scale biofuels industry, such as Brazil or the US. There is a good case for protecting new **infant industries** until they are strong enough to be competitive. The government can then gradually reduce the protective measures.
- To protect small industries that are important to an economy: for example, **small island economies**, such as Mauritius, will not be able to produce agricultural goods, such as sugar cane, or manufacture products, such as packet sugar, on the same scale as large countries. However, the small country may want to develop the sugar industry because the climate and conditions in that country are favourable for sugar production.
- To protect local jobs against cheap imports from large countries: many people in a country might depend on, for example, work in the textile industry. A strong argument for protection is to protect domestic industries against dumping (selling at a price that is below the cost – technically the marginal cost – of producing a product). This occurs when a business takes advantage of different price elasticity of demand in two markets. It may sell mass-produced goods at a relatively high price at home, but the goods will also be exported and sold at a very low cost overseas.

- To protect the current account of the balance of payments: the case study in section 6.2.4 showed how Ecuador has imposed tariffs on over 600 products to reduce imports and prevent the country getting into debt.
- To protect domestic industries from cheap subsidised imports: solar power manufacturers in the US receive government subsidies to protect this important industry from cheap, state-subsidised solar panels from China. China has rapidly become the world's biggest producer of solar panels (two thirds of global production in 2017), and competing countries have raised tariffs to prevent dumping.
- To protect strategic industries, e.g. electricity, gas, nuclear, wind and solar energy: without steady energy supplies a country's industries could be forced to shut down. Governments try to make sure that a large percentage of energy is supplied within the domestic economy. In the UK the government has been subsidising the development of wind, wave and nuclear energy, as well as low carbon-emitting coal-fired power stations.
- To encourage green and environmentally friendly technologies: the government may subsidise these technologies within the domestic economy. Industries that are less cost-efficient but more environmentally efficient are protected against lower-cost but less environmentally efficient imports.
- To protect intellectual property rights (IPRs) such as the formula for a new medicine or scientific invention: it may take years of research to develop these and it may be argued that individuals, businesses and countries should be able to protect them against copying.

Consequences of protectionism

Many economists believe that the key consequence of protectionism is a reduction in world trade, output and jobs. Once barriers go up, they tend to be reciprocated in what have been referred to as '**beggar my neighbour**' policies.

Tariffs and quotas are seen as a means to protect domestic industry (particularly new industries). However, competitors tend to take a dim view of them, and often take retaliatory action when they are imposed. For example, US President Trump threatened to impose tariffs on a range of industrial goods imported from Mexico, even when those goods are produced by US companies operating there. It is likely that Mexico will retaliate by imposing tariffs on goods from the US. The net effect will be a reduction in global trade.

Protecting home industries from cheap foreign imports means that on an international scale there will be a reduction in economic efficiency (unless those goods are being artificially subsidised by the foreign government). Economies are most efficient when they use resources (land, machinery, etc.) in the most productive way. Subsidies and tariffs distort patterns of efficiency by enabling less efficient producers to survive.

Protectionism may protect jobs in the short term, but it is likely to lead to slower economic growth overall. Not only does the home country lose out but, in addition, its trading partners will suffer from the loss of trade, jobs, and reductions in growth.

ACTIVITY

Find a story in the national press about the protection of a national industry. Then produce a balanced editorial article, setting out details of the protective measure and why it has been introduced. Present arguments in your editorial for and against the protective measure from the perspective of the home economy.

DID YOU KNOW?

Some Americans argued that the US should not join NAFTA. They argued that American jobs would be lost to Mexican workers who would be willing to work for lower wages. It was also argued that Mexico's lower environmental standards would give Mexican firms an unfair comparative advantage.

KEY POINTS

1. Protectionism can be used to support infant industries and strategic industries.
2. Protectionism helps against the effects of dumping and against imports from countries with a poor environmental record.
3. All countries protect their industries in some ways.

SUMMARY QUESTIONS

1. Set out three arguments for protectionism that you feel are valid.
2. Identify two arguments for protectionism that you feel have less merit.
3. In what situations are all countries likely to protect their industries?

6.3 Foreign exchange rates
6.3.1 Exchange rates

TOPIC GUIDANCE

Students should be able to:
- define exchange rates
- explain how exchange rates are determined
- compare floating and fixed exchange rate systems.

DID YOU KNOW?

The main determinant of an exchange rate is the demand and supply of currencies. the key influence on demand is the extent to which foreigners want to purchase the goods and services traded by a country.

For example, if Indian importers want to purchase more goods from China, they will need Chinese yuan (*remnimbi*) to buy the goods.

The exchange rates of international currencies (say, for example, the US dollar) are determined both by the demand for US goods and the wider demand for dollars in global saving and trading.

ACTIVITY

Find out the current exchange rate of your currency against the euro, US dollar, yuan and Indian rupee. After two weeks, check the exchange rates again. How have they altered? What explanations can you provide for this? Produce a graph or chart that shows the rates over six weeks.

The exchange rate

When you buy t-shirts or other items of clothing produced in China you will want to pay for them in the currency of your own country (unless of course you live in China). The t-shirts will most likely have been imported into your country by a specialist importer or by a large retailer. The Chinese manufacturer that made the t-shirts may not want to be paid by the importer in the currency of your country. This is because the Chinese manufacturer will need to pay its own workers and suppliers of cotton in the currency of China, the yuan. The importer will therefore need to purchase yuan to pay the Chinese manufacturer. Foreign currency can be bought and sold in the foreign exchange market (or forex). This market specialises in exchanging dollars, yuan, rupees and other currencies.

The exchange rate between the US dollar and the Indian rupee is determined by demand and supply in international currency markets

The **exchange rate** between two currencies is determined by demand and supply. If the demand for US dollars by Indians (to buy US goods) rises quickly while the demand for rupees by Americans (to buy Indian goods) remains steady, then the value of the dollar will rise against the rupee, e.g. from US$1 = 65 rupees to US$1 = 67 rupees.

You can see from this analysis that a major determinant of the value of a currency is how popular the currency is – that is, the strength of demand for it. One of the major factors influencing demand is the extent to which foreigners want to buy goods from that country. For example, the Singapore dollar tends to be a relatively strong currency because many foreigners buy goods from Singaporean companies.

Another factor strengthening a currency is its use for international trading. For example, the US dollar has for many years been used by countries for trading because it tends to keep its value over time. It is therefore both a means of exchange and a store of value (see Unit 3.1).

Multiple exchange rates

There is not just one exchange rate for a currency: it can often be exchanged for the currencies of many other countries, e.g. the yuan against the dollar, the yuan against the euro, the yuan against the rupee. This means that there can be multiple exchange rates.

Exchange rate systems

A country's government must decide how to manage (influence) the exchange rate. There are two main approaches.

- **Fixed exchange rates**: the value of the currency is fixed against another currency or group of currencies. This fixed rate is maintained by the government. For example, the government could set the exchange rate such that two dollars of your currency might be exchanged for one US dollar. This helps to make the currency stable. However, it may make it difficult for the country to sell its goods on international markets if the exchange rate is set at too high a level for exporters to be competitive. A disadvantage of having a fixed rate is that the government has to support the existing rate even when the rate makes it difficult for exporters to sell their goods competitively.

- **Floating exchange rates**: the value of your currency changes from day to day according to the demand for, and the supply of, it. If we are finding it difficult to sell exports the currency will fall in price (as demand falls). Lowering the price of the exports makes them more competitive – and so sales should improve.

CASE STUDY | The Eurozone

Most of the countries in the European Union have a shared currency, the euro. These countries include France and Germany, and smaller economies such as Luxembourg and Greece. An advantage of having a common currency is that there is no need for the paperwork and costs involved in exchanging money. This makes trade within the Eurozone more efficient. Management of the euro is carried out by the European Central Bank in Frankfurt. The euro has become an important international exchange currency. Exporters from smaller countries are happy to be paid in euros or US dollars, knowing that these currencies are likely to retain their value.

Questions

1 What benefits would there be to an individual country from being part of a common currency zone?
2 Why might German manufacturers be pleased that their country is part of the Eurozone?

DID YOU KNOW?

The equilibrium exchange rate between one currency and another is the price where the demand for that currency is equal to its supply. It is important for central banks to know what this price is so that the exchange rate is not set artificially high or low.

STUDY TIP

You should be able to demonstrate an understanding of the various advantages and disadvantages of these two types of exchange rate system.

KEY POINTS

1 The exchange rate is the rate at which one currency exchanges for others.
2 A country's currency will have multiple exchange rates.
3 Exchange rates can be fixed against other currencies or be free to float according to the laws of supply and demand.

SUMMARY QUESTIONS

1 Define the term 'exchange rate'.
2 What factors determine the exchange rate of one currency against another?
3 What are the benefits to producers of having a freely floating exchange rate rather than a fixed one?

6.3.2 Causes of foreign exchange rate fluctuations

TOPIC GUIDANCE

Students should be able to:
- discuss the causes of exchange rate fluctuations.

The US dollar is used widely as a generally acceptable international exchange currency

DID YOU KNOW?

A destabilising effect on currencies can be caused by speculators – people who make money from trading in currencies. Sometimes they will sell a country's currency, and others rush to do the same. The speculator might then buy the currency back at a much lower price and gamble that it will rise again.

Appreciation and depreciation

Another way of looking at the exchange rate is as the price of buying the currency of one country with that of another country. Like other prices, the exchange rate will then be determined by the demand for, and the supply of it.

If more people in India want to buy US dollars, the demand curve will shift to the right and the price of dollars will increase when bought with rupees. This may be because more Indians want to import goods from the US. Figure 6.3.2.1 shows this change. It is referred to as an **appreciation** in the price of the dollar. (In contrast, if Indians want to buy fewer goods from the US, this leads to a fall in demand for dollars and a fall in value – that is, **depreciation** – of the dollar.)

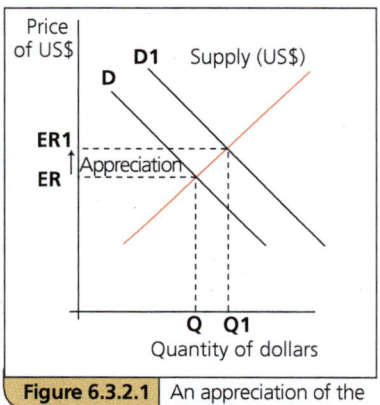

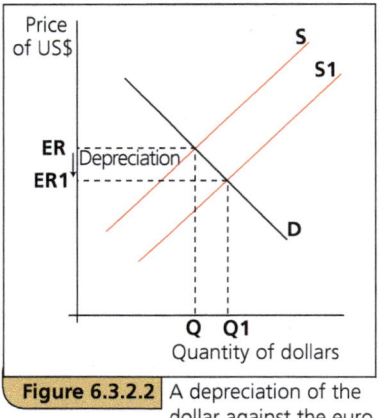

Figure 6.3.2.1 An appreciation of the dollar against the rupee

Figure 6.3.2.2 A depreciation of the dollar against the euro

The price of a currency may fall as a result of an increase in the supply of that currency, e.g. as a result of citizens of that country using their domestic currency to buy more imports. An example of this is that the US dollar is accepted widely as an international trading currency and more and more dollars have been entering the international exchange market. The increase in supply of dollars over time (see Figure 6.3.2.2) leads to its depreciation against other currencies, such as the European Union's euro. For the last 25 years the US has been running large current account deficits with the rest of the world. This has helped the world economy because US dollars are widely accepted as a means of international exchange.

Under a system of freely floating exchange rates the value of currencies will appreciate and depreciate continually, in line with changes in demand for, and supply of, currencies for international exchange.

Foreign exchange is bought and sold for trading purposes and also for investment, such as buying shares in companies in other countries. Some people also buy currency in order to speculate, e.g. to buy at a low price and sell when prices rise.

> **DID YOU KNOW?**
>
> Currency price can also be affected by the interest rate in one country compared with interest rates in other countries. Investors want to invest where interest rates are higher: raising the rates can encourage an inflow of capital, increasing demand for the currency and leading to a rise in its exchange value. When money is moved from one country to another to take advantage of differences in interest rates, it is known as 'hot money'.

Devaluation and revaluation

Revaluation of a currency occurs when its value is adjusted. For example, the rate of exchange between a country's currency and the US dollar was previously 10 units to one US dollar. Now the government changes the rate to 5 units equal to one US dollar. This would make the dollars half as expensive to people wanting to buy them with the revalued currency.

In a system where exchange rates are fixed against other currencies, they may become overvalued over time. For example, a country might find that at the existing exchange rate it is difficult for exporters to compete with cheaper (or better-quality) products from rival countries. The government may then have to act and **devalue** the currency – that is, force the exchange rate down. The central bank would be instructed to supply an increased quantity of the currency onto international markets. This would reduce its price and bring about **devaluation** (see Figure 6.3.2.3), and at the same time make imports more expensive. These two effects would help to improve the current account balance (see Unit 6.4).

> **KEY POINTS**
>
> 1. Fluctuations in exchange rates are caused by changes in the supply and demand of international currencies.
> 2. Changes in demand and supply for currencies result from the demand and supply of currencies for trade purposes, and for capital flows.
> 3. Speculation can lead to unsettling changes in the price of foreign exchange.

> **SUMMARY QUESTIONS**
>
> 1. How might a change in the demand for the Indian rupee, by people in the Eurozone buying more Indian goods, lead to a change in the exchange rate of the rupee against the euro?
> 2. How might a change in the supply of the New Zealand dollar lead to a change in its exchange rate against other currencies?
> 3. Explain the difference between:
>   a depreciation and devaluation
>   b appreciation and revaluation.

> **DID YOU KNOW?**
>
> Devaluation is a serious step to take – before it takes place, foreign exchange dealers lose confidence in a currency and try to sell it, often leading to a greater fall in the currency than the government devaluing their currency would wish.

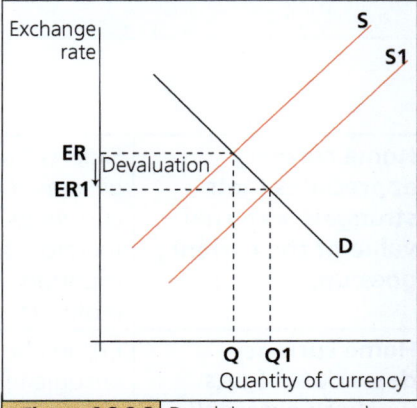

Figure 6.3.2.3 Devaluing a currency by increasing its supply

> **STUDY TIP**
>
> Make sure that you understand the difference between an appreciation and a revaluation, and a depreciation and a devaluation of a currency.

> **DID YOU KNOW?**
>
> Multinational companies affect exchange rates because they are responsible for most global trade. For example, if a large Chinese company starts to purchase large quantities of resources from Mongolia, or builds a new plant there, the Mongolian currency (the tugrik) will not only appreciate against the yuan, but also against other currencies.

6.3.3 Consequences of fluctuations

> **TOPIC GUIDANCE**
>
> Students should be able to:
> - discuss the consequences of exchange rate fluctuations.

Fluctuating exchange rates

Changing exchange rates affect those most concerned with the trading process – exporters and importers. They also have knock-on impacts on the economy. For example, they cause price changes for consumers (of imported goods), and for producers whose inputs have an imported component, such as the cost of raw materials, and energy costs.

The table below shows the effect of rises and falls in the value of a currency.

Home currency appreciates (gets stronger); external value of the currency goes up.	Exports from home country become more expensive to customers from other countries, therefore more difficult to sell. Exporters will sell less/make less profit. Value of exports decreases.	Imports from other countries become cheaper, including raw materials and finished goods. Importers will find goods from other countries cheaper to buy, so they can sell more in the home country, enabling them to make more profit. Value of imports increases.
Home currency depreciates (gets weaker); external value of the currency goes down.	Exports from home country become less expensive to customers from other countries, therefore easier to sell. Exporters will sell more/make more profit. Value of exports increases.	Imports from other countries become more expensive, including raw materials and finished goods. Importers will find goods from other countries more expensive to buy, so they can sell less in the home country/make less profit. Value of imports increases.

Strong demand for Australian coal in recent years was one factor leading to an increase in demand and hence the price of the Australian dollar – increasing profits in Australian mining

> **STUDY TIP**
>
> Make sure that you can show an understanding of both the causes and the consequences of exchange rate fluctuations.

> **CASE STUDY** | **The Malaysian ringgit**
>
> The Malaysian ringgit (MR) is the official currency of Malaysia. It is made up of 100 sen (cents). The currency is printed by Bank Negara Malaysia, which also intervenes to ensure a certain level of stability.
>
> Between 1997 and 2005, the currency was pegged against the US$, but today it is allowed to float against a number of currencies. It is not freely tradeable outside of Malaysia.
>
> China is the major trading partner of Malaysia, so events in China impact on the stability of the ringgit.
>
> The US is another of Malaysia's major trading partners. When Donald Trump was elected president in 2016, this led to a fall in the value of the rinngit. The reason for this was Trump's protectionist policies, which risk reductions in trade with countries such as Malaysia. In December 2017, one ringgit was worth 0.21 euro, 0.18 GBP and 1.62 yuan.

> **Questions**
>
> 1 Why does the Malaysian central bank allow the ringgit to change value over time? Why does it limit the degree to which it is allowed to fluctuate?
>
> 2 How is the value of the rinngit influenced by Malaysia's trade with other countries?
>
> 3 Why does Malaysia have multiple exchange rates against overseas currencies?

Price elasticity of demand for exports and imports

The consequences of exchange rate fluctuations depend on the elasticity of demand for traded goods. In the first decade of the 21st century, the Australian dollar was a popular currency, due to the high demand for Australian goods, particularly from China (for Australian coal and minerals). Demand for Australian goods was inelastic, as too was the demand for the Australian dollar, which peaked at an exchange rate of AUS$1 to US$1.10 in July 2011. The table shows the effect of this.

Australian exporters	Exported goods with an inelastic demand benefited from higher sales revenues. (Other exporters selling goods with elastic demand were not able to benefit.)
Australian importers	Imported goods more cheaply, leading to increasing profit margins.
Australian consumers	Benefited from cheaper prices of imported goods.
Australian importers	Benefited from cheaper fuel, raw materials and part-finished goods.
Australian government	Benefited from a healthy economy with a strong foreign trade sector.

The consequences of a depreciating currency

There are also advantages to the depreciation of a country's currency. In 2010, the British pound (GBP) depreciated against the euro because of the weakness of the UK economy in the 2008–09 recession. This fall in the value of GBP was a major factor in helping to pull Britain out of the recession in 2010. In 2010, UK manufacturers reported increases in exports, particularly of modern engineering products, because their goods were less expensive for foreign buyers. There was another depreciation in the value of the GBP in 2016, as Britain voted to leave the European Union.

The effect of a depreciating currency depends on the price elasticity of demand for exports and imports. If demand for exports is elastic, a fall in the currency will lead to a greater than proportional increase in sales of exports. If the demand for imports is also elastic, a depreciating currency could lead to a more than proportional fall in imports.

> **ACTIVITY**
>
> Search newspapers and the internet to find a country where the exchange rate has been rising and a country where it has been falling. Create a short newspaper report highlighting the reasons for the change in the value of the currencies in question.

> **KEY POINTS**
>
> 1 Changes in the exchange rate influence five major groups.
>
> 2 An appreciating currency can help most groups in a 'strong' economy.
>
> 3 A depreciating currency can help exporters to sell more, while leading to a fall in imports.

> **SUMMARY QUESTIONS**
>
> 1 What impact is an appreciating domestic currency likely to have on
>   a exporters
>   b importers?
>
> 2 Why is it important to consider the price elasticity of demand for exports when discussing the impact of a depreciation of a currency?
>
> 3 How might consumers in a particular country be affected by the appreciation of their currency?

6.4 The balance of payments

6.4.1 The current account of the balance of payments

TOPIC GUIDANCE

Students should be able to:
- describe the structure of the current account of the balance of payments.

Food products such as olives and feta cheese are one of Greece's main exports. They appear as an export good in Greece's current account of the balance of payments

ACTIVITY

Find out the top 10 imports and exports of your country. Using this information, and material gathered from the activity in section 6.1.1, create a poster to display this information.

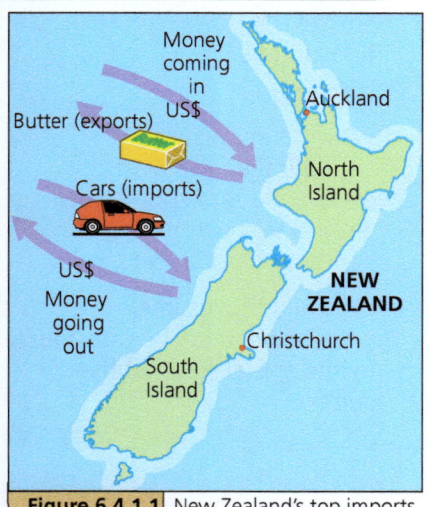

Figure 6.4.1.1 New Zealand's top imports and exports include cars and butter

The current account

The **current account** of the balance of payments shows the income earned by a country and the expenditure it makes in dealings with other countries. It consists of four elements:

- trade in goods
- trade in services
- primary income
- secondary income.

The balance of trade in goods and services

The **balance of trade in goods and services account** shows the flows of money coming into and going out of a country as a result of trading.

- **Trade in goods**: these are literally items that you can see, physical goods that a country trades. For example, in 2015 New Zealand's top exports were goods: milk powder, oil, meat, butter, cheese, fish, fruit, wood, machinery and equipment.
  - Goods exports are goods sold by New Zealanders to foreign countries bringing revenue into New Zealand.
  - Goods imports are purchases by New Zealanders of goods from other countries.
- **Trade in services**: these are non-physical traded items. The UK's main services include banking, insurance and transporting goods.
  - Services exports consist of services sold to foreigners, bringing revenue into the UK.
  - Services imports consist of expenditures on services bought from outside a country. For example, when a UK company hires an overseas shipping company to transport goods for it, the payment is counted as a services import.
- **Exports** – lead to inflows of money.
- **Imports** – lead to outflows of money.

The balance of trade in goods and services account can therefore be set out as shown in the box opposite.

Debits represent payments to countries where goods and services are imported from. **Credits** represent receipts from sales of exports.

This is how to calculate the balance of trade in goods and services.

1. Find the balance in goods. In the illustration the balance in goods is US$10 million.
2. Find the balance in services. In the illustration the balance in services is US$300 million.

	Credits (US$ million)	Debits (US$ million)	Net difference (US$ million)
Goods			
Food, beverages, tobacco	100	40	60
Oil and fuel	0	100	–100
Manufactured goods	400	350	50
Total goods	500	490	**Balance in goods 10**
Services			
Transport	200	100	100
Financial services	300	100	200
			Balance in services 300
Current total			**Current balance 310**

> **STUDY TIP**
>
> The IMF identifies three elements of the current account. 1. The goods and services account (the overall trade balance); 2. The primary income account (factor incomes e.g. from loans and investments); 3. The secondary income account (transfer payments).

3 Find the balance of trade by combining the totals from the balance in goods and services. In the illustration the country has a surplus on both goods and services trading, giving it a positive current balance. The current balance is US$310 million.

Balance in goods = US$10 million

Balance in services = US$300 million

Current balance = US$310 million

The economy of the country would benefit from exporting more goods and services than it imports.

Primary income

The current account also records two other types of primary income flow between a country and the rest of the world. Taking the example of Germany:

1 Add wages, salaries and other benefits received by Germany's residents who are working abroad. Deduct wages, salaries and earnings of foreign nationals working in Germany.

2 Add investment income earned by Germans from overseas investment, e.g. profits. Deduct investment income paid to overseas citizens with investments in Germany.

Secondary income

Secondary income is an entry in the accounts for transfers of goods, services or financial assets where there is no corresponding transfer of economic value, e.g. the sending of gifts, donations to charities and government transfers to entities such as the International Monetary Fund.

KEY POINTS

1 The balance of trade in goods and services account shows the goods and services trade of a country.

2 Imports appear as debit items in the account. Exports appear as credit items.

3 Also included in the current account are movements of money resulting from income payments and current transfers.

SUMMARY QUESTIONS

1 Barbados has many nationals working in the United States. Where would their wages and other incomes appear in the current account?

2 A country's exports of goods in July were US$60.5 billion and its imports were US$105.8 billion. Exports of services were US$24 billion and imports of services US$20.7 billion. Calculate the balance of trade in goods and services.

3 A country typically imports more than it exports, but receives large sums in charitable donations. How would these movements of money affect the current account balance?

6.4.2 Current account deficit and surplus

TOPIC GUIDANCE

Students should be able to:
- define current account deficit and surplus
- discuss the causes and consequences of current account deficits and surpluses.

Germany is frequently able to run a balance of payments trade surplus based on its high-quality engineering industries including motor vehicle manufacture

DID YOU KNOW?

Bangladesh has run trade deficits since it became independent in 1971. In recent years Bangladesh has developed a reputation as one of the world's finest high-quality textile producers, and is the largest exporter of fresh water prawns in the world; however, it continues to have to import large quantities of food and manufactured goods.

DID YOU KNOW?

A current account deficit results when receipts from exported goods and exported services, income flows and current transfers are less than expenditure on imported goods and imported services, income flows and current transfers.

Deficit and surplus

The current account of the balance of payments is the section of the account that shows trade in goods and services.

The current account is in deficit when the total value of goods and services exported is less than the total value of goods and services. We will use the symbol X to refer to exports and the symbol M to refer to imports.

The current account is in surplus when the total value of goods and services exported is greater than the total value of goods and services imported:

$X < M$ = trade deficit $X > M$ = trade surplus

Trade deficits and surpluses relate either to trade with a particular trading partner, e.g. the US and China, or trade between a country and the rest of the world.

Causes and consequences of a trade deficit

Causes of a trade deficit are often related to other factors that make an economy weak, e.g. insufficient resources, poor infrastructure, corruption and weak economic decision-making.

- If a country has insufficient domestic resources it has to import lots of goods and services.
- Poor organisation of production: inefficient organisation of production and distribution systems on a national scale resulting from poor transport links, the use of inefficient technology and the widespread nature of corruption will result in low levels of output and reliance on imported goods.
- The value of the country's currency makes the price of exports too high and imports too low. If the currency of the country is overvalued then this will make it difficult for exporters to sell goods because they will be overpriced on world markets.

When a country suffers from a trade deficit, particularly where this is prolonged over a period of time, this will lead to these issues.

- Debt increases. The debt will have to be repaid, so the country will have to put aside part of its GDP each year to pay off foreign debt (providing less for domestic consumption and investment).
- Sovereignty is lost. Domestic governments lose power as they have to accept terms and conditions imposed on them by foreign lenders including the International Monetary Fund, the World Bank, and foreign banks. Foreign lenders will impose conditions about the type of economic policy that they want to be in place to continue to lend to a country.

- The value of the currency of the deficit country falls. As the value of its currency falls it will need to sell more and more goods to earn the same amount of money from foreign trade as before.
- Imports become more expensive. Where these consist of oil, food etc. then this makes life increasingly hard for people in a country.

Causes and consequences of a trade surplus

A country will typically build up a trade surplus if the following applies.

- Its exports are in strong demand in other countries. For example, in recent years China has become the world's number one manufacturer of a wide range of goods, enabling it to build up considerable trade surpluses.
- Its exports are competitively priced as a result of a relatively low exchange rate against other currencies. Some economists argue that one of the reasons that China has been able to build up such large surpluses in recent years is because the price of the yuan has been relatively low (particularly against the US dollar).

The main benefits from having a trade surplus are as follows.

- The surplus will arise because exporters are able to sell a lot of goods on international markets, typically resulting in higher profits. Export industries are able to recruit more labour and carry out more investment – providing people with jobs and money.
- The country with the trade surplus will be able to build up reserves of foreign currency which if it so chooses can be used to invest in other countries, or simply to build up reserves.

The following are the main drawbacks.

- Business activity is focusing on producing goods for export at the expense of producing goods for consumption in the home market. Domestic consumers may become frustrated if they receive fewer goods because production is being exported overseas. This benefits the shareholders in export industries at the expense of domestic consumers.
- A trade surplus will lead to a rise in the value of countries' currency (because foreigners are demanding more of this currency to make purchases). In the medium term this will make the countries' exports more expensive and reduce the balance of payments surplus.

SUMMARY QUESTIONS

1. Identify one country (apart from Bangladesh) that has a current account deficit. What are the causes of the deficit in this country?
2. Germany is a country which typically has a surplus on its current account because of its highly competitive exports. What other examples can you find of other countries with current account surpluses? What are the main reasons behind the surplus?

STUDY TIP

Make sure that you understand the difference between a deficit and a surplus.

DID YOU KNOW?

A current account surplus results when receipts from exported goods and exported services, income flows and current transfers are more than expenditure on imported goods and imported services, income flows and current transfers.

DID YOU KNOW?

The countries with the biggest surpluses on current account – given here as percentage of GDP – are Switzerland (about 12 per cent), China (6 per cent), Germany (5 per cent) and Japan (3.5 per cent).

KEY POINTS

1. A trade deficit results from weaknesses in a domestic economy.
2. A trade deficit will result in increasing debt, and loss of sovereignty in a domestic economy.
3. A trade surplus arises when exports are strong in comparison to imports.
4. A trade surplus is likely to lead to increasing profits, wages and employment. It may increase the price of the currency. The surplus country will be able to build up its foreign exchange reserves.

6.4.3 Policies to achieve balance of payments stability

> **TOPIC GUIDANCE**
>
> Students should be able to:
> - outline policies for stability of current balance
> - discuss the effectiveness of policies for stable current balance
> - explain the impacts of deficit or surplus.

The importance of stability

Macroeconomic management thrives on **stability**. Uncertainty leads to volatility, making it difficult for businesses and governments to make appropriate forecasts and decisions. This slows investment and trade which are vital to international growth. Running an overly large surplus or deficit on the current account of the balance of payments can cause wider economic problems.

The impact of surplus

A country will tend to run a **surplus** if it is efficient and produces goods that are in demand. The main result of a country running a surplus is the rise in the value of its currency. On the foreign exchange market there will be higher demand for its currency in order to buy its goods and invest there. In addition, if one country has a surplus, one or more countries will have a **deficit**, and countries that are persistently in deficit will see their currency's value fall. Countries with balance of payments surpluses find that the extra money flowing into their economy leads to rising prosperity and wages, and higher levels of inflation.

Policies for surpluses

Countries with huge surpluses can cause problems for the global economy unless they reinvest the surplus. Surpluses can only exist if other countries run deficits, but other countries cannot run deficits forever. When a surplus country allows the value of its currency to rise, the costs of its goods and services rise and are less attractive to buyers. A key remedy for a surplus is to allow currencies to appreciate, or to reduce or eliminate the surplus. Another policy is to reduce restrictions on imports. Both policies will help deficit countries, but, surplus countries may want to keep their advantage.

China is the country with the largest balance of payments surplus. Manufactured goods such as textiles provide an important component of this surplus

> **DID YOU KNOW?**
>
> The term 'Dutch disease' is used to describe a situation where a country exports a lot of natural resources (natural gas, in the case of the Netherlands). The high level of exports of natural resources leads to a rise in the value of the currency as foreigners seek to buy it. The consequence is that the export of other goods and services becomes increasingly difficult because of the rising price of the currency.

CASE STUDY: Germany's current account balance in 2015

The table gives figures for Germany's current account balance, 2015.

Item	Euros (billions)
Current account	1179.6
Exports	916.6
Imports	257.0
Services	−30.2
Primary income	63.7
Secondary income	−39.5

(Source: Deutsche Bundesbank Monetary Report, March 2016)

The account is typical of Germany's position in recent years. There was a strong surplus on visible trading from sales of pharmaceuticals (e.g. to the US, UK and the Netherlands), cars, computers, optical instruments and machinery.

Primary income involves considerable investment inflows, as international investors seek opportunities in Germany. Secondary income sees outflows because of contributions to bodies such as the International Monetary Fund and the European Union.

Germany benefits from being a member of the Eurozone. As most economies in the European Union are weaker economically, the value of the euro is much lower than if Germany was the only country in the Eurozone. German exports are thus relatively affordable on international markets and this – combined with the quality of German products – enables continual surpluses to be made on the balance of payments.

Germany benefits from being a member of the European Union because: there are no internal trade restrictions; and Germany is trading with a currency that makes its goods highly competitive.

Questions

1. How does Germany benefit from trading with the euro rather than its previous currency, the Deutsche mark?
2. How might Germany reduce surpluses on its current account?
3. Who else would benefit from this?

STUDY TIP

Make sure you can differentiate between policies to deal with surpluses and those to deal with deficits and explain their merits and weaknesses.

ACTIVITY

A country's debt : GDP ratio shows what proportion of its GDP consists of government debt. It indicates: how much a country has borrowed to finance balance of payments deficits and investment projects; and how much the country owes as a percentage of how much it produces. A figure greater than 100 per cent means that the country has borrowed more than its current annual GDP.

Find out your country's current debt : GDP ratio. Try to find an explanation for the ratio.

KEY POINTS

1. Stability in the balance of payments encourages long-term planning and growth.

2. Sustained surpluses can lead to a long-term appreciation of the currency, can be inflationary and can lead to problems for other countries.

3. Sustained deficits lead to rising debt which can only be financed by borrowing and are likely to lead to a currency crisis.

The impact of deficit

When a country has a persistent negative current account balance, it will become increasingly indebted to international financial institutions. For example, between 1987 and 2017 Jamaica ran average deficits of US$66.5 million per year. This is unsustainable and requires regular interest payments at the expense of investment in the economy. Additionally, Jamaica's macroeconomic policy is limited by requirements from donor bodies. Jamaica has to borrow more in order to finance the deficit. Deficit countries:

- have to borrow or run down reserves to pay for deficits
- face increasing interest rates as they borrow more
- see a loss of value in their currencies.

Policies for dealing with deficits (and their disadvantages)

Policy	Disadvantage
Restrict imports through quotas and tariffs	Likely to lead to retaliation from trading partners
Encourage exports through subsidies	Likely to lead to retaliation
Reduce taxes and raise interest rates	Produces increased domestic costs
Allow currency to depreciate so that exports become cheaper and imports more expensive	Requires an elastic demand for exports and an elastic demand for imports
Use macroeconomic monetary policies to deal with domestic inflation, e.g. higher interest rates, and fiscal policy to stimulate growth, e.g. lower taxes on business	The choice of such policies is highly dependent on advice and 'instruction' from international lenders

SUMMARY QUESTIONS

1 How might a sustained surplus in a large trading country have negative impacts for the growth of the global economy?

2 What is the likely impact of surpluses and deficits in the balance of payments on:

   a exchange rates   b economic growth

   c international confidence?

3 A country has run a sustained deficit for 25 years and is forced to borrow from international institutions that impose increasingly high interest rate penalties. What might the country do to try and reduce its deficit?

Unit 6 — Test yourself

SECTION 1: Multiple-choice questions

1. Which of the following is an NOT advantage to a country of international specialisation?
   a. The country can produce increased total output
   b. The country has the ability to increase efficiency
   c. The population gain a range of skills
   d. The population gain access to a wide range of goods through trade

2. Which of the following may be a disadvantage to a country that specialises in the production of ready made garments?
   a. Workers earn low hourly wages
   b. Garments may be sold at low prices to other countries
   c. Economies of scale lead to lower production costs
   d. Export sales rely on the demand from other countries

3. Which of the following best defines 'Globalisation'?
   a. Free movement worldwide of workers
   b. Free movement worldwide of products
   c. Free movement worldwide of capital
   d. All of the above

4. Which of the following is NOT an advantage to a multi-national company of operating in many different countries?
   a. The ability to sell in different markets
   b. Consumers may have different tastes
   c. Lower wage costs in developing countries
   d. Access to new sources of raw materials

5. Which of the following best describes the principle of comparative advantage?
   a. Countries produce all goods and services for their own citizens
   b. Countries specialise in only primary or secondary production
   c. Countries produce products in which they are relatively efficient
   d. Countries encourage competition among producers

6. Which of these sets of initials represents the organisation that was set up to promote free trade for the benefit of all?
   a. WTO
   b. NAFTA
   c. ASEAN
   d. EU

7. Which of the following may be a reason for a country to introduce protectionism?
   a. To protect consumers against high prices
   b. To protect the government against tax fraud
   c. To protect the environment
   d. To protect infant industries

8. A floating exchange rate for a country's currency means that:
   a. The currency is always worth the same against other currencies
   b. The currency exchange rate is set by the central bank
   c. The currency goes up or down in value according to supply and demand
   d. The currency exchange rate is supported by government intervention

9. If demand for a country's exports is relatively price inelastic, this means that:
   a. A 5% appreciation of the country's currency will lead to a less than 5% decrease in sales
   b. A 5% appreciation of the country's currency will lead to a more than 5% decrease in sales
   c. A 5% appreciation of the country's currency will lead to no change in sales
   d. A 5% appreciation of the country's currency will lead to a 5% decrease in sales

10. Which of the following may lead to a country's balance of trade deficit increasing?
    a. An appreciation of the country's currency
    b. A depreciation of the country's currency
    c. An increase in efficiency in export production
    d. An increase in consumer demand for home-produced goods

SECTION 2

Country C is a developed nation, which is currently a member of a free trade area. The country specialises in selling financial services worldwide and most of the population are employed in the tertiary sector.

Country C has a large, persistent deficit on its balance of payments current account, due to the reliance on imported consumer goods and food. In recent years the currency of Country C has depreciated against other major currencies, due to the government's decision to exit from the free trade area and seek free trade agreements with other countries.

The government of Country C would like to achieve the following objectives:

- Free trade agreements with major world economies, such as USA and China
- An increase in the productivity of the country's workforce
- An improvement in the competitiveness of manufacturing, in order to boost export sales in this area
- An increase in investment from multi-national companies, who will be encouraged to locate factories in Country C.
- A reduction in the deficit on the current account of the balance of payments

    a Explain what is meant by 'deficit on the balance of payments current account?' (2)

    b Explain what is meant by 'financial services' and give an example of an organisation in this sector (2)

    c Explain what is meant by a 'free trade area' and give an example of a free trade area in your part of the world. (3)

    d Explain the difference between currency depreciation and currency appreciation. (2)

    e Explain how being a member of a free trade area may benefit businesses and consumers in Country C. (6)

    f Explain why the government of Country C may want to 'increase workforce productivity' (3)

    g Discuss the possible benefits and drawbacks of more investment by multi-national companies in Country C (6)

    h Discuss what may be the opportunities and threats to the economy of Country C of the decision to exit from the free trade area. (6)

SECTION 3

Country D is a developing country, made up of a number of islands. The main industries are fish processing and tourism. The population are mainly employed in connection with one or other of these activities. Fish canning factories are located on the main island, where most people live. The airport is located on a nearby island and the remaining islands are tourist resorts, run by multi-national travel companies. These resorts cater for high income travellers, who look for luxurious accommodation, international food menus and activities such as diving and other water sports. The currency exchange rate of Country D is fixed against the US Dollar. The government of Country D is committed to free trade, although there is import tax on processed fish products from other nearby countries.

1 a Identify and Explain TWO examples of specialisation in Country D. (4)
  b For one example from (a), explain how the economy of Country D may benefit from comparative advantage. (4)
  c Discuss whether increasing globalisation in the future may be seen as an opportunity or a threat to Country D. (6)
  d Explain TWO external factors that may cause Country D to consider aiming its tourism services at middle income as well as high income tourists.

2 a Identify and explain what is meant by 'free trade' (4)
  b Explain how free trade with nearby countries may benefit the population of Country D. (4)
  c How might the multi-national companies that run the tourist resorts on islands in Country D benefit from free trade? (6)
  d What are advantages and disadvantages to Country D of the involvement of multi-national companies in their tourism industry. (6)

3 a Explain what is meant by 'trade protection' (4)
  b Identify and explain ONE reason why the government of Country D impose an import tax on processed fish products from other countries. (4)
  c Explain TWO reasons why the government of Country D may offer a subsidy to a new domestic tourism company, aiming to set up a new hotel on one of the smaller islands. (6)
  d Explain how the government of Country D may use import licensing to allow more opportunities for local water sports operators. (6)

4 a Explain ONE reason why the government of Country D may have decided to fix its currency exchange rate against the US Dollar.
  b Identify and explain ONE item that would be a debit and one that would be a credit on the balance of payments current account for Country D.
  c Discuss the likely impact of an appreciation of the US Dollar on the lfish processing and tourism industries in Country D.
  d Descuss whether Country D benefit from changing to a floating exchange rate system? Justify your answer.

Glossary

A

Absolute poverty a measure of the number of people with income below a certain figure, often UN figure of US$1.25 per day.

***Ad valorem* tax** a tax levied as a percentage of the value of the item it is imposed on (e.g. value added tax and many import taxes).

Ageing population a population with increasing average age, usually resulting in increased proportion of older to younger people.

Appreciation of currency rise in the value of the currency in terms of other currencies for which it can be exchanged.

Average fixed cost (AFC) total fixed cost of a business divided by the number of units produced or sold.

Average revenue (AR) average receipt to a business from the number of units sold.

Average total cost (ATC) total cost of production of any given output divided by the number of units sold; also referred to as average cost (AC).

B

Balance of payments account setting out financial flows resulting from a country's trading and financial exchanges with other countries.

Barter exchange of one good for another; relies on a double coincidence of wants (i.e. that two people each require what the other is offering).

Base year a year used as a basis for comparison when creating an index. The base year is given a figure of 100. Comparisons can then be made against the base year (e.g. 110 would represent a figure 10 per cent higher than the base figure).

Budget plan for the future set out in numbers. A national budget sets out government spending and expected tax and other revenues in the period ahead (often one year).

C

Capital refers to items that go into further production (e.g. machines, factory buildings). Can also be used to refer to the finance acquired by a business to pay for its activities.

Capital employed relates to financial definition of capital: total amount of finance used by a business to support its activities.

Central bank a country's main monetary authority (e.g. the United States Federal Reserve) controlling the supply of money and supervising other banks.

Choice opportunity to select from alternative end products and between alternative actions.

Company a business that is recognised in law as being separate from its owners, who are its shareholders.

Comparative advantage being relatively more efficient at certain activities compared with others that can be carried out using the same resources.

Complements goods demanded for use together (e.g. laptop computers and the computer software that can be installed on them).

Consumer Prices Index (CPI) measure of the change over time in the cost of a fixed basket of goods and services, including food, housing, transport and electricity.

Contraction in supply/demand a decrease in quantity demanded or supplied resulting solely from a change in the price.

Co-operative organisation set up by a group to further their mutual interests (e.g. farmers for joint marketing of their crops).

Core worker full-time, relatively well-paid employees typically working on long-term employment contracts.

Cost-push inflation general rise in prices resulting from increases in production costs, such as an increase in the price of imported raw materials or energy.

Credit card used for making purchases; the user pays for items by a stipulated later date. A set credit limit determines how much can be spent in this way. The amount of interest charged depends on the length of the credit period.

Current account a bank account enabling an account holder to deposit and withdraw sums and make payments using their bank card. The account holder pays interest on negative balances.

Current account balance the four elements of income and expenditure resulting from the dealings of one country with other countries. The balance is made up of the trade in goods, the trade in services, income flows and current transfers.

Cyclical unemployment unemployment resulting from downturns in the trade cycle (i.e. when there is a general fall in demand in an economy).

D

Debit card enables the holder to make payments and to withdraw cash from their current account. The money is deducted immediately (compare credit card).

Deflation a general fall in the level of prices in a country.

Demand the quantity of a good or service that will be purchased at a particular price. Effective demand describes the desire to purchase goods backed up by the money to pay for them.

Demand-pull inflation general rise in prices resulting from a general increase in the demand for goods in an economy.

Demographic transition stages in the development of population structures from low life expectancy, with high birth and death rates, to longer life expectancy, with falling birth and death rates.

Depreciation of currency fall in the value of an international currency on international exchange markets.

Derived demand demand for a product or service resulting from its use in producing some other demanded good or service.

Glossary

Devaluation fall in the value of a currency, usually brought about by the central bank. Action is taken, such as selling the domestic currency to lower its price and make a country's goods more competitive.

Developed country country characterised by relatively high GDP per head and HDI indicators, low birth and death rates, allowing 'all … citizens to enjoy a free and healthy life in a safe environment' (Kofi Annan, former Secretary General of the UN).

Developing country low- or middle-income country, characterised by lower levels of GDP per head and industrialisation, with higher birth and death rates than developed countries (World Bank definition).

Direct tax a tax that has to be paid directly (e.g. by the income earner (income tax) or the householder (government rates)) (compare indirect tax).

Discrimination favouring or showing preferential treatment to one group or individual over others.

Diseconomies of scale the result of a firm becoming too large, when inefficiencies occur, leading to rising costs.

Disposable income money available for spending after tax and other compulsory deductions.

Division of labour concentration of workers on specific specialist work tasks.

Dumping increasing sales by exporting goods into a foreign market at lower prices than the goods cost to make in the domestic market.

E

Economic growth the increased efficiency of an economy to produce goods over time, measured by rising GDP.

Economic indicators measures used to record changes in economic performance (e.g. GDP per head in 2013 compared with 2012).

Economic problems issues that arise from balancing uses of scarce resources and goods. An opportunity cost is involved.

Economic system the ways in which resources are allocated in an economy.

Economies of scale the advantages of a larger firm over a smaller one, enabling it to produce larger outputs at lower unit cost.

Equilibrium price the price at which quantity demanded equals quantity supplied to a market, and at which demanders and suppliers are content.

Equity shares in a business.

Euro international currency of most of the countries in the European Union.

Eurozone area in which the euro is the generally accepted currency (e.g. France, Germany, Belgium, Netherlands, Italy, Spain, Ireland). At the start of 2014 there were 18 countries in the Eurozone.

Exchange control limiting the quantity of foreign currency available to the general public and to business, as well as controlling the purposes for which foreign currency can be used.

Exchange rate amount at which one country's currency can be bought with another's (e.g. the Mexican peso against the US dollar).

Extension in supply/demand an increase in the quantity demanded or supplied resulting solely from the change in the price of that good.

Externalities effects resulting from a particular activity, such as pollution caused by a production process. Externalities can be positive or negative.

F

Factors of production resources used in production: land, labour, capital and enterprise.

Fiscal policy deliberately adjusting the relationship between government taxes and spending in order to achieve government policy objectives.

Fixed costs (FC) any costs that do not vary with the level of output (e.g. rent and rates).

Fixed exchange rate established rates at which one currency will exchange for another. The government can fix the exchange rate between its currency and one or more other currencies; difficult to maintain over time.

Fixed incomes incomes not related to the rate of inflation in a country, and tend to remain stable because the earners have little bargaining power (e.g. pensions of older people).

Floating exchange rate an exchange rate between one currency and others determined by their relative demand and supply; changes from day to day.

Free trade carrying out trade without tariffs, quotas or other restrictions on trading.

Free trade area region in which there are no restrictions on importing and exporting (e.g. North American Free Trade Area (NAFTA)).

Frictional unemployment employment resulting from a lack of smoothness in demand and supply adjustments. Tends to be of a relatively short duration.

Fringe benefits non-monetary work-related advantages, such as subsidised travel or low-price company canteen meals.

G

Government intervention government actions to regulate and control market forces (e.g. through taxing and subsidising business activity).

Gross Domestic Product (GDP) the value of the output of an economy in a given period. Also the value of all earning and spending in an economy within a time period.

Gross Domestic Product (GDP) per capita or per head the value of total output of the economy in a given period, divided by the population.

H

HIV/AIDS Acquired Immune Deficiency Syndrome (AIDS) is an infectious disease caused by the Human Immunodeficiency Virus (HIV).

Human Development Index (HDI) an index used to measure human well-being. It is made up of three elements of human

Glossary

development: life expectancy, education and standard of living.

I

Incidence of tax the burden of a tax: the extent to which the burden falls on the end consumer or the business selling to the end consumer.

Indirect tax a tax that is paid by an intermediary who then passes the tax on to an end payer (e.g. taxes on the purchase of goods are first paid by a business, which then passes some or all of the tax on to the purchaser/consumer).

Inelastic demand demand that changes by a smaller proportion than the change in price that instigated demand to change.

Inequality differences in income and living standards between members of a society.

Infant industry an industry that is in its earliest stages of development in a particular country.

Inflation a general increase in the level of prices in a country over time.

Integration the bringing together of businesses and their operations (e.g. through merger and takeover). Vertical integration involves taking over an earlier or later stage of production. Horizontal integration involves the joining together of businesses at the same stage of production.

Interest rate the price charged for borrowing or saving money.

International Monetary Fund (IMF) an international body set up to provide finance for countries that need relatively short-term financial support (e.g. because they are not able to meet international debts in the short term).

International specialisation countries focusing on lines of production at which they are relatively efficient.

J

Joint supply two or more goods that are produced as part of the same production process (e.g. by-products created in the production of sugar from sugar cane can be used as fuel for sugar mills).

Joint venture an organisation jointly set up by two organisations; frequently set up when one international company wants to enter a new market.

L

Labour the human resource enabling both physical work and intellectual work.

Land a general term used to describe the gifts of nature. It not only includes farmland, but also other gifts of nature, such as oil contained in an oilfield.

Legal tender currency that is recognised in law as suitable payment in a given country.

Life expectancy the average age that a person can expect to live to in a particular country.

Limited liability the greatest amount that a company's owners might have to pay out to meet debts, the maxium being the sum that they invested in the business.

Loan a sum of money advanced to a borrower, usually in return for a payment of interest as well as the repayment of the loan.

Loan capital that part of the finance of a business that is borrowed rather than raised by the owners from their own resources.

M

Market any situation where buyers and sellers come into contact.

Market capitalisation the value of all the shares of a company on a particular day.

Market clearing price the price at which the quantity supplied to the market will be bought in its entirety (with no unsatisfied demand).

Market demand the total value of the demand in the market arrived at by adding together the individual demands of all buyers.

Market economy an economy in which most economic decisions are made freely by buyers and sellers, with only a very limited amount of government intervention.

Market failure inefficient allocation of resources by the market such that another outcome would have led to participants in the market being better off.

Megacity a city with over 10 million inhabitants.

Merger an agreement between two businesses to join together to create a single enterprise.

Merit good a good that it is judged an individual should have on the basis of need (e.g. food provided to the poor through a public distribution system). Merit goods result from the existence of information failure.

Microbusiness a business that employs fewer than five people.

Mixed economy an economy in which decisions are made through a combination of buyers and sellers deciding what to buy, produce and sell, coupled with government intervention, such as taxing or subsidising the production of some goods.

Monetary policy regulations created by the government and monetary authorities to control the supply of money in an economy and the level of interest rates.

Monopoly existence of only one firm in an industry. Businesses with monopoly powers are able to exercise some control over the supply to the market and the prices charged.

Mortgage borrowing to purchase land or property that is secured against the land or property.

Multinational a business that operates in two or more countries. Most large multinationals have a presence in several countries across the globe.

Multiplier effect the ripple of ongoing spending that results from an initial increase in spending in an economy.

N

NAIRU the Non-Accelerating Inflation Rate of Unemployment: defines a level of unemployment below which there is an increase in inflation.

National debt the sum of money owed by the government as a result of borrowing, usually through the issue of government bills and bonds (promises on paper to repay in the future coupled with additional interest payments).

Glossary

Natural increase in population increase in population resulting from the birth rate exceeding the death rate.

Natural monopoly a monopoly resulting from natural factors (e.g. minerals being found only in a certain region).

Newly Industrialised Countries (NICs) countries such as Brazil, Russia, India and China that are experiencing rapid industrial growth.

O

Opportunity cost the next best alternative that is given up when a decision is made.

Optimum population the most efficient size of population in terms of combining the other resources in the economy with the number of people.

Overpopulation in a country, too many people relative to the availability of other resources, leading to an inefficient use of resources.

P

Participation rates number of people who are prepared to work; number of people within working age range.

Partnership a business owned by two or more people, often carrying out professional work or a business service on a local scale.

Perfect competition a situation in which there are many buyers and sellers in a market, each of whom has knowledge of all of the prices being offered in the market. Their products are identical. New firms can readily enter or leave the market.

Population pyramid a diagram indicating the numbers of people in a country, by age and gender groups.

Price competition situation in which businesses seek to sell at lower prices than rivals.

Price elasticity the responsiveness of quantity demanded of a product to changes in price.

Price elasticity of demand the responsiveness of quantity demanded to a change in the price of a specific item.

Price elasticity of supply the responsiveness of quantity supplied to a change in the price of a specific item.

Price maker a firm that is able to decide what price it will charge for goods and services.

Price stability a situation in which prices stay more or less the same over a period.

Price taker a business that can only sell at the market price (i.e. a firm in a perfectly competitive market).

Prices and incomes policy a government-imposed limit on wage increases and prices that businesses can charge.

Primary industry the first stage in a production process that uses natural resources (e.g. land for farming).

Private benefits advantages to an individual or group resulting from their economic actions.

Private costs the disadvantages to an individual or group resulting from carrying out an economic action.

Private sector the part of the economy owned by private individuals and organisations, not the government.

Privatisation the transfer of a business from government to private ownership.

Productivity the output per factor of production, e.g. labour, per period of time.

Profit the reward for risk-taking; the sum that remains after all costs have been subtracted from revenues.

Profit maximising point the production or sales level at which there is the greatest difference between total revenue and total cost.

Progressive tax a tax by which richer people pay a higher proportion of their income than poorer people.

Protection measures to limit import quantities, or to raise the price, in order to give domestic industries an increased advantage.

Public corporation government-owned firm, such as the public railway network or a state-owned airline. Senior government-appointed officials manage the firm on a day-to-day basis. Government approval is required for major expenditure decisions.

Public expenditure government spending.

Public good a product (e.g. street lighting), consumption of which by one person does not reduce the possibility of someone else consuming it (referred to as non-rivalry), and where no one can be excluded from consuming the good.

Public sector part of the economy run and managed by the government.

Q

Quality of life measurement of the benefits to living, such as the built environment, health and leisure activities, not just material goods or income.

Quota limitation on the numbers of items that can be exchanged between countries.

R

Rate of unemployment percentage of the working population who are unemployed.

Real GDP the real value of national income (or national output) when inflation is taken into consideration.

Recession two or more consecutive quarters (three-month periods) in which there is a fall in GDP.

Regional specialisation the focus of a geographical area on certain lines of production.

Regressive tax a tax by which poorer people pay a higher proportion of their income than richer people.

Regulations rules and laws.

Relative poverty state of being poor resulting from one individual or group receiving relatively less than others (e.g. less than half the average national earnings).

Revaluation an increase in the value of a currency usually resulting from deliberate actions by government and/or monetary authorities (e.g. through the purchasing of the currency in international exchange markets).

Glossary

Revenue the value of total sales made by a business within a period, usually a year.

S

Savings income that is set aside for a purpose.

Savings account a bank account designed to encourage regular savings. The interest rate is usually higher than for a current account.

Scarce used to describe a resource or good in limited supply compared with the demand to use it.

Seasonal unemployment unemployment resulting from the change in demand for workers in response to seasonal changes, especially in agriculture and tourism.

Secondary industry the stage in the production of goods concerned with making or using raw materials from primary industry.

Shift in demand/supply curve the effect of a change in factors other than the price of a good (e.g. a demand curve will shift to the right if a good becomes more popular, or if consumers' incomes rise; a supply curve will shift to the right if technological improvements make it easier to produce that good).

Social benefits the advantages of a particular activity to members of a society. Social benefits consist of both private benefits and external benefits.

Social costs the negative effects to members of a community resulting from a particular activity or production of a good or service. Social costs consist of both private costs and external costs.

Specialisation concentrating on one or a small range of activities.

Specific tax a tax levied at a fixed rate per unit of output regardless of its price.

Standard for deferred payments a measure for making payments in the future.

Standard of living the basket of goods and services that an individual is able to purchase and enjoy with their income (including access to health and education services).

Stock exchange a building in which stocks and shares are traded by dealers.

Structural unemployment unemployment resulting from a major restructuring of industries in an economy (e.g. from the shift from labour-intensive agriculture to capital-intensive manufacturing).

Subsidies money granted by the state to keep down the price of goods and maintain the supply.

Substitutes alternatives that can replace others (e.g. travelling by bus instead of by car).

Supply the quantity of a good that will be produced or sold at a particular price.

Sustainable economic growth ongoing increases in GDP or living standards over time.

T

Takeover the acquisition of 51 per cent or more of the shares of another business in order to take over control of that business.

Tariff a sum of money that an importer or exporter has to pay to trade goods across borders.

Technological unemployment unemployment resulting from new developments in technology (e.g. automatic machinery replacing human labour for certain tasks).

Tertiary industry service industries that provide value for people (e.g. postal services, insurance and banking services, leisure industries).

Total cost (TC) the sum of all the fixed and variable costs at a given level of output.

Total revenue (TR) the average revenue multiplied by the number of units sold. The total receipts of a business from selling activities.

Total variable cost (TVC) the sum of all the variable costs at a given level of output.

Trade cycle increasing and falling levels of economic activity over time. After four or five years of upswing (increasing production), there may be a downturn.

Trade in goods exports and imports of physical goods.

Trade in services: non-physical traded items (e.g. banking, insurance, transport).

Trade union body, recognised in law, of employees with a common work interest who seek to further this through bargaining with employers.

Trader buyer and seller of commodities and paper assets such as shares; buyers and sellers on stock exchanges and other financial exchanges (e.g. a trader in foreign exchange).

U

Underpopulation too few people in a country to make efficient use of the resources available.

Unit of account one of the functions of money; money can be divided into separate units (e.g. dollars and cents), which can be used to record the value of transactions, loans and other financial deals.

V

Variable costs (VC) expenses that vary with the level of output (e.g. fuel costs, raw material costs).

Virtual monopoly an organisation, though not an absolute monopoly, able to exert considerable monopoly powers in terms of setting prices or the quantity supplied to the market.

W

Wage gap difference in money earned by sectors of the workforce (e.g. male and female earnings).

Weighted price index a way of calculating price changes. Items on which more of a typical person's income is spent are given the greatest weighting in the index. The index is thus weighted to give greater consideration to relatively important items of expenditure.

Weighting importance attached to items appearing in an index; the greater the weight, the more account is given to a particular factor that appears in an index.

World Trade Organization (WTO) international body supervising international trading. It actively seeks to encourage the removal of tariffs and quotas and to create regulations governing fair trading between nations.

Index

A
age 31, 183, 193, 194
aggregate decisions 22–3
agriculture 85
angel investors 94
appreciation 218–19
automatic stabilisers 137
average cost 108, 110, 117
    shape of the average cost curve 108–9
average fixed cost (AFC) 106
average revenue (AR) 112–13, 117
average variable cost (AVC) 107

B
balance of payments 127
    balance of trade in goods and services 222–3
    current account 222–5
    deficit and surplus 224
    importance of stability 226–7
    primary income 223
    secondary income 223
banks 70–3
barter 68
beggar my neighbour policies 215
biofuels 164
birth rate 186, 187
bonds 73
bonuses 78
borrowing, 74, 75
brain drain 28
budgets 130–1, 179
    balanced budget 131
    budget deficit 131
    budget surplus 131
    impact of different budget positions 136
business growth 94, 115
    external growth 95
    internal growth 94–5
businesses 78, 92–3
    inflation 167
    unemployment 159

C
capital 6, 7, 8, 9
    capital-intensive production 103
capitalism 46
career prospects 79
central banks 72–3
commercial banks 70
    governments and commercial banks 71
    main activities 70–1
    other banking services 71
commission 78
comparative advantage 210–11
competition 116–17
complementary goods 51
complements 30
construction industries 90, 152
consumer price index (CPI) 160–3, 170
consumers 12, 24
    consumer durables 74
    propensity to consume 75
consumption 55, 74, 76
contraction in demand 30
contraction in supply 33
costs 106–7
    cost-push factors in inflation 164–5
    costs and output 110–11
    key terms 111
    opportunity cost 3, 10–13, 15
    total and average costs 108–9, 110–11, 117
credit cards 70
credits 222–3
current accounts 70

D
death rate 186, 187
debit cards 70
debits 222–3
debt 73
deficit 131, 224, 226
    causes and consequences of a trade deficit 224–5
    impact of deficit 228
    policies for dealing with deficits (and their disadvantages) 228
deflation 166, 168
    causes of deflation 168–9
    consequences of deflation 169
    price stability policies 170–1
demand 28
    demand changes 25, 30
    demand-side growth 145
    derived demand 80, 85, 100
    effective demand 18, 48
    factors of production 100–1
    recording demand 28–9
    wage determination 80
demand curves 28
    age distribution 31
    changes in the conditions of demand 30
    contraction and expansion 30
    demand curve under monopoly 118–19
    income 31
    movement along the demand curve 30
    popularity 30–1
    price of other products 31
    shifts in the demand curve 30
    straight-line demand curves 29
demand graphs 28
demerit goods 55
demographic transition 190
depreciation 218–19
    consequences of a depreciating currency 221
deregulation 141
devaluation 219
direct provision 57
direct taxes 132, 134
discrimination 84
diseconomies of scale 99
disequilibrium 25

E
earnings 78, 82
    average earnings 83
    public and private sectors 83
    skilled and unskilled workers 82, 151
economic development 175, 196–7
    criticisms of using GDP as an economic indicator 177–8
    development as freedom 197
    factors impacting on development 198–9
    Human Development Index (HDI) 178–9
    inequality as uneven development 197
    making comparisons using GDP 176–7
    poverty 182–5
    standard of living 176, 180–1
economic growth 126, 142–3, 148, 184
    causes of economic growth 144–5
    consequences of economic growth 145
    government and economic growth 148
    illustrating economic growth 146–7
    nature of recession 145
    sustainable economic growth 148–9
    trade cycle 149
    what is economic growth? 144
economic migration 187
economics 1
    basic economic problem 2–3
    making choices 3, 12, 15, 49
    making sacrifices 3, 15
economies of scale 93, 98–9
    external diseconomies of scale 99
    external economies of scale 98, 99
    internal diseconomies of scale 99
    internal economies of scale 98–9
education 11, 141, 199
elasticity 63
    elasticity and impact of direct taxes 135
    price elasticity of demand 40–3, 62–3, 135, 221
    price elasticity of supply 44–5
embargo 212
employment 60–1, 127, 150
    full employment 154–5
    industrial structure 151–3
    participation rates 151
enterprise 6, 7
equilibrium 25
    equilibrium price 36–7
equity 134
exchange control 212
exchange rates 43, 165, 216–17
    causes of fluctuations 218–19
    consequences of fluctuations 220–1
    exchange rate manipulation 212
    exchange rate systems 217
    fixed exchange rates 217
    floating exchange rates 217
    multiple exchange rates 217
    price elasticity of demand for exports and imports 221
expansion in demand 30

Index

expenditure 76–7
exports 221, 222
extension in supply 33, 44
externalities 53
   negative externalities 53
   overconsumption of goods with external costs 55
   positive externalities 53
   underconsumption of merit goods and goods with external benefits 55
extractive industries 90, 152

F
factors of production 6, 100, 102
   combining factors of production 101
   definitions 6–7
   illustrating the demand for factors of production 100–1
   mobility 8–9, 54
   quantity and quality 9
fertility rate 186, 187
financial regulations 72
firms 90–1
   growth of firms 94–5
   making a profit 115–16
   mergers and integration 96–7
   other goals of business organisations 115
   profit maximising point 114–15
   small firms 92–3
fiscal policy 130–1, 136
   automatic stabilisers 137
   discretionary fiscal policies 137
   impact of different budget positions 136
fixed costs (FC) 106, 110–11
food costs 164
foreign currency 72
free markets 46–7
free trade 210
   comparative advantage 210–11
   free trade areas 210
   other benefits 211
   World Trade Organization (WTO) 211
fringe benefits 79

G
gender 192, 195
   gender work gap 83–4
geographical mobility 8, 54
globalisation 206
   benefits 206–7
   disadvantages 207
goods 60, 104
   balance of trade 222–3
   economic goods 4–5
   free goods 4, 5
governments 13, 123
   budget 130–1
   budget possibilities 131
   conflicting aims 128
   economic growth 148–9
   fiscal policy 130, 136–7
   full employment 154–5

government failure 56
government intervention 26, 57
government policy and wages 81
government policy to address market failure 56
government roles 124–5
governments and commercial banks 71
indirect taxes 62–3
macroeconomic aims 126–7
monetary policies 138–9
price stability policies 170–1
reasons for government spending 131
reasons for taxation 131, 132
regulations 58–9
subsidies 60–1
successful economies 129
suitable mix 128
supply-side policies 140–1
trade-offs 128
unemployment 159
grievances 89
gross domestic product (GDP) 142
   criticisms of using GDP as an economic indicator 177–8
   GDP per head 143
   making comparisons using GDP 176–7
   measuring by expenditure 142
   measuring by income 143
   measuring by output 142
   nominal GDP 143
   problems in measuring GDP 143
   real GDP 143

H
health 183, 199
HIV/AIDS 191
households 74–5
   household consumption 76
Human Development Index (HDI) 178–9
hyperinflation 167

I
imports 132, 221, 222
   import licensing 212
   import quotas 212
   import tariffs 212
   taxes 133
incidence of tax 63
income 31
   balance of payments 223
   differences in income 198
   disposable income 31
   high income 196
   income distribution 126–7
   income tax 133
   inflation 167
   low income 196
   middle income 196
   patterns of income and expenditure 76–7
   prices and incomes policy 171
   redistribution 132, 185
indirect taxes 62, 132, 135

effective taxes 63
elasticity and impact of direct taxes 135
incidence of sales taxes and price
elasticity of demand 62–3
   indirect sales taxes 62
   where knowledge of elasticity is useful 63
industries 60–1, 90, 151–3, 199
   infant industries 214
inequality 182–3, 197
inflation 161, 170
   causes 164–5
   consequences 166–7
   cost-push factors 164–5
   demand-pull inflation 164, 165
   hyperinflation 167
   mild inflation 167
   price stability policies 170–1
   who loses out in a period of inflation? 166–7
integration 96
   types of integration 97
interest 70
   interest rates 72
international government 125
International Monetary Fund (IMF) 73
international trade see trade
investment 94, 141, 199

J
job satisfaction 79
joint supply 35

L
labour 6, 7, 8, 9, 60–1
   division of labour 86–7
   labour market reforms 141
   labour-intensive production 102
land 6, 7 8, 9, 164–5
legal tender 72
lending 70
life expectancy 197
loans 70
local government 124

M
M & A 96
macroeconomics 22, 123
   balance of payments 127
   conflicts between government aims 128–9
   economic growth 126, 142–9
   employment 127, 150–5
   fiscal policy 130–1, 136–7
   government responsibility 126
   income distribution 127
   key decision-makers in the macro-economy 23
   macroeconomic aims 126
   monetary policies 138–9
   prices 126
   supply-side policy 140–1
   unemployment 156–9
manufacturing industries 85, 90, 152
market clearing price 37
market failure 50
   causes of market failure 54–5

Index

consequences of market failure 55
government policy to address market failure 56
not producing public or merit goods 50–1
markets 21, 48
  bringing together buyers and sellers 48
  competition 116–17
  coordinating decision-making 49
  keeping prices down 49
  market allocation of resources 25, 48
  market economy 26–7
  market equilibrium and disequilibrium 25, 36–7
  market systems 24, 46–7
  providing choice 49
  sectors in a market economy 47
  weaknesses of the market economy 49
megacities 193
mergers 96
merit goods 51, 54, 55
micro-businesses 78
microeconomics 22, 56
  indirect taxes 62
  microeconomic decision-makers 67
  regulation 58–9
  subsidies 60–1
mixed economies 27, 56
  effectiveness of government intervention 57
  government policy to address market failure 56
  illustrating government microeconomic policies in the market 56
  nationalisation, privatisation and direct provision 57
mobility 8–9, 54
monetary policy 72, 138–9
  monetary policy helps a government to achieve economic aims 139
  use of monetary policies 139
money 68
  medium of exchange 69
  standard for deferred payments 69
  store of value 69, 70
  unit of account 69
monopoly 54, 118
  advantages and disadvantages of monopolies 119
  demand curve under monopoly 118–19
  features of a monopoly 119
  price makers 118
mortality rate 186
  infant mortality rate 186
  maternal mortality rate 186
mortgages 70
multinational companies 208
  benefits and disadvantages of operating in many countries 209
  benefits and disadvantages to host countries 209
  measuring the size of multinationals 209
multiplier effect 159

N
NAIRU (Non-Accelerating Inflation Rate of Unemployment) 128
natality rate 186
national debt 73
national government 124–5
nationalisation 57
net migration rate 186, 187
newly industrialised countries (NICs) 152–3

O
occupational mobility 8, 54
opportunity cost 3, 10–11
  consumers 12
  economic actions 12
  government 13
  opportunity cost in education 11
  producers 13
  production possibility curves 15
  workers 13
output 110–11
  costs and output 110–11
  optimum output 109
overdrafts 70
overtime 78

P
patents 43
pay 78
  differences in pay 83
payment 69, 71
perfect competition 116
  illustrating average cost and average revenue in perfect competition 117
physical conditions 35
popularity 30–1
population 186
  age structure 194
  ageing populations 193
  consequences of population change for developed countries 191
  consequences of population change for developing countries 190–1
  demographic transition 190
  dependent population 191
  gender structure 194, 195
  natural increase 187
  optimum population 192
  overpopulation 192–3
  population growth (or fall) 187, 198–9
  population growth in developing and developed countries 188
  population growth in Uganda and the UK 188–9
  population pyramids 188
  underpopulation 192
  urban/rural divide 194, 195
poverty 167
  absolute poverty 182, 184
  causes of poverty 183
  dealing with poverty 184–5
  inequality and poverty 182–3
  poverty line 183
  relative poverty 182, 184
price competition 116
price elasticity of demand 40
  elastic demand 41
  exchange rate changes 43
  exports and imports 221
  illustrating price elasticity of demand 42
  indirect taxes 62–3, 135
  inelastic demand 41
  making simple calculations 41
  measuring price elasticity 41
  revenue implications 42–3
  tax decisions 43
  total revenue 43
price elasticity of supply 44
  factors influencing price elasticity of supply 44–5
  making simple calculations 45
  perfectly inelastic supply 45
prices 26, 31, 49, 126
  changes in market conditions 38–9
  equilibrium price 36–7
  market clearing price 37
  maximum prices 56
  minimum prices 56
  price controls 171
  price makers 117, 118
  price stability policies 170–1
  price takers 117
  prices and incomes policy 171
prices index 160
  base year 161
  basket of goods 160–1
  calculating average price changes 162
  inflation 161
  problems involved in using a prices index 163
  weighted price index 162
  weighting 161
primary industry 90, 152
private benefits 52
private costs 52
private sector 47, 83, 91
privatisation 57
producers 13
production 60, 102, 104, 105
  capital-intensive production 103
  labour-intensive production 102
  overproduction of demerit goods 55
  production costs 34
  underconsumption of merit goods and goods with external benefits 55
production possibility curves 14
  illustrating choice and allocation 15
  illustrating economic growth 146
  illustrating opportunity cost 15
  illustrating recession 146–7
  movements along a production possibility curve 16–17
  points under a production possibility curve 16
  shifts in the production

Index

possibility curve 17
production possibility frontiers 14
productivity 105, 198
products 46–7
   development 60
   taxes 133
profit 114–15
   profit maximising point 114–15
   taxes 133
protectionism 61, 212
   consequences of protection 215
   limiting numbers or prices 212
   methods of trade protection 212–13
   reasons for protection 214–15
public corporations 57
public goods 50, 54
public sector 47, 83, 91
purchasing taxes 133

Q
quality of life 181
quantitative easing 139
quantity of money controls 171
quotas 212

R
raw material costs 164
recession 72, 145
   illustrating recession 146–7
regulations 58
   advantages 59
   disadvantages 59
   financial regulations 72
resources 1–3, 15, 26
   allocation of resources 25, 26, 48
   finite resource base 2
   government influence on economic decision-making 26
   market and economic decision-making 26–7
   mixed economies 27
retail 95
retail price index (RPI) 160–3
retirement 151
revaluation 219
revenue 42–3, 112, 132
   average revenue (AR) 112–13, 117
   total revenue 43, 112, 113
ripple effect 159

S
sales taxes 62
saving 69, 74, 199
   inflation 167
   motive for saving 70
   savings accounts 70
   savings ratio 70–1
scarcity 2
secondary industry 90, 152
service industries 85, 91, 104, 152
   balance of trade 222–3
shareholders 95
small businesses 92–3
small island economies 214
social benefits 53
social costs 53
social welfare 115, 183
specialisation 86
   how does specialisation occur? 204–5
   international specialisation 204
   regional specialisation 204
   specialisation according to comparative advantage 210–11
spending 74
   motives for spending 74
stability 137, 170–1, 226–7
standards of living 176, 180
   differences between countries 181
   differences within countries 180
   indicators 176–7
   quality of life 181
statements 70
statutory boards 57
subsidies 35, 212
   illustrating the effect of subsidising a supplier 61
   reasons for subsidies 60–1
substitutes 31
suppliers 24, 61
supply 32
   effect of changes in supply on the market 35
   extensions and contractions in supply 33, 44
   individual and market supply 32–3
   supply changes 25, 34–5, 44
   supply-side growth 144–5
   wage determination 80
supply curves 32
   individual and market supply 32–3
   shifts in the supply curve 34
supply-side policies 140
   deregulation 141
   education and training 141
   effects on macroeconomic aims 141
   incentives to work and invest 141
   labour market reforms 141
surplus 131, 224
   causes and consequences of a trade surplus 225
   impact of surplus 226
   policies for surpluses 226–7
survival 115

T
takeovers 96
tariffs 132, 212
taxes 35
   ad valorem taxes 132
   common taxes 133
   direct and indirect taxes 132, 134–5
   effective taxes 63
   indirect taxes 62–3
   progressive taxes 132–3, 185
   proportional taxes 133
   qualities of a good tax 134
   reasons for taxation 131, 132
   regressive taxes 133, 185
   sales taxes 62
   value added tax (VAT) 62
tertiary industry 90, 152
total cost (TC) 108, 110–11
total revenue 43, 112, 113
trade 203
   administrative complexity 212
   causes and consequences of a trade deficit 224–5
   causes and consequences of a trade surplus 225
   free trade 210–11
   globalisation 206–7
   multinational companies 208–9
   protectionism 61, 212–15
   specialisation 204–5
   trade cycle 149
   trading 205
trade-offs 128
trade unions 83, 88
   benefits of membership 89
   impact on the economy 89
   negotiation 88
training 141

U
underemployment 183
unemployment 154, 156, 183
   causes of unemployment 156
   consequences of unemployment 158–9
   cyclical unemployment 157, 158–9
   dealing with unemployment 155, 157
   demand-deficient unemployment 157
   frictional unemployment 157
   impact on businesses 159
   impact on communities 159
   impact on government 159
   impact on people 158–9
   impact on the economy 159
   measuring unemployment 156
   rate of unemployment 154
   search unemployment 157
   seasonal unemployment 157
   structural unemployment 157
   technological unemployment 157
   temporary unemployment 157
universal education 11
urban/rural divide 194, 195

V
value added tax (VAT) 62
variable costs (VC) 106, 110–11

W
wages 78, 164
   agriculture, manufacturing and services 85
   gender work gap 83–4
   government policy and wages 81
   non-wage factors 79
   strength of bargaining power 81
wants 2, 28
   double coincidence of wants 68
workers 13, 141
   demand and supply 80
   differences in earnings 82–5
   different types of occupation 78–9
World Trade Organization (WTO) 211